The Weak in the World of the Strong
*The Developing Countries in the International System*

# The Weak in the World of the Strong

## The Developing Countries in the International System

Robert L. Rothstein

COLUMBIA UNIVERSITY PRESS
*New York*

**Library of Congress Cataloging in Publication Data**

Rothstein, Robert L
  The weak in the world of the strong.

  Includes bibliographical references and index.
  1. Underdeveloped areas—Foreign economic
relations.  2. Underdeveloped areas—Foreign
relation.  3. International economic relations.
I. Title.
HF1413.R66    382.1'09172'4    77-7889
ISBN 0-231-04338-4 (cloth)
ISBN 0-231-04339-2 (paper)

Columbia University Press
New York  Guildford, Surrey

To

Mark and Jane Pisano

# Contents

# Preface

This is a book in international relations. I note this fact here only because much of the subject matter covered trespasses on areas of concern that have not generally fallen within the traditional domain of international relations. Discussions of the internal politics and policymaking styles of the developing countries, economic development doctrines, and orientations toward the international trade and aid systems have usually been left to their own disciplines and specialists. I have not been able to comply with this useful—or at least economical—form of academic boundary maintenance in this book because the external policies of the developing countries and the problems and pressures they have created for the international system cannot be understood by concentrating on either the internal or external dimension: the interaction between the two is critical.

To argue that the developing countries cannot be successfully integrated into the international system without both internal or external changes is hardly novel. But the internal dimension of change frequently seems to fade from view or is not sufficiently connected to changes sought or changes occurring in the external realm: in reality, though not in rhetoric, the international debate on development and on the problems of the Third World has come to focus on what the rich must do for the poor—not on what the poor must do for themselves—before any of the external changes can have much effect. As we shall see, this is a necessary focus, but hardly sufficient.

A recent United Nations study, *The Future of the World Economy*, which appeared after this book went to press, illustrates the problem. In technical terms, this is a valuable study. But after a passing bow to the need for both international and internal change, the study concentrates almost exclusively on the need for a range of external change that is politically improbable, that may raise expectations that are bound to be frustrated, and that sanctifies a goal—sharp and rapid reductions in the per capita income "gap" between rich and poor—that may be the wrong goal for many developing countries (see chapter 5). At any rate, in what follows I shall not neglect the external dimension, but I shall also attempt to indicate why the truism about the need for both internal and external change is usually honored more in the breech than in the observance, and what needs to be done about it in practical terms. I shall be concerned analytically with how we have reached the current state of affairs and prescriptively with how we might begin to alter it.

This is a long book and I have felt the need to cut short or eliminate the discussion of a few topics. For example, I have not discussed foreign investment and the role of multinational corporations in chapter 3 primarily because these issues have been well covered elsewhere and because I could not say anything useful in a summary fashion. I do believe, however, that the material in chapter 3 and in other places provides a more general framework for the discussion of a narrower issue like foreign investment. As another example, the discussion of institutional problems in chapter 11 can only be taken as indicative, a deficiency I hope to remedy in a forthcoming book. Still, much has been covered in many domains, some of them not my own, and I apologize for any indiscretions or distortions.

I wrote the first draft of this book in residence as a Fellow of the Woodrow Wilson International Center for Scholars. I am very grateful to the Center not only for generous financial support but also for the provision of a delightful working atmosphere. I am especially grateful because two of my colleagues at the Center, Professor Raymond Hopkins of Swarthmore College and Professor Douglas Chalmers of Columbia University read my manuscript with great care and were a constant source of intellectual and personal support.

Professor Bela Balassa of Johns Hopkins University and the World Bank has made a valiant effort to reduce my economic ignorance not only by reading much of the manuscript but also through many personal discussions of the issues. I have never failed to learn something useful from him—usually that I had better think again. Jane Pisano, formerly of Georgetown University and currently a White House Fellow, also read the manuscript with great care and was always ready to discuss the issues when I felt the need to do so. In any case, to Jane and Mark Pisano I owe a debt of friendship that extends well past this book.

I am pleased once again to have my book published under the auspices of the Institute of War and Peace Studies at Columbia University.

Shorter and earlier versions of chapters 4, 7, 9 and 11 have appeared in *International Affairs* (London), *World Development,* and the *International Studies Quarterly.* I thank the editors of those journals for permission to reuse this material.

Responsibility for any errors or omissions in what follows is mine alone.

Robert L. Rothstein

*New York*
*April 1977*

# The Weak in the World of the Strong
*The Developing Countries in the International System*

*Institute of War and Peace Studies*

# Part One

# Setting and Questions

# 1

# The Third World in the
# International System:
# Perspectives on Past and Future

The attempt to establish a satisfactory relationship between the underdeveloped and the industrial countries is likely to be one of the dominant themes of the next 25 years. The desire of the underdeveloped countries to overturn the existing international order or to establish patterns of exploitation in their own favor has been stimulated by the spectacular successes of the petroleum-exporting countries. But the relationship between small and underdeveloped countries, bitter with memories of generations of colonial exploitation, and the complex and sophisticated international systems established and dominated by the industrial countries was troubled—and troubling—well before the Organization of Petroleum-Exporting Countries (OPEC) began to reorganize our political, economic, and perceptual universes.

This is an extraordinarily difficult time to write about the relationship of the underdeveloped countries to the international systems in which they must operate. The uncertainties are staggering. The crisis of the old order is readily apparent, but the shape of a new order is only dimly visible. Short-term forecasts are futile, for they are undermined by the next day's headlines. But even longer term forecasts are not much better, for the answer to one uncertainty seems inseparable from the answer to all the others. Will the industrial countries regain control of their resource environment, or will they drift on unable to overcome the inertia of institutions and ideas—and politicians—created for a different kind of world? Will the Third World hang together and extract higher and higher prices for its resources, or will it disintegrate into hostile fragments? Will nuclear weapons begin to proliferate, and will they create a world of unimaginable insecurity, or will they be integrated into the fabric of international security? Are we in an unmanageable universe in which the interlocking problems of nonrenewable resources, energy, food, population, and pollution will shortly compel a "lifeboat ethic"? And would our own moral values and self-image be able to survive the starkly controlled and selfish world implied by this ethic?

There are no single answers to these questions, nor is it clear that joint answers can be or will be negotiated (unless one shares the faith of an official at the World Food Conference who claimed that "Chaos must surely show that a new order is possible"). Nevertheless, no matter what the order of difficulty, we must seek some judgment of where we are heading, for we have no other way (except "muddling through" by doing what we have always done) of organizing our priorities and taking immediate actions to avoid the worst kind of future.

The relationship between rich and poor is never likely to be without tension and conflict. The needs of the poor are too great and the sense of exploitation too salient to expect that demands upon the rich will rapidly diminish or that satisfaction with whatever the rich are willing to offer will rapidly increase. There are, however, substantial moral and practical reasons to seek to ameliorate tension and conflict and to avoid unnecessary provocations and confrontations. But to do so will be difficult, for an improved relationship between the rich and the poor will require significant changes in attitude, expectations, and behavior on the part of both groups. We are primarily concerned in this book with two levels of change for the underdeveloped countries, but one obvious point ought not to be forgotten: All the changes, domestic and external, for rich and for poor, are interconnected.

[4]

For the developing countries there are clearly important and objective reasons to worry about the nature of the external environment and to seek to change it in a number of ways. The need to trade to overcome the deficiencies of inadequate domestic markets, the need for aid and investment to supplement domestic resources, and the need for protection against adverse external developments from which these countries suffer, but which they can barely influence—like the oil crisis, recession, and inflation—testify to the necessity for an abiding concern with external developments. And yet, one of the major themes of this book suggests that the underdeveloped countries have placed a disproportionate emphasis on external change by blaming too many of their problems on the international systems, by assuming that most of their problems can be solved by transforming these systems, and by believing that recent events have actually given them the power to achieve revolutionary external goals. Until these views are altered, and until a proper balance is established between internal and external factors, I doubt the possibility of fundamentally diminishing the degree of conflict between rich and poor.

I am not arguing that an objective concern with external developments is wrong or misconceived. A number of factors have, however, transformed an objective concern with external developments into an obsessive preoccupation for many developing countries—at the expense of what should be an equal, or perhaps predominant, concern with domestic change. These factors include bitterness at past exploitation, a persisting influence of external values on elite groups, and substantial benefits to some elite groups from the export–import sector. But these factors have been strongly reinforced by two others: the influence of theories (or doctrines) about the need for rapid industrialization and the ideological debate that attributes underdevelopment itself (and thus the right to reparations) to the developed countries. I comment here briefly about these two factors, the first to illustrate some of the interconnections I shall examine and the second to explain some of the issues that I shall not discuss.

During the 1950s and the early 1960s industrialization via import substitution seemed to be the only road to economic development for the majority of the underdeveloped countries. Prospects for primary product exports seemed bleak, and the possibility of exporting low-level manufactured goods or components of final products seemed likely to run into tariff or nontariff barriers or were a relatively late-arriving development. I discuss these issues in more depth in chapter 3. Here I note only that the choice of a strategy of rapid industrialization had two important consequences. On the one hand it meant domestically that one series of choices was neglected: Too little attention was paid to agricultural productivity, to family planning, to improving the conditions of supply within traditional export industries, to low-level local planning, and to slower, more qualitative growth strategies. On the other hand the choices made guaranteed that the relationship between the underdeveloped countries and the international systems would become more and more inextricable and thus more and more prone to tensions and conflicts. In part this was because the strategy of import substitution industrialization itself left the developing countries more—not less—dependent on the industrial world for the imports necessary to create and operate new industries. In part also, however, since this strategy could be implemented only at the expense of other parts of the domestic society, and since it was not successful enough to begin to compensate the losers, internal conflicts were exacerbated. A new development strategy was clearly necessary; given the power of the entrenched interests that benefited from import substitution, and given the reluctance of the ruling elites to risk major domestic transformations, the only recourse seemed to be increased demands for external support.

I have recorded this development here because it should alert us to how domestic failures can lead to increased pressures on the international systems. This is particularly true in the context of underdevelopment, for few of the countries I discuss have the resources (or, in some cases, the domestic political power) to alter major policy commitments sharply. I discuss the significance of this in a subsequent chapter on the problems of policymaking. But the prevailing theories of development also have become more sophisticated and more differentiated; there is at least some hope that they will be applied more prudently and that the interrelationships between domestic and external factors will be perceived more accurately.

I have tried to avoid the ideological warfare that dominates much discussion about the relationship between the underdeveloped countries and the existing international order, for three fundamental reasons.[1] The first is that many of the issues in dispute seem beyond useful resolution—except to those already committed to one or another unassailable truth. For example, I believe that the contentions that the economic growth of the industrial countries rests upon colonial exploitation or that the industrial countries cannot maintain high levels of prosperity without continuing to exploit the poor countries cannot be sustained. I do not mean to assert that participation in the international systems is entirely or always beneficial to the underdeveloped countries—as some of the more orthodox defenders of the international division of labor frequently assert—but rather only that the more extreme arguments for the inevitability of exploitation (which is not equivalent to dependence, for dependence is the fate of all small countries) are incorrect and misleading.

The second reason why I have tried to avoid many of the ideological conflicts, except as they intrude into the decisionmaking process, is that I believe excessive concern with questions of guilt and responsibility has distracted the attention of many underdeveloped countries from a more profound effort to deal with their own problems as quickly as possible or to see the external world in a sufficiently differentiated manner. Even if the underdeveloped countries could establish the responsibility of the industrial countries for existing patterns of underdevelopment, it strains credibility to imagine that the industrial countries would accept the judgment or would do very much about it in practical terms. Concentration on such issues yields only rhetorical successes; worse yet, it fosters a tendency to await the arrival of external salvation.

1. The literature on dependence and its significance is now massive. See, for example, James D. Cockcroft, André Gunder Frank, and Dale L. Johnson, *Dependence and Underdevelopment: Latin America's Political Economy* (Garden City, N.Y.: Anchor Books, 1972). For a critical analysis, see David Ray, "The Dependency Model of Latin American Underdevelopment," *Journal of Inter-American Studies and World Affairs*, 15, 1 (February 1973):4–20.

## SETTING AND QUESTIONS

Even if all the demands of the Third World were granted—more aid, more access to developed markets, debt relief, more influence on international monetary affairs, and so on—the benefits would not help all the underdeveloped countries, and many of the benefits would go to the wrong groups or not enough groups domestically. The central point is that most of the demands can help only the most advanced developing countries (who have almost competitive export sectors or good prospects for commodity exports or have seemed credit worthy enough to be granted large loans). Moreover, only those countries with a reasonably effective policymaking system and a ruling elite committed to national development are likely to be able to take advantage of existing opportunities. I do not argue that these demands ought to be rejected; rather I insist that their effectiveness cannot be isolated from domestic conditions. These comments also show that the proposition that the underdeveloped countries have become too concerned with external events is not equally applicable to all developing countries: It may be more or less true for all, but it is also definitely much more true for the poorest and least developed countries who cannot benefit very much from the items currently on the international agenda.

The final reason I have not discussed ideological issues at great length is that I believe many or most of the problems of the underdeveloped countries can be adequately explained by fundamental differences in power and capacity. Poor and weak states have always had great difficulty in establishing a satisfactory relationship with the existing international systems. Underdevelopment has clearly added a new dimension to this problem but has not made the problem itself any less relevant. We do not need elaborate theories of "dependencia" or exploitation to understand the problems of the underdeveloped countries: Poverty and weakness in the context of a complex environment are usually sufficient. (As noted, I do not ignore the ideological debate where it has affected actual decisions or the perception of available alternatives.) The position I have adopted also means, in contrast to many ideological discussions, that I do not argue that any single decision is correct for all the underdeveloped countries. A number of different decisions about the external world are viable for different groups of underdeveloped countries; in any case, this is a choice that must be left to each country itself, not imposed by outside observers. I argue in later chapters for a particular style of decisionmaking and for particular improvements in the process of decision but not for any single decision by all the underdeveloped countries.[2]

The position I adopt explicitly challenges the contention of many radical critics that the underdeveloped countries do not have any meaningful choices because they are controlled—directly or indirectly—by external influences. I do not assert that cases in which small and poor countries have become satellites or appendages of foreign countries or companies cannot be found: "Banana republics" have not yet completely disappeared. Nor do I assert that the underdeveloped countries have a wide range of easy or painless choices. There are, nevertheless, many cases in which the range of choice for underdeveloped countries is not completely determined by external forces, and not all these choices are trivial or meaningless. The available choices may be sharply circumscribed by the weakness and poverty of the underdeveloped countries, and the options considered may be heavily conditioned by the attitudes and assumptions of the Great Powers, but even within these boundaries the possibility of better or worse decisions for each country has frequently remained open. Moreover, the persistent impact of nationalism, the growth of indigenous capabilities, and the aid of experts from international institutions have increased the desire and the ability of the underdeveloped countries to make their own decisions—and, in some cases, their own mistakes.

That the distinction between domestic and external policy is merely an analytic convenience—especially for poor and weak states—is, of course, virtually a truism. But it is a truism that needs to be strongly reaffirmed, for the difficulties and dangers of dealing with domestic problems have made it too easy to blame too much on, and to expect too much from, the external world. The need to

2. I do believe, however, that a policy of domestic redistribution to benefit the very poor, which is morally justified and would also increase the ability of governments to cope with their own problems, is increasingly important, although in different ways, to all developing countries. This presumes that the elites in both developing and developed countries can be induced to take the idea of redistribution seriously. See chapters 8 and 9 for more detailed analysis.

perceive this issue with more clarity is particularly strong if the developing countries do have increasingly meaningful choices to make about external orientations. These choices must reflect a more sophisticated perception of what the external world is likely to do and what difference it makes to each country; in turn, the ability to evaluate external opportunities and to take advantage of them is likely to be effective only if serious efforts are made to improve the quality of the domestic process of decision. Even a benign and cooperative international environment will make little difference to countries that remain content with a decisionmaking style that is *ad hoc*, episodic, and excessively ambitious.

There are two other reasons for spending a great deal of time on the problems of domestic policymaking in a book concerned with the external policy of developing states. First, although poor and weak states—OPEC apart, or a truly unified Third World bloc apart—cannot normally fundamentally influence the external world, improving the domestic process of decision is well within the capabilities of a great many developing states. Second, insufficient attention has been paid to the fact that one reason why the poor countries have placed disproportionate stress on external salvation is the persistent failure of domestic policies. The changes probable within the international order are not likely to be sufficient unless the developing states achieve better results domestically; until they do, they will place demands on the international order that are bound to engender conflict and strain the capacity of external systems already flawed and weak.

---

I am arguing two parallel propositions about the relationship between the developing countries and the international systems. For most of the developing countries, and for most of the time, efforts to improve the domestic policymaking system ought to have first priority; the stress on external change has been misguided or deliberately designed to avoid dealing with domestic problems. This argument is especially compelling because even a thoroughly benign environment cannot help a corrupt or dysfunctional domestic system, and a thoroughly malign environment can do much less damage to a country that has a degree of flexibility and efficiency. In Chapters 3 and 4 I illustrate why domestic change has come to seem less compelling—except rhetorically—than external change.

But this is hardly the whole story, for not all problems are domestic in origin. There have been, and there continue to be, external forces that take advantage of poor and weak countries. Beyond this, all the developing countries can be injured or overwhelmed by external events for which they bear no responsibility—like the oil crisis or inflation. The international systems impose a hierarchy of hindrances or dangers that affect different developing countries in different ways but that nonetheless do create patterns of injustice or indifference—hindrances like trade barriers and other obstacles that impede primarily those countries that are closest to being able to help themselves, or dangers like recession and inflation that injure all. I argue that efforts to remove these hindrances, diminish the dangers, or compensate for unfair costs are necessary; I do not argue that those changes are more important than domestic changes or that they can overcome problems created by corrupt and conservative ruling elites.

⬤•••▶

The oil crisis has had an extraordinary impact on the Third World. In one sense it is the limiting case in any argument for a better balance between internal and external factors, for it is difficult to imagine a more brutal and dominating external "shock," although, perversely, the main purveyors have been other underdeveloped countries. In another sense, however, the oil crisis provides an excellent illustration of some of the themes of this book, especially the tendency to seek salvation by external change, and an unrealistic inflation of expectations about what can be achieved either quickly or externally.

The oil crisis has simultaneously sharply increased the dependence of most of the non-OPEC developing countries on external resources (to pay for imports of oil, fertilizer, and food) and engendered a rather desperate, now-or-never desire to establish a "new international economic order." Both the need to give aid and the need to deal with the challenge to the existing order have compelled the industrial countries to rethink their relationship to the Third World. Consequently, in addition to commenting on the oil crisis and its aftermath, I comment in the next section on some more general questions about the relationship between rich and poor. In particular I discuss the threat from the Third World and how we might begin to alter the terms of a relationship that is becoming increasingly tense and bitter.

## THE OIL CRISIS, THE TACTICS OF CONFRONTATION, AND THE QUEST FOR A NEW INTERNATIONAL ORDER

Traditionally, international systems have been Great Power systems. What the Great Powers have wanted, what values they have sought to implement, and what patterns of behavior they have chosen to reward or punish have created and dominated the structure of world politics and the international trading system. A hierarchy of interests has tended to prevail: In the first instance the Great Powers have determined their own interests; in the second instance they have sought to ensure the survival of the international systems that reflect their values and capabilities; residually they have sought to provide for the poor and the weak. The norms of behavior have been norms of convenience for the Great Powers, or have been norms that do not inconvenience very much.[3]

Before OPEC's extraordinary successes radically altered perceptions of the range of the possible for poor countries, the only alternative left to underdeveloped countries intent on extracting increasing amounts of external support seemed to be pleas for more charity, open or disguised, or a strategy of deliberate disruption. The level of charity has not kept pace with either demands or needs. As a result much public discussion in both developed and developing countries—and well before the oil crisis—has been devoted to the dangers and possibilities of the sustained and deliberate use of terrorism, nuclear proliferation and nuclear blackmail,

3. On some of the changes in the last 100 years that have affected the role of small countries in international relations, see Robert L. Rothstein, *Alliances and Small Powers* (New York: Columbia University Press, 1968), Ch. 1.

expropriation of foreign assets, default on debts, and calculated attempts to destabilize the international monetary system. These are nuisance strategies designed to compel the rich countries to pay a price to restore tranquility. They do not threaten the basic structure of the international order, and they are apt to lose more than they gain if they engender retaliatory action on the part of the industrial countries.

These threats are, nevertheless, not entirely specious or irrelevant. Complex societies are increasingly vulnerable to tactics that have no other purpose than to intimidate or disturb: The threat of terrorist actions against specified national airlines, for example, could have catastrophic effects on air travel and tourism. Nuclear proliferation need not end in nuclear attacks to be dangerous: Contamination of the environment through increased testing or accidental explosions threatens everyone. And the revival of biological warfare capabilities—the "poor man's nuclear weapon"—is not improbable. Whatever the psychic costs of living with these threats, and they may be high, there are also material costs involved. In particular the advanced nuclear powers may feel compelled to invest in defensive systems (like the ABM) that are both costly and a destabilizing factor in the central strategic balance. Similarly a unified default on debts might threaten the viability of some of our leading banks, and a successful effort to withhold some critical commodities from our industries could have severe shortrun effects on our prosperity. Finally attempts to create links with domestic minority groups might become a significant factor in the domestic political process in the industrial countries—the notion that Black Africa might become the Israel of the 1980s is not entirely fanciful.

In sufficiently desperate circumstances one or a number of these actions might be attempted. And the threat of doing so will surely persist, if only because a number of dissident groups see some virtue in acting as if the rhetoric of irrational actions is meant to be taken literally. There are, however, two factors that make an orchestrated attempt to implement such actions improbable and unlikely to succeed. First, unified support within the Third World is not likely to be achieved, for interests and perspectives are too disparate. Second, the industrial countries have the means to protect themselves against such actions—at the expense of the Third World. What has seemed to give special currency to these threats is, of course, the oil crisis. A fourfold or fivefold rise in price within a year for an irreplaceable and nonrenewable resource is hardly part of a "nuisance" strategy. But OPEC has also simultaneously emboldened and impoverished much of the rest of the Third World, and the quest for its support in efforts to create a new international economic order has not only raised the possibility of new support for threatened actions but also created a wholly new range of threats.

That the devastating shortrun—and uncertain longrun—effects of a massive transfer of financial power to the oil producers have had a galvanizing impact on the rest of the Third World is not surprising. But there are peculiarities in this situation that need to be examined: *Schadenfreude,* joy at the suffering of another, is an understandable reaction on the part of the underdeveloped countries, but Third World importers of oil (and food and fertilizer) have suffered even more grievously than the rich countries. An enormous redistribution of income from the poorest less-developed countries (LDCs) to the OPEC countries has been one of the most salient effects of the recent crisis.[4]

But OPEC's victims have barely protested. Happiness at the discomfiture of the industrial countries is part of the explanation for their silence. So, too, is fear that OPEC will become even greedier. And for the producers of other critical primary products, the desires not only to emulate OPEC but also to receive OPEC's support in a challenge to the existing international order are responsible for what otherwise would be an irrational degree of joy at subsidizing the bankrolls of the oil producers. This is a fundamentally unstable situation, for ultimately it rests on the doubtful proposition that OPEC's successes can be repeated; if these efforts fail, the clash of

4. The immediate impact of the rise in oil (and food) prices on the non-OPEC LDCs was to double their balance of payments deficits (from $10 billion to $20 billion in 1974), virtually destroying the effects of present flows of loans and grants. See Hollis B. Chenery, "Restructuring the World Economy," *Foreign Affairs* 53, no. 2 (January 1975):258. The $10 billion is equivalent to about 15 percent of the total import bill of the underdeveloped countries and has hit some countries like India very hard (India's oil payments would eat up about two-thirds of her foreign exchange reserves).

interests within the Third World bloc are likely to become bitter.

There are many technical reasons (e.g., market structure, availability of substitutes, political and economic differences) that make the longrun success of future OPECs improbable.[5] Nor is it necessarily true, from the perspective of the Third World as a whole, that providing substantial benefits for a relatively small number of raw materials producers is the fairest way for the industrial countries to help the poor countries. Nevertheless a cartel strategy is either under way or threatened, and some of these efforts may succeed in extracting substantial shortrun gains.[6] The prospects that such efforts will produce even more short-term disruptions of the international trading system may also be reasonably good, for even advanced economies need time to adjust to rising resource costs. As a result, if OPEC hangs together, and if it decides to fund a number of raw materials cartels (or to fund an integrated commodity program without Western participation), a marked rise in economic conflict—perhaps even military conflict—is very likely.[7]

A decision on the part of OPEC itself or a number of its leading

5. There have been many discussion of the difficulties of emulating OPEC. See, for example, Marian Radetzki, "The Potential for Monopolistic Commodity Pricing by Developing Countries," in G. K. Helleiner, ed., *A World Divided: The Less Developed Countries in the International Economy* (London: Cambridge University Press, 1976), and Anthony Edwards, *The Potential for New Commodity Cartels* (London: The Economist Intelligence Unit, 1975).

6. The developing countries within the United Nations Conference on Trade and Development (UNCTAD) have been seeking developed country support for commodity agreements that rest on joint producer-customer cooperation. At the time of writing, the success of this venture remains problematic. Moreover, the UNCTAD program does not preclude unilateral producer action (where possible) but merely subordinates it (where necessary) to joint action. Clearly, from the perspective of many developing countries, producer cartels are a "first-best" choice because concessions (e.g., on price ceilings) would not have to be made to consumers and producer-consumer cooperation is a "second-best" choice necessitated by economic, financial, or political weaknesses. If the UNCTAD program fails, which is a very real possibility, the likelihood of a resort to cartel action will surely rise. For a detailed discussion of these issues in the UNCTAD context, see Robert L. Rothstein, "Global Bargaining: Commodities and the Quest for a New International Economic Order" (forthcoming).

7. How generous OPEC has been depends on the eye of the beholder. For example, Jonathan Power, writing in the *New York Times* (March 15, 1975), observes that OPEC's aid level in 1974 reached almost $10 billion, which is about what the LDCs lost, in the aggregate, from oil price increases. Yet this is deceptive, for only $2.6 billion of the $10 billion was actually disbursed in 1974; almost 70 percent of the total went to Egypt, Syria, and Jordan; future aid levels may decline as more of the OPEC members learn how to spend their revenue on themselves.

members to support efforts to overturn the existing economic (and political) order is far from self-evident: A continuing resource crisis may slow the growth rates of the industrial countries, which will reduce demand for all raw materials; the higher prices likely to result from an OPEC-supported cartel strategy would also raise the prices of the commodities and manufactured goods that the OPEC countries themselves must import; and, finally, it is not clear how long OPEC (especially its conservative members) will support efforts to destabilize a system from which OPEC is the greatest beneficiary. If OPEC begins to invest in raw materials industries in the Third World, a strategy designed to increase and stabilize the prices for such goods makes more sense but OPEC has thus far not gone much beyond merely talking about such investments, for they are not as safe as investments in the industrial countries, and they may well engender a nationalist reaction from underdeveloped countries that have no desire to replace one set of foreign owners with another. At any rate, OPEC's charity has thus far been limited (in both actual disbursements and the range of recipients), and many of its members (e.g., Indonesia, Ecuador, Nigeria) have already begun to complain that they do not have spare funds for external aid. And OPEC itself is becoming increasingly dependent on Western imports that its members will not be able to forgo easily. But, whatever the likelihood or the effectiveness of OPEC's support, it is clear that the Third World's current efforts to construct a "new international economic order" rest on the hope that OPEC will provide the necessary funds and leverage; if that hope is disappointed, the "new" order may not be very different from the old order.

The likelihood that a cartel strategy will fail over time is hardly

---

Still, OPEC aid levels, according to Power, were about 2 percent of their combined GNP in 1974, which is well above Western (or Soviet) aid levels. And OPEC has pledged to help other LDCs form their own OPECs.

It is clear that one reason that criticism of OPEC by non-OPEC LDCs has remained muted is fear that OPEC will raise prices again. Another factor is the obvious desire to get more aid from OPEC. How long fear and greed will keep the non-OPEC LDCs from protesting about what OPEC has done to their growth prospects—which are now negative in some cases for the period 1975–1980, and rarely above 1 percent per year in the other cases—is a mystery I cannot solve. For more recent figures on OPEC's aid, which confirm the preceding comments, see Maurice J. Williams, "The Aid Programs of the OPEC Countries," *Foreign Affairs*, 54, 2 (January 1976):308–24.

grounds for complacency among the industrial countries. Political problems could easily turn the arena of resource diplomacy into an arena of "hot" or "cold" wars: for example, through another Middle East war, an invasion of part of OPEC's territory, or the radicalization of OPEC as a result of leadership changes. But even a series of failures in a cartel strategy might be very destabilizing in the short run. The level of uncertainty could increase, governments could begin to feel the necessity of subsidizing high-cost domestic production or of guaranteeing external supplies by bilateral "deals," prices might rise too rapidly, and the inflationary consequences might compel "beggar thy neighbor" and deflationary policies that reduce everyone's welfare—including Third World exporters and Third World aid recipients. Deliberate efforts on the part of the cartels to turn the industrial countries against each other by selective bargaining might increase the likelihood of this outcome. A series of failures could also make the irrational disruptive tactics already discussed seem more and more necessary. This is especially likely because euphoria about the prospects of overturning the existing order may prevent or delay a number of underdeveloped countries from immediately adopting domestic policies that might help them deal with some of the incredible human problems they confront (for further comment, see chapter 9). And when these problems are confronted, they are apt to have deteriorated even further and thus to constitute an even heavier charge on the charity of the rich.

But can the Third World remain sufficiently unified behind a confrontational strategy? The poor countries surely have some shortrun power to disrupt and to increase the degree of uncertainty, especially if an opportunity for pressure and blackmail, like another Middle East war, intersects with a rising demand for resources. More power than this, the power to transform radically the international systems, the poor countries do not have—even, I believe, with the committed support of OPEC. Two factors in particular suggest that perhaps even the ability (or the desire) to inflict major shortrun disruptions on the external systems may be exaggerated: The first is the range of attitudes within the Third World (and within OPEC) and the second is the range of response open to the industrial countries.

## SETTING AND QUESTIONS

In the present atmosphere a kind of Gresham's Law seems to hold: the rhetoric of confrontation tends to prevail over the rhetoric—and even the deeds—of moderation. This is likely to persist for some time, for the great majority of underdeveloped countries share the desire to see the existing international order transformed. Nevertheless, it ought not to be assumed that all share the expectation that transformation is either imminent or probable. Elements of moderation persist within large parts of the Third World, for the need for immediate help, increasing doubts about OPEC's charity, and many beneficial (or at least lucrative) ties with the developed world compel some degree of prudence. Thus the argument that the poor countries have little to lose and can therefore easily risk radical and dangerous confrontations is sharply overdrawn: Many countries have done well enough to have something of value to lose, and all the elites have a great deal to lose. The interrelation between prosperity in the industrial countries and that in the developing world—especially a developing world that wants to industrialize and must export—has also become even more painfully apparent as a result of the recession; the perception that what benefits the rich does not *necessarily* impoverish the poor is becoming slightly less abstract.

A more radical approach to rich–poor relations might be more easily translated into a unified action strategy if interests and attitudes within the Third World were not so disparate. Unity has been relatively easy to sustain on the level of general principles, particularly in declarations that simply add together everyone's demands, but has tended to break down or be radically diluted when actual negotiations on specific topics are scheduled. For the most part this reflects the fact that almost none of the issues on the international agenda—commodity agreements, more preferences or access for manufactured exports, debt negotiations, food and financial aid—benefit every underdeveloped country equally, and some (e.g., commodity agreements) might inflict severe costs on some parts of the Third World.

I do not imply that the radical demands implicit in various proposals to create a "new international economic order" (NIEO) will not have strong support from some countries and a good deal of tacit and opportunistic support from even the moderate countries.[8] The moderates are not really hostile to the aims of the more radical Third World countries: What restrains them is a combination of present needs and differing perceptions about the immediate feasibility of overturning the existing order. Bitterness toward the industrial countries, as well as the unlikelihood that they will receive all the aid or trade benefits they want, is likely to make them quick converts to the radical cause. In this sense the recession in the industrial countries may have created a lull in the strategy of confrontation, which could be shattered when rising demand once again gives OPEC and a few other mineral exporters a great deal of leverage. (I discuss the reaction of the industrial countries to this situation a little later.)

OPEC's successes have obviously given radical arguments about the possibility of creating a new order great currency. But other developments have also played a part. Current fears of resource depletion and food shortages are a case in point. Contentions that the citizens of the rich countries consume far more resources (both minerals and foodstuffs) per capita than those of poor countries and that these resources are steadily being depleted by excessive use in the rich countries are transformed into accusations that the overdevelopment of the rich is responsible for the underdevelopment of the poor and that the consumption of resources by the rich must be slowed or there will be none left for the poor.[9] This is a dangerous argument, because it is doubtful that the rich countries can help the poor countries by slowing their own rates of growth (which would happen if resource usage was cut quickly) and because it oversimplifies the relationship between resources and

8. Among the many proposals in the NIEO are the following: demands for an integrated commodity program, more domestic processing of commodity exports, more access for manufactured exports, national ownership of national resources, renegotiation of debts, and more aid under less stringent terms.

9. This fear gains some force from the fact that the growth rate of resource usage by the LDCs will increase more rapidly than the growth rate for the rich countries (who have passed the per capita income level at which resource usage begins to decline). Still, even with these high rates of growth, the LDCs will use only about 15 percent of total world resources by the year 2000, an increase of only 5 percent over current figures. See Wilfred Malenbaum, "World Resources for the Year 2000," *The Annals* 408, (July 1973):30–46.

wealth. Resources are not a fixed inventory that can only be depleted, and "the poor nations are not poor because other nations are using large amounts of natural resources, but because those poor nations suffer from low overall levels of productivity which prevents them from making good use of their potential resources. . . ." [10]

A more radical approach may also be the result of other factors. Some elites may see desperate attacks on the system, no matter what the odds on beneficial results, as the only way to attract sufficient support to deal with monumental problems or to provide a scapegoat for not dealing with them at all. Others may be deliberately disruptive because of the pleasure they feel at the discomfiture of the rich—at watching us worry about "dependence," "the futility of self-reliance," "the costs of interdependence." And for those elites who hope to move their countries toward increasing self-reliance and a "bicycle culture," sacrificing long-term benefits in exchange for putative shortrun benefits is not even an issue; the only benefits the systems can pass on are shortrun (but see chapter 9, for I disagree with this view).

The radical countries do not, however, have the power by themselves to achieve massive gains. The tacit or rhetorical support of the moderate countries is thus not likely to be sufficient: They too must be willing to take risks and to sacrifice some shortrun benefits if a strategy of confrontation is to succeed. But this is unlikely, because immediate national needs are too pressing and because too many elites have no real desire to alter the existing order or because they are genuinely committed to principles of moderation. In sum, only a unified Third World strategy has even slightly more than a marginal probability of fundamentally restructuring the international order, but real unity—one for all, and all for one—is likely to founder on conflicts of national (and personal) interest. In any event, how much shortrun uncertainty and how much disruption actually ensue are not completely within the control of the

10. Mogens Boserup, "Sharing is a Myth," *Development* 3, no. 2 (March 1975):3. Some of the same countries who accuse the rich countries of using too many resources are in the forefront of those demanding that the rich countries also import more from the LDCs.

Third World; even more critical will be the reaction by the industrial countries.

In the abstract the industrial countries are rich and flexible enough to develop substitutes or synthetics in place of necessary resources, to decrease the amount of natural resources used per unit of output, to improve the technology of exploration and extraction, and to cut unnecessary consumption.[11] These propositions suggest that natural resources (except for oil) constitute a fluid, changing, and changeable inventory that need not be exhausted if technology and the price system are allowed to function, if governments plan for the future carefully, and if they intervene to deal with short-range problems. Future OPECs are also likely to be much easier to disrupt, for few will have members (like Kuwait) with a declining marginal utility for current income or the ability to take the brunt of production cutbacks. The reserve positions of the United States, Canada, and Australia in many of the major minerals will also affect the viability of other cartels. It is this (potential) combination of strengths that has led two recent analysts to the sanguine judgment that "The so-called resource crisis will have very little long-term effect on the balance of power between economies because it is only a temporary phenomenon."[12]

What the industrial countries can do is obviously not necessarily what they will do. The reaction of the industrial countries to the resource crisis thus far hardly seems to justify much optimism about a willingness to pay substantial costs now to ward off only potentially larger costs in the future. Moreover, in contrast to the inane arguments of the "new isolationists" (now the "new inter-

11. Is this judgment too optimistic? No clear answer is really possible, for much of the debate between resource pessimists (like the "Club of Rome") and resource optimists rests on guesses about future rates of use: If the industrial countries use resources at current or higher rates, pessimism may well be justified. Optimists argue that shortages will increase prices and thus stimulate the use of other materials and/or the search for better extraction techniques. Whether we will make the effort to develop new technologies in time is clearly uncertain. Even if we do, however, the shortrun problems of adjustment to higher resource costs, different life-styles, new patterns of international tensions, and so on may sharply increase the level of conflict within the international system. For a good discussion of the resource issue see *The Future of the World Economy* (New York: United Nations, 1976).

12. Philip Connelly and Robert Perlman, *The Politics of Scarcity—Resource Conflicts in International Relations* (London: Oxford University Press, 1975), p. 46.

ventionists"), our ties with the Third World are no longer trivial. When the bulk of our imports from the underdeveloped areas consisted of coffee, tea, and spices, we could easily adjust to their absence (and perhaps even improve our economic performance by investing the saved income appropriately). Conversely we now import raw materials essential for major industries, and when there are no alternative sellers, or their prices are much higher, or the prices of substitutes are prohibitive, the effects of deprivation or scarcity on our economy could be quite severe. The fact that our consumption of mineral resources in 1968 (in 1973 dollars) constituted only 4.3 percent of our GNP (of which energy accounted for 2.3 percent) is not an indication of the real importance of these resources, for they are necessary to keep a much larger part of our economy functioning. In addition, although the bulk of our overseas investment has gone to other industrial countries, expropriation of whatever assets we do have in the LDCs would still be costly (especially if the losses were insured by the American Government).

If the industrial countries have the will to do so, they are likely to be able to regain control of the resource environment within a few years. The shortrun costs may be severe, but they may also be manageable—barring another oil embargo by OPEC. But the very effort to regain control of the resource environment puts a large premium on quick results for the LDCs: There is an unfortunate paradox at work here, for the more the rich countries work to free themselves of dependence on the resources the poor countries have, the more it pays the poor countries to be as demanding and disruptive in the short run as they can be. The desperate need of the underdeveloped countries for short-term help merely reinforces this pattern of conflict. And the industrial countries, conversely, have not appeared willing to take out much insurance—in the form of immediate redress of some of the grievances of the poor countries—against threatening and uncooperative behavior.

This is a dangerous and explosive situation, for each group of countries may act on perception of shortrun interests that not only guarantee immediate losses for all but also increase the possibility of even worse longrun disasters. Simple-minded arguments about

[22]

the necessity of understanding that all of us, rich and poor alike, now live in an interdependent world are not likely to be persuasive in these circumstances: The rich countries are too intent on reducing their "interdependence" with the poor countries, and the poor countries are too mistrustful to see interdependence as much beyond the current euphemism for dependence. There is no point in bemoaning the irrelevance of nationalism either, for nationalism is both a powerful and potentially useful force for the governments of underdeveloped countries.[13] Nor is the well-meant advice that bargaining must replace a strategy of confrontation especially useful, for the real problem is much more complex: how to create the conditions in which bargaining becomes possible when the parties to the bargain distrust each other and have different sets of priorities, in which many problems cut across the traditional hierarchy of the state system and cannot be dealt with by self-regulation or the unilateral use of force, in which nationalism and interdependence seem to exert a contrary force on most issues, and in which there are both general recognition that the old rules of the game no longer work very well and no agreement on what the new rules should be.

The temptation to cut through this extraordinarily complex situation with a "simple" solution like military intervention is obviously strong.[14] But the necessity of resisting a new generation of "terrible simplifiers" is also strong, for their fantasies and the fantasies of some of the more radical spokesmen of the Third World

13. For comments on the potential benefits of nationalism, see Constantine V. Vaitsos, "Foreign Investment Policies and Economic Development in Latin America," *Journal of World Trade Law* 8 (1973):632–33. But see also chapter 3 for some of the costs of nationalism.

14. Some of the arguments for military intervention are almost breathtaking in their intellectual (and one would add moral, except that is obviously an irrelevant category to those who believe the world suffers from an unwillingness to use force) vulgarity. The astonishing contention of one "unknown soldier" (Miles Ignotus) is that we can maintain a 10-year occupation of the oil fields—not to say, while also defending tanker routes, ports, refineries, and so on—ignore the Soviet Union, handle guerrilla conflicts with ease (because, as our "experts" apparently have just discovered, the deserts have no trees; clearly however they have lots of mirages), and also, when the rest of OPEC retaliates, just pick up another piece of territory (with no trees, presumably). Another publicist, who apparently has plagiarized our unknown soldier, tells us that, after all, the oil countries have no right to their oil just because they happen to be living on top of it. This novel principle could have some striking consequences, for by the same reasoning our resources would not really be ours.

could collide in a violent and unpredictable fashion. Talleyrand's warning that you can do everything with bayonets but sit on them ought to be reemphasized for those who believe they can resolve our problems by dispatching the marines; Bismarck's definition of preventive war as suicide for fear of death must also be noted in an era of potential thermonuclear conflict.

There is some evidence recently of more willingness on the part of the rich countries to accommodate some of the demands of the underdeveloped countries. But reluctant concessions to discuss food and commodity problems to entice the oil producers into substantive negotiations are unlikely to be sufficient. Even the major proposals contained in Secretary Kissinger's speech to the Seventh Special session of the General Assembly in September 1975, which appeared to constitute an important shift in the official position of the United States on several critical issues, will not quickly transform distrust and bitterness into a spirit of mutual accommodation. This is especially true, not only because the suspicion arises that the speech was a venture into public relations that will be quickly forgotten (or destroyed by Congress or by other parts of the Executive branch), but also because so many of the critical issues do not have simple solutions that will immediately benefit more than a limited number of underdeveloped countries. Even so, another aspect to a strategy of confrontation is frequently ignored by the more radical spokesmen of the Third World. Improved relations are unlikely unless the underdeveloped countries recognize that agreements are not necessarily wise, or just, or viable that benefit only small groups of commodity exporters, or that guarantee a system-wide increase in inflationary pressures, or that presume there is no connection between prosperity in the rich countries and that in the poor countries.

On balance, I would argue that, if the reaction of the industrial countries simply reflects an effort to deal with the range of threats we have already discussed—the nuisance tactics either joined to or separated from an OPEC-supported cartel strategy—the grounds for an improved relationship between rich and poor will remain tenuous and transitory. In these circumstances, accommodation will represent only tactical moves in response to momentary shifts in leverage and influence, and the more significant underlying reality will primarily reflect efforts to regain dominance or to destroy existing patterns of interaction. A more lasting improvement of relationships, one designed for long-term viability in the context of a fairer international order, must rest on other perceptions of the obligations that each group of countries has to the other. The first of these obligations is moral, and I postpone discussion of this issue to the concluding chapter. But the other obligations reflect more practical concerns, for they involve judgments about the ability of the Third World to impede global settlements important to all of us and their ability to undermine increasingly the stability of existing international institutions.

In the first sense the underdeveloped countries may not have the power to achieve many of their external goals, but in a number of important cases they may have the power of preventing any other group of states from achieving theirs—or at least of making them pay a heavy premium to do so. Where only cooperative and voluntary agreements are useful—pollution, the oceans, population, food, access to resources, nuclear proliferation—the underdeveloped countries may have a strong veto (or delaying) power. In most instances these are system issues, not simply in that they can be resolved only at the global level, but also in that the way they are dealt with will have a profound effect on the universe all of us inhabit. This means that some potential for disruptive action is only a small part of the reason why we need to be concerned about the attitudes of the Third World toward the international system: more critically we need their cooperation to make the international order more stable and prosperous.

In the second sense the numerical dominance of the Third World in many international institutions gives them the leverage to transform—and distort—these institutions so that they inhibit the solution of non-Third World issues or so that solutions reflect prevailing Third World perceptions and prejudices. This tendency has already begun to undermine support for international institutions in the industrial countries and to increase the quest for alternate arenas of decision. This could be an unfortunate development, especially if it proceeds in a random fashion, for in an era of increasing interdependence, and in an era in which multilateral, global solutions may be becoming increasingly necessary, the proliferation of institutions creates confusion, incoherence, and enormous loss of time (and money). But the importance and effectiveness of the major international institutions can be reasserted only if both groups of countries perceive the need to do so and if the Third World countries in particular are convinced that they do not need to use their blocking power to ensure fair and persistent concern for their problems.

A strategy of confrontation could have one other cost. Splits and tensions within the Organization for Economic Cooperation and Development (OECD) (and indeed within each country) are likely to escalate if common policies toward the Third World cannot be devised, and this too could impede or delay agreements on many critical issues. These splits and tensions reflect two factors. In the first place the developing countries clearly intend to follow a policy of isolating the more vulnerable Europeans and Japanese from the United States—primarily by emphasizing the short-term effects of resource boycotts on resource-dependent economies. In the second place, tensions between the more conservative and the more liberal OECD countries are likely to cause increasing internal bitterness, irrespective of the outcome of the resource conflict. The Scandinavians and the Dutch already have accused the United States, West Germany, and Japan of greed, of unwillingness to share a prosperity that owes much to unfair bargains with the Third World, and of an inability to see where their true long-term interests lie. Conversely the conservative countries have accused the Scandinavians and the Dutch of fake generosity, of being "free riders" on conservative policies, and of knowing full well that the "concessions" they offer will not have to be implemented or will not cost them very much. The dangers in this situation can be diminished only if the OECD countries make a more serious effort to establish common policies toward the developing countries—and if those policies manage to produce substantial, widespread, and rapid results within a good part of the Third World.

Continuation of the present pattern of confrontation, latent and overt, thus seems likely to increase the uncertainty and dislocation in the international systems and to prevent much more than transitory accommodations. The results could be doubly disastrous: Many underdeveloped countries are liable to delay imperative domestic reforms while they await salvation by an external miracle, and cooperative agreements among the rich countries, on which the prosperity of many poor countries remains dependent, and global agreements among all countries in areas like the oceans and pollution, as well as the international institutions that must mediate such agreements, will become increasingly improbable or ineffective. Finally, apart from the practical dangers of increased conflict, the moral obligation to provide as much help as possible—at least to those countries that deserve help—remains strong.

The developing countries now believe that the existing rules of the international system are unfair and discriminatory. To some extent these views are justified, but to some extent they are also unconsidered and ideological (see chapter 2). But no lasting improvement of rich–poor relationships is likely until this belief is altered, which means that we need to consider the creation of a set of norms and rules that seem fair to both sides. We can no longer define what is fair by reference to rules that we ourselves have created. If it is impossible to reach agreement on mutually beneficial norms, and if each side seeks only to protect its own shortrun interests, we may be compelled to pay severe costs—in welfare losses, rising arms budgets, increasing inwardness—at a not too distant date. I return to these issues briefly in chapter 11. In the next section I comment briefly on the need for this kind of normative quest.

--------◆◆◆◆◆--------

Third World threats to the industrial countries—irrational nuisance tactics, a cohesive cartel strategy, inhibition of global solutions to some problems, distortion of the existing institutional structure—are not overwhelming, and they ought not to elicit hysterical reactions by Western governments or publicists. Many of the threats reflect the rhetorical desperation of frightened countries that confront massive problems without the means (and sometimes without either the will or the knowledge) to seek solutions. Rhetorical threats are unlikely to be converted into action unless something akin to another oil crisis generates a real unity within the Third World and unless the industrial countries fail to develop a coherent policy toward these threats. Neither another crisis nor the continued "muddling through" of the rich countries is wildly improbable. It seems, therefore, that the rich countries must think of establishing better grounds for their relations with the Third World, for the following reasons: (1) There is a degree of danger and a higher level of uncertainty (and irritation) from the shortrun tactics of the Third World; (2) the degree of danger could become a good deal greater in some circumstances in the years ahead, and it makes sense to pay a premium now to ward off worse costs; (3) we have not only a moral obligation to the poor countries but also the desire to create and maintain an international system that is both stable and just, which means we must respond to their real needs. Obviously this response will be useless if the developing countries do not set their own houses in order, but some developing countries are making the effort, and others may be encouraged or compelled to do so if the international system begins to alter in important ways and its utility as a scapegoat begins to decline. Still, the proposition that both sides must alter current patterns of behavior cannot be overemphasized; changes by the developed countries alone are not likely to be granted or to be sufficient if the developing countries ignore what they must do for themselves or seek too rapid and extreme external change.

## ON THE PRACTICALITY OF NORMS

An international order—especially one in which there is a high degree of interdependence—in which each state seeks more autonomy as the first goal is inherently unstable. The first movement away from this condition can come, however, only from the strongest state: The leader of the system, who benefits most from its persistence, must also make the initial and the largest sacrifice to the ideal of cooperation and mutually beneficial interdependence. The United States is also in the best relative position to take the first step, for we are likely to endure smaller costs from concessions to more cooperative forms of interdependence, and our actions are likely to have the widest ramifications. Such first steps cannot come from those who feel that they have been exploited in the past and will be exploited in the future—who feel, that is, that the system itself is inherently unjust. This means, I believe, that merely articulating the proposition that we shall all share a similar fate is not enough (for it may not be true and will surely be greeted with cynicism by the poor); also necessary is some realization that the shortrun agreements we seek are more than compromises or settlements of particular issues. They are also first steps in the difficult process of creating an international system in which even the poor and the weak have an expectation that their interests will not be forgotten the moment that the industrial countries regain their economic (and political) strength.

In a world sharply divided over values and principles, the need to seek agreement on normative rules that will provide guidance for behavior, or rules by which behavior is to be judged, is especially important. Indeed it is virtually a tautology to assert that explicit concern for the normative structure of the system is likely to be particularly important when values are in conflict. Normative concerns would be less consequential in a system in which consensus was high and the meaning of desirable behavior could be left implicit. The quest for normative agreement is not an irrelevant venture into utopian speculation, for no lasting agreement with the underdeveloped countries is possible until they are convinced they will be treated fairly within the international order. We cannot understand what norms and principles are likely to be acceptable to the underdeveloped countries (and to their ruling elites, on whom we shall focus) until we examine some of the critical decisions they have made, why they have made them, and what might be done to improve the quality of choice within the context of underdevelopment. I do this in chapters 3, 4, and 5.

Perhaps the most we can initially expect from this effort is agreement on procedural norms, on how we should go about seeking solutions, rather than on the substance of solutions. There have been a number of attempts to establish stable and reliable procedural norms, but they have faltered because they have not taken sufficient account of the differences in perspective between large, rich, and stable countries and small, poor, and dissatisfied countries. For example, the reasonable rule in trade negotiations that the costs of trade distortions ought to be borne by the state that imposes them, and not transmitted to other states, is less than helpful to the LDCs, who can usually (with a few exceptions) trade in manufactured goods only with the aid of deliberate distortions of free trade principles. Principles that promise to treat all states equally are even less useful to manifestly unequal states, and principles that defer benefits to the future are not much better.[15] Too many of the suggested norms reflect the desire of rich and powerful states for stable, conservative behavior: Note, for example, frequent injunctions not to use power arbitrarily, to negotiate everything, and to define interests so that they are mutually compatible. But the underdeveloped countries need rules for changes, for disproportionate benefit and unequal treatment, for getting somewhere fast rather than remaining somewhere long. And they need some assurance that efforts to deal with their problems will persist as long as necessary. I discuss these issues in more detail in chapter 11.

## THE STRUCTURE OF THIS BOOK

Part one of this book consists of this and the next chapter. Chapter 2 sets out the characteristics of the countries I deal with and attempts to justify a decision to focus on a rather unusual set of distinctions. This is not an academic exercise, for it not only distin-

15. Thus commonsense propositions about the need for commodity agreements that benefit both producers and consumers, or new international rules on investment policies that do not injure U.S. interests, do not—I think—take sufficient account of the fact that the LDCs are unlikely to accept any agreement that does not provide salient, disproportionate, and immediate benefits to themselves. In any case, given the fact that the LDCs are all in favor of the same kind of resource policies (i.e., demands for increased national ownership, control, and revenue, more local processing of raw materials, indexation to protect against inflation, control of market forces) and are increasingly in favor of group bargaining through cartels like OPEC, the possibilities of mutually satisfactory agreements may be on the decline—unless the rich countries decide to pay a subsidy to avoid even worse conflicts. The difficulties of reaching agreement within UNCTAD on an integrated commodity program clearly reflect the divergences between (and frequently within) both groups.

guishes the states I discuss from other groups of states but also provides the more specific distinctions within the Third World group itself that will be necessary when we move from analysis to policy. I conclude with a general statement of the relationship between poor and weak states and the international systems. I hope this provides a useful introduction to the more specific material that follows.

Part two consists of three chapters. Chapters 3, 4, and 5 look back at a series of major decisions about relations with the external world that were made by the majority of underdeveloped countries in the years before the oil crisis. I have tried to understand why certain policies became prominent, how internal and external pressures bore down upon the ruling elites to lead to a particular kind of decision, and what results ensued. These are analytic and interpretive, not historical, chapters: I have been more interested in extracting the general themes that appear crucial to me than in providing a detailed history of any particular policy.

Generalizing about a small number of critical decisions across a wide range of Third World countries obviously has its costs in specificity and comprehensiveness. Nevertheless, since common patterns and reactions are present, I think it is a justifiable and useful approach. At any rate, it is the compromise I have chosen between detailed case studies of a few countries and macroscopic generalizations that seem to bear little relationship to the process of decision within the context of underdevelopment. Moreover, the current challenge of the underdeveloped countries to the existing international order cannot be understood *de novo:* The decisions that have preceded the challenge, the rationale that inspired each decision, and the results that followed must also be understood. This point is particularly important in the context of poor and underdeveloped societies, for early decisions that commit a great part of available resources to a single choice are difficult to control or to reverse.

Chapters 3, 4, and 5 are also relevant in another sense, for the factors that have impeded more effective decisionmaking in the past are still present. In addition many of the decisions I discuss at roughly the point in the 1950s and 1960s when they first became prominent are still very much part of the internationl debate on development. For example, regional cooperation, nonalignment, and the problems of aid and trade are still on all Third World agendas. This is hardly surprising, given the limited range of choice before poor and weak countries and given the different periods in which many of these countries achieved independence.

Part three, which consists of chapters 6 through 9, reflects one of the central concerns of this book: the attempt to restore some balance to the discussion of the external orientation of the developing countries by stressing the extent to which an improved decision-making style and a more objective consideration of the range of policy options are imperative. In one sense this is almost a truism, for few analysts will deny that there is no response from the external world that can overcome fundamental deficiencies in the domestic political and economic systems of the underdeveloped countries. But it is a truism that has not been taken seriously, and I examine the reasons why this is so. In addition the analysis in these chapters is designed to take account of the limitations that have appeared in preceding chapters. As such, I suggest reforms that are practical and feasible, and not merely academic statements of ideal policymaking systems or romantic evocations of revolutionary transformations.

Chapter 6 discusses the nature of politics in underdeveloped countries and comments in particular on the contentions that the ruling elites are thoroughly corrupt and self-interested and that they are likely to be overwhelmed by the revolutionary expectations of the masses. Chapter 7 attempts to set out the basis for a more effective approach to policymaking in developing countries. Chapters 8 and 9 directly connect the discussion of domestic decisionmaking with the problem of establishing a satisfactory relationship with the external world. Chapter 8 discusses the conventional orientations of relatively open and relatively closed economies and the countries for which these options are likely to remain attractive. Chapter 9 discusses the new emphasis on redistribution and self-reliance, suggests some necessary changes, and indicates its relevance for a large group of very poor LDCs.

I do not argue that any orientation is clearly superior for all the developing countries: Conditions and attitudes are too disparate. Also, I discuss political decisions about economic orientations, not economic decisions. Finally, these are not "pure" either/or decisions but relative, more or less decisions to move toward a particular external orientation. Inherited patterns are too mixed, decision-making has been too *ad hoc,* and power is too limited and dispersed to permit quick and massive movement toward a single, elegant choice.

Part four, which consists of chapters 10 and 11, balances the emphasis on domestic policymaking by suggesting changes in the way that the international systems ought to be operated. Chapter 10 is speculative and seeks to forecast a range of probable behavior by different groups of developing countries; this is a necessary preface to the concluding chapter, for we need to have some sense of the kind of world for which norms and rules must be prescribed. Chapter 11, finally, suggests a number of rules and precepts for both groups of countries that might make the emerging international order more stable, more bearable for all its members, and more just.

———◆•◆•◆———

I have already alluded to the fact that, though this book is about the external orientations of the underdeveloped countries, it is not an essay in economics. The choice of broad economic strategies and of the stance to be taken toward the outside world is never wholly an economic issue. Ultimately the crucial question in all the decisions we examine concerns choosing who is going to gain and who is going to lose, and in what time period, from the operation of the economy. This is, of course, a political question about the allocation of resources. This means that we need to know a good deal about the operation of the political system and about the value preferences of the ruling elite. I do not assert the simple-minded proposition that politics must prevail over economics, or vice versa, or that the domestic political and economic systems are always more critical than the international systems, or vice versa; what I do assert is that the nature of the mix between these considerations is what really concerns us.

I am concerned, moreover, with what practitioners and publicists believed about economic development, not with whether the views they accepted were necessarily true or false. This is an important qualification, for I hope it permits me to avoid the charge that I have oversimplified the discussion of prevailing theories of economic development. I am well aware, for example, that economic theorists disagreed about "balanced" versus "unbalanced" growth, or about the relationship between industry and agriculture, or about the type of industry that ought to be emphasized, or about the relative virtues of planning and the market—among other things. But the practitioners with whom we are concerned are obviously not economic theorists, and they fastened upon those aspects of the theoretical debate that seemed to fit their own purposes, which were never completely economic. I seek to understand, not only what theories they adopted as their own, but also why they did so.

Problems with values, conscious or unconscious, are bound to affect any book about the problems of the Third World. The first problem concerns my own values. I have attempted to limit the impact they might have by concentrating on the problems confronting the ruling elites and working "upward" from problems to available theories, rather than "downward" from theories to the world of the practitioner. This does not eliminate the impact of my beliefs, but I hope it does limit them and reduce the scope of whatever distortions personal beliefs produce.

More specifically I have worked with a simple set of premises that ought to be set down, if only to avoid unnecessary misunderstandings. I believe that we have a persistent moral obligation to help the poor countries as much as we can—and more than we have—(but I also believe there are increasingly important practical reasons for us to examine their problems and their needs more sympathetically); that the stability of the international systems themselves—especially the relationship between the major powers—is an absolutely critical variable for both groups of countries; that the tangle of distrust and suspicion now dominating the relationship between rich and poor can be broken or diminished only if the rich countries make the first sacrifices (but they can do so only if they adopt a sufficiently long-range perspective); and, finally, that the poor countries themselves must begin to perceive the relationship between their needs and problems and the problems and possibilities of the external world in a more sophisticated and differentiated fashion.

Values can also intrude in other ways. Anyone who becomes involved in research on the Third World soon confronts a series of statements that are simply taken for granted or a set of beliefs or perspectives that are beyond objective confirmation or refutation. I think it useful to conclude this chapter with a brief statement about a number of these propositions, either to make my own position clear or to help the reader reach his own judgments. Perhaps more critically, continual awareness of the impact of subjective judgments on various issues may help avoid a number of errors or oversimplifications.

## THE DOMINANCE OF POLITICS

No theme is more pervasive in the literature on underdeveloped countries than the dominance of domestic political considerations on all issues. This would probably be surprising only if untrue, for it is difficult to see what else could be dominant in societies where questions of legitimacy, authority, and national identification remain unsettled. Unfortunately, too many of the "politics is everything" analyses seem to presume that the meaning of the statement is self-evident. I believe that this is not true. In the chapters that follow (especially chapter 6) I examine why politics is crucial, but I also attempt to specify more precisely what this means in terms of acceptable policies and policymaking styles, and what elements of the political process are more or less amenable to useful change. This is an issue, I think, in which detail is more important than broad generalizations. We need to know what kind of politics is dominant, not simply that many issues involve the "allocation of scarce values."

Three aspects of the domestic political process are especially crucial in the chapters that follow. The first concerns elite purposes and elite attitudes. Are the elites concerned only with personal survival, and are all the elites corrupt and incompetent? How one answers these questions has much to do with how one stands on an issue that we shall shortly discuss: reform or revolution. The second

*[35]*

political issue concerns the dangers implicit in overcomitting the few resources that an underdeveloped country is likely to have to a single policy choice. Such decisions are apt to be based on information that is insufficient or doubtfully accurate; they may require more talent and skill than LDC governments usually possess; and, once made, they are difficult to unmake, for additional resources may not be available, and vested interests may object to any change. These considerations suggest the need for a cautious policymaking style, but whether such a style can be created, or whether it can be an adequate response to the problems confronting most underdeveloped countries, is unclear. Finally, throughout this book I am concerned with how political and economic factors interact and with what relationship there is between domestic and international pressures.

Another aspect of this issue is a more direct reflection of conflicting (or potentially conflicting) beliefs. By what standards should we evaluate the political performance of underdeveloped countries? Attachment to democratic forms is no longer much of a candidate, but what is a viable alternative? Rhetorical commitment to development is insufficient, but even a suspension of judgment until the results are in is not much better—what shall we consider a good result (e.g., high rates of growth, more equitable distribution, high levels of employment, or what)? I have noted these issues here only to highlight my own bias toward improving the quality of life for the great mass of citizens, but I do not believe—as many advocates of redistribution seem to—that this means growth rates can be ignored. (See chapter 9 for more discussion of this issue.)

THE DISCOUNT RATE ON THE FUTURE

How much current consumption are we willing to sacrifice now to ensure a more beneficent future for our progeny? This is an extraordinarily complex question even for very rich countries. In a way a rather strong (and apparently justified) faith in the idea of progress in the developed countries has seemed to eliminate the need to face the question: If the mere accumulation of technologic progress guarantees that future generations will be more prosperous than present generations, nothing much deliberately needs to be set aside for future needs. Clearly, this oversimplifies, since both governments and people do sacrifice some current consumption and do invest in enterprises that will begin to pay off well into the future. Lately our faith in progress has been considerably eroded, as has our faith that technologic fixes will automatically provide solutions to future needs, and the question that now concerns us is whether we can get governments and people to put a much lower discount rate on the future—that is, to sacrifice more current consumption than ever before, perhaps enough so that even well-off people begin to feel it, to ward off potential disasters for the next generation.

As we are all aware, this issue is creating enormous difficulties for the advanced countries. The issue is, however, even more stark for the underdeveloped countries, for sacrifices of current consumption are obviously extraordinarily difficult for countries living near the subsistence level—and for governments too insecure to take the risk of exacerbating domestic discontent. The LDCs desperately need high rates of investment to begin creating relatively modernized economies, but they also need high rates of current consumption to provide for the poor (and for investments in human capital). Western governments and aid agencies have offered the LDCs much free advice about the necessity of "biting the bullet," about the virtues of sacrifice, and about the dangers of not taking the long run seriously enough. No doubt, this is well-meant advice, but it also reflects a failure to think contextually about the dilemmas confronting weak and poor governments. Thus, for example, the demands for financial orthodoxy on the part of the International Monetary Fund (IMF), or the demand for detailed plans before foreign aid will be granted, seem to reflect judgments on the part of Western analysts about how they would run a development program in a developed country. I raise this issue here only to emphasize the importance of thinking about the different time perspectives of rich and poor governments and the different costs for each of current sacrifices.

ATTRIBUTIONS OF GUILT AND CRITERIA OF SUCCESS

Radical spokesmen attribute the problems of the underdeveloped countries, indeed underdevelopment itself, to the operation of the international system. Conservative spokesmen attribute guilt to the policies followed by the underdeveloped countries themselves. Others blame the corruption and incompetence of the ruling elites. Variations on each of these themes abound.

Who is right, or rather, is anybody right? The answer, in my judgment, is that any argument that attributes responsibility for the problems of the underdeveloped countries to a single factor is vastly oversimplified. All these factors—the international system, domestic political and economic constraints, elite attitudes and behavior—are mixed together in complex ways and can be separated only as a matter of analytic convenience. I stress this commonplace because it is so frequently ignored and because it creates a bias toward simplistic solutions.

This issue is closely related to another: the inflation of expectations. The first generation of development "theories," like Walt Rostow's "stages of growth," seemed to promise easy and virtually automatic progressions from poverty to prosperity. The ruling elites who adopted these theories were too credulous and expected results too quickly and too painlessly. Policies were adopted with inflated expectations of the effects they could produce and then dropped when they failed to produce—or, more accurately, produced only the slow and moderate success that should reasonably have been anticipated. Regional cooperation, as we shall see, is an excellent illustration, for it was adopted without any clear understanding of the limited results it could achieve among very poor economies and then criticized for failing to produce a socioeconomic transformation. Such a result was improbable from the start, but disappointment when it was not achieved created an indifference to the limited gains that regional cooperation could (and did) produce.

REVOLUTION AND REFORM

Many of the problems confronting the underdeveloped countries appear so overwhelming that only revolutionary solutions seem to make sense. The impossibility of achieving much progress in the face of archaic socioeconomic institutions and corrupt leaders is especially apparent. But how widespread are these deficiencies? Can they be blown away only by revolution? [16]

16. Since this theme appears in a number of places in this book, a strict definition of terms might seem appropriate here. But a completely satisfactory definition of

More and more analysts, in despair over the extraordinary range of human problems that seem to be accumulating in many underdeveloped countries, have adopted a revolutionary perspective. This book is built on a different premise. I am in complete agreement that some LDCs face some problems that require a revolutionary solution. I think, however, that too many judgments of the need for revolution are merely extrapolations from the problems of a few desperate cases like Bangladesh. Not all the underdeveloped countries face problems so intractable that reasonable policies of reform are irrelevant. Or perhaps I should say they do not face such problems yet.

The argument that nothing less than a revolution is acceptable suffers from the vice of aggregation: All problems are seen as a reflection of the problems of some. Moreover, I think too many of the advocates of a revolutionary strategy are willing to sacrifice small improvements in the lot of the desperately poor and hungry for a romantic vision of what the future might bring. Indeed, in many underdeveloped countries the very conditions that seem to make revolution necessary may make the success of a revolution improbable. The revolutionaries, once in power, must still deal with the structures of underdevelopment that created the need for revolution. The revolution may succeed only in replacing one group of corrupt, reactionary, and self-interested elites with another group of corrupt, ostensibly radical, and self-interested elites.

As we shall see, this issue is not entirely abstract. It appears most acutely in decisions about whether to support particular regimes and whether to oppose ruling elites that seek to ensure

---

either revolution or reform has been extremely difficult to devise. See, for example, the essays in Carl Friedrich, ed., *Revolution* (New York: Atherton, 1966). We shall employ the terms only in a very loose sense implying a more-or-less (not either/or) distinction between evolutionary change that does not seek the immediate destruction of the existing political and socio-economic orders (or, following Webster, "to amend or improve by change of form or by removal of faults or abuses") and violent and/or extreme change that seeks to uproot the existing orders immediately (or, again following Webster, "a sudden, radical, or complete change"). The ambiguity of this distinction, particularly in establishing where one form of change begins and the other ends, is not significant in the context of this book: in substantive terms, I am primarily concerned with measures of reform throughout, and when the discussion concerns the choice between revolution or reform, what is generally at issue is the state of mind or the attitudes with which analysts approach the problems of the developing countries.

their own survival. I believe general rules are not very useful in this situation, for a concern with personal survival seems to transcend ideological differences among the elites themselves. Left, right, or center, nothing can be accomplished unless the regime feels secure enough to begin thinking about national (i.e., not personal) strategies. In no way does this imply that distinctions cannot be made between the Duvaliers and the Somozas and the Nyereres and the Houphouet-Boignys. But for the most part, distinctions between elites on this issue tend to appear after the elites have become convinced that they are in sufficient control of the available levers of power.

I am not completely negative about the need for revolution or the possible fate of a revolutionary strategy. I am trying to emphasize that too much may be expected from a revolution in the context of underdevelopment and that substantial human costs are implicit in the argument that only a revolutionary strategy will work. There is also something of a self-fulfilling prophecy at work here. If we act *as if* only a revolutionary strategy makes sense, we shall force the elites into even more regressive and self-protective behavior and thus make revolution necessary. In addition I believe that many LDCs confront problems that can be dealt with by reform strategies. In any case I doubt that large numbers of revolutions are about to occur, and it thus seems to me absolutely imperative that we begin to do what we can as soon as we can.[17]

A HIERARCHY OF VALUES

There is an obvious asymmetry between Great Powers with global interests and small countries with primarily local or regional

17. One ought not to mistake my doubts about the likelihood of many revolutions for doubts that violent change and continuing instability are probable. Indeed violence and instability seem inevitable. But I doubt that the results of violence or instability are likely to lead consistently to revolutionary socioeconomic transformations that benefit the bulk of the population, for I believe that there are no changes that can quickly and effectively overcome the deficiencies of underdevelopment. We need to end the illusion that there is some magic key by which desperately poor and inefficient societies can suddenly be transformed into Denmark's or Switzerland's. Improvements are possible and imperative, but it remains an open question whether they can be achieved more readily by steady reform or massive revolution. The Ethiopian muddle may be illustrative: the overthrow of the corrupt, incompetent, and repressive Selassie regime by corrupt, incompetent, and repressive (ostensibly) radicals seems to mean only more of the same for the majority of the populace: brutalizing poverty.

[40]

interests. This asymmetry is sometimes reflected in different value hierarchies. The Great Powers' central concern is always the stability of their own relationships, which may, on occasion, seem to require the sacrifice of other values that concern the small countries—especially equality and justice. Such sacrifices of their interests and values may be one price that small countries have to pay for coexistence in an international system dominated by the quest for security.

I stress this point only to make it clear that the values the LDCs seek to achieve are not the only ones at stake in the international system. Peace between the Great Powers and prosperity among the Great Powers are values that can benefit all members of the international system, for the poor countries are unlikely to achieve either stability or prosperity independently of stability and prosperity among the Great Powers. For the poor countries to act as if this is not true reflects a dangerous misperception of their own interests. Unfortunately, some of the rhetoric surrounding recent efforts to increase "collective self-reliance" among the developing countries seems particularly irresponsible in this regard.

Part of the confusion over this issue reflects a pattern of divergent and sometimes conflicting desires on the part of the underdeveloped countries: They want increased prosperity, but they also want or are pleased by actions that injure the industrial countries or reduce their wealth. Thus we shall see, for example, demands that the industrial countries reduce their use of raw materials joined to demands that they increase their imports from the underdeveloped countries. Or we see demands for higher prices for raw materials joined to demands for trade preferences or for more foreign aid from the industrial countries. Understandably the underdeveloped countries are obsessed with solving their own problems, but they must also begin to understand the interconnections between their interests and those of the rich countries. So long as the underdeveloped countries remain in the international systems, they cannot escape some degree of dependence on the behavior of the industrial countries.

# 2

## Third, Fourth, and Other Worlds: Getting the Labels Straight

### ON THE PROBLEMS OF BEING SMALL AND POOR

All the states I deal with share some characteristics and some patterns of behavior. On the most general level they are what Professor Keohane has called "system-ineffectual" states that "can never, acting alone or in a small group, make a significant impact on the system."[1] In addition, if they confront a major security threat, all weak states must rely on essentially ambiguous external aid to ensure survival, and all must work with a very narrow margin of safety. As the Greek dictator Metaxas once observed, muddling through is a prerogative granted only to Great Powers.[2]

But the fact that all small states are "consumers" (and not "producers") of security and "price-takers" in economics and thus share a common grievance against the Great Power systems is only part of the story. There are also some important differences among small states, in the first instance, differences between small developed countries and small underdeveloped countries, and in the second

1. Robert O. Keohane, "Lilliputians' Dilemmas: Small States in International Politics," *International Organization* 23 (1969):296.
2. See Rothstein, *Alliances and Small Powers*, p. 18. The obvious point that not all underdeveloped countries are small (although all are weak) will be dealt with below. I want to avoid this complication in this and the next section to concentrate on general differences between developed and developing small countries.

[42]

instance, differences among the underdeveloped countries them-selves. I examine each of these sets of differences in turn, the first only to provide a brief background for the second.

ON BEING SMALL: IS SIZE ENOUGH?

Some obvious differences exist between the older, mostly Euro-pean and the newer, mostly Afro-Asian small countries. For one thing the problem of security has been transformed, not only be-cause nuclear weapons have unique effects, but also because so few of the newer small countries have actually faced a security threat. Geography made security the dominant concern of the European small countries, for most were likely to be implicated in any Great Power war; conversely the newer small countries might be sought as allies or supporters of the Cold War antagonists, but major war was itself less likely because of nuclear weapons, and local wars were likely to be manageable unless they became part of the Cold War struggle itself.[3]

The European small countries also shared political tradition and political language with the European Great Powers. Their leaders came from the same social class, they were committed to the same ideas about the necessary primacy of foreign policy, and they did not question the value of preserving the existing international sys-tem. The Afro-Asian small countries could hardly be more different: Western forms of government have been loosely imposed on much different indigenous political traditions, the leaders of the new states do not come from a single social class (and they are frequently much younger than their counterparts in the industrial world), do-mestic politics is more important than foreign policy, and there is little commitment to the preservation of an international system identified with imperialism and exploitation. Dissatisfied, bent on change, not always very concerned about the systemic virtues of stability, the new states have become unpredictable and unsettling elements in a dangerous international system. The concerns of the least stable subsystem may tend to dominate any larger system;

3. Increasing intraregional tensions, joined to rising arms budgets, may make local wars more dangerous and more prolific in the years ahead—even without a strong Cold War context. See chapter 4 for further comment.

perhaps only the vast disparity of power between the new states and the industrial states and the extraordinary care with which the nuclear powers have had to manage their own relationship have kept the underdeveloped countries from exerting a more destabilizing effect on the international system.

The most important difference between the older and the newer small countries is, of course, economic. Size imposes some common limitations on all small countries. They cannot have certain industries, because they cannot exhaust the relevant economies of scale (e.g., in aircraft, automobiles, locomotives); their industries are less specialized, for much specialization depends on market size; and small markets tend to be less competitive than large markets and thus lose whatever gains might result from rigorous competition.[4]

Foreign trade presumably provides small countries with an escape from the limitations of a small market (i.e., a market under 10 to 20 million people). Dependence on foreign trade involves, however, high risks, for it means that the prosperity of the small country is at the mercy of changes in foreign demand (e.g., tastes may change, or synthetics may be created), tariff and nontariff barriers, competition from new producers, currency manipulations, and changes in political outlook in foreign markets. The degree of dependence on foreign trade varies with a number of factors: ratio of exports to GNP, average and marginal propensities to import, domestic demand pressures, diversity of exports, and the diversity of export markets. Other factors may also be important, including the government's reserve holdings, the policies that the government seeks to implement, the political constraints under which it operates, and its market position (a large share of an important market, for example, may make dependence bearable—if the resource is in high demand).[5] What is at issue is not dependence but the quality and kind of dependence. And this is where differences between de-

4. See the "Introduction" in E. A. G. Robinson, ed., *Economic Consequences of the Size of Nations* (New York: St. Martin's Press, 1960).
5. Several of these factors are discussed in T. Balogh and P. Balacs, "Fact and Fancy in International Economic Relations," *World Development* nos. 1 and 2 (February 1973):85.

veloped and underdeveloped small countries begin to be significant, for the developed small countries are in a much stronger position on almost every variable. Consequently dependence may entail high risks, but it usually also repays the risk taker with high income; dependence for an underdeveloped country is more profound and thus more risky, and the returns may be less certain, less extensive, and more variable.

No small state can ignore the limitations of its domestic market, the high unit costs of production, and the intrinsic uncertainties of external market dependence. Nevertheless size is only one variable, and it can easily be swamped by the action of other variables. The effects of underdevelopment—especially low levels of industrialization, of per capita incomes, of productivity, and of administrative competence, and long distance from major markets— generally overwhelm the effects of size alone. Small developed countries have a wider range of choice, depending on their factor endowments: They usually have a high trade ratio, because they are capable of competing internationally, but they can have either a high or low index of concentration (i.e., dependence on a small number of exports and/or a small number of buyers), corresponding to their export structure. Small underdeveloped countries, conversely, have very high levels of concentration but a somewhat lower trade ratio than might be expected.[6] The lower trade ratio is a direct reflection of underdevelopment. Whereas some aspects of underdevelopment usually imply high foreign trade ratios (especially the low levels of income and national product), most of the characteristics of underdevelopment sharply lower the ability to trade by lowering the ability to compete effectively.[7] One of the ironies of this conclusion is that most of the underdeveloped countries who complain bitterly about the effects of dependence on foreign trade actually trade less than their small size would suggest; as they develop, perhaps perversely from their point of view, they will become more dependent on foreign trade. (They should also, *ceteris*

6. See Peter J. Lloyd, *International Trade Problems of Small Nations* (Durham, N.C.: Duke University Press, 1968); and Nadim G. Khalaf, *Economic Implications of the Size of Nations, with Special Reference to Lebanon* (Leiden: E. J. Brill, 1971).

7. See Simon Kuznets, *Modern Economic Growth* (New Haven, Conn.: Yale University Press, 1966), pp. 430, 431.

*paribus*, be better able to protect themselves against the effects of dependence and to earn fair rates of return for their labor.) [8]

In short, all small countries are dependent, but some are more dependent than others. And in the contemporary period efforts to diminish the degree or the costs of dependence have become vastly more difficult, for the international environment has become complex and sophisticated, and the underdeveloped countries are relatively much poorer and less developed than their predecessors. Furthermore the very existence of the huge "gap" in living standards between the rich and the poor countries has itself become a significant moral and political issue.

---

One other difference between developed and underdeveloped small countries ought to be isolated. One dimension of "smallness" is frequently overlooked: organizational and administrative capacity. A state with a small GNP and a small population is likely also to have few trained people and few resources to devote to learning about and dealing with the external world. Underdeveloped small countries are especially deprived, for they tend to have small Foreign Ministries, they cannot afford to establish many embassies abroad, information sources are usually limited and frequently controlled or dominated by foreign interests, and there are few indigenous experts to call upon when problems arise.[9]

These deficiencies can have important practical implications, for they may mean that the policymaking system will perceive developments incorrectly or late and that the capability of effective or timely response will not exist.[10] It is also likely to mean prolonged dependence on external advice and information. As one illustration

8. There are other important differences between the older small countries and the underdeveloped countries, especially the rate of population growth and the changing nature of the international system. Since I discuss these issues in later chapters, I do not deal with them here—except to say that they make the differences between the two groups of small countries even more salient.

9. See Maurice A. East, "Foreign Policy Making in Small States: Some Theoretic Observations Based on a Study of the Uganda Foreign Ministry," *Policy Sciences* 4, no. 4 (December 1973):491–508; and Marvin C. Ott, "Foreign Policy Formulation in Malaysia," *Asian Survey* 12 (1972):225–91.

10. See the interesting analysis in Maurice A. East, "Size and Foreign Policy Behavior: A Test of Two Models," *World Politics* 25 (1973):556–76.

the French West African states who negotiated with the European Economic Community (EEC) in the early 1960s had to rely on foreign (mostly French) advisers to establish their own positions. In addition, failure to acquire knowledge about foreign market conditions can result in lost opportunities or persistence in developing exports with low demand prospects. These deficiencies are, however, neither absolute nor irremediable. On some issues, especially local issues, an underdeveloped country may have as much of the relevant information—if not more—than a distant Great Power. And the underdeveloped countries are also slowly improving their capacity to deal with the issues that affect their fate. Recent efforts to control the operations of multinational corporations or to take over foreign-owned extractive industries indicate that knowledge and skill are not in the sole possession of the developed countries.[11]

DOES THE THIRD WORLD EXIST?

We shall be concerned in the rest of this book solely with underdeveloped countries. The preceding discussion has indicated how small underdeveloped countries differ from small developed countries. In this section I discuss how underdeveloped countries differ among themselves.

Does the "Third World" exist? No one raised the question in the 1950s and through much of the 1960s. Apart from the Latin

11. There are also analysts who argue that international stratification (hierarchy) itself explains state behavior. See, for example, Johan Galtung, "A Structural Theory of Aggression," *Journal of Peace Research* 2 (1969):95–119. I have not dealt with this approach, in part because empirical tests of the effects of stratification have been inconclusive, and in part because the argument seems to define away what needs to be demonstrated—that "top dogs" always exploit "underdogs." Indeed exploitation itself is never adequately defined in this approach. In addition it is far from clear that other factors (e.g., perceptions of leaders, historical experiences, the climate of opinion) are less important than stratification. There are also problems in determining where divisions in the hierarchy ought to be made and in providing evidence that the ruling elites actually perceive and act on their perceptions of "rank disequilibrium." Still, I believe it is likely that the felt significance of rank disequilibrium may have risen in recent years. But the poor countries themselves, rather than merely increase aggressive behavior as a result of these status deprivations, can also reformulate their goals or change the model of success they hope to emulate—that is, attempt to alter the dimensions by which rank is established. And the rich countries may also take actions that appear to reduce the significance of wide disparities between different hierarchical ranks.

## SETTING AND QUESTIONS

Americans, the underdeveloped countries tended to have a common past, common attitudes toward the former colonial rulers, and a common set of problems. They also shared the same intellectual baggage: nationalism, anticolonialism, nonalignment, "socialism." More critically, the new states did not seem to be in competition with each other. They had few ties with each other, trade was concentrated with the former colonial power, and external security threats were minimal. Joining together in support of the ideas they shared was thus relatively simple, for membership in the Third World was not onerous: No one had to sacrifice anything, and nothing much was required beyond verbal commitment to a few slogans. The illusion of power, the ostensible equivalence with the "First" and "Second" Worlds, was no doubt an added attraction; so, too, perhaps was the publicity attendant on summit diplomacy.

Within the past decade many critics have challenged the notion that the "Third World" usefully describes a coherent bloc of underdeveloped countries. Doubts have arisen because of a number of developments. On the broadest level there are so many underdeveloped countries, and there are so many differences between them, that any single label is bound to be misleading. Whatever indicator we choose to highlight, the range of variation is enormous: level of development, per capita income, political forms, culture, historical experience, or ideology. In fact, the variations among underdeveloped countries are probably much wider than those among developed countries, if only because of the absence of the advanced technology and heavy industrialization that tend to create similar institutional patterns and problems. Anticolonialism is a less powerful unifying force as few colonies remain; nonalignment has lost significance with the decline of the Cold War and with the increasing need to seek help from all the industrial countries; and socialism has been undermined by the practical necessity of mixed economies (especially the need to make some concessions to both domestic and foreign capitalists, and the absence of sufficient administrative skill to run a centralized economy). Only nationalism remains strong, but by its nature it cannot be a powerful agent of mutual cooperation.

Another change is perhaps even more important. As the underdeveloped countries began to concentrate on problems of economic development, and as their policies toward the external world began to be increasingly critical, sharp differences began to appear between various groups within the Third World bloc. Regional groups that benefited from preferential arrangements with the industrial countries did not want to share their benefits. The more advanced LDCs were reluctant to accept agreements that subsidized their poorer neighbors. And the poor neighbors were reluctant to become closed markets for the benefit of their more advanced neighbors. Those LDCs capable of exporting manufactures to the industrial countries were in competition with each other but also did not want to see more competition arise from within the Third World. Exporters of primary products wanted to exclude new producers from the market and to maintain high prices. The point is, of course, that national interests no longer necessarily coincided—at least in the short run—with the "general interests" of the Third World, and the possibility of competition and divergent interests within the larger bloc frequently eroded the possibility of meaningful cooperation. As a result Third World summit meetings could do little more than enunciate "maximum common denominator" positions.

None of this means that the Third World no longer "exists." What it does mean, I believe, is that the term can be used only in a narrow and precise sense. Common attitudes and shared responses to the behavior of the industrial countries still unify the underdeveloped countries on specific issues. Indeed, despite the many specific differences between the underdeveloped countries, the Third World group actually broadened its membership and developed a sharper focus in the 1960s. The addition of the Latin American countries to the Third World bloc in the 1960s clearly illustrates these developments: The Third World group was increasingly becoming a pressure group aimed at altering the policies of the industrial countries, not merely a residual part of the Cold War struggle. The oil crisis, at least for the moment, has intensified these trends and solidified an unusual degree of Third World unity (on principles, if not on detail): The need to hang together to alter the existing system, or the fear of the consequences of not hanging together, have turned the Third World into an increasingly critical political and economic force. Indeed unity itself has become so powerful a symbol within the Third World that increasingly strenuous and difficult efforts are made to overcome conflicts in interest—usually by simply adding together everyone's demands or by complex measures designed to compensate potential losers. In any case I shall continue to refer to the Third World when I discuss a pattern of behavior that cuts across the characteristics that separate one group of underdeveloped countries from another or that attempts to unify all the poor countries against all (or most of) the rich (and socialist) countries.

What are the characteristics of these countries? In a general sense I could argue—as Lloyd Reynolds does—that all the underdeveloped countries share, in some measure, these characteristics: the dominance of subsistence production and self-employment, low per capita incomes and unequal distribution of incomes, imperfect markets, low productivity, dependence on export earnings and foreign capital flows, and small public sectors and minimal modern industrial sectors. Obviously wide variations exist between countries on all of these characteristics, but Reynolds (and, of course, many other analysts) argues that this problem can be dealt with by focusing on the median behavior of these countries, rather than on the particular characteristics of one or a few countries.[12] This is clearly unsatisfactory, for it imposes an artificial similarity on disparate groups of countries. It has to recommend itself only two rather negative virtues: It has been difficult to find a better way of discussing the behavior of all the underdeveloped countries (not so difficult for those who fail to see the problem at all), and it is probably not much more of a distortion than the tendency to discuss the behavior of the

12. Lloyd G. Reynolds, *The Three Worlds of Economics* (New Haven: Yale University Press, 1971), pp. 97, 98. Political scientists would, of course, provide a different list of characteristics, including a tendency toward single-party states, a low level of social mobilization, the development of bureaucratic organizations, and the persistence and transformation of important traditional institutions. For one version of such a list of characteristics, see S. N. Eisenstadt, "Social Change and Modernization in African Societies South of the Sahara," in Marion Doro and Newell M. Stultz, eds., *Governing in Black Africa—Perspectives on New States* (Englewood Cliffs, N.J.: Prentice-Hall, 1970), pp. 236–50.

"West," or the "Free World," of the "Soviet Bloc," or the "industrial countries" as unique entities.

Listing the characteristics that the members of a group "more or less" share—in contrast to nonmembers, who may share some of the characteristics but not all of them—is a useful device when a more precise definition cannot be articulated. In the present case, however, even when we merely seek to distinguish the underdeveloped countries from more developed small countries, this approach is inadequate, for it leaves out two crucial dimensions of the difference between the underdeveloped countries and earlier generations of new and poor states. Both dimensions are primarily subjective and thus extraordinarily difficult to isolate on any conventional index.

The first dimension that has tied the underdeveloped countries together, above and beyond the shared problems of weakness and poverty, comprises a strongly felt sense of deprivation and resentment against the developed countries and a growing conviction that the rules of the international systems are deliberately rigged against them—so much so that fair treatment is impossible without a fundamental restructuring of the principles of world order. The predecessors of this generation of underdeveloped countries were touched by many of the same attitudes and feelings, but the difference, I believe, is more of kind than of degree. In any event, without some attempts to add this dimension to the objective list of shared characteristics, we shall not be able to understand some aspects of the behavior of the underdeveloped countries—for example, their support for OPEC policies that injure the rest of the Third World severely or even the support of OPEC itself (at least rhetorically) for actions that threaten the systems from which OPEC benefits.

The second dimension may be even more difficult to isolate. The context of weakness and insecurity within which the leaders of the developing countries must operate may also engender common psychologic attitudes. As an illustration James Scott has remarked of Malaysian civil servants:

Never absent from their political thoughts is the obvious fragility of their nation, the awareness that the future is uncertain and that all could be lost tomorrow or the day after, and a general apprehension that cool heads may not, in the end, prevail. [13]

Pye, speaking of the Burmese elite, makes a somewhat similar point:

Feeling that they may not have ultimate responsibility for their own national fate, they are tempted to seek security by publicly articulating an image of their nation's development in which they do not fully believe. [14]

President Nyerere of Tanzania rather graphically illustrates another aspect of the state of mind engendered by the difficulties of governing permanently inferior (in power and wealth) states: "Small nations are like indecently dressed women. They tempt the evil-minded." [15]

What effects can be attributed to these attitudes? One result may be a vacillation between the desire (as one observer has commented about the Danes) to "lie dead" to avoid involvement in Great Power conflicts and the desire to be recognized as an equal, to participate in all the system's activities. This ambivalence may also take a slightly different form, for the developing countries want economic independence, which implies separation from the rich countries, but also need external support even to begin to create the conditions of independence. Another result may be to create a despair about the possibility of any meaningful choice at all. [16] This may create a sense of futility about the prospects for having an influence on events, or perhaps even a degree of irresponsibility in critical situations. Thus an Estonian diplomat noted in the 1930s: "We do not take sides . . . we do not want to be placed in a posi-

13. James C. Scott, *Political Ideology in Malaysia—Reality and the Beliefs of an Elite* (New Haven, Conn.: Yale University Press, 1968), p. 14.

14. Lucian W. Pye, *Politics, Personality, and Nation-Building: Burma's Search for Identity* (New Haven, Conn.: Yale University Press, 1962), p. 130.

15. Quoted in Reginald H. Green and Ann Seidman, *Unity or Poverty—The Economics of Pan-Africanism* (Baltimore, Md.: Penguin, 1968), p. 130.

16. Similarly this leads to many comments about the "importance of being unimportant," for it may mean that the Great Powers will be indifferent to what the weak do. It also leads to judgments that "small nations don't have a foreign policy . . . they have merely a policy of existence." C. S. Sulzberger, *The New York Times,* October 20, 1974.

tion of risk which taking sides would involve. We tell both sides frankly that we will go with the majority." [17] Clearly these attitudes are not the exclusive property of this generation of new and weak states; nevertheless I believe they are somewhat more prominent now, if only because of the especially severe problems that confront many developing countries.

But as this book will indicate, these arguments are misleading and oversimplified. Weakness is not impotence, and small countries—even small, poor countries—not only have better or worse choices in different international systems but also can take advantage of their opportunities in a better or worse fashion. I have emphasized these points here, however, only to make clear that we cannot understand the behavior of the developing countries solely by reference to shared conditions of poverty and weakness, for we need also to be constantly aware of the influence of subjective attitudes and fears.

---

What criteria should we use to understand differences among the underdeveloped countries themselves? On what basis should we distinguish more specific groups of underdeveloped countries? Caplow distinguishes between developed countries, developing countries that are partially industrialized and that import capital and technology, and underdeveloped countries in which technology has not yet taken root. [18] Adelman and Morris discern three groups of underdeveloped countries: small, primary product exporters; small, manufacturing exporters; and all large LDCs (markets over 20 million). [19] Bergsten has categorized an emerging "middle class" of developing states (those with a competitive manufacturing sector, a key raw material, or a large domestic market) and a "Fourth World" group of "have-nots." [20] The World Bank, as a

17. Quoted in Rothstein, *Alliances and Small Powers*, p. 28.
18. Theodore Caplow, "Are the Rich Countries Getting Richer and the Poor Countries Poorer?" *Foreign Policy*, no. 3 (Summer 1971):91.
19. Irma Adelman and Cynthia Taft Morris, *Economic Growth and Social Equity in Developing Countries* (Stanford, Calif.: Stanford University Press, 1973), p. 106.
20. C. Fred Bergsten, "The Response to the Third World," *Foreign Policy*, no. 17 (Winter 1974–75), p. 10. Many of Bergsten's middle-class countries have taken large

result of the oil and energy crisis, has divided the underdeveloped countries into four groups: (1) the OPEC countries; (2) mineral exporters (Chile, Bolivia, Jamaica, Zaïre, Zambia, etc.); (3) countries with more than $200 per capita income (Egypt, Argentina, Brazil, Mexico, Colombia, South Korea, Malaysia, the Ivory Coast, Senegal, etc.); (4) countries with less than $200 per capita income (Bangladesh, India, Pakistan, Ceylon, Ethiopia, Tanzania, Uganda, etc.).[21] These efforts hardly exhaust the possibilities: Others have used geographic distinctions, or political differences, or variations in population growth rates.

There are also analysts who do not make any distinctions at all. But treating the Third World in an undifferentiated fashion, except in reference to certain shared attitudes or to a general range of characteristics, can be misleading. The danger is especially apparent when generalizations are based on aggregated statistics: India, Pakistan, Bangladesh, Nigeria, Indonesia, and Brazil dominate such statistics to the extent that whatever is happening to them can appear to be happening to all of the underdeveloped countries. Sometimes, of course, the fate of the very large LDCs does mirror that of the rest of the LDCs. And sometimes there is so much variance among the large LDCs that any consistent influence on statistical profiles is likely to be canceled out. But it may also be true that the particularly intractable problems of a few large LDCs can create unwarranted despair or cynicism about the problems of other LDCs. This may create the impression that only revolutionary policies make sense, a position already taken on faith by too many commentators.

This argument necessarily implies that the large underdeveloped countries ought to be treated as a separate category in this book. If it was my intention to discuss the specific policy choices

---

gambles on the viability of an outward orientation, and the oil crisis may make the payoff increasingly dubious. And many of these countries also have significant internal problems, which may make the maintenance of middle-class standards problematic. Perhaps they should be described as a very fearful and insecure lower middle classe—a category that suggests more problems for the international system than a simple middle-class category.

21. The fourth group has slightly more than 50 percent of the Third World population; the World Bank has estimated that they will have negative growth rates over the period 1974–80.

confronting individual countries, then countries like India and Indonesia would indeed have to be treated separately: On technical grounds alone, possession of a (potentially) large domestic market gives these countries choices (and problems) that the small underdeveloped countries do not have. India, for example, is (relatively) more immune from trade fluctuations because exports have generally been only 4 to 6 percent of GNP. Nevertheless, for most of the purposes of this book, it does little harm to presume that whatever generalizations are made apply to both large and small underdeveloped countries. The primary reason for this is that the large countries, apart from the size factor, share most of the other characteristics of underdevelopment already noted. Furthermore that the large LDCs have potentially wider markets and more numerous choices has not been as important as it might seem, because these countries have frequently remained as dependent on foreign aid and foreign resources as the smaller LDCs. One reason for this is that they have had high import needs, especially for capital goods and intermediate goods in order to industrialize, and thus external developments have been critical.

Classification schemes are not necessarily right or wrong; rather, they are more or less useful. In chapters 3 and 4 I discuss not merely what policies the underdeveloped countries have followed but also why they have chosen to do so. Consequently analytic categories or classes that primarily reflect the analyst's effort to disaggregate an arena of analysis to facilitate more precise hypotheses or more sophisticated policies are not completely adequate for my purposes. What we need are analytic categories that attempt to illuminate the process of choice within Third World countries, not ones that help an external observer organize a universe of discourse. As we shall see, the categories I have chosen cut across many of the distinctions that separate the underdeveloped countries and thus permit a reasonably broad level of generalization.

Three factors decisively affect the relationship between the underdeveloped countries and the international political and economic systems in which they find themselves, and these are useful for my purposes. The first factor is the ruling elite's perception of the stability and security of its own tenure, for this ultimately determines what risks can or will be taken. This factor is specially important in terms of time perspectives, for insecure elites cannot risk programs that pay off only in the future. What is involved here is more than the personal perspectives of the elite; equally crucial is the ability of the policymaking system to produce tangible and widespread benefits. Radical critics have protested that emphasis on elite security is conservative or reactionary and may justify a concern for maintaining the status quo. I would agree that this may well be true, but I am not arguing that these are morally good or bad criteria; rather, I only point out the importance of the connection between this factor and the attitudes likely to be taken toward the external world. In addition this factor is likely to affect the actions of a radical elite just as much as a conservative elite—the specific decision about the external world might be different for the two elites, but the security concern would be present in both cases. Finally I am not arguing that all LDC governments ought to be helped to ensure their own survival or that it is necessary to support all stable regimes: Neither international agencies nor national governments can or should avoid practical and moral judgments about which regimes are worth stabilizing or worth supporting.

How can we estimate the stability of a regime, and how can we estimate an elite's perception of its own security? Unfortunately I think the best we can do is infer both estimates from a number of external signs: the gap between available food resources and the population growth rate, unemployment figures, measures of domestic violence (e.g., riots, strikes, guerrilla warfare), the rate and direction of military spending, the rate of inflation, and certain aspects of the behavior of the elites themselves (e.g., are they sending capital abroad, are they investing in government bonds, what is the rate of domestic savings?). None of these criteria, singly or jointly, are completely adequate, and it is unlikely that inferences from these indirect data are ever completely adequate. The fundamental difficulty is, of course, that ultimately elite security is a subjective index.

We have one additional resource, however, in terms of estimating the elite's perception of its own security, for an insecure elite is not likely to be able to make a sustained, long-term commitment to economic development. This is the second of the three factors that affect the relationship between the LDCs and the international system. Although it is obviously related to the first, I have separated the two factors to make it clear that there are likely to be significant policy differences between an elite that merely seeks to ensure its own survival and one that is concerned with its own problems of survival but also wishes to begin the process of creating a national economy.

Rhetorical commitments to economic development are nearly universal. Real commitments are far more limited, not simply because of the obvious fact that the process of development itself is intrinsically destabilizing—resisting development may also be destabilizing—but also because the gains from development may go to the wrong groups or be delayed too far into the future. The elite commitment may also be only to growth, not development, and be limited to prestige projects or tangible programs with quick payoffs (in contrast, for example, to more long-term investments in human capital). Still, on balance, a secure elite committed to development is likely to concentrate on raising the domestic savings rate, on reforming the tax structure, on controlling corruption, on limiting luxury imports and frivolous investments, on reducing inequities in income distribution (or ensuring that those who receive disproportionate benefits actually invest it wisely), and on controlling spending on premature public services or the military budget.

The third factor affecting the relationship between the LDCs and the international system is the attitude that the ruling elite takes toward the international economic system. Are the elites committed to the notion that the international division of labor is inherently unfair? Do the elites believe they can (or must) overcome dependence and that self-reliance is a meaningful alternative? Do they see the international system as Senghor once did—as a "necessary evil"—or do they see only the evil? This set of attitudes is crucial for any underdeveloped country, for it is likely to determine the general direction that any development policy takes—that is, whether the country will follow a more or less inward orientation, a more or less outward orientation, or even a more or less radical version of redistribution and self-reliance (see chapters 8 and 9).

[57]

## SETTING AND QUESTIONS

Economists may object that I have left out of this discussion the most important factor in determining a small country's response to the international system. This factor is, of course, the economic structure of the country: level of development, resources, location, skills, the availability of capital, and so forth. International relations specialists may also object that I have left out an equally critical factor. How can one explain the choices a small country might make without discussing the nature of the international system within which it must operate? What are the relations between the Great Powers, what is the technologic environment, what is the intellectual frame of reference, what are the prevailing trade and aid patterns?

My answer to these objections is that these factors are not in any way excluded from the chapters that follow. I have selected different factors here, however, because I am intent on illuminating the range of choice that the small countries have had over the past 30 years. The point I am making is that the three factors I have discussed are not necessarily any more or less important, either in general or in detail, than the impact of a small country's economic structure and the nature of the international system. But these three factors are the primary ones *within the immediate control of the governing elite*. They have a crucial impact on the range of choice the ruling elites are likely to contemplate, on whether, for example, redistribution may seem too dangerous or relying on external support too contaminating. The other factors, at least within any period of a few years, are essentially givens for the elite: They can decisively affect the fate of a poor country, but there is little a poor country can do about altering their shape or direction. The one partial exception to this is, I think, the nature of the contiguous environment with which the poor country must deal; I discuss this at a number of points in the following chapters, especially in reference to regional opportunities. The basic points remain, nonetheless, that poor countries have only limited room in which to maneuver and that how they respond to what opportunities and choices they do have is strongly affected by the elite's stability, commitments to development, and attitudes toward the international economic system.

Chapters 6 through 9 combine analysis with some discussion of policy choices. For the sections on policy I need not only to incorporate the implications that can be drawn from the material in chapters 3 and 4 but also to devise a classification scheme that takes more direct account of the assets that each group of countries possesses. A fourfold breakdown of Third World countries, which will be explained more adequately later, seems useful and realistic (although it is obviously not the only one possible): manufacturing exporters, commodity exporters, and separate categories for the very large LDCs and for the very poor (and numerous) LDC's who have none of the assets the others possess.[22]

Interpretations of the impact of the international system on the developing countries have become heavily ideological. Too much is simply taken for granted by both critics and proponents. Consequently in the next section I lay out some of the factors I believe must be considered if the relationship between rich and poor is to become more cooperative and less ideological. We are, however, dealing with only part of the problem: Domestic changes are also necessary, or new perceptions are unlikely to emerge or to be acted upon.

## THE DEVELOPING COUNTRIES AND THE INTERNATIONAL SYSTEMS

The advantages of staying within the international system for a small country are obvious. Presumably the knowledge, skills, and

22. There have been numerous efforts to establish criteria for the countries in the last category. The UN has a list of countries "most severely affected" by the oil crisis, UNCTAD has a list of 29 "least developed" countries, and there are other lists of relatively worse-off countries (e.g., landlocked or island countries, or regionally backward countries, or countries with low per capita incomes). These lists are not identical, but there is a great deal of overlap between them. Adding them together suggests a rough total of 60 or 70 eligible countries—with a great deal of shifting at the margins. These countries have certain special characteristics that need to be kept in mind: They have done less well than the other LDCs since 1960 in growth rates of GNP or per capita income or food production; they are least likely to benefit from current aid and trade packages; and they are least able to protect themselves against adverse external developments. I return to their problems in chapter 9.

technology of the industrial countries provide some shortcuts to development and indicate some roads that do not have to be taken or some errors that can be avoided. Another advantage is, of course, that the rich countries can potentially provide bountiful markets for the exports of small countries; this is a substantial improvement over the last century, when there were fewer rich countries and less impressive levels of prosperity. How bountiful these markets are tends to depend on how fast the rich countries are growing. In addition, increased productivity in the rich countries might mean a fall in LDC import prices, and increased prosperity in the rich countries could mean higher levels of foreign aid and private investment. Increasing aid and investment levels in the first half of the 1960s, as well as high aggregate rates of export growth for the LDCs, were thus clearly correlated with rapid growth rates in the major Western economies.

The disadvantages of remaining in the international system for a small country are also obvious. In comparison to the nineteenth century, disparities between rich and poor countries are now on the order of 18 or 20 to 1; in the earlier period they were not much more than 2 to 1.[23] The available technology is also generally more capital intensive, with externalities and invisibilities more important, and is usually created expressly for large-scale, complex, and labor-scarce societies. But beyond these technologic constraints, one other factor is especially critical: The underdeveloped countries must compete with an existing group of advanced countries that have established patterns of behavior that reflect their interests and values.

The existence of the advanced countries may create problems for the poor countries in a number of ways. The demonstration effect, for example, may develop taste or expenditure patterns that are inappropriate or premature for poor countries; luxury imports and government services that drain the investment budget are promi-

---

23. R. B. Sutcliffe, *Industry and Underdevelopment* (London: Addison-Wesley, 1971), p. 324, reports that the average cost of capital in a single industrial operation in nineteenth-century France equaled 6 to 8 months' wages for the average worker; for the LDCs in the current system the average cost of capital in a single industrial operation is now about 350 months' wages—almost 30 years.

nent illustrations. The poor countries may also fear, perhaps rightly, that the superior productivity of the industrial countries, as well as the deliberate policies of powerful multinational corporations, may force the great majority of the LDCs to remain "hewers of wood and drawers of water"—excluded from the most advanced industries, left only to exchange their primary products for more costly manufactured goods. The governments of the rich countries may also reinforce their dominance by supporting only conservative LDC governments and by insisting on the universal validity of theories and doctrines that reflect their own experience. Moreover the "welfare nationalism" of the rich countries may dim the prospect of reforms beneficial to the poor. Even if the rich countries are generous, the benefits may be limited to a few underdeveloped countries: Competition among the poor themselves may rise in significance if the markets of the rich are opened freely to all LDCs, but only a limited number are capable of grasping the opportunity before the rich countries retreat behind carefully drawn escape clauses. And, finally, all of these pressures bear down upon the LDC governments in a period when their own citizens are increasingly aware of the distance between their aspirations and their expectations or between what they have and what the citizens of the rich countries have.[24]

One other factor must be mentioned, however briefly, for it has a profound impact on perceptions of necessary or feasible policies. The population growth rate of the LDCs is much faster than that of the nineteenth century. Current rates of population increase in some LDCs are well over 3 percent per year, and the aggregate figure is between 2 and 3 percent. In the nineteenth century the figure rarely went beyond 1 percent per year and began to rise only after a degree of industrialization had already occurred. For the LDCs the result has been rising levels of unemployment, increases in food

24. There is a useful discussion of the advantages and disadvantages of the international system for the LDCs in Paul Streeten, "More on Development in an International Setting," in Dudley Seers and Leonard Joy, eds., *Development in a Divided World* (Harmondsworth: Penguin Books, 1970), pp. 34–44. There are other factors, for example, the "brain drain," problems of capital flight, and the need for more government intervention, affecting the position of the LDCs that I have not mentioned in this discussion.

imports, and sharp increases in the costs of some social services. The need to deal with these problems cuts the investment rate (particularly because of increases in the number of dependent children and mothers) and creates pressures on LDC governments not faced by their nineteenth-century predecessors.

The underdeveloped countries thus face a double burden. They must deal with an international system of increasing complexity, but they must do so from a domestic base that is less secure and less manageable. Nationalism and a felt sense of injustice about past treatment have also created a severe bias against foreign contact and a strong suspicion that whatever the rich countries do reflects a pattern of deliberate exploitation. The problems of decisionmaking in these circumstances are enormous, for the range of uncertainty is wide, and the costs of miscalculation can be overwhelming. For example, even sound development programs can be undermined by a sharp drop in export receipts (as happened to Ghana with cocoa or Zambia with copper or Ceylon with tea) or by a sharp rise in prices for necessary imports.

There is also usually a fundamental asymmetry in the bargaining positions of the weak and strong. Once committed to a particular set of trading relations, especially with richer and more powerful partners, a small country stands to lose much more (relatively) from interruption of relations than a Great Power does. The absence of a domestic market for previously exported goods, the limited amount of diversification possible in either the range of exports or the number of export markets, and the more difficult adjustment problems for small and underdeveloped economies mean that a small country risks more than a large country in any exchange relationship. Indeed the small country may lose control over a great deal of its foreign policy (economic and political); we need only to recall the experience of the Eastern European countries with Nazi Germany in the 1930s.[25] Beyond these considerations, once a small country—especially an underdeveloped small country—does make a decision to participate or not to participate in the international sys-

---

25. See Albert O. Hirschman, *National Power and the Structure of Foreign Trade* (Berkeley: University of California Press, 1945), p. 25.

tem, it is much less able to reverse or alter the decision: Resources are too limited and too immobile to be easily shifted to new tasks. Note the difficulties that Burma has had in trying to "reopen" its economy or that many Latin American countries have had in moving from import substitution to a more open, export-oriented policy.

That the underdeveloped countries face great risks and uncertainties in joining the international systems is clear beyond reasonable doubt. But does participation also guarantee exploitation and injustice? The evidence that "surplus capital" has to be invested in the underdeveloped countries, or that the rich need the markets of the poor, or that the rich could not prosper without the raw materials of the poor is generally unpersuasive.[26] No simple formula—economic, political, or psychologic—has ever been able to explain the full range of behavior between weak and strong states. Patterns of exploitation dominated colonial relationships in the past and continue to dominate many relationships. But they are not the whole story, not only in the sense that not everything done in the past was evil, but also in the sense that the patterns of the past need not be repeated.

I do not mean to leave the impression that I am an apologist for the record of the past or that I have a naive faith that the international systems can or will be transformed to benefit the poor countries. The international systems are not neutral: They are biased and unfair because they have been constructed to reward the virtues and talents of the dominant powers. The advantages that participation offers may well require capabilities that only a few LDCs possess. The risks may seem too high to some elites, and the benefits may appear insufficient or badly distributed to others. Sometimes meaningful choices may be eliminated by the behavior of the most powerful states. The discipline of playing by the rules of the system is harsh, failure is easy, and the virtues that are rewarded may be almost impossible to acquire by underdeveloped countries. These are powerful constraints and cannot be ignored, but they do

26. These issues are discussed in Benjamin J. Cohen, *The Question of Imperialism—The Political Economy of Dominance and Dependence* (New York: Basic Books, 1973), pp. 132 ff.

not mean that the decision to participate in the international system is always wrong or that the alternatives to participation are necessarily more beneficial.

A number of reasons justify a more sophisticated and differentiated approach to participation in the international system. In the first place some underdeveloped countries are in a much better position than others to extract fair (or even superior) bargains from the dominant powers and their institutions. The degree of benefit a poor country can expect from participation and the degree of protection it can provide for itself against external "shocks" are not fixed and invariable sums: They can be altered by careful and prudent efforts to diversify exports and markets, to create industries that are competitive and likely to provide useful linkages with the rest of the economy, to cut unnecessary imports, and to develop the capacity to respond to whatever opportunities appear.[27] Obviously the very nature of underdevelopment means that it will be difficult to implement such actions effectively. Nevertheless they can be usefully approximated, they are not wildly utopian, and—especially important—they can be accomplished by each national government alone.

Other reasons justify an attempt to perceive the international system in a more differentiated fashion. The international systems are not unchanging and perfectly consistent monoliths. The political structures of these systems can evolve in useful ways, the goals of the major actors may shift, the means they are willing to use in pursuit of their goals may become less violent, and the intellectual climate may become relatively more favorable to the interests and values of the weaker states (as has happened, fitfully, with the slow evolution of a more egalitarian, liberal, and internationalist ethic). Failure to comprehend and to take advantage of these changes could cost the underdeveloped countries substantial benefits. What can be got from aid agencies, international and regional banks, and some advisers and investors is not always sufficiently understood by ref-

27. These issues are discussed from a different perspective in *ibid.*, pp. 168 ff. Charles P. Kindleberger, *Foreign Trade and the National Economy* (New Haven, Conn.: Yale University Press, 1962), is also useful.

erences to the machinations of ITT, the CIA, military advisers, and the United Fruit Company.

Even an intrinsically unfair relationship may provide more benefits than a fair relationship that must be based on isolation and learning by doing without. This is especially true if the dominant powers appear willing to offer more concessions to the subordinate powers and if the bargaining power of the latter group appears to be on the rise. Furthermore some of the development theories now emerging are much more sophisticated than those of the 1950s and 1960s: Many of the newer approaches begin with the problems of the underdeveloped countries, not the experiences of the industrial countries, and they are more concerned with what the developing countries can do, not with what would be most convenient for the rich countries.

These changes do not mean that there is some prospect for the underdeveloped countries of ending dependence. What is at issue here is the possibility of creating a more realistic calculus of choice: a choice between participating in the international system with the intention of slowly and painfully altering the quality and quantity of dependence—but not the fact of dependence—and accepting new approaches that may reduce dependence but carry costs and dangers of their own. There are, of course, variations of each of these choices in which the primary goal is only the survival and enrichment of the elite.

These are stark choices, but they only recognize the limitations imposed by the burden of underdevelopment in a complex international system. Whatever the underdeveloped countries have attempted to do, they have remained dependent: Exporting primary products has meant dependence on foreign demand; import substitution led to even higher import coefficients, as well as dependence on foreign private investment; export of labor-intensive manufactured products is again dependent on foreign demand and foreign investment; and a foreign policy of nonalignment has not generally provided the benefits its proponents have envisaged. Trade with other LDCs has never amounted to enough to alter the basic picture, and it will be some years before current efforts at "collective self-reliance" can have more than a marginal impact. Nor have deliberate attempts to withdraw from the international system led to real autonomy; one needs only to examine the sorry record of Burma in the last two decades. Whether the new emphasis on redistribution and self-reliance can alter these judgments is a complex and unclear question that I discuss in some detail in chapter 9.

Too frequently the elites, as well as many radical analysts, have simply taken it on faith that the industrial countries are a power elite intent solely on exploitation and that the international systems are intrinsically and unalterably imperialistic. But the existence of a power elite means only that the opportunity to exploit exists; it does not mean that the opportunity will be always and everywhere grasped.

A number of factors have inhibited more objective elite calculations or expectations about the nature of the external environment. One is simply the contemporary record itself: bribery, overpricing, and other machinations by some multinational corporations, overt and covert interventions into the domestic affairs of many developing countries, high levels of protection when LDC exports threaten some industries in the developed countries, and so on. Another factor has been the lack of sufficient expertise within the developing countries to bargain effectively or to be able to make the best judgments about the available range of choice—although this is clearly changing. Two other factors seem, however, to be particularly important. The first factor reflects the inability or reluctance of the ruling elite and its supporters to confront domestic problems directly and honestly. As the prime beneficiaries of the existing order and of the emphasis on rapid growth (which justified sharp inequities in income distribution), the elites have responded to escalating domestic problems by seeking external scapegoats and by demanding external relief for internal deficiencies. In some instances this response may have been justified, and in most instances it was at least understandable, but it was also simplistic and insufficient in the great majority of cases. I discuss this factor in more detail in the next chapter. Here I want only to comment briefly on the other major inhibiting factor: the failure to make a distinction between dependence and exploitation.

Dependence and exploitation sometimes have been and sometimes are equivalent terms, but they have not always been so, nor do they need to be so in the future. Exploitation is rarely defined in a precise fashion. Barrington Moore, for example, has argued that exploitation "forms part of an exchange of goods and services when 1) the goods and services exchanged are quite obviously not of equivalent value, and 2) one party to the exchange uses a substantial degree of coercion." [28] How does one measure what is "of equivalent value"? Or suppose we argue that exploitation exists when a powerful state takes unfair advantage of its superiority. How shall we determine what is fair and unfair? Does a rich country exploit a poor country when the rich country buys the poor country's raw materials cheaply if they are cheaper because they are in abundance and cost less to extract? There is no abstract answer to this question. The distinction between an acceptable commercial exchange and exploitation may not always be easy to make—and, indeed, may not be present—but unless the attempt is made, any discussion is entirely rhetorical or ideological. Failure to do so has meant that foreign investment and foreign ties have usually either been attacked and eliminated on spurious grounds or attacked but granted access in exchange for favors and bribes.

The problem of distinguishing between normal commercial exchange and exploitation would, of course, be much easier if a generally acceptable definition of exploitation existed. But no such definition does exist, nor is one likely to be created: Ultimately, the meaning of exploitation seems to rest on an underlying notion of the distinction between what is fair and what is unfair, but this distinction is too entangled with values and beliefs to be stated in a fashion that would engender universal agreement. At the extreme most of us might agree whether a particular action is fair or unfair, but the majority cases seem to fall somewhere in the middle of the spectrum, where either/or judgments are misleading. There is some virtue in these circumstances in self-consciousness: that is, in at least recognizing that interpretations of exploitation are usually value laden and that what is frequently involved is the need to

28. Barrington Moore, Jr., *Reflections on the Causes of Human Misery and upon Certain Proposals to Eliminate Them* (Boston: Beacon Press, 1972), p. 53.

make careful judgments about trade-offs between the costs and benefits of each case.

Few of the elites have made these calculations. For the most part what many of them have done is clear: They have adopted an aggressive posture rhetorically but in reality have attempted to decide as little as possible or risk as little as possible. Incrementalism has seemed much less costly and has reduced the degree of uncertainty in the short run. The order of the day, consequently, has been accommodation with foreign capitalists and other domestic elites. The loss of control, the dangers of competition, and the risks (real and imagined) attendant upon participation in the international trading system explain why the elites have been so reluctant to open their economies to the outside world, but the limited benefits from closing off their economies or from capitulating to foreign interests and tastes explain why there has been so much vacillation and "muddling through" in the decisionmaking process.

I am not arguing that participation is always the best choice or indeed that any simple statement about the relationship between the developing countries and the external environment is justified. Specific decisions by an individual country must take much more into account than the general considerations just noted: a country's level of development, its export prospects, what it desires from its economy (e.g., growth, distribution, more autonomy, national strength), its judgment of the future, and its own willingness to take risks. The dangers move, moreover, in both directions, for an undiscriminating rejection of external involvement is as futile and costly as an undiscriminating acceptance of every value or product the external world offers. What I have been arguing for, therefore, is, not a particular decision, but a less ideological and more pragmatic way of thinking about the external world and its opportunities and dangers.

In particular the possibility of reforming the international systems and of dealing with them more selectively must be weighed against the other alternatives that are in fact open to poor and weak countries: Romantic notions about the possibility of going it alone or going it with a union of the poor may be as dangerous and futile as the notion that the existing international system is equally fair to all. The developing countries do not have a wide range of viable alternatives *especially in any short- or medium-term perspective:* Even leaving the international system could be accomplished only after a period of extensive external involvement to acquire the imports that might make self-reliance feasible. The constricted range of real choice ought never to be forgotten by those who jump so easily from the notion that the external world is unfair to the notion that there are easy alternatives to learning how to deal with it. The developing countries, like the hedgehog, have learned one big thing about the international system—that it exploits poor countries (or that the charge that it does so is useful) and consequently must be overthrown. Now the underdeveloped countries also need to learn, like the fox, the many small things that might enable them to establish a more profitable balance in international transactions.

If we can navigate the current crisis without disaster, it seems to me that the possibility of extracting a better bargain from various parts of the international systems may be improving—from government and international aid programs, from trade preferences, from a growing understanding of the methods of controlling the behavior of multinational corporations, from improved bargaining leverage in the resource arena, and perhaps even from the development of more appropriate theories and attitudes. By themselves, however, these changes are important but insufficient. In one sense they do not go far enough, for they do not reflect a coherent and lasting commitment to integrate the developing countries more thoroughly into the international system.[29] And they do not yet provide the developing countries with what may be—I believe—the irreducible minimum obligation of the rich countries: protection against external developments for which the poor countries are not responsible

29. Another argument is sometimes raised against the changes I have just listed: that they are incremental and are not sufficiently revolutionary to solve most Third World problems and that they are simultaneously sufficiently supportive of the existing elite structure to prevent others from implementing radical reforms. There are cases in which I would accept the main thrust of this position, if not all the details, but there are more cases in which I would disagree. The argument suffers from many problems: the vice of aggregation (see chapter 1), a reluctance to look closely at the record, romanticism about the options really open to very poor countries, and so on. I do not, however, deal with this issue in detail here but reserve comment to chapters 5 and 11.

but from which they are the first victims. I return to these issues in the concluding chapter.

The other sense in which existing changes are insufficient is, of course, that they guarantee nothing to those countries that cannot take advantage of existing or emerging opportunities. For this problem the ultimate responsibility belongs to the developing countries themselves. Help can be sought from friendly and competent international organizations, and perhaps even from a new Third World research organization (much discussed lately), but priorities can be established and translated into action, and trade-offs can be evaluated between various forms of domestic control and various forms of participation only if the ruling elite is committed to national development and only if the policymaking system is capable of achieving steady and sustained results. Chapters 6 and 7 confront these issues directly.

# Part Two

## From the Cold War to the Oil War

# 3

## External Policy: The First Decade

The developing countries that achieved their independence in the first decade or so after World War II tended to adopt a number of similar policies. Economic nationalism, import substitution industrialization, nonalignment, and regional cooperation were not universal policy choices, but they were certainly widely accepted. We look briefly at these policies in this and the next chapter, not to provide a detailed analysis, but rather to seek some insight into two questions. First, what effect did these policy choices have on the relationship between the developing countries and the external world? And second, what can the experience with these policies tell us about the problems and limitations of policymaking in the context of underdevelopment?

### ECONOMIC NATIONALISM: THE COSTS OF "INDIGENISM"

Economic policies frequently seem paradoxical. Does a cut in consumption really raise incomes in the long run? Is it really necessary to distribute income inequitably in the short run to achieve a more equitable distribution in the long run? To anyone who understood the prevailing growth theories, the answers were obvious. But to a weak government, confronting demands from an aroused populace for some immediate return from independence, the injunction to demand sacrifices—not to offer rewards—seemed willful and dangerous. A development policy not only failed to provide shortrun benefits (except to a favored few) but also implied a long period of instability as new groups emerged and demanded instant recognition, and old groups resisted any loss of wealth or status.

For elites concerned with domestic stability and personal security, economic nationalism was a rational response to the circumstances in which they found themselves. Economic development was concerned with increasing national income; economic nationalism, conversely, was concerned with how the national income was divided. The goal, simply put, was to expel foreigners, to take over their investments, and to limit the terms under which future foreign investments might be made. This did not necessarily or even usually imply the nationalization of domestic industries (that is, ownership by the state itself). "Indigenism"—the replacement of foreigners by native proprietors and workers—was at least the ostensible goal; more precisely the major goal was to transfer national wealth into the hands of whatever group controlled the government.[1]

Significant costs were attached to a policy of economic nationalism, especially if it was seriously implemented. There were obvious costs in investments foregone and in higher interest rates on whatever investments did take place, as well as the costs of paying for expropriated assets—if they were paid. There were also costs in efficiency if the new owners and workers were less productive than the foreigners they displaced. Perhaps even more important were the effects not simply on existing enterprises but on the order of future priorities that the government felt compelled to establish. Thus industrialization—the great symbol of national development in the modern world—took precedence over agricultural productivity, even though the vast majority of the population lived (barely) off the land; within an industrialization policy, certain industries like steel were favored, even if it meant producing well above the world

1. On this theme, with much detail from one area, see Frank H. Golay *et al.*, *Underdevelopment and Economic Nationalism in Southeast Asia* (Ithaca, N.Y.: Cornell University Press, 1969).

market price; products were required to have the highest possible domestic content, even if this meant higher costs and lower quality; immediate, visible symbols of national standing (like armies, dams, and monuments) were favored over less dramatic achievements; and public enterprise was inevitably favored over private, for there were not enough indigenous entrepreneurs both to replace for-eigners and to create new industries.[2] The status aspects of eco-nomic nationalism were particularly costly, for they tended to imply too much imitation of capital-intensive Western technology and premature acquisition of Western institutions like labor unions or social welfare services before the state could afford to pay for them.

Why bear such costs? In the first place, costs were measured in terms of their presumed impact on economic growth. But economic growth was not the only, or even the primary, goal of many leaders. Inheriting states that were barely unified and badly integrated, what the leaders sought were policies that helped to create a sense of identity with the nation and a sense of legitimacy for the govern-ment. Economic nationalism responded to these needs, for the ex-pulsion of foreigners provided the "we" against "them" symbolism that seemed necessary. Moreover the economic losses attendant on nationalism were not likely to be immediately apparent—in fact, to the unsophisticated, simply taking over prosperous enterprises seemed all that was necessary to ensure domestic prosperity—while the psychic and symbolic returns could be put to use at once.[3]

Only a few elite groups came to power intent on major struc-tural transformations of their societies. Naiveté about the ease with which economic growth could be achieved—fueled in part by the simplistic growth theories then prevalent—and about the extent to which political independence also implied economic autonomy

2. For interesting comments on the costs of nationalism, see Harry G. Johnson, "A Theoretical Model of Economic Nationalism in New and Developing States," in Harry G. Johnson, ed., *Economic Nationalism in Old and New States* (Chicago: Univer-sity of Chicago Press, 1967).

3. If in fact the benefits of growth are inequitably distributed, economic nation-alism may not be so irrational—over the long run. If the country develops capabili-ties that it would otherwise leave unused, and if it does learn by doing, short-term losses may be offset by gains over time. This calculation was not, however, made at the time, and the elites generally adopted economic nationalism in terms of its short-run advantages.

were partially responsible. In addition the ruling elites were rarely in a sufficiently strong position to risk the dangers and dislocations of fundamental change. In these circumstances economic nationalism once again seemed appropriate, for it was hardly a revolutionary policy; changing owners did not change the underlying economic structure. Indeed it probably made major change even more difficult by creating a new domestic class with a vested interest in maintaining the status quo. Thus "Africanization" or "Asianism" were primarily (though not exclusively) conservative strategies aimed only at changing which small group profited at the expense of the others.[4]

Economic nationalism provides psychic benefits for all the citizens of a new state, and this is particularly useful for elites intent on bolstering a sense of national unity. But economic nationalism also provides tangible returns to the small group that inherits the jobs and businesses of the expelled foreigners. As Breton notes, this creates disproportions in the distribution of benefits, for the jobs and businesses tend to go to the middle class: They, in effect, share the costs of economic nationalism with all their fellow citizens but keep the tangible benefits for themselves.[5] The political elite may actually favor this outcome, in spite of its inequities, for it enables them to pay off their own supporters quickly and safely—at an apparent cost only to foreigners.

Finally, the costs of economic nationalism were bearable not only because it provided important returns to the elite but also because the costs themselves were not allowed to get out of hand. The quest for national unity and the desire to assert the state's independence and autonomy were facilitated by attacking foreigners (especially the more vulnerable foreigners) and replacing them with natives, but there was only so far that such a policy could go before

4. See Henry Bienen, *Tanzania: Party Transformation and Economic Development* (Princeton, N.J.: Princeton University Press, 1967), pp. 218, 219, and 305.

5. Albert Breton, "The Economics of Nationalism," *Journal of Political Economy* 72, no. 4 (August 1964):376–86. Aggregate income may go up after confiscation: Previously a share of the national income went abroad, and that share now stays home. Obviously the share that now stays home is likely to be smaller than it was when repatriated (because of inefficiency, etc.), but the fact that all the national income does stay home means that the total may decline, but the income of individual citizens may go up. The key is how well the citizens do with the expropriated assets.

the economic losses would begin to outweigh the political and economic gains. Few LDCs had the skilled manpower to take over foreign enterprises, especially if those enterprises were export oriented—as many obviously were—and thus required the talent and knowledge to deal with the external world. In any case the foreign response was unlikely to be sympathetic to the new managers of confiscated enterprises. Beyond this many of the elites shared the values of foreign investors and had their own economic and political fortunes closely tied to the foreign sector.[6] Consequently, while the domestic elites could see the advantages of attacking an easy scapegoat like foreign capitalists, they also saw the dangers to themselves of carrying that attack too far and threatening the entire economic structure that they had inherited—and from which they benefited.

In most cases pragmatism prevailed over ideology. Promises of "reclaiming the national patrimony" were never completely redeemed, especially in enterprises that had to deal with the external world. And even with wholly domestic firms, nationalization tended to be limited to those areas where the domestic entrepreneurs seemed likely to be able to operate successfully—that is, in consumer industries, where the local pattern of demand had already been mapped out. In many cases the foreign owners simply hired a few supporters of the ruling elite, or bribed them, and managed to hang on. Even a country as ideologically committed as the Ghana of Nkrumah found that it had to compromise with foreign capitalists or its export earnings would drop sharply.[7] The same held true for Indonesia, which discovered that expelling the Dutch was too costly, or Burma, whose leaders felt that they either had to yield to the foreign capitalists or turn sharply inward and leave the international economic system.[8] And the Ivory Coast, aware of its heavy dependence on France, did not bother even to seek whatever politi-

6. On these points, see especially Henry L. Bretton, *Power and Politics in Africa* (Chicago: Aldine, 1973).

7. See Roger Genoud, *Nationalism and Economic Development in Ghana* (New York: Praeger, 1969), pp. 159 ff.

8. Bruce Glassburner, "Economic Policy-Making in Indonesia, 1950–57," *Economic Development and Cultural Change* 10, no. 2 (January 1962):113–33; Hans O. Schmitt, "Decolonization and Development in Burma," *The Journal of Development Studies* 4, no. 1 (October 1967):97–108.

cal benefits economic nationalism might create: Houphouët-Boigny simply accepted the necessity of a heavy French "presence" and was rewarded with high levels of foreign aid and investment (and very high rates of growth).[9]

These examples reflect different ways of dealing with the same basic dilemma: the need to attack foreigners for domestic political reasons, but the need for continued foreign support to keep the domestic economy going. The result was that while economic nationalism was never completely a rhetorical policy—for foreign enterprises were taken over to one degree or another in most developing countries—it was rarely carried on to the point where it would constitute a fundamental challenge to the status quo. Potential clashes with the external world—investors and their governments—were generally averted, for the rhetoric of economic nationalism and the provision of jobs and benefits for the elites and their supporters seldom threatened the underlying reality of continued foreign control.

———————————

Economic nationalism could be conceived as a short-term policy designed to buy time and support for an incumbent regime while it seeks to consolidate its power. And in a more extended perspective, economic nationalism could be a useful instrument of economic development, for it justifies the development of the local skills and capital necessary to compete in the international trading system. But economic nationalism was also never really a viable long-range economic strategy. A poor country intent on rapid growth must also develop an economic strategy designed to make the most of its limited resources within the context of a particular international environment.

What this obviously means is that, after the initial political struggles are resolved, external policy in its broadest sense—that is, both foreign policy and international trade policy—must become

9. See Elliot J. Berg, "Structural Transformation versus Gradualism: Recent Economic Development in Ghana and the Ivory Coast," in Philip Foster and Aristide R. Zolberg, eds., *Ghana and the Ivory Coast: Perspective on Modernization* (Chicago: University of Chicago Press, 1971), pp. 187–230.

increasingly important. Economic nationalism may well influence the nature of the choice made, but the necessity of choosing an orientation toward the external world cannot be avoided. The gap between available resources and needed resources can be filled only by foreign resources (or so the prevailing theories argued), and the elite itself was bound to become concerned with its place in the growth rate sweepstakes, not only because of domestic pressure, but also because the need for rapid growth was one of the more salient "demonstration effects" that the rich countries passed on to the elites of the poor countries.

Import substitution industrialization (ISI) was the economic response to these circumstances. Nonalignment was the foreign policy response. And regional cooperation sought to overcome some of the limitations of both ISI and nonalignment.

## IMPORT SUBSTITUTION INDUSTRIALIZATION: THE PERIPHERY RESPONDS TO THE CENTER

### IMPORT SUBSTITUTION: DEFINITIONS AND DIRECTIONS

Import substitution seeks to increase the share of total consumption satisfied by domestic production. Primarily it involves an effort to take over the existing domestic market from foreign producers by prohibiting their imports (usually by high tariffs and other import controls).[10] To the extent that the new industries created to supply domestic demand could one day be competitive with the displaced foreign producers—an important qualification—high rates of protection could be justified by reference to arguments for protection of infant industry. There were also, as we shall see, other economic arguments for import substitution, especially the need to stimulate domestic entrepreneurs by providing them with a captive market. But ISI cannot be understood in wholly

10. See Stefan H. Robock, "Industrialization Through Import-Substitution or Export Industries: A False Dichotomy," in Jesse W. Markham and Gustav Papanek, eds., *Industrial Organization and Economic Development* (Boston: Houghton Mifflin, 1970), pp. 350–65; and Jose A. Datas-Panero, "Import-Substitution," *Finance and Development* 8, no. 3 (September 1971):34–39.

economic terms, for political and psychologic factors were equally important.

Import substitution did not work out very well. We discuss some of the economic reasons for this below and in chapter 8. In the next section, however, we ask why ISI was so appealing to so many developing countries.

THE POPULARITY OF ISI

There were a number of developing countries that did not adopt inwardly oriented policies of ISI—Taiwan, South Korea, Hong Kong, Singapore, Malaysia, the Philippines, the Ivory Coast, and Pakistan (for a period in the 1960s). Many of these countries faced a major security threat, which meant—among other things— that they needed and received high levels of foreign aid. Some (like Hong Kong and Singapore) had no choice but to adopt an export orientation. In addition, for various reasons few of these countries could hope to ameliorate their problems by regional agreements. Finally the majority of these countries were run by strong military regimes or a powerful political leader; consequently to some degree domestic pressures could be contained or suppressed. For the most part these governments were also pro-Western—or at least heavily dependent on Western support.

Conditions were considerably different for most of the other developing countries. In particular, while the ruling elites were at least ostensibly committed to rapid growth, they were generally in a weak position domestically and without access to substantial external resources. What the elites needed was a growth strategy that was not too destabilizing domestically, that seemed to make economic sense, and that responded sufficiently to nationalist pressures. Import substitution was popular because it satisfied all these constraints: It was not really revolutionary, it provided an acceptable interpretation of how to achieve high growth rates in a hostile world, and it was created or popularized primarily by a number of Third World elites—and sharply criticized by many Western economists. All these factors made ISI extremely useful politically and psychologically to the elites who adopted it.

In retrospect the economic growth theories of the 1950s seem vastly oversimplified responses to complex problems. This is usually attributed to two factors: the need for a clear and attractive alternative to the Soviet model of development and the tendency to use the relatively uncomplicated history of Western economic growth as a relevant analogy for the LDCs. As Hirschman remarked, most of the available theories stressed easy "stages of growth" in which, once a missing link had been provided (usually capital or technology or entrepreneurship), economic growth would follow more or less automatically.[11] Other problems, like population growth, income inequities, or political development, would presumably disappear as incomes rose.

The growth theories said very little about the international economic system itself, but implicitly they rested on the notion that the system—that is, the pattern of relations established by the major economic powers—would have a benign effect. The theories acted *as if* the behavior of the industrial countries could be treated as a constant and as invariably providing fair opportunities to all, and not merely to the rich countries. This implied that the underdeveloped countries could safely concentrate on solving their internal problems without worrying too much about biases or "shocks" from abroad. But if this judgment was incorrect, the developing countries could follow the theories perfectly—and still find themselves impoverished as a result of protection, excessive profits for foreign investors, declining aid levels, and a structure of production that benefited primarily the rich.

In whatever choice they made, therefore, the underdeveloped countries had to make a critical calculation about the likely behavior of the industrial countries. A long history of colonial exploitation meant that suspicion and fear dominated most calculations: The international system would have to appear very benign to make the risk of joining it attractive. Everyone might indeed be better off in an open system, but the system was never that open for the LDCs—one needs only to note, for example, that the rich countries spent at least three times as much on direct and indirect support of domestic production of importable primary commodities as they did on

11. Albert Hirschman, *The Strategy of Economic Development* (New Haven, Conn.: Yale University Press, 1958), pp. 7 ff.

foreign aid.[12] In these circumstances the ruling elites were likely to be predisposed toward any economic strategy that promised not only more growth but also—and perhaps especially—more autonomy.

In the abstract these goals might have been sought by a number of different approaches. In practice, however, rapid industrialization became the order of the day, not only because it seemed to be a symbol of modernity (to the elites), but also because the agricultural sector was a symbol of the colonial era. In addition, according to conventional theory, industrialization seemed to provide better returns on investments and more prospects of increased employment opportunities.[13]

The decision to concentrate on industrialization meant that an effective relationship with the external world had to be established. Maintaining a steady stream of imports was imperative for any industrialization process—as distinct from, for example, merely increasing national income by exchanging primary products for manufactured goods—for the necessary capital goods could only be imported. If imports were imperative, foreign exchange was also imperative. Other than running down reserves (which few underdeveloped countries had), or relying on the profits of the industrial sector itself (which were too small), or taking money from the other sectors of the economy (which were too poor to pay the industrialization bill), or receiving high levels of foreign aid and investment (which only a few countries got, usually close allies of the United States), the only other alternative was a high rate of export growth. Since few LDCs had any manufactures to export, and since the few that did (usually in Latin America) faced tariff and nontariff barriers in the industrial countries, the only thing left to export seemed to be the traditional primary products that the LDCs had always exported. Some countries that possessed the right mix of primary products—and sufficient faith that their markets would remain open—did try this alternative, for example, the Ivory Coast

12. See Ignacy Sachs, "Outward-Looking Strategies: A Dangerous Illusion?", in Paul Streeten, ed., *Trade Strategies for Development* (London: Macmillan, 1973), p. 56.

13. R. B. Sutcliffe, *Industry and Underdevelopment* (London: Addison-Wesley, 1971), has a good discussion of all these issues.

and Malaysia. But the vast majority of LDCs either did not have promising primary product exports or were convinced that continuing to rely on such exports would leave them underdeveloped, dependent, and exploited. The arguments that appeared to justify export pessimism for the LDCs—and consequently an emphasis on import substitution industrialization—were usually identified with the name of Raul Prebisch, the Argentine economist who was the Director of the Economic Commission for Latin America.

Prebisch's central argument was that the terms of trade for Latin America's primary product exports were falling because the benefits of economic progress were being monopolized by the rich countries. Increased productivity in the rich countries did not lead to lower prices for the manufactured goods that the Latin Americans wanted to import: The power of labor unions to force wages up and to keep them there and of large corporations to maintain artificially high prices meant that the "center" did not pass its gains back to the "periphery." Conversely increases in productivity in the periphery were passed on to the consumer in the industrial countries via lower prices. The periphery needed the manufacturing imports that only the center could provide more than the center needed the raw materials that only the periphery could provide: Declining demand for primary products as incomes rose, increased efficiency that lowered the raw materials content of many manufactures, the increased use of synthetics, and increases in the service sector of the advanced economies all meant that the demand for primary goods would fall. Producers and consumers in the rich countries both benefited, by higher prices for their exports and lower prices for their imports, while LDC producers and consumers were both victimized. The result was exploitation, for the strong were taking unfair advantage of the weak.[14]

Prebisch's pessimism about the prospects for primary product exports was supported by several other economists. H. H. Singer, for example, argued that, since much of the investment in primary products was foreign, and since foreign investors repatriated high rates of profit, the secondary effects of the investment process

14. Prebisch's papers are conveniently collected (although somewhat shortened) in *Development Problems In Latin America* (Austin: University of Texas Press, 1970).

would be lost. The "spread effects" or the "linkage effects" of specialization in primary products were thus likely to be limited. This specialization also presumably allowed less scope for technologic progress or for economies of scale.[15]

Prebisch's arguments provided a strong justification for rapid industrialization. Since the developing countries could not earn sufficient foreign exchange by exporting primary products, and since manufacturing exports were minimal, and since foreign aid was insufficient, the only alternative was import substitution. Thus ISI was designed—or rationalized—in terms of the foreign exchange it would save. By prohibiting imports of consumer goods, they could spend the money saved on imports of the essential capital goods necessary for industrialization. Necessary imports henceforth would displace unnecessary imports, and new domestic industries would supply the missing imports. The new industries would also provide employment for rapidly growing populations.

These arguments completed the circle. An economic attack on the traditional export policies of the LDCs was joined to an economic argument for a particular (though not really new) strategy of industrialization. Prebisch performed two services for the ruling elites: He provided an intellectual rationale for rapid industrialization, which was what the elites wanted to do anyway, and for rejecting dependence on the export of primary products, which was what the elites did not want to do. Perversely the effort to end dependence resulted in even more dependence for the developing countries, for imports of capital goods to create a domestic industrial base could not be foregone—as consumer goods imports could—in an ensuing crisis.

Prebisch's views were sharply challenged by many economists. The critics disagreed with his contention that there was a secular decline in the terms of trade for primary products, or that instability in commodity prices was especially disabling, or that the failure of benefits to "trickle down" to the periphery was due more to exploitation by the center than incorrect policies followed by the periph-

15. H. H. Singer, *International Development: Growth and Change* (New York: McGraw-Hill, 1964), p. 165.

[84]

ery.[16] Nevertheless, whatever the long-term trend, commodity prices were sharply falling from their Korean War highs, instability did exist and made planning very difficult, and the developed countries were not making a fundamental effort to deal with the problems of the developing countries. Moreover, Prebisch's emphasis on industrialization was shared by virtually all of the prevailing development theories: Disagreement centered on means, not ends. Import substitution was also a low-risk strategy—in the short run. The domestic market had already been mapped out by foreign importers, and the new industrialists who replaced them had guaranteed gains. Finally Prebisch provided the elites with a rationale for doing what they wanted to do anyway, for primary product exports evoked memories of a colonial past, and industrialization evoked visions of an autonomous future. This was particularly important because the elites wanted not only rapid growth—and the status and prosperity it implied—but also increased autonomy and self-reliance.

If import substitution had been implemented carefully, and if it had been limited to industries likely to become competitive in the future—either internationally or regionally—it would have been a sensible part of an industrialization strategy. But its main attractions, I believe, were political and psychologic, not economic. Domestically it could be seen as an expression of nationalism, as a means to transfer resources to allies, as a relatively risk-free strategy (to both foreign investors and indigenous entrepreneurs, protected by the new tariff barriers), and as an acceptable way to begin a process of industrialization. Externally, in a negative sense, it was not a radical threat to the existing order, for the goal of rapid industrialization was widely sanctioned, and the means employed did not totally exclude foreign investment. And in a more positive sense a partially closed strategy that attempted to import only the goods necessary to industrialize was not an irrational response to a

16. See, for example, Theodore Morgan, "Economic Relationships Among Nations: The Pattern of Commodity Trade," in Bert Hoselitz, ed., *Economics and the Idea of Mankind* (New York: Columbia University Press, 1965), pp. 143–91; and H. Myint, "Economic Theory and Development Policy," *Economica* 34, no. 134 (May 1967):119 ff.

world in which rapid growth was a prime value, in which the prospects for primary products seemed bleak, and in which the continuation of traditional patterns of exchange seemed likely only to increase the gap between rich and poor.

### CONSEQUENCES: ANTICIPATED AND UNANTICIPATED

Most of the ruling elites probably adopted rapid growth and rapid industrialization via import substitution with mixed motives and without much thought about the long run. The climate of opinion within many developing countries, the pressure of example from other Third World countries, and the ease with which the decision responded to both the domestic and international pressures confronting the ruling elites all played some role in popularizing a particular pattern of development and a particular response to the external world. But the failure to think through longrun consequences or to understand the difficulties of controlling the effects of shortrun decisions in countries with weak policymaking systems has had profound and lasting effects on the prospects and problems of the developing countries.

Criticisms of import substitution have tended to focus on the short-term economic costs.[17] Thus it has frequently been claimed that the substitution process usually ground to a halt after the creation of low-level consumer goods industries, for most domestic markets were too small to make the production of intermediate or capital goods feasible. The new industries also tended to be high cost and inefficient, for they had no need to learn how to compete once protected by tariffs and other devices. Inefficiency also hindered exporting, an effect exacerbated by overvalued exchange rates (to facilitate imports of necessary inputs) and administrative difficulties with export and import controls. As a consequence, for example, Latin America's share of world trade dropped from 1950 to 1970, with little domestic compensation, since the manufacturing sector of the GDP went up only from 19 percent to 25.6 percent.[18]

17. See Robock, "Industrialization Through Import-Substitution or Export Industries"; and Albert O. Hirschman, *A Bias for Hope: Essays on Development and Latin America* (New Haven, Conn.: Yale University Press, 1971), pp. 85–123.

18. Miguel S. Wionczek, "Latin American Growth and Trade Strategies in the Post-War Period," *Journal of Developing Areas* 8, no. 4 (1973):9.

Moreover, the new industries did not help the employment problem very much, both because of population growth rates and because of the adoption of capital-intensive techniques that required skilled labor.

Domestic agriculture also suffered from the adoption of import substitution policies. Agricultural exports were hurt by overvalued exchange rates, and the costs and quality of the goods that had to be bought domestically were affected by inefficiency and the lack of competition. The justification for this rested on the assumptions that only manufacturing could provide rapid enough growth, that industrialization was likely to provide far more "linkages" with the rest of the economy, and that increased investment funds for manufacturing had to come from some other sector of the economy.[19] What was not sufficiently foreseen was the extent to which weakening the largest economic sector would slow the growth of a domestic market to buy industrial products and the extent to which scarce foreign exchange would have to be spent on food imports. This illustrates, again, that import substitution was primarily adopted as a reflex response to immediate pressures, and not as a carefully analyzed long-term strategy.

The emphasis on rapid growth and rapid industrialization also tended to create a particular kind of society with particular patterns of production. One result was increased inequality in income distribution.[20] Presumably the inequities would be reduced or eliminated either by direct government efforts to redistribute income (e.g., by taxes or subsidies) or by the operation of a "trickle down" mechanism. This has not happened, perhaps because there were administrative weaknesses, or because the elites were unwilling to redistribute, or because the very adoption of modern technology (which requires highly skilled workers and an unequal distribution of income to purchase modern consumer goods) requires an unequal society. In any event, as Stewart and Streeten note, a reinforcing cycle develops:

19. See Hirschman, *The Strategy of Economic Development*, pp. 109, 110.
20. See Irma Adelman and Cynthia Taft Morris, *Economic Growth and Social Equity in Developing Countries* (Stanford, Calif.: Stanford University Press, 1973), pp. 182, 183.

high growth leads to the adoption of Western technology, which tends (for technical reasons) to generate inequalities; those who benefit also gain power, and set in motion further policies reinforcing the inequalities and the pattern of development which gave rise to it.[21]

There is some irony in the fact that ISI was ostensibly adopted to save foreign exchange yet not only failed to do so but also left each country more dependent on even more critical imports. External shocks would no longer inhibit imports of cigarettes, soft drinks, or textiles but would inhibit imports of vital equipment and supplies to keep the industrial sector operating. In any case, since many of the new industries were foreign owned and repatriated high rates of profit, borrowed on the local capital market, manipulated transfer prices to keep tax payments low, and overwhelmed indigenous entrepreneurs, they provided only minimal benefits for the local economy. And neither the foreign-owned nor the locally owned industries had much incentive to export—domestic profits were high enough.

Import substitution also had an unforeseen effect on the prospects for regional integration (or even wider forms of Third World collaboration like collective self-reliance). On the one hand each developing country tended to create domestic industries producing the same low-level range of products and thus complicating the development of trading relationships. On the other hand the new import-replacing industries themselves required imports primarily produced by the industrial countries and thus reinforced dependence on traditional trading ties.[22]

The unfortunate effects of an excessive emphasis on rapid growth and import substitution industrialization are thus clear. Domestically a production pattern was created that deflected attention away from the agricultural sector and increased income inequities. Externally dependence on the developed countries increased, and

21. Frances Stewart and Paul Streeten, "New Strategies of Development: A Comment" (unpublished paper), p. 15.
22. On this point, see the comments by Douglas Paauw in Theodore Morgan and Nyle Spoelstra, eds., *Economic Interdependence in Southeast Asia* (Madison: University of Wisconsin Press, 1969), p. 375.

ties with other developing countries became more difficult to negotiate. These effects were compounded by virtue of the fact that developing countries lack the resources and the flexibility to alter
course easily, even when the need to do so becomes apparent.

But why did these policies lead to such bad results, and why
were more efforts not made to alter them? And what lessons can we
extract from this discussion about the limits of policymaking in the
context of underdevelopment?

IMPORT SUBSTITUTION INDUSTRIALIZATION: AN INTERPRETATION

Some of the reasons for the failures of import substitution are
implicit in what has already been said. The ruling elites and their
supporters were the prime beneficiaries of the industries created
and obviously were unlikely to contemplate changes that might
threaten their own interests. But if the elites can fairly be indicted
for corruption and conservatism, I think some compassion is also
necessary in light of the problems they confronted. The goals they
were seeking—rapid growth and rapid industrialization—were
sanctioned by the prevailing development theories, and other approaches to development (e.g., via slower growth, redistribution,
and self-reliance) were not available or were under sharp attack
(e.g., autarky as in Burma).

Apart from those who were wholly corrupt and intent only on
enriching themselves and their supporters, many elites may have
adopted their goals in reasonably good faith that they were setting
their countries on the right path. The simplistic nature of the existing development theories, which seemed to promise virtually automatic results, undoubtedly facilitated the decision; so too did the
fact that the theories could also be used to justify the immediate
provision of benefits for friends and allies. If no one was looking
very far ahead, that was also due, in part, to the nature of theories
that seemed to imply that existing problems—inequity, population
growth, agricultural inefficiencies—would be easily resolved in the
process of growth itself, and, in part, to the difficulties that weak
and insecure leaders had in thinking very far ahead.

Perhaps this puts a somewhat different perspective on the contention that import substitution failed because it did not lead to any fundamental changes in the socioeconomic order.[23] This is generally true: For the most part what happened was that some goods were now supplied domestically that previously had been imported, and a different elite group usually profited at the expense of everybody else. Existing demand patterns, already distorted by the demonstration effect, and the existing distribution of income, already skewed in favor of the middle and upper classes, were simply reinforced.

Two things ought, however, to be said about this criticism. In the first place rapid growth and rapid industrialization were not designed to freeze the existing order: Most of the elites, few of whom were economically sophisticated, thought (or at least appeared to think) that they were adopting policies that would gradually and steadily benefit everyone and create the basis of a modern economy. In the second place, if these policies had seemed revolutionary, they would never have been chosen by elites in constant fear that they were about to be overthrown. The question is not really why import substitution failed as a revolutionary strategy, for it was never meant to be revolutionary, but why a strategy that was meant to produce progressively beneficial results was converted into a reactionary defense of an increasingly inequitable status quo.

I think a good part of the answer to this question can be found in the context of decisionmaking in developing countries. New and inexperienced elites were forced to decide critical strategic issues without much knowledge or expertise, without many useful precedents, and in the face of sharp domestic cleavages and serious foreign pressures. Choices in these circumstances were not likely to be the result of measured attempts to establish long-range goals and to determine the best means of achieving them. Consequently the elites tended to act like Simon's "satisficers," not seeking optimal solutions but settling for the first tolerable alternative they could discover.[24] The policies chosen were clearly not likely to be revolu-

23. This argument is made by Wionczek, "Latin American Growth and Trade Strategies," pp. 14 ff.
24. Herbert A. Simon, "A Behavioral Model of Rational Choice," *Quarterly Journal of Economics* 69 (February 1955):99–118.

tionary but were likely to respond to elite desires to reward supporters and to diminish immediate pressures.

This is a style of decisionmaking that emphasizes the shortrun virtues of agreement on policy, rather than the quality of the policy itself. (I discuss the strengths and weaknesses of this approach in more detail in chapter 7.) Here I note only that policies made in this fashion are prone to drift or inertia, for they are too often chosen simply in response to immediate tactical needs. Problems tend gradually to accumulate, and originally manageable problems become unmanageable, because there is no effort to move steadily or consistently in a defined direction; there is only an effort to stay afloat. In this sense the policies we have been discussing, which were not initially irrational or imprudent, were chosen because they responded in a satisfactory way to the immediate pressures that the elites had to deal with, but these policies were also carried too far and were not cut off at the point where they became increasingly inefficient, because it always seemed easier (or safer) to yield to the demands of the vested interests that had been created and to continue doing a little more of the same thing than to risk the conflicts and uncertainties of reversing course. This decision to continue "muddling through" was also facilitated by the general unavailability of viable or attractive alternatives to rapid growth and rapid industrialization and by the difficulties of reversing course in societies that lack resources and flexibility, especially when the prime beneficiaries of the status quo would have had to put their own gains at risk.

The elites, I believe, got caught in a trap, which was only partially (or sometimes) the result of their own corruption and incompetence, when it became apparent that prevailing policies were not working and new policies were necessary. One way out was an effort to restructure radically the domestic socioeconomic structure, but this was clearly threatening and promised few shortrun gains to elites whose time horizon was constricted. The only other way out was to stumble forward and hope (or at least assert for public consumption) that the policies would ultimately produce the promised results.

◀•••▶

There are three reasons why the discussion of rapid growth and industrialization via import substitution is important. First these policies are still popular in many developing countries and thus need to be understood. Second, and perhaps more critically, the decision to adopt these policies, and the results that ensued, have tended to set—or heavily condition—the relationship between the developing countries and the external world. Import substitution not only made the developing countries more dependent on the external world but also exacerbated a number of domestic problems. And it created a bias among the elites to seek solutions to these problems through increased pressure on the international systems. We shall see the effects of this in the next two chapters.

Finally, since I am concerned in later chapters with establishing the grounds for a better relationship between rich and poor, this discussion may have provided some hints about the directions we shall need to go. In the first place it emphasizes the necessity of understanding the dilemmas that confront developing country elites more contextually: that is, not simply criticizing them for corruption and incompetence but also understanding their problems, the theories with which they had to work, and the limits within which they can make (or are willing to accept) major changes. In the second place it suggests the need to create a policymaking system that takes account of these conditions but nonetheless offers some possibility of steady and tangible movement in a desired direction. Chapters 6 and 7 discuss this issue directly, and chapters 8 and 9 attempt to apply the results to the external orientations that the developing countries are likely to adopt. There are also lessons in the preceding discussion that need to be pondered about inflating expectations too drastically and about promising easy results on the basis of uncertain doctrines. There may also be a useful warning here about the facile assumption that only a revolution can deal with the problems of most developing countries: A revolution, even if its leaders are genuinely committed to national development, must still deal with the underlying conditions of underdevelopment. Revolution may alter the way alternatives are perceived, and it may create the opportunity to move in new drections, but it is not a solution in and of itself: Honest elites, an effective policymaking system, and a relatively benign international environment are still necessary. The last comment suggests a final lesson: Domestic change, however necessary, will be insufficient unless the external world makes a more sophisticated effort to help the developing countries. I discuss this in chapter 11.

Before concluding this chapter, I comment on another way in which the developing countries have attempted to deal with domestic and international pressures: regional integration.

## THE POLITICAL ECONOMY OF REGIONALISM

### REGIONALISM: THE COOPERATION OF THE VICTIMS

Regional cooperation has always seemed to make a great deal of sense for small and poor states. Whatever else the developing countries have in common, they share the need to make more commitments to each other. Regionalism does not, of course, necessarily lead to more security, more peace, more prosperity, more—or less— anything.[25] But properly used, regionalism does seem to offer some opportunities that are beyond the range of small domestic markets and some protection against the pressures of the international economic and political systems. Regionalism cannot solve the problems of the LDCs, but it might be able to ameliorate some of them. Such modest virtues have, however, seemed insufficient: What developing country elites have wanted, and what regionalism can provide, have only rarely converged.

The region has always been symbolically important, perhaps as a repository of shared experiences and resentments. It has not been much more than symbolically important, because the practical problems—both political and economic—that the developing countries confront do not seem to have regional solutions. The problems appear either local or global in origin, and regional institutions and processes have seemed too weak to deal with pressures or conflicts

---

25. Perhaps the best study of regionalism is J. S. Nye, *Peace in Parts, Integration and Conflict in Regional Organization* (Boston: Little, Brown, 1971); also useful is Ronald J. Yalem, *Regionalism and World Order* (Washington, D.C.: Public Affairs Press, 1965).

from either direction. Moreover, in contrast with either import substitution or nonalignment, the political and economic arguments for regionalism have frequently clashed. Consequently, regional organizations have rarely been given either the resources or the authority to act autonomously in pursuit of regional goals. The region has thus remained a negative and defensive arena, turned to only as a last resort when local problems threaten to get out of hand, and international solutions are unavailable or unappetizing.

Regional economic integration became a fashionable topic in the early 1960s. Import substitution was running into trouble, for it was neither saving foreign exchange nor transforming domestic economies so that they could produce intermediate or capital goods. The growth rate for primary product exports had also slowed, apparently justifying Prebisch's export pessimism for the LDCs.[26] But the need to export to acquire foreign exchange for financing necessary imports was still strong. Since the advanced countries were not providing much help in either foreign aid or trade preferences, the only solution seemed to be regional integration. In addition the success of the European Common Market was important, for it not only provided a concrete illustration of the potential of an integrated regional market but also was a potential threat to the exports of some underdeveloped countries. But the integration schemes of the developing countries were designed primarily only to extend the range of domestic import substitution to the entire region. Given the limitations of even regional markets, such arrangements were not likely to yield substantial benefits.

Regional integration thus began as a classic foul-weather measure, a response to domestic failures and international indifference. One needs only to note, for example, that regional cooperation almost invariably slowed when export prospects for primary products brightened: When commodity prices for Latin American exports went up 25 percent from 1963 to 1968, integration in Latin America ground to a halt, and as long as prospects for Southeast Asian exports remained buoyant, regional cooperation never went much

26. See R. S. Bhambri, "Customs Unions and Underdeveloped Countries," *Economia Internazionale* 15, no. 2 (1962):237 ff.

beyond rhetoric.[27] The promise of special trade preferences by one of the industrial countries was also usually enough to undermine regional cooperation: Whatever benefits such agreements promised to the local recipients, they also engendered regional conflicts between those within the agreement and those on the outside.[28] Potential global benefits generally seemed to outweigh potential regional benefits, and indeed to do so without asking much by way of sacrifice in return.

Since regional trade in the Third World was low, there was bound to be room for expansion—if only because so many existing industries within the LDCs were working well below capacity. There is especially a large potential market for regional sale of manufactures. For example, in Southeast Asia, 82 percent of the region's exports of machinery and transport equipment were within the region, but this constituted only 4 percent of total import requirements for these products.[29] As a result most regional organizations had substantial growth rates for intra-area trade, although usually only for the first 5 or 6 years. Intra-area trade within the Central American Common Market went up 28.8 percent per year from 1960 to 1968, the Central African Customs and Economic Union went up 23.2 percent per year, the Latin American Free Trade Association (LAFTA) went up 7.4 percent, and the East African Community went up 7.9 percent.[30] Nevertheless the figures were somewhat deceptive, not only because the initial trade figures were so low, but also because the trade that did occur tended to be limited to non-

27. See Miguel S. Wionczek, "The Rise and the Decline of Latin American Economic Integration," *Journal of Common Market Studies* 9, no. 1 (September 1970):61; on Southeast Asia, see the various essays in Theodore Morgan and Nyle Spoelstra, eds., *Economic Interdependence in Southeast Asia* (Madison: University of Wisconsin Press, 1969).

28. For Nkrumah's fears that regional agreements would pit African against African, see I. William Zartman, *The Politics of Trade Negotiations Between Africa and the European Economic Community* (Princeton, N.J.: Princeton University Press, 1971), p. 21.

29. See Morgan and Spoelstra, *Economic Interdependence in Southeast Asia*, p. 19.

30. These statistics, as well as other material, can be found in Felipe Pazos, "Regional Integration of Trade Among Less Developed Countries," *World Development* 1, no. 7 (July 1973):1–3. Statistics illustrating the decline of integration are also cited by Pazos as well as by Wionczek, "The Rise and the Decline of Latin American Economic Integration."

competitive items. Such trade was also only a small percentage of total trade: For example, intra-LAFTA trade went up only from 8 percent to 11 percent of total Latin American trade from 1960 to 1968.

The fact that the poor countries were doing badly was only part of the reason for the new appeal of regional integration. The poor countries were also beginning to feel victimized by the global system. They were doing badly at precisely the moment the rich countries were flourishing; correctly or not, these developments were perceived as interconnected. The developing countries began to fear that they were irremediably losing their place in the international system. The "gap" psychosis began to dominate their calculations, the assumption that relative differences between the rich and the poor were somehow more important than the absolute level of income of the poor.

Regional integration was a defensive reaction to this sense of losing place. Regional cooperation seemed particularly appropriate because the recently formed European Economic Community (EEC) seemed to be responsible for a large measure of Western Europe's progress and prosperity. The EEC appeared to be a threat aimed directly at the LDCs, a "consumers' union" that could be met only by a "producers' union." [31] As the President of Uruguay noted in 1961:

> The formation of a European Common Market and European Free Trade Association constitutes a state of near-war against Latin American exports. Therefore, we must reply to one integration with another one; to one increase of acquisitive power by internal enrichment by another, to inter-European cooperation by inter-Latin American cooperation. [32]

The fear was not only that the powerful "consumers' union" would exploit the LDCs directly but also that it would favor one group of LDCs—essentially the former French colonies and potentially the former British colonies—against another. These arguments were frequently supported by large exporting groups or by investors who

31. For the quoted phrases, see Edward S. Milenky, *The Politics of Regional Organization in Latin America* (New York: Praeger, 1973), p. 14. Milenky also notes that one reason for LAFTA was a "pervasive sense of loss of status" (p. 177).

32. Quoted in Sidney Dell, *Trade Blocs and Common Markets* (New York: Knopf, 1963), p. 211.

hoped to establish profitable new industries within the protected area.

Doing badly engendered a willingness to experiment with regional integration, but it also engendered the fear of doing even worse within a customs union or free trade area. Free trade has always been the doctrine of the strong, of those who had faith that they could compete, and it was no less true when applied within a particular area.[33] What the weak states feared was that Prebisch's vision of the international system, in which the center exploited the periphery and compelled the periphery to live by exchanging primary products for manufactured goods, would be repeated within the region. Thus each group sought to use the regional framework for different purposes: the weaker to compensate for their backwardness and to build an industrial base, the stronger merely to widen the available market and to improve their export performance.[34] The weaker always wanted concessions to their weakness, but the stronger were sufficiently satisfied with the status quo so that the need to sacrifice to ensure a better future never seemed overwhelming. As a result most of the regional integration schemes worked at cross-purposes: National interests dominated regional interests, and the region remained an afterthought to more pressing concerns.

In the next section I briefly examine some of the reasons for these judgments.

REGIONAL ECONOMIC INTEGRATION: LIMITS AND POSSIBILITIES

Whatever form it took—free trade area, customs union, common market—regional integration usually involved trade liberalization, the removal of discrimination between the members of the arrangement.[35] In the abstract the potential benefits could be quite substantial. In general these benefits have been grouped into three

33. See Joan Robinson, *The New Mercantilism* (Cambridge: Cambridge University Press, 1966), p. 24.
34. Milenky, *The Politics of Regional Organization in Latin America*, stresses this theme in a number of places; for the same theme in Eastern Europe, see Henry Wilcox Schaefer, *Comecon and the Politics of Integration* (New York: Praeger, 1972), p. 49.
35. The standard work is Bela Balassa, *The Theory of Economic Integration* (Homewood, Ill.: Richard D. Irwin, 1961).

areas: static benefits, dynamic benefits, and improvements in bargaining power with the rest of the world. For technical reasons, however, these benefits were unlikely to be very large for arrangements that grouped together developing countries. Since this point has been amply documented in the theoretical and empirical literature on integration, I briefly illustrate it only in passing.

In terms of static benefits, for example, the amount of trade creation that could be engendered among the developing country members of a regional arrangement was bound to be limited: Too little preintegration trade took place within the region, and too much went to the outside world; the regional tariff level was, moreover, likely to be higher than previous national tariffs, for the members were seeking to promote trade among themselves, not free virtually nonexistent trade to improve efficiency.[36] Nationalism magnified these limitations, for each country normally sought to industrialize and was reluctant to enter any arrangement that might threaten—through regional competition—the few industries that had been created. Consequently, almost by default, integration concentrated primarily on agreements about which country was to get what new industries. And this meant that the immediate benefits of integration were not likely to be large.

The dynamic effects of integration—internal and external economics of scale, competition, increasing specialization, new incentives to entrepreneurs—were also likely to be long range. These benefits look beyond existing patterns of trade to the creation of trade patterns that will be based on regional comparative advantage (and protection against the rest of the world), but such benefits will be large only for countries that have already created a functioning modern economy.[37] Again, wholly apart from the question of whether the ruling elites are willing to risk transforming the existing socioeconomic order, only longrun benefits are really possible. Finally, bargaining positions are not likely to be much improved,

36. One useful discussion is R. G. Lipsey, "The Theory of Customs Unions: A General Survey," *The Economic Journal* 70, no. 279 (September 1960):496–513.
37. See R. F. Mikesell, "The Theory of Common Markets as Applied to Regional Arrangements Among Developing Countries," in Roy Harrod and Douglas Hague, eds., *International Trade Theory in a Developing World* (New York: St. Martin's Press,

*[98]*

for the market strength of a regional arrangement among poor countries is usually too weak to affect prices decisively, and the national incomes of the members are not likely to rise enough to increase demand for imports from the rest of the world.

Since few of the regional agreements had a significant impact on agricultural production, in part because the partners tended to produce similar commodities with similar cost structures, success came to be measured by the degree of stimulation for manufacturing exports to the region. Nationalism (and the power of the vested industrial interests created by national import substitution policies) impeded agreements on existing production, and attention had to center on coordination of future industrial programs. But even this degree of cooperation was difficult, for specialization and a regional division of labor ran against the grain for states that had come to identify dependence with specialization in primary product exports and independence with a symbolic industrialization.[38] In addition many of the new industries created within the region were foreign owned, a circumstance that limited their economic impact (because of profits remitted, the wrong kind of technology, etc.) and frequently engendered sharp domestic conflicts over exploitation and autonomy.

The potential benefits of integration must also be weighed against a number of costs that emerge (or can emerge) during the operation of a regional agreement. There are, for example, revenue losses from tariff cuts to the partners within an agreement and potentially higher prices for imports if a partner's price for an item is above the world market price. Equity in the distribution of benefits is also likely to create problems, since the benefits from the agreement usually tend to cluster around a few "growth poles," and the weaker partners tend to fall even further behind the stronger.[39]

---

1963), pp. 205–29; and *Trade Expansion and Economic Integration Among Developing Countries* (UNCTAD: 67.II.D.20, 1967), p. 10.

38. See Joseph Grunwald, Miguel S. Wionczek, and Martin Carnoy, *Latin American Economic Integration and U.S. Policy* (Washington, D.C.: The Brookings Institution, 1972), p. 12. In some countries the military elites also wanted high degrees of self-sufficiency—steel mills, auto factories, and so on—which impeded agreement.

39. Miguel S. Wionczek, "Latin American Growth and Trade Strategies in the Post-War Period," *Journal of Developing Areas* 4, no. 2 (1973):20, 21.

LAFTA has experienced especially severe difficulties with the equity problem, but the Andean Pact, the East African Common Market, and the Central American Common Market have not escaped sharp internal conflicts over the distribution of benefits.[40] And there seems to be no way the problem can be avoided, since there are disparities in levels of development within each region.[41] The problem might be ameliorated, however, if the elites in the stronger countries were willing to make some short-term sacrifices for the benefit of the regional agreement and to establish prior agreements on the distribution of benefits—but few elites have been willing to make this commitment.

REGIONAL INTEGRATION: ELITE PERSPECTIVES

Regional integration confronted the ruling elites with a number of dilemmas. The benefits from integration were likely to be long term, major changes in domestic institutions and processes seemed necessary, the quest for national autonomy might be undermined by relinquishing industries (or power) to regional institutions, and it was not always clear that the right groups within the state (i.e., nationals, not foreigners) or all the states within the region would actually benefit. Moreover the slow and modest progress implicit in regional integration among developing countries was not very attractive psychologically to elites schooled in the simplistic notion that rapid growth and rapid national industrialization were both possible and the solution to all their problems.

But escalating domestic problems and increasing dependence on an uncertain and complex international environment meant that some response to the opportunities—and dangers—of regional integration was necessary. What most of the elites seemed to do was hedge: They made a rhetorical commitment to regional integration, but they turned it into a minimal extension of national import sub-

40. *Ibid.* See also Edward S. Milenky, "Developmental Nationalism in Practice: The Problems and Progress of the Andean Group," *Inter-American Economic Affairs* 27, no. 4 (Spring 1973):54; on Kenya, see Philip Ndegwa, *The Common Market and Development in East Africa* (Nairobi: East African Publishing House, 1965), pp. 39–72; on Central America, see James D. Cochrane, *The Politics of Regional Integration: The Central American Case* (New Orleans, La.: Tulane University, 1969), p. 111.

41. See the interesting discussion in G. K. Helleiner, *International Trade and Economic Development* (Baltimore: Penguin Books, 1972), pp. 146, 147.

stitution policies, excluding existing industrial interests and limited to swapping markets for future industries. This was a low-risk, shortrun strategy, for it offended as few domestic interests as possible and made no effort to transform the prevailing socioeconomic structure. By the same token it was a low-gain, high-risk strategy over the long run, for by failing to confront domestic problems and to make a genuine commitment to a dynamic form of regional cooperation, the elites made it likely that the region would soon run into the same constraints that had brought national import substitution policies to a halt.

Prudence about a fundamental commitment to regional integration is neither completely irrational nor simply another illustration of the dysfunctions of nationalism. Cooperation with poor, weak, and potentially unstable partners is clearly risky, especially for countries with small margins of error and a need for substantial shortrun benefits. In this sense, improvements in the national market can always yield more benefits than regional agreements to distribute future industries.[42] Nevertheless regional integration has the potential to make a reasonably important contribution to the solution of some of the problems that the developing countries face. But more serious efforts to cooperate have failed—or not even been attempted—because the political will to cooperate has not been sufficiently strong.

Cooperation without an underlying political commitment to create a genuine regional institution is inevitably limited and tenuous. Only agreements in which all members benefit immediately are really feasible. In addition, cooperation is unlikely if it threatens existing bilateral aid and trade arrangements, if it appears to impede national development plans, and if it endangers national elites or threatens to diminish their status.[43] If neither the weak nor the the strong partners are willing or able to sacrifice in the short run,

42. It is not without interest that most of the "success stories" of the past 25 years—success in terms of rapid rates of growth—were not in regional agreements: South Korea, Taiwan, Hong Kong, Singapore. See Chenery, "Growth and Structural Change," pp. 21–23. I do not imply that regional integration is irrelevant, but rather that it is not the only way for an LDC to improve its economic performance.

43. See Aaron Segal, "The Integration of Developing Countries: Some Thoughts on East Africa and Central America," *Journal of Common Market Studies* 5, no. 3 (March 1967):262.

regionalism will never be much more than a last, reluctant resort when all else has failed. It is hard to escape the impression that, despite all the rhetoric, when faced with a choice between depending on the developed countries or depending on neighbors, most of the elites really prefer dependence on the developed countries.[44]

———◆••••▶———

I do not intend to discuss regional political organizations separately, primarily because they have never become very significant, and because their weaknesses are similar to those of regional economic organizations.[45] In general, institutions like the Organization of African Unity have been too weak to impose solutions to regional conflicts and have been limited to peripheral—but occasionally useful—tasks such as seeking a truce between combatants, peace-keeping after hostilities have ended, and legitimization of whatever compromise has been finally negotiated.[46]

In terms of elite perspectives the desire to create a sense of national identity could hardly be facilitated by creating a new and presumably superior center of power and influence—in this sense, regional institutions may have been decidedly premature. Regional institutions also did not provide much (if any) help against domestic coups or dissidence, for regional forces did not exist and probably would not have been allowed to intervene if they did. All that the regional group seemed capable of doing was providing *ex post*

44. The Andean Pact, one of the most recent ventures into integration, is interesting in that it has attempted to work within the context of a strong "developmental nationalism." Nevertheless one may be permitted doubts about the long-term viability of an agreement that is so nationalistic and inwardly oriented. At a minimum this kind of approach limits the benefits that can be expected, although this may be balanced by various gains from controlling foreign investment—if the gains are actually achieved. For a discussion of the early years of the Pact, see Milenky, "Developmental Nationalism in Practice."

Since writing this, new evidence has appeared that amply justifies the pessimism displayed. The Pact is now virtually moribund as a result of Chile's defection on both economic and ideological grounds, the stiff rules on foreign investment have not worked, the benefits of trade liberalization have not been equitably distributed, and harmonization agreements on the creation of new industries have foundered. See *The Economist*, November 13, 1976, p. 129.

45. See Nye, *Peace in Parts* for a careful analysis.

46. See *ibid.* and Gordon Connell-Smith, *The Inter-American System* (London: Oxford University Press, 1966), pp. 303, 304.

*facto* legitimization to the new rulers. Finally, in contrast to non-alignment (see the next chapter), a commitment to regionalism had few symbolic or psychic rewards, for neither elite nor masses cared enough about, or knew enough about, the region to get exercised about the fate of regional cooperation.

REGIONAL INTEGRATION: NEW DIRECTIONS

What alternative is there to regional cooperation that merely attempts to extend national import substitution policies? There is at least one orthodox alternative: more outwardly oriented export promotion policies. There is no necessary incompatibility between regional cooperation and the export of manufactures, for a coordinated regional industrial policy based on comparative advantage would surely facilitate an export policy.[47] Conversion to such a policy would, however, be difficult, for it would increase dependence on the international trading system. In these circumstances I believe that more outwardly oriented regional agreements are not likely. In fact more closed forms of integration, in which nationalism is the dominant force and strong efforts to control foreign investment are made—as in the Andean Pact—seem much more probable in the years ahead.

Efforts to increase cooperation among the developing countries have also begun to move in other directions in recent years. There have been, for example, some movement away from efforts to construct elaborate regional mechanisms and some tendency to substitute more narrowly conceived practical measures of cooperation. Arrangements such as the Senegalese river basin organization have been constructed without any promises of wider cooperation but simply to earn the obvious gains from cooperation. This kind of cooperation is eminently sensible, but it provides few of the wider benefits implicit in integration—though it also avoids the problems of more extensive forms of cooperation. But even the more traditional ventures into integration seem to be moving in the same direction: The attempt to coordinate and harmonize national policies on resource allocation, a slow and difficult task, has taken prece-

47. Wionczek, "Latin American Growth and Trade Strategies in the Post-War Period," pp. 34, 35.

dence over the broad quest for reductions in tariff and nontariff barriers.

There is another sense in which the regional focus has been broadened, for efforts at "collective self-reliance" within the Third World—locally, regionally, globally—have become increasingly prominent. This movement (to which I return in chapter 9) is partly a reflection of disenchantment with the record of regional integration and partly a reflection of new patterns of thought within the Third World about the possibility of commodity cartels, preferential schemes limited to other underdeveloped countries, and fiscal and monetary cooperation. Surely the effort to increase intra-Third World trade and to reverse the trends toward declining interdependence make a great deal of sense. But this judgment also presupposes that too much is not expected from such ventures—for they face even more severe practical problems than regional integration—and that they do not deflect attention from more critical and immediate problems.

---

Regional integration was one way to try to deal with difficult domestic problems and the powerful pressures of a sophisticated external environment. But the results were disappointing, in part because too much was expected from any attempt to integrate poor countries, and in part because the elites were increasingly unwilling to risk the domestic transformations that might have increased the range of benefits that integration could offer. The elites had obviously benefited from past policies, but they had been joined by too few others; rather than risk their own gains in an effort to spread the benefits of growth around, they increasingly sought to blame existing problems on the external world and to demand support from it. Before examining these demands in chapter 5, I illustrate in the next chapter the way in which foreign policy itself, in the period with which we are concerned, began to reflect the increasing tendency to seek more help from abroad and to see the solution to domestic problems in external changes.

# 4

## Foreign Policy
## and Development Policy:
## From Nonalignment
## to International Class War

### UNDERDEVELOPMENT AND FOREIGN POLICY

Foreign policy is important to any new state, for it helps the state to reaffirm its independence and articulate its identity. But foreign policy is also rarely critical for a new state—especially an underdeveloped new state—for the first order of business is inevitably domestic. Foreign policy, except when the new state perceives a direct external threat, thus tends to be a residual category, dominated not only by domestic politics but also by rhetorical and ideological preoccupations.

Foreign policy rarely serves a single purpose. Goals tend to mingle together: Even after the fact sharp lines between the quest for security, or aid, or trade, or status and prestige are frequently difficult to discern. The goals of foreign policy are also only rarely a matter of entirely free choice: What "stands to reason" as a goal usually emerges from a complex interaction between areas of constraint and areas of choice. The constraints are both external and internal. Externally they include the international system, the existing technology, the intellectual models that provide the conventional wisdom and form the prevailing climate of opinion, and the contiguous environment (an especially crucial factor for new and weak states). Internally they include the limitations set by size, the level of development, and the political system. For developing countries, constraints clearly dominate choices. What does get chosen, moreover, tends to be heavily conditioned by the personality and priorities of the dominant leader and his friends. Why (and to what degree) this is so needs to be carefully stated.

Governments always have intentions. Whether they also have the capabilities to achieve their intentions is another matter. Developing countries are a classic case in point: As one text after another has demonstrated, they abound with organizational and informational deficiencies.[1] These deficiencies may be even more profound in foreign affairs, for the skills and knowledge to deal with the external world may be particularly hard to come by. Most of the LDCs have small foreign affairs bureaucracies, few embassies abroad to collect information, and few alternate sources of information. The foreign news that the local media features also tends to be drawn from a single source: the news agencies of the former colonial mentor. There are, finally, few interest groups with a large stake in foreign affairs and little public interest in what happens outside the immediate environment.

Something of a commonplace about foreign policy in underdeveloped countries emerges from these conditions: With few experts at home and few embassies abroad, with few interest groups and little public interest, and with few sources of knowledge, foreign policy tends to be the unfettered preserve of the leader and his friends. The result is a highly personalized foreign policy. When the dominant leader is particularly popular and his rule unchallenged, the distinction between personal views and state policies may disappear. As some observers have reported, India may not have had a foreign policy, but Nehru certainly did.[2] And the

1. See, for example, Maurice A. East, "Foreign Policy-Making in Small States: Some Theoretic Observations Based on a Study of the Uganda Ministry of Foreign Affairs," *Policy Sciences* 4, no. 4 (December 1973):491–508; Marvin C. Ott, "Foreign Policy Formulation in Malaysia," *Asian Survey* 12 (1972):225–41.

2. K. P. Misra, ed., *Studies in Indian Foreign Policy* (New Delhi: Vikas, 1969), p. 218.

same point has been made about Nkrumah in Ghana and Sukarno in Indonesia.[3]

Personalized foreign policy is not, after all, a monopoly of the LDCs. Benes dominated Czech foreign policy for 20 years, Titulescu dominated Rumanian foreign policy for nearly the same amount of time, and Lange in Norway, Spaak in Belgium, and Luns in the Netherlands were not far behind. These countries are all small, but they are also relatively more modernized than the current generation of LDCs. Why were these leaders so little constrained by whatever bureaucracies, interests groups, and mass media existed in their countries? Are we to assume that personalized foreign policy is a characteristic of size and not the level of development?

When Benes et al. dominated the foreign policy of their countries, they did so because of an underlying consensus within the country about what the foreign policy ought to contain. When Nehru et al. dominated the foreign policy of their countries, however, they did so because of their own personal power and because of the remoteness of foreign policy issues from the people. If Benes had died or been replaced (before, say, 1938), Czech foreign policy would not have altered very much; when Nehru died, and when Nkrumah and Sukarno were overthrown, foreign policy took on a wholly new dimension. The personalization of foreign policy in the context of a developed state, large or small, means different things than it does in the context of underdevelopment. For an LDC, personalization diminishes continuities between regimes, lowers predictability, and perhaps even encourages foreign meddling to replace unfriendly leaders. It may also affect the willingness of foreign aid agencies and private investors to make long-term commitments to what may be a short-term government. In this sense there is something of a self-fulfilling prophecy at work: Expectations that a regime will not survive long may engender behavior on the part of the regime itself (e.g., repression, arms spending, irrational investments, corruption) and on the part of foreign governments that enhance instability.

Illustrations of the discontinuities attendant on personalized

3. See W. Scott Thompson, *Ghana's Foreign Policy, 1957–1966* (Princeton, N.J.: Princeton University Press, 1969); and Franklin B. Weinstein, "The Uses of Foreign

foreign policy are abundant. The sharp reversals in both economic and political policies in Indonesia after the fall of Sukarno and in Ghana after the fall of Nkrumah are indicative. Even in India, with a relatively more developed and competitive political system, the replacement of Nehru by Shastri led to important changes. The influence of the bureaucracy increased, since Shastri lacked the knowledge and influence of Nehru; substantively the global emphasis of India's policy was replaced by more concern with local and regional matters.[4] The general point is obvious: Policies are followed because they are favored by a leader; conversely the leader is not followed for his choice of one foreign policy over another. Within limits foreign policy becomes readily manipulable, for the leader is usually not locked in by public or bureaucratic pressures. Trade-offs between different issues and various compromises and bargains are thus presumably easier to arrange.

The personalization of foreign policy in the developing countries has another effect not sufficiently stressed. Since the elites have usually been educated by the former colonial rulers, and since the main sources of information still tend to flow from the colonial states, indifference and ignorance about regional matters tend to dominate.[5] This is surely not the only reason that regional cooperation among the LDCs has never got very far, but it is an important supplementary factor, for it has meant that efforts to improve regional ties have come rather late in the game—usually after domestic problems have mounted, and the response of the former colonial ruler has come to seem inadequate.

The propensity on the part of the elite to manipulate foreign policy for domestic purposes also has some important costs. For one thing it simply may not work. For example, Ben Bella's attempt to use foreign policy successes to overcome domestic weakness was

---

Policy in Indonesia: An Approach to the Analysis of Foreign Policy in the Less Developed Countries," *World Politics* 24 (1972):356–81.

4. See Michael Brecher, *Succession in India: A Study in Decision-Making* (Oxford: Oxford University Press, 1966). Mexico's sudden shift from an ostensibly radical foreign policy under Echevarria to a more conservative policy under his successor is also illustrative.

5. For example, Nehru cared about regional matters only in terms of preventing Great Power interventions. See Michael Brecher, *India and World Politics* (London: Oxford University Press, 1968), pp. 314–15.

turned against him by his domestic enemies: They accused him of spending too much time on establishing an international role for himself and too little time on substantive domestic problems.[6] There is no simple trade-off in which success in one realm can balance failure in the other; domestic weaknesses may be diminshed by foreign successes, but they can rarely be eliminated or controlled in that fashion. The leader, initially unconstrained, may also discover that rousing the masses against real or imagined foreign enemies is dangerous: Nehru ignored his own "public opinion," then rather belatedly attempted to rouse it against the Chinese in 1962, and then discovered that he had lost control of the situation. Previously acceptable solutions had to be rejected, because the "public" would accept only something that could be defined as a victory.[7] Finally the attempt to use foreign policy for personal ends risks creating real external threats where none existed: Defense budgets may have to be raised, and foreign investors may be reluctant to make any new commitments.

The influence of individual leaders has tended to decline over time. With the disappearance of the first generation of nationalist leaders and with the growth of concern for tangible successes in economic development, the influence of professionalized bureaucracies has generally increased.[8] Successors to the original leader have usually lacked his prestige and popularity and tend to be bound by the need not only to consult other sources of power but also to produce real results. Indeed the absence of interest groups and bureaucracies does not always mean that the elite can operate without domestic constraints. In many LDCs sharp domestic cleavages and the high potential for instability mean that the leader must consult with or take into account the views of various domestic groups before acting. This is another way of stating an earlier point:

6. David and Marina Ottaway, *Algeria—The Politics of a Socialist Revolution* (Berkeley: University of California Press, 1970), pp. 147–48.

7. Neville Maxwell, *India's China War* (New York: Doubleday, 1972), p. 133.

8. See Brecher, *Succession in India*, pp. 167–68; W. Scott Thompson, "Ghana's Foreign Policy Under Military Rule," *Africa Report* 14, nos. 5 and 6 (May–June 1969):8–13; David C. Cole and Princeton N. Lyman, *Korean Development: The Interplay of Politics and Economics* (Cambridge, Mass.: Harvard University Press, 1971), p. 219.

personal control of foreign policy means different things when it rests on a domestic consensus than when it rests on the power and popularity of a single leader.

In the years immediately after independence, unity on foreign policy seems much easier to achieve than unity on domestic policy.[9] Domestic conflict may be sharp and pervasive, but the contending groups can usually agree on the elemnts of an external policy: economic nationalism, anticolonialism, nonalignment, and so forth. Foreign policy may thus be used to achieve domestic goals in this period, but the goals tend to be symbolic and psychologic: to create a degree of identity with the nation, to affirm a new status, and to enhance national unity. Negatively the leader also has to be careful not to choose policies that alienate important domestic groups (a significant reason for nonalignment as we shall see). Again, foreign policy unity does not reflect an underlying consensus; only commitment to some rather rhetorical and nebulous goals is really at issue. And just as the influence of personality tends to decline over time, so too does the ability to use foreign policy to achieve essentially symbolic purposes. As the developing countries come to understand that they need tangible things from the external world and that political independence does not imply economic autonomy, domestic conflicts begin to be mirrored in foreign policy choices. Foreign policy has come to seem more important to many LDCs because, as a group, they have become more sharply aware of how much their domestic options depend on the policies they adopt toward the external world.

Foreign policy has never been an entirely autonomous realm. There is no way that foreign policy decisions can be completely isolated from the domestic political system, except perhaps when an irrational leader is indifferent to the support his policies engender or the costs they inflict on his citizens. The notion of the "primacy of foreign policy" has always been more ideology than history. Thus an analysis of foreign policy that does not include an analysis of the domestic political system is always incomplete.

I want here to emphasize, however, only one aspect of the

9. John M. Ostheimer, *Nigerian Politics* (New York: Harper and Row, 1973), pp. 166–67.

domestic political process, for it has affected—in varying degrees—the form and content of foreign policy. LDC political systems are extremely unstable, for none of the groups that compete for control of the state really has the power to establish a stable equilibrium. If social cleavages are especially profound, pervasive distrust destroys the possibility of compromise; consequently the various conflicts merely reinforce each other, for an economic or political conflict also becomes an ethnic, or racial, or class, or regional conflict. Even if a dominant leader emerges, or if the army takes over, they usually lack the power (and the will) to attempt to create a truly integrated state. For the most part they can do little more than ensure their own continuance in power. They must use what power they have to reward supporters, bribe potential allies, and thwart enemies. The danger of being thrown out of power concentrates attention, but only on matters of the moment. The temptation to corruption and the quest for immediate wealth, as a hedge against an uncertain future, are bound to be strongly appealing.[10]

Domestic instability, or the fear thereof, tempts insecure leaders to use foreign policy as a supplementary resource in their political struggles. A rising defense budget, or efforts to secure high levels of military assistance, may be a way to keep the army happy, and not a response to an external threat. Foreign aid may be sought to pay off supporters, not to raise domestic investment rates. Summit meetings and speeches at the U.N. may be designed to alleviate psychic insecurities, not to deal with substantive problems. And so on. For leaders who feel constantly threatened, a foreign policy that reflects an "objective" interpretation of the national interest—if any such thing exists—is likely to appear as something of a luxury; if they do not use foreign policy to increase their own domestic strength, they may not be around to use it at all.

I do not mean that foreign policy only or always responds to domestic imperatives in the Third World. These are "more or less," not "either/or" distinctions. Clearly there are cases in which foreign

10. Very useful on the nature of the domestic political systems are Aristide R. Zolberg, *Creating Political Order—The Party-States of West Africa* (Chicago: Rand Mc-Nally, 1966); James C. Scott, *Political Ideology in Malaysia—Reality and Beliefs of an Elite* (New Haven, Conn.: Yale University Press, 1968); and Ruth First, *The Barrel of a Gun—Political Power in Africa and the Coup d'Etat* (London: Allen Lane, 1970).

policy takes priority over domestic policy, either because the state faces a real external threat (e.g., in Cambodia or South Korea) or because the dominant leader wants to enlarge his domain (e.g., Nkrumah and Sukarno).[11] But for most of the LDCs, foreign policy is clearly a derivative of domestic politics.

These comments provide a more general context for an analysis of the transformation of nonalignment, the major foreign policy orientation of most developing countries, from the realm of symbolic rhetoric and domestic stabilization into a doctrine of class warfare with the rich countries.

## NONALIGNMENT AND THE COLD WAR

If statesmen always made their foreign policy choices in response to an objective determination of the nature of the international system, the rationale for a policy of nonalignment would be quite clear. Nonalignment—literally, not taking sides—has almost always appealed to the weaker members of a bipolar international system. Nonalignment is especially attractive when the two antagonists are neither at war nor willing to cooperate with each other— which is to say, in periods of "cold war." In such circumstances the weaker states may find themselves the objects of competition but not the victims of war. From this perspective, nonalignment is obviously not a foreign policy; it is simply a tactical response to a particular distribution of power between the Great Powers.[12]

J. W. Burton has argued that nonalignment "does not necessarily rest upon the continued existence of rivalry between two power groupings." [13] This is surely a misleading argument. Nonalignment

11. On Cambodia, see Bernard K. Gordon, *The Dimensions of Conflict in Southeast Asia* (Englewood Cliffs, N.J.: Prentice-Hall, 1966), p. 67. Leonard Binder, "The New States in World Affairs," in Robert A. Goldwin, ed., *Beyond the Cold War* (Chicago: Rand McNally, 1965), pp. 209 ff., argues that only charismatic leaders really considered foreign policy more important than domestic policy, although for declaratory not operational reasons.

12. For a discussion of nonalignment in these terms, see Robert L. Rothstein *Alliances and Small Powers* (New York: Columbia University Press, 1968), pp. 237–64.

13. J. W. Burton, *International Relations: A General Theory* (Cambridge: Cambridge University Press, 1965), p. 167.

cannot be explained by bipolarity alone, but it also cannot be explained without bipolarity. The viability of nonalignment is directly related to the power balance between the Great Powers. It is decisively affected by that balance, and it in turn exercises some influence over its operation. Nonalignment would hardly be attractive— to the nonaligned—if the Great Powers were at total war or total cooperation: The possibility of attracting benefits from both sides would have disappeared. Nor would it be attractive in a balance of power system (as in most of the nineteenth century) where the Great Powers primarily sought the support of their peers rather than of their inferiors.

Shortly after Communist China exploded its first nuclear device in October 1964, an Indian commentator noted: "Nonalignment has always been, in reality, an informal, unstated, unilateral alignment with unnamed Powers." [14] And a few years later another avowed apostle of nonalignment, Prince Sihanouk of Cambodia, declared that "in case of a massive Viet Minh invasion we will count on the aid—material and armaments—of the United States. . . ." [15] These comments indicate why nonalignment is a tactic, not a foreign policy: When a weak state, presumably committed to nonalignment, suddenly finds itself threatened by a Great Power, it must rapidly become aligned with another Great Power. Those who were threatened, or those who desperately needed external aid, were aligned, not nonaligned, for example, South Korea, Taiwan, Thailand, Pakistan, Jordan. If nonalignment had been something more, if it had really altered the international system, as Burton and others argued, threatened states would have been provided with something more than the traditional option of scurrying for cover under the wing of a willing Great Power.

Not all bipolar systems are identical. There are differences in means and ends between such systems that make a purely structural analysis inadequate. In terms of present concerns the critical question is this: Granted that the weak get certain opportunities to maneuver in a bipolar system that they do not get in other systems,

14. Raj Krishna, "India and the Bomb," *India Quarterly* 21 (1965):122.
15. Quoted in Roger M. Smith, *Cambodia's Foreign Policy* (Ithaca, N.Y.: Cornell University Press, 1965), p. 53.

why do those opportunities become so prominent in the Cold War system?

One answer is, of course, is there are simply so many more new states that they are bound to be more noticeable parts of the landscape. More significantly, however, differences between the Cold War bipolar system and earlier bipolar systems are usually attributed to the impact of nuclear weapons on Great Power relations. Nuclear weapons have made Great Powers' wars too dangerous, but they have not eliminated the conflicts and disagreements that lead to war. The conflicts have instead been transferred to areas where nuclear weapons cannot be used effectively or where the stakes involved would not justify their use. The dangers of escalation have also meant that much conflict remains at the political, economic, or paramilitary level.

In the past the influence of Small Powers rose only when they were sought as allies on the eve of Great Power conflicts. In the Cold War, with Great Power military conflict limited, Small Powers were still sought as allies or friends—but in place of, not because of, an imminent Great Power war. They were sought as symbols of victory in a political struggle never meant to erupt into major war. Small Powers remained targets of Great Power policies, but they had more means to defend themselves in a political conflict, and the costs of losing were likely to be (relatively) more bearable. Direct military intervention by the Great Powers was also somewhat less likely: Fears of escalation, or of being bogged down in a quagmire, or of offending the rest of the Third World induced caution on intervention—though surely not abstinence—on the part of the Great Powers. All these developments thrust the weak into a position of unaccustomed prominence.[16]

———————◆◆◆◆———————

The systemic perspective on nonalignment is useful. It shows why nonalignment seemed to be so rational a choice for weak states, for it had always been a sanctioned tactic within bipolar systems. Nuclear weapons, which compelled the Great Powers to tread

16. For a more extensive treatment of these developments, see Rothstein, *Alliances and Small Powers*, pp. 245 ff.

carefully and to seek the support of the LDC's, reinforced the appeal of nonalignment, for it at least seemed as if the possibilities of maneuvering for aid from both sides were wider than ever.

But a perspective that analyzes nonalignment primarily as a derivative of the patterns of relationships created by the Great Powers is necessary but not sufficient: Some understanding of the domestic process of choice, of why so many ruling elites found nonalignment appealing, is also necessary. This does not mean that the significance of external configurations of power can be forgotten: If nonalignment had been an irrational response to external pressures and opportunities, it would have been much more difficult to make sensible use of it domestically. Indeed what seems to have made nonalignment so widely popular is that, as with import substitution industrialization, it seemed to respond to both domestic and international needs and pressures.

The nationalist movements that had had to fight for their independence frequently developed a great deal of expertise about foreign affairs. But the diplomacy of the independence struggle was difficult to convert into the diplomacy of independence. The rest of the nationalist movements, who were simply granted independence, were in no better position: Few of them came to power with clear and definite ideas about foreign policy. Energies were primarily directed toward domestic problems, and there was indeed an instinctive bias against too much involvement with the industrial world. A real security threat—as in South Korea or Taiwan—could, of course, alter priorities quickly, but few developing countries actually faced such threats. In addition most lacked a tradition of foreign policy that might have compelled some attention to the external world through custom or habit. Beyond this, information about the external world was sparse and public interest minimal. It was also some years before the elites began to recognize how dependent on the international system they remained. Without the pressures of the Cold War and without a demonstration effect from peers intent on creating an anticolonial bloc, many would probably have ignored foreign policy altogether.

Once Cold War pressures began to develop, nonalignment seemed to have some defensive virtues. Small Powers have always sought to keep the Great Powers out of regional affairs—usually without success, especially if one of the Small Powers is dissatisfied with the status quo—and this was clearly one goal of the non-aligned movement.[17] On the one hand this meant that the non-aligned had to reject alliances with East or West, military bases, and any other behavior that seemed to imply partiality toward one side or the other. (In practice, of course, there were many ambiguities, and debates about acceptable behavior and about who was or was not truly nonaligned went on endlessly. Were the West African states, dependent on French expatriates, French aid, French currency, and—in extremis—the French army, really nonaligned? The answer is, it all depends—on what you mean and when and why you ask.) On the other hand, using nonalignment to balance between the Great Powers and to exclude them from regional affairs also required the interest and cooperation of both sides. If the Soviet Union had not decided to compete for the allegiance of the Third World, and if containment had not been extended to the "grey areas," nonalignment might have seemed irrelevant.

The primary elite goals, in general, were personal security and the creation of some sense of national unity. At first glance personal security seemed to have little to do with foreign policy (unless the state confronted an external threat). But some foreign policy choices could exacerbate domestic conflicts: Lining up with one side or the other in the Cold War, for example, was bound to intensify the antagonism between ideological enemies.[18] Nonalignment provided the leaders with a popular policy alternative that obviated the need to choose sides in the Cold War. In this sense, nonalignment both reflected and provided an alternative to a domestic stalemate between opposition groups that were in fundamental conflict but too weak to resolve the conflict in any single direction. A foreign policy that had the support of all the major domestic competitors would at least have the negative virtue of not making a difficult situation

17. See *ibid.* for an analysis of the efforts of various Small Powers to exclude Great Powers from regional matters.
18. For comments on this theme, see Michael Leifer, *Cambodia—The Search for Security* (New York: Praeger, 1967), pp. 65–70; and J. Bandyopadhyaya, *The Making of India's Foreign Policy* (Bombay: Allied Publishers, 1970), p. 257.

worse. It would keep conflicts at one level from reinforcing those at another level.

Nonalignment also facilitated the quest for national unity and a national identity. The developing countries wanted very much to have their independence reaffirmed and their sovereign equality recognized. Establishing a position separate from, and implicitly morally superior to, the Great Power blocs was thus enormously appealing. As Ali Mazrui observed, nonalignment always reflected an emotional desire for equal dignity and for the right to be one's own policeman.[19] Nonalignment seemed to symbolize freedom and independence and the right to decide important issues without Great Power meddling. All the conferences of the nonaligned, the summit meetings, and the declarations of Third World brotherhood (and First World duplicity) may have seemed meaningless and hypocritical rhetoric, but the goals the elites sought were primarily ceremonial and symbolic. From this perspective, nonalignment was not a policy but—as Sayegh noted—a "frame of mind" that sharpened and highlighted the distinction between "we" and "they." [20]

A brief comment on the states that did not choose nonalignment may provide a useful counterpoint. Most of the states that rejected nonalignment had to deal with threats beyond their meager resources. In some cases they were classic external threats, aggression across an international boundary. More often, especially at the height of the Cold War, the threatened states feared some mixture of aggression and internal subversion. In other cases the decision to align reflected rather simple ideological distaste for the other side—as with some of the traditional monarchs—or a desire to gain resources to use in conflict with a local rival—as in Pakistan. At any rate, insofar as they can be usefully separated, many of the LDCs who aligned because of essentially internal threats tended to fear a threat to particular regimes rather than to the state itself. Binder reports, for example, that the Shah of Iran joined the Western alli-

19. Ali A. Mazrui, *Towards a Pax Africana* (Chicago: University of Chicago Press, 1967), p. 141.
20. Fayez A. Sayegh, ed., *The Dynamics of Neutralism in the Arab World: A Symposium* (San Francisco: Chandler, 1964), p. 93.

ance system primarily to bolster his own power, not because he expected an external attack.[21]

The ceremonial and symbolic virtues, and the practical deficiencies, of nonalignment presented the threatened LDCs with an acute dilemma. In contrast to the more or less mythical argument that nonalignment provided an opportunity to get aid from both East and West, the major aid recipients were the countries that aligned with one side rather than the other. Egypt and India were partial exceptions, but even in these cases the dual donors tended to succeed one another rather than provide aid simultaneously. The aid givers, after all, wanted more than high rates of economic growth and did not like sharing recipients. In any case the road to aid tended to be the road to alignment. But the decision to align neither attained popularity nor provided the regime much beyond money and guns; it did not help much in creating a sense of national identity, for it evoked too many memories of past dependence. Thus the need for foreign aid had to be strong to compel alignment. Karl van Vorys, for instance, argues that the Pakistanis always envied the Indians' success with nonalignment and aligned with the United States only because there seemed to be no other way to balance India's local superiority.[22] The aligned, in fact, frequently seemed to be looking for an opportunity to move toward nonalignment, balancing between the blocs, as the subsequent behavior of Pakistan and South Korea indicates. In a way the general fuzziness of nonalignment, of who or what constituted nonalignment, provided a sensible way out for some states: Like the Ivory Coast, they could accept all sorts of foreign ties in practice but still insist that they were nonaligned because they did not—formally— belong to one of the blocs. This tactic might even survive foreign military intervention to save the regime in power, as it did several times in Africa. All this was possible, of course, because nonalignment was never very important to more than a handful of LDCs.

21. Leonard Binder, *Iran—Political Development in a Changing Society* (Berkeley: University of California Press, 1962), p. 393; I. William Zartman, *International Relations in the New Africa* (Englewood Cliffs, N.J.: Prentice-Hall, 1966), pp. 34 ff., makes the same point in reference to West Africa.

22. Karl von Vorys, *Political Development in Pakistan* (Princeton, N.J.: Princeton University Press, 1965), p. 165.

And these tended to be countries with transient delusions about the possibility of converting external ceremonial successes into internal (or regional) coin of the realm.

Nonalignment always referred to global issues. Even when nonalignment was adopted because of its domestic utility, its rhetoric was concerned with the overarching issues of the Cold War and anticolonialism. Conversely nonalignment had little if anything to say about either local LDC conflicts or economic relations among the LDCs themselves. Many of the potential conflicts within the Third World were simply not foreseen, perhaps because primary attention still focused on the former colonial mentors or on Cold War dialectics.[23] At any rate, attempts to solve intra-LDC conflicts would have destroyed the facade of unity before it could be put to any use. Economic issues were never seriously discussed at Bandung in 1955: Despite all the effusions of Third World brotherhood, most developing countries were too concerned with economic ties to the industrial world to raise the issue of economic relations within the Third World.[24] Consequently, throughout this period and indeed throughout the 1960s, trade between the LDCs themselves actually fell as a percentage of world trade.

There were, of course, different emphases within the non-aligned movement. As Kimche points out, two major strands were especially prominent.[25] The first was tactical and opportunistic and reflected the desire to take advantage of a particular structural configuration within the international system. Nasser's comment about Tito illuminates this perspective: "Tito is a great man. He showed me how to get help from both sides—without joining either." [26] Thus any decline in the Cold War would be unfortunate, for it would remove opportunities to maneuver and to balance between the antagonists. These tactical opportunities began to disappear as

23. On the failure to foresee the potential conflicts within the movement, see G. H. Jansen, *Nonalignment and the Afro-Asian States* (New York: Praeger, 1966), p. 17.

24. See Lalita Prasad Singh, *The Politics of Economic Cooperation in Asia* (Columbia: University of Missouri Press, 1966), p. 7.

25. David Kimche, *The Afro-Asian Movement—Ideology and Foreign Policy of the Third World* (Jerusalem: Israel Universities Press, 1973), pp. 22–23.

26. Quoted in Peter Lyon, *Neutralism* (Leicester: Leicester University Press, 1963), p. 86.

the Cold War declined in intensity and as the industrial countries began to concentrate on their own domestic problems.

The other major strand in nonalignment was much more moralistic. It was related, however distantly, to the persistent Small Power illusion that the small were somehow intrinsically more moral than the large.[27] Nehru's desire to establish a "zone of peace"—implicitly a morally superior zone—between the Great Power blocs was the latest version of this presumption. In the abstract this was a much more radical interpretation of the meaning of nonalignment, for it sought to alter the system, not merely to take advantage of the opportunities it provided. Wholly apart from the moral hypocrisy of its leading proponent (Nehru's behavior during the Sino–Indian conflict and the acquisition of Goa was less than edifying),[28] the desire to establish a zone of peace between the Great Powers was far beyond the capacity of any Third World movement.

Whatever strand of nonalignment we select, the direction of interest was toward the global system. If a scale of priorities could have been established for the LDCs in the 1950s and early 1960s (and there is surely some fuzziness in these dates, especially for the Africans who became independent only in the 1960s), it would have rested, I believe, on a distinction between two areas of symbolic concern and two areas of substantive concern.

1. The global arena was fundamentally an area of ceremonial and symbolic concern, used to create a national identity, to reaffirm the acquisition of independence and sovereign equality, and to provide the elites with the status and prestige attendant on international statesmanship. In some ways the global arena could be used in this fashion only because the elites were primarily concerned

27. Thus a Swedish newspaper could write in 1923 that "the interests of the weaker always coincide with those of justice," and Arnold Toynbee, a few years later, could argue that "if there were no 'Great Powers' in the world there would be no danger to the peace of the world was a thesis which could hardly have been contested, in 1932, by any impartial student of public affairs." Both quotes are from Rothstein, *Alliances and Small Powers,* chapter 1. More recently, Ben Bella stated: "We are aligned with all just causes. We are aligned with good and nonaligned with evil." Quoted in Ottaway, *Algeria—The Politics of a Socialist Revolution,* p. 146.

28. See especially the comments by Maxwell, *India's China War,* p. 134 and *passim.*

with domestic political stability and did not fully understand the extent to which the patterns and trends of the international economic system affected the alternatives they had.

2. The regional level has always seemed more important than it actually was; that is, it has seemed as if the region ought to be important for states manifestly too weak to go very far on their own. But rhetoric dominated substance here also. Regional partners were too weak to be of much material use; even if they had wanted to cooperate, communications, transportation and trading ties were still directed toward the former metropolitan areas. What was left were expressions of brotherhood—pan-Africanism, pan-Asianism, and so forth—and marginal peacekeeping activities by institutions like the Organization of African Unity. As Zartman remarks of West Africa, intra-African affairs had so little to do with the dominant domestic conflicts in each of the states that leaders could do pretty much as they wanted in that arena: Since it was not very important, whim, old friendships, and transient ties could determine particular outcomes.[29] Howell also reports that leaders of Kenya had more freedom to do as they wished on the regional level than on any other level.[30]

In some cases, of course, regional cooperation did not get very far, not only because neighbors were too weak to be useful, but also because active mistrust and fear of neighbors existed. In these cases mutual antipathy destroyed the flexibility provided by mutual indifference. Singh, for example, emphasizes the extent to which dislike for each other and fear of large neighbors like Japan and India have kept the Asian LDCs from more than marginal cooperation. All wanted to ensure national before regional development; none have been willing to sacrifice special arrangements with extra-area Great Powers, or any revenue from substituting a regional for a national tariff boundary. One delegate to a joint meeting thus commented, "Right now, when we talk aid, we talk directly with Washington. We don't want to create the possibility of having to go through a third party and being told some day our needs must be

29. See Zartman, *International Relations in the New Africa*, pp. 53–55.
30. John Howell, "An Analysis of Kenyan Foreign Policy," *Journal of Modern African Studies* 6 (1968):45 ff.

subordinated to greater Asian good." And a Burmese speaker, alluding to the Japanese, was even more revealing: "It was terrible to be ruled by a Western Power, but it was even more so to be ruled by an Asian power." [31]

Material weakness, the reluctance of elites in new states to surrender any aspects of the sovereignty they had so recently acquired, and either indifference to or dislike of neighbors combined to limit the practical significance of regionalism.

3. Objective calculations of real interests prevailed at two levels. Bilateral Great Power relationships, usually with the former colonial rulers, were generally perceived as too important to sacrifice to ideological rhetoric. These relationships can be usefully separated from the wider systemic relationships because they were always considered unique and different: While colonialism and neocolonialism were universally attacked, the rhetoric did not prevent persisting and profound ties with the "former" rulers. For those elites who were especially conscious of their countries' weakness and of the need for aid and investment from the West, conservative behavior seemed imperative. Senegal and the Ivory Coast in French West Africa, Kenya in British East Africa, and the Philippines and Malaysia in Southeast Asia were careful not to act in too radical a fashion: Foreign private investment was sought and protected, expatriate officials exercised significant power, and foreign policy behavior within the Third World was restrained and moderate.[32] None of this, of course, prevented any of these states from being members in reasonably good standing of the nonaligned movement. The costs of ignoring the importance of bilateral ties or of granting precedence to other concerns were usually high: When Ghana became increasingly radical under Nkrumah, when Guinea refused to join the French system in West Africa, when Tanzania recognized East Germany and broke diplomatic relations with the British for their policy in Rhodesia, and when Guatemala and Cuba (and later Allende's Chile) offended American norms in Latin

---

31. Singh, *The Politics of Economic Cooperation in Asia,* pp. 5 and 11.
32. On Senegal, see W. A. E. Skurnik, *The Foreign Policy of Senegal* (Evanston: Northwestern University Press, 1972); on Kenya, see Howell, "An Analysis of Kenyan Foreign Policy," p. 44.

America, all suffered immediate and substantial losses in foreign aid and investment—at a minimum. These relationships ought to have been calculated with great care—although in many cases they were barely calculated at all—for they provided the major portion of the resources each LDC could hope to extract from the external world and also the major threat of intervention or retaliation in the case of recalcitrant behavior.

4. The other arena in which objective calculations prevailed might be called the contiguous environment or local areas of discord. Border areas were too important and potentially dangerous to be analyzed either ideologically or in romantic terms of brotherhood. Levi may go too far in asserting that power politics always prevailed locally, but it is surely clear that some degree of prudence and careful calculation of real interests were imperative.[33] Domestic weakness in and of itself dictated a conservative local policy, for whatever threats to security materialized were likely to be heavily dependent for success on sanctuary and support from a hostile neighbor.[34] The nonaligned always advocated peaceful settlement of Great Power disputes, whatever the merits of the case at hand, but they were careful to say nothing about how intra-LDC disputes were to be settled. Thus a member of the movement could not expect much help from its peers if a festering dispute erupted into war; consequently vigilance and preparation were imperative.

Given the weakness of the states involved and the wide number of actual and potential conflicts over borders and treatment of minorities, it is probably surprising that more local wars did not occur. But the very weakness that made the outbreak of conflict so dangerous to a local government also engendered prudence about getting involved in "foreign adventures." Moreover most of the LDCs were aware that they too were vulnerable to some boundary claim or minority conflict.[35] Commitment to the status quo thus had

33. Werner Levi, *The Challenge of World Politics in South and Southeast Asia* (Englewood Cliffs; N.J.: Prentice-Hall, 1968), p. 76.
34. On Kenyan fears in this regard, see Howell, "An Analysis of Kenyan Foreign Policy," p. 41.
35. Saadia Touval, *The Boundary Politics of Independent Africa* (Cambridge: Harvard University Press, 1972) also stresses the impact of domestic weakness on the decision to accept the status quo.

far more to do with careful calculations of self-interest than normative calculations about the need to establish the principles of international law.

Commitment to the status quo at the local level may not survive
for long. Weakness engendered a willingness to accept peaceful
nonsettlement of disputes, but it did not remove the disputes themselves. Any number of developments could suddenly overturn the
tacit agreement not to contest borders: for example, the emergence
of a new leader(s) in one of the large LDCs intent on a venture into
regional imperialism, or the eruption of conflicts in outlying areas
that feel they are being treated unfairly by the central government.
The fact that some developing country leaders have now solidified
domestic control may also make them more willing to launch external attacks: Once held back by the fear that domestic control would
crumble if conflict was risked, these leaders may now be emboldened to seek to right old wrongs or to attempt to deal with resource
constraints by acquiring neighboring resources. The rising arms
budgets in many LDCs underscore the point. Increasing domestic
discontent may also engender willingness to risk local wars, although this well-known hypothesis has been difficult to verify. A
sense of unfairness about the distribution of the world's natural
resources may also create pressures toward forced sharing: The
LDCs have demanded that the rich countries distribute the resources of the international system more equitably, but they have
not displayed a similar interest in sharing what resources they do
possess with each other. Why should Zambia and Gabon prosper
simply from inhabiting one part of the geological universe, while
the less fortunate must do without? In any case, whereas local conflicts were fairly muted in the 1950s and 1960s, the potential for future conflicts is high.

## THE DECLINE OF NONALIGNMENT

Nonalignment as either a tactic of maneuver between the Cold
War blocs or as a means of establishing a zone of peace began to

decline in the mid-1960s.[36] This decline has usually been attributed to the diminution of Cold War tensions and to a tendency on the part of the Great Powers to become preoccupied with their own internal problems. Anticolonialism also began to decline as a unifying force as more and more colonies achieved independence. The notion of playing both sides against each other—the classic tactical and systemic rationale for nonalignment—thus began to lose much of its appeal: It was harder to balance between increasingly disinterested Great Powers, and the issues for which balancing made sense (anticolonialism and the extraction of aid from both sides) either dissipated or took on a new form.

The other external rationale for nonalignment was to create a "zone of peace" between the Cold War antagonists. This goal also obviously lost most of its appeal as the Cold War declined. Perhaps even more significantly, conflicts within the nonaligned movement began to grow. This may have been inevitable, for it is surely unlikely that the movement could long remain neutral or indifferent to issues that were crucial to some of its members. The outbreak of the Sino–Indian war in 1962 was particularly important: When the rest of the nonaligned countries did not support the Indians, and indeed turned nonalignment against the Indians (i.e., being nonaligned between India and China), India rapidly lost interest in nonalignment. With India gone—into something resembling alignment with both sides—even the nominal attempt to create a zone of peace in the Cold War virtually disappeared.

These changes in the Cold War context and in relations within the nonaligned movement itself made it increasingly difficult to justify nonalignment with a few general references to bipolarity and Third World brotherhood. I would argue, however, that there were more fundamental reasons for the decline of nonalignment. What nonalignment did not do was respond to the domestic problems that began to beset the LDCs within the last decade. As a second generation of leaders emerged, and as they were forced to deal with a range of explosive problems—population pressures, food pres-

36. Skurnik, *The Foreign Policy of Senegal*, p. 245, argues that nonalignment grew in importance as bipolarity declined but cites no evidence that supports his views.

sures, unemployment pressures, declining trade and aid prospects, rising debts, and so on—a foreign policy that responded primarily to the aftermath of independence no longer made much sense. Symbolic and ceremonial payoffs were no longer sufficient. Elite survival became bound up not only with silencing domestic opposition and expelling a few foreign capitalists but also with achieving some degree of success in dealing with the problems of economic development.

A serious concern for economic development, especially in the light of prevailing theories about the need for foreign exchange to import capital goods, inevitably meant a serious concern about relations with the international economic system. The developing countries had to begin worrying not only about aid relationships with the major donors but also about general prospects for both traditional and new exports.[37] To improve these prospects required pressure against both Cold War sides—that is, against all the industrialized countries—rather than a balancing between them. Small and weak states could develop rapidly only by taking advantage of the opportunities created by the international economic system. What had previously been a nebulous arena for displays of rhetoric and status was increasingly becoming the (apparently) determining factor for domestic growth and prosperity.

In contrast to Bandung in 1955, when economic problems were barely touched, tangible gains now had to be extracted from the industrial world. The Latin Americans joined in this new effort: The Third World was no longer merely new and Afro–Asian states, for the common denominator was now poverty and a shared resentment of unfair treatment. Escalating domestic problems (apparently) could be dealt with only by aid, investment, and trade through the medium of the international economic system. In any case this was surely true for increasingly conservative ruling elites

37. As a rough guide, approximately 75–80 percent of the foreign exchange available to the LDCs has come from trade, and only about 20 percent from aid. Since the foreign exchange earned by traders could be spent as they wished, which sometimes meant on luxuries, an aid dollar might be worth more than a trade dollar—on the assumption that the aid dollar was not wasted, lost to corruption, and so forth. In any case the general point still holds: Most of the foreign exchange available had to come from trade, especially as aid levels declined.

who were unwilling to risk the turbulence of a fundamental restructuring of domestic socioeconomic institutions. As domestic economic problems began to be *the* domestic political problems, a foreign policy of nonalignment simply seemed increasingly irrelevant. It did not even get aid from both sides, and aid levels (after a brief rise in the early 1960s) began to level off and then decline.

What was necessary was a foreign policy that served objective needs and interests in a way that nonalignment neither did nor could. Nonalignment was an attractive policy for a period when first priority went to establishing national identity, avoiding foreign policy choices that exacerbated domestic conflict, and affirming a unique role for new and insecure states. It served the elites in this fashion, for it contributed to their ability to stay in power, but it had much less to contribute to a period in which economic development had a high priority. In the new circumstances the nonaligned still needed each other, for group pressure was likely to be more effective in extracting concessions than individual action. That meant action in two directions. The weak themselves had to form stronger regional groups to overcome the limitations of market size and to improve their bargaining positions: This meant an effort finally to treat intra-Third World cooperation seriously. But the developing countries also had to establish some kind of position toward the international economic system itself. This effort, which has attempted to define the terms that the developing countries consider fair for remaining within the system, has centered on the various United Nations Conference on Trade and Development (UNCTAD) meetings. Something of a trade union of the poor against the rich has emerged from these efforts—perhaps even the notion of class war. I discuss these matters in the next chapter.

## FROM NONALIGNMENT TO CLASS WAR

The nonaligned movement is not, of course, dead. It has, instead, been transformed into something quite different: a joint alignment against all the industrial countries. That this has nothing to do with any traditional meaning of nonalignment is probably of

*[127]*

little importance. But it is important to understand the change that has taken place, for it reflects the end of a period—with a rough closing date sometime in the mid-1960s—in which external rela-- tions performed primarily ceremonial functions for the developing countries and the beginning of a period in which the quest for changes in the operation of the international aid and trade systems became increasingly prominent.

What relationship was there between nonalignment and domestic economic policies like import substitution industrialization? Is there any evidence, for example, that nonalignment was chosen because it might make import substitution easier? The answer is no, for the decisions seem to have been compartmentalized, emanating from the same set of conditions but related only as spokes in a wheel. In reprospect there might have been a closer relationship between the two policies if either policy had been more successful in achieving its goals. If import substitution had actually saved large amounts of foreign exchange, a foreign policy aimed at acquiring more aid and trade might have been less necessary. Successful import substitution policies would have made the developing countries less dependent on the international system and perhaps more willing to continue a foreign policy that was primarily rhetorical, but an unsuccessful import substitution policy increased dependence. Conversely, if nonalignment had actually managed to raise aid levels from both sides, the failures of import substitution might have been more bearable. But neither policy achieved its ostensible external goals, and thus they seemed to bear very little relationship to each other.

The compartmentalization of foreign policy and domestic development policy also could not survive escalating domestic problems. This was especially true because of two factors: the reluctance of most elites to risk their own gains by fundamentally transforming domestic socioeconomic structures and the influence of prevailing economic doctrines that not only argued that a small and poor country could prosper only by participating in the international division of labor but also emphasized the need for rapid industrialization, which meant increasing and undiscriminating involvement with a sophisticated and demanding international environment.[38] Consequently the economics and the diplomacy of development have become increasingly difficult to separate, and "foreign policy," in this sense, is no longer a residual category of domestic policy.

I do not mean that foreign policy in any of its more traditional meanings has completely disappeared from the nonaligned movement, for declarations on the arms race, East–West relations, the remnants of colonialism, and disputes like the Arab–Israeli conflict continue to emanate from the regular summit meetings of the nonaligned. Nevertheless the axis of real concern has shifted. This has meant that Third World concerns have become an increasingly important part of the international agenda. These concerns tend to be defined, debated, and negotiated within international institutions like UNCTAD. As such the regular summit meetings of the nonaligned now seem to perform primarily a legitimizing function for the assertion of demands that must be negotiated in other fora. This might change if the Third World set up its own "OECD," outside of the U.N. system, for there would presumably be less need to rely on the intellectual support of the international secretariats, but this much-discussed proposal remains mired in the internal politics (and finances) of the Third World.

One last point needs to be made. The Third World has sought to put increasing pressure on the industrial countries to extract tangible benefits. The only leverage that the developing countries have seemed to possess—especially before the oil crisis, but even after it—is their unity. The quest for unity has thus become a major preoccupation of the Third World. But how is it possible to maintain unity among so many countries with so many different or even conflicting interests? Compromising conflicting interests would be difficult in any circumstance, but it is especially difficult for poor

38. In recent years some interesting and provocative defenses of self-reliance have begun to appear. Nevertheless, in earlier years—and indeed by many at the present time—it was virtually taken for granted that small and poor countries could not separate themselves from the international trading system without paying severe costs—Burma was a convincing case in point. But when we move away from simple choices—"join or not join"—to a discussion of selective and discriminating strategies that emphasize various degrees and kinds of participation, the possibility of relative self-reliance begins to look less dangerous for some developing countries. For further discussion, see chapter 9.

countries that cannot afford to sacrifice present gains for future benefits. Consequently no one has been asked to sacrifice anything; negotiating proposals simply add together everybody's demands or promise losers that they will somehow be compensated. Such proposals make meaningful bargaining difficult, for any compromise threatens to unravel the whole package unless all can gain something, but this is surely unlikely in a bargaining universe in which only some demands can be met and in which almost nothing benefits all the developing countries. This is an issue that the Third World has not yet faced, preferring to maintain the fiction of unity. I discuss some aspects of these difficulties in the next chapter (and, once again, in chapters 10 and 11).

# 5

## The Rich against the Poor: International Class Warfare from UNCTAD-I to the Oil Crisis

### TOWARD A FOREIGN POLICY OF DEVELOPMENT

By some standards the developing countries did very well in the 1960s. The link between high growth rates and the growth of exports seemed clear, and Third World exports had indeed done quite well. Exports had gone up 67 percent from 1959 to 1969, and the yearly average was 5.9 percent. Imports went up 5.4 percent per year in the same period, with more than 90 percent of the costs met by export receipts.[1] The overall growth rate averaged about 5 percent, although per capita growth was only about half that because of population increases.[2]

In relative terms the picture was less impressive. The LDC share of world exports declined from 27 percent in 1953 to 19.3 percent in 1968. In addition the share of primary products in world trade declined from 54 percent in 1953 to 37 percent in 1967, and more than 80 percent of LDC exports still came from primary prod-

---

1. See Leslie Stein, "Developing Countries and International Trade—An Alternative View," *Journal of Modern African Studies* 8, no. 4 (1970):605–6.

2. Harald B. Malmgren, "Trade for Development," in Charles R. Frank, Jr., *et al.*, *Assisting Developing Countries—Problems of Debts, Burden-Sharing, Jobs and Trade* (New York: Praeger, 1972), pp. 383–84.

ucts. And since demand for tropical-zone products was rising less rapidly than that for temperate-zone products, the LDC share of primary product exports also declined from 40.5 percent in 1961 to 38.2 percent in 1966.[3] Their terms of trade had also fallen: From 1955 to 1970, the prices for Third World exports had fallen by 6 percent, while the exports of the rich went up 8 percent.[4]

Manufacturing exports had increased during the decade from about 13 percent to about 19 percent of total LDC exports. These exports were, however, concentrated in a few countries. In 1968, for example, Hong Kong, Taiwan, South Korea, and Israel accounted for 42 percent of the total of manufactured exports, and the top eight countries had two-thirds of the total. These figures reflect one fact obscured by aggregate growth figures: Most of the gains were going to a small group of higher income developing countries, while the poorest developing countries were not doing very well at all. Moreover, despite a potentially large market for such goods among themselves, the LDCs did not export many manufactures to each other; exports to other LDCs grew more slowly than those to the advanced countries, and the same small group of LDCs dominated intra-LDC trade in manufactures. Indeed the poor countries traded less with each other at the end of the decade than they did at the beginning, such trade dropping from 23 percent to 20 percent of total LDC trade.[5]

The more general picture provided by overall growth rates was also not as reassuring as first appearances might suggest. According to U.N. statistics, for example, the averge GDP growth rate declined from 4.6 percent per annum in 1955–60 to 4.4 percent in 1960–65, and per capita growth rates decined in the same period from 2.3 percent to 1.9 percent. The performance of the Latin American states in these years was slightly worse than the average record (e.g., per capita growth rates declined from 1.9 percent to 1.7 percent), which may provide part of the explanation for the growing tendency of many Latin American states to move toward increased participation in the Third World. Finally income distribution figures were also beginning to be worrisome: The share of world in-

3. Stein, "Developing Countries and International Trade," p. 607.
4. Malmgren, "Trade for Development," pp. 393–94.     5. Ibid.

come held by the poorest 60 percent of the world's population declined from 13.2 percent in 1950 to 11.1 percent in 1964. The faith that rapid growth would ultimately diminish income inequities might still persist, but the dangers of waiting until (if ever) the fruits of growth began to "trickle down" to the poor were becoming more and more apparent.

Why had the LDCs done reasonably well in absolute terms but much less well in relative terms? A good part of the answer is that the rich countries had done even better: The overall growth rate and the export growth rate of the industrial countries went up faster in the 1960s than the equivalent rates for the poor countries. Consequently the poor countries had a declining share of world trade, even though absolute increases were impressive.[6] But there has been a positive correlation between high rates of growth in the advanced countries and those in the poor countries: When the economies of the rich have been booming, so have the economies of the poor, if at a relatively slower pace. One reason for this connection is that the LDCs must export to achieve high rates of growth; the only markets for the bulk of their exports (both primary products and labor-intensive manufactured goods) are in the industrial countries, and demand for LDC exports thus goes up (although not equivalently) when the industrial countries are doing well. The industrial countries are also likely to be more generous and to invest more in the LDCs when they are doing well.

The connection between high rates of growth in the advanced countries and those in the LDCs has seemed very close in the past. It has been at the center of the "trickle down" theory of development and has provided a good deal of support for the notion that special privileges for the poor were not really necessary if the rich managed their own affairs well (and if the poor followed correct domestic policies). The developing countries clearly hope that this relationship can be altered in the future by means of improved bargaining and increasing degrees of collective self-reliance within

6. For a useful analysis of trade relations between particular rich countries and the Third World, see David Wightman, "The Export Stake of Industrial Countries in the Third World," in *The Case for Development* (New York: Praeger, 1973), pp. 157–248.

the Third World. In the medium and longer term some movement in this direction seems both necessary and justified. Nevertheless, in the short run, the correlation between growth rates in the rich countries and those in the poor countries seems likely to persist. There is only fragmentary evidence that the growth rates of the poor can persistently outpace those of the rich countries: For example, from 1968 to 1972, the growth rate of the developed countries was 4.5 percent per annum but 6.2 percent per annum for the developing countries (per capita rates were 3.5 percent and 3.7 percent respectively). But it would be dangerous for the poor countries to assume that this reflected a fundamental reversal of roles or that support from the industrial countries would shortly be unnecessary.

A 6 percent per year export growth rate for the LDCs in the 1960s may—or may not—seem impressive, but it was definitely unexpected. The decade began with a great deal of export pessimism by the developing countries. The prices for many primary goods dropped from their Korean War highs during the years from 1957 to 1962. How well the rich countries would do, or continue to do, was also unclear. In any case, demand for primary products seemed likely to decline. This was due, as Maizels claimed,

> to changes in the pattern of demand in the industrial countries; to technological developments, particularly the use of synthetics for natural materials in industry; and to fiscal and protectionist policies in the field of foodstuffs, beverages and manufactures which limit the expansion of exports of these goods from primary producing countries.[7]

To continue to depend on primary product exports to the rich countries was also psychologically unappealing, for it perpetuated a pattern of dependence from the past.

What could the developing countries do? The obvious answer was to diversify, to move into exports for which world demand was likely to continue high. This meant that they would have to develop an export capacity in manufacturing. Unfortunately this seemed difficult to do, for converting an economy from import substitution—

7. A. Maizels, "Recent Trends in World Trade," in Roy Harrod and Douglas Hague, eds., *International Trade Theory in a Developing World* (New York: St. Martin's Press, 1963), p. 43.

with overvalued exchange rates, protected domestic markets, and no competition—to "export substitution" was difficult.[8] And it was risky, for it was not clear that the industries that did manage to become competitive would be allowed access to the markets of the industrial countries; in any event, prospects for success seemed likely to be limited to a few countries, not the bulk of the Third World.

But everything else the LDCs had tried had not worked—or had not worked sufficiently. Economic nationalism, import substitution, regional cooperation, exporting primary products, all worked to a point but not beyond. And growth rates in per capita income seemed to be steadily declining.[9] Stagnant agriculture, rapidly rising levels of unemployment, declining export receipts and mounting import bills, and low levels of foreign aid and investment forced the LDC elites to contemplate a confrontation with the international trading system itself—for it was becoming clear to the elites that they could not successfully trade within that system unless they received special dispensations. This shift in perspective toward the international trading system was not primarily a reflection of the advice of outside experts and doctrines: It reflected the experiences of the underdeveloped countries themselves and the beginnings of an adversary relationship with the industrial countries.

The inwardly oriented policies of the 1950s had not succeeded in saving enough foreign exchange to pay for the imports of the capital goods needed for industrialization. There was a gap between the foreign exchange that the LDCs could earn through their exports and what they needed to continue their industrialization programs; estimates of the size of the projected gap in the early 1970s varied from a little less than $10 billion to a little more than

8. On the various structural and policy factors that impede exporting, see Angus Maddison, *Economic Progress and Policy in Developing Countries* (London: Allen and Unwin, 1970), pp. 199–206. The phrase "export substitution" was a play on import substitution and implied moving into exports that seemed to have good long-term demand prospects.

9. Benjamin I. Cohen and Gustav Ranis, "The Second Postwar Restructuring," in Gustav Ranis, ed., *Government and Economic Development* (New Haven, Conn.: Yale University Press, 1971), p. 440.

$20 billion. To close the gap, the LDCs needed more foreign aid and foreign trade, especially trade in low-level, labor-intensive manufactures with the advanced countries. They could get more aid and trade only by applying whatever pressure they could muster against the rich countries. The international arena was no longer, therefore, a residual category for the LDCs, an arena for symbolic or ceremonial exercises. If industrialization was imperative, imports were imperative; if imports were imperative, aid and trade (usually as a disguised form of aid) were imperative. A foreign policy of development, manipulating the international system for domestic economic goals, became the central feature of Third World policies in the 1960s.

I mentioned earlier the significance of the foreign exchange gap. It was not the only gap, for gaps existed wherever the observer looked: in savings, technology, productivity, and so on. But there was also a free-floating gap between the rich and the poor that came to symbolize the moral basis of the demands the poor were asserting. Surely an enormous gap existed between per capita incomes in the rich and the poor countries; more critically the gap was surely increasing in absolute terms and possibly or occasionally in relative terms also. The necessity of diminishing this gap, perhaps even by some kind of redistribution of income, has become one of the major themes of the past decade and continues to exert a profound influence on public discussion. Why this may be unfortunate, even pernicious, is discussed in the next section.

## THE GAP BETWEEN RICH AND POOR: SYMBOL AND SUBSTANCE

Before the oil crisis per capita income in the United States was projected to be $10,000 in the year 2000. Per capita income in India was expected to reach about $200 in the same year—if India managed to get enough foreign aid. Estimates of absolute income differences between the rich and the poor by the year 2000 varied between $7,000 and $9,000 per capita.[10] The absolute gap between the

10. For various projections of likely gaps by 2000, see Richard Jolly, "The Aid Relationship: Reflections on the Pearson Report," *Journal of International Affairs* 24,

rich and the poor was thus likely to increase sharply, and the relative gap might also increase if population growth rates were not slowed quickly.

Projections such as these have led to a number of demands for crash programs to reduce the gap, usually by a massive international redistribution of incomes. Pestel and Mesarovic, for example, in the latest Club of Rome book, contend that income disparities between Latin America and the industrial countries must be narrowed to 3 to 1 by 2000, and 5 to 1 for Asia and Africa, if we hope to avoid an international system dominated by desperate acts of terror and destruction by the poor. To accomplish this, they maintain that the rich countries must transfer $250 billion per year (and $500 billion if we delay much longer) to the poor countries.[11]

These are astonishing figures: They amount to 25 to 50 times the amount of current resource transfers. As such they are obviously politically absurd (so much so that they might merely induce apathy and indifference). Still, if Pestel and Mesarovic have indeed identified the correct goal—reducing disparities of income to 3 and 5 to 1—and if they have indeed identified the correct means of achieving it, the figures they cite would remain astonishing—but they would not be absurd. The burden of proof would rest on those who maintain the superiority of other goals and other means.

Suppose the rich countries agreed to transfer $250 billion a year to the poor countries. Could sums of that magnitude be transferred without destabilizing the international economic system? It is surely unlikely. Could the funds be absorbed by the recipients? It is again surely unlikely, for it is unclear how they could be usefully invested. But suppose the funds were simply doled out in equal amounts to all the citizens of the poor countries, so that in 25 or 50 years the accumulative sum would presumably have reduced income disparities to 3 and 5 to 1. Would the gap really have begun to disappear? Perhaps—but only for a short time, for once payment

no. 2 (1970):164–80; and Paul Streeten, *The Frontiers of Development Studies* (New York: Wiley, 1972), p. 300.

11. For these any other estimates of aid needs to reduce the gap, see Mihajlo Mesarovic and Eduard Pestel, *Mankind at the Turning Point* (New York: Dutton, 1974), pp. 58–64.

*[137]*

came to an end, the factors initially responsible for creating the gap would begin to work again. The gap between the rich and the poor is not just an income gap: It is also a gap between modernized, industrialized societies with particular kinds of institutions and processes and rural, traditional societies with very different institutions and processes. These distinctions—or gaps—create sharp differences in productivity, which is what ultimately distinguishes a developed from an underdeveloped economy, that cannot be eliminated simply by transferring money.[12] And if we did not simply dole out the money for consumption purposes but instead attempted to use it for investment, there is no way that $250 billion per year could be sensibly invested.

At the root of proposals for radical and immediate redistributions of income is the simple-minded notion that the way to make the poor richer is by making the rich poorer. The rich countries might indeed become poorer by virtue of such transfers, but it is far from clear that the poor countries would really become much richer. As growth rates slowed in the rich countries, growth rates would probably also slow in the poor countries; the transfer of funds might do no more than allow the poor countries to tread water until demand for their exports began to grow again.[13]

The notion of the gap is also misleading in other ways. As a number of economists have pointed out, international comparisons of income tend to underestimate real incomes in poor countries. The statistics on which such comparisons are based are not very reliable, and the exchange rates used to convert local currencies into dollars can have a sharp effect on the range of disparity. Moreover, some things tend to be left out or badly estimated in national income statistics within the developing countries—for example, subsistence output and intra-family services. There is also an implicit tendency to assume that what people demand from their economies in the rich countries is what they will demand in the poor countries

12. See the "Introduction" in Gustav Ranis, ed., *The Gap Between Rich and Poor Nations* (London: Macmillan, 1972), p. 4.
13. I have already noted, earlier in this chapter, my doubts about the likelihood that recent changes in commodity prices and terms of trade portend the end of the close relationship between growth rates in the two groups of countries.

and that income disparities thus accurately reflect differing abilities to buy the same set of goods.[14]

Aggregate income comparisons between the rich and the poor may also mislead in other ways. In the first place the world is not in fact sharply divided into two groups, one rich and one poor. There is a continuous gradation between the very poor and the very rich, and there are countries scattered throughout the spectrum. Indeed, insofar as one wants to be accurate about the gap, it would be more precise to say that the gap between the developed countries and the lower income underdeveloped countries is widening but that the gap between the developed countries and the top level of the underdeveloped countries (over, say, $600 per capita income) is narrowing. And, of course, the revolution in oil prices, and the potential increases in the prices of some other raw materials, may also alter the gap—not necessarily for the better for the great majority of underdeveloped countries. In any case the growing gap within the Third World can be seen from Table 1.

Acting as if there were only two groups of countries clearly sep-

TABLE 1. RELATIVE GROWTH RATES OF THE DEVELOPING COUNTRIES: DIFFERENCES IN AGGREGATE GROWTH RATES

|  | All Developing Countries | All Developing Countries (excluding major petroleum exporters) | Least Developed Countries |
|---|---|---|---|
| Total GNP |  |  |  |
| 1960–70 | 5.2 | 5.1 | 3.4 |
| 1970–73 | 5.7 | 5.3 | 3.2 |
| 1970–80 target | 6.0 |  |  |
| Per capita GNP |  |  |  |
| 1960–70 | 2.6 | 2.5 | 0.8 |
| 1970–73 | 3.1 | 2.7 | 0.6 |
| 1970–80 target | 3.5 |  |  |

SOURCE: *Review of Progress in the Implementation of Special Measures in Favour of the Least Developed Among the Developing Countries* (UNCTAD, TD/B/AC.17/3, June 10, 1975).

14. For interesting discussions of these matters, see P. T. Bauer, *Dissent on Development* (Cambridge, Mass.: Harvard University Press, 1972), pp. 52 ff.; and the comments by Mahbub ul Haq in Ranis, *The Gap Between Rich and Poor Nations*, pp. 48–49.

arated from each other may create the belief that only extreme solutions make sense or that the problem of helping the poor is unmanageable. In addition aggregate statics tend to mask the impact of a few large LDCs: China apart, India, Pakistan, Indonesia, Bangladesh, and Brazil constitute about two-thirds of the population of the Third World, and whatever happens to them seems to be happening to all the LDCs. I assert, not that the other LDCs are all doing well, but rather that the desperate condition of India, Pakistan, and Bangladesh, in particular, has exerted a negative effect on the statistical profile of the Third World. Note, for example, as another illustration of growing divergences within the Third World, the differences between India, Bangladesh, and Pakistan and two other groups of developing countries (Table 2).

TABLE 2. INDIA, BANGLADESH, AND PAKISTAN AND OTHER DEVELOPING COUNTRIES

| Countries with: | GNP per capita 1973 (dollars) | GNP in real terms 1960–70 | 1970–73 | GNP per capita in real terms 1960–70 | 1970–73 |
|---|---|---|---|---|---|
| | | (percentage change per annum) | | | |
| GNP per capita over $250 | 530 | 4.9 | 6.5 | 2.2 | 3.8 |
| GNP per capita under $250 | 115 | 4.2 | 3.0 | 1.7 | 0.5 |
| India, Bangladesh, Pakistan | 100 | 3.9 | 2.0 | 1.6 | −0.3 |

SOURCE: UNCTAD Secretariat data.

The divergences would be even sharper, of course, if petroleum exporters or fast-growing manufacturing exporters were added to the table. In sum, then, the use of aggregate rich versus poor statistics may obscure more than it reveals and divert attention away from policies that at least can help the developing countries that do not face overwhelming immediate problems. These distinctions are necessary to note, for lumping all the developing countries together distorts the significance of the gap.[15]

The evidence I cited in the first section of this chapter has already indicated that some poor countries did well in the 1960s. Caplow has cited other evidence, however, indicating that the rank

15. It also confuses public discussion and hinders the development of sensible policies.

order of states in the international system is very stable. The rich are getting richer, but the poor (or all the poor) are not getting poorer; they are getting richer at about the same rate as the rich, but the initial differences are so wide that absolute disparities are increasing. Caplow also shows that the time lag for catching up is lengthening, so that equality between the rich and the poor is inconceivable.[16] Statistics such as these have to be used with great caution, for they mask important differences within each group of states. Nevertheless the general point here seems valid: The absolute gap between most of the rich countries and most of the poor countries is unlikely ever to disappear (short of nuclear war or some other action that would drive the living standards of the rich sharply downward).

How important is this? Is reduction of the gap between the rich and the poor the proper goal for the international system? If not the absolute gap, should we aim to reduce the relative gap? What are we trying to say with the notion of the gap? I would argue that the answer is that it is indecent and immoral for the rich to expend vast sums on luxuries when vast numbers of people must endure every conceivable physical degradation. We have, I take it, a moral obligation to help those who need and want our help. But we have no moral obligation to ensure that everyone has one-fifth or one-third or one-tenth the income of the rich countries by any known date. Such a goal is politically meaningless and practically impossible, which is to say that we do not have a moral obligation to do what cannot be done—or, anyway, what we do not know how to do.

This means, I believe, that the simple goal of reducing the gap between the rich and the poor may be the wrong goal *for the Third World as a whole*. There is simply no feasible way that such a goal can be accomplished for the vast majority of LDCs, and the effort to do so may end only by making everyone worse off—unless someone can demonstrate that the prosperity of the poor bears no relationship to that of the rich. I do not mean to argue that some countries will not or cannot move up (or down) the international hierarchy, for some clearly will. But, apart from a few oil producers

16. Theodore Caplow, "Are the Rich Countries Getting Richer and the Poor Countries Poorer?," *Foreign Policy*, no. 3 (Summer 1971):90–107.

this is not going to happen in a wholesale fashion, and when it does happen, the root cause is likely to be increases in some form of comparative advantage, not the transfer of large sums of money. In fact the transfer of such funds would probably be economically useful (as distinct from useful for primarily humanitarian purposes) only to those countries already capable of helping themselves—and not to those who need help the most.

I do not want to leave the impression that I am in any sense against helping the poor and increasing our aid efforts. I think, however, that sole concentration on reducing a gap of such magnitude is apt to do quite the opposite: that is to say, compel apathy in the face of an impossible task or create the illusion that the only way in which the poor can be helped is by turning the international economic system on its head. I am not arguing that the gap is irrelevant, either as a political symbol or as an indication of our moral responsibilities, or that I feel that it ought not to be narrowed. But concentration on the gap may deflect concern from more practical and immediate tasks that need to be accomplished. In addition an obsession with the need to reduce the gap tends to make relative growth rates the central issue in the development debate: This may be unfortunate, not because growth rates are unimportant, but because even rapid growth by the poor countries that did manage to narrow the gap would not really solve many of their problems—unless the gains from growth were more equitably distributed than they have been in the past. Moreover the belief that the international system is going to be torn apart to benefit the poor is politically absurd. And, for the reasons I have outlined, even if such an attempt were made, there is little reason to believe it would greatly help either many of the poor countries or many of their poorest citizens.

What we should primarily be concerned with is, not the gap between the rich and the poor, however useful that gap has been as a symbol of desperation, but provision of a decent standard of living for those who live in poverty, degradation, and hunger. How to do this is a complex and difficult issue that requires some understanding of the trade-offs between growth and equity and between elite security and elite responsiveness to change. I take up these matters again in chapter 8. Here I note only that it may be possible to achieve increased equity without sacrificing growth and with resource transfers that are both politically and economically feasible. In the short run this goal is not likely to have much to do with whether the income gap between rich and poor (externally) is increasing or decreasing. In the long run a program fundamentally aimed at providing a decent standard of living as quickly as possible for the poorest citizens may be the only way that the poor countries themselves can begin to reach the points where the gap is irrelevant—because incomes at the bottom of the scale have been sufficiently raised—or can be diminished by their own efforts.

Whatever the validity of this argument, emphasis on the gap between the rich and the poor dominated the discussion of trade and aid in the 1960s. For radicals the existence of the gap itself was the direct result of colonial exploitation, and the exploiters now owed massive reparations to the exploited. To others the gap was attributed to the inequities of an international trading system that insisted on treating unequals as if they were equal. For others responsibility for the gap was irrelevant; what was critical was simply the need to eliminate it.

That the poor needed external aid was a nearly universal proposition.[17] But there were sharp disagreements about the form and the amount of help to be given. To make their case more strongly, the poor countries banded together to increase their bargaining power against all the industrial countries. What began to emerge, as a replacement for traditional Cold War distinctions, was the notion of an international class war between the rich and the poor.


## UNCTAD: TRADE UNION OF THE POOR
## IN A CLASS SYSTEM?

The creation of the United Nations Conference on Trade and Development (UNCTAD) was a reflection of the Third World's

17. Doubts about the necessity of aid really began to appear only in the late 1960s, although there were always a few heretics in the early years, for example, P. T. Bauer.

changing perceptions of its own needs and its own relationship to the international economic system. The nonaligned movement was losing whatever internal cohesiveness it once had, for the LDCs were discovering, as Nyerere observed, that "all that the non-aligned nations have in common is their non-alignment." [18] Anticolonialism could no longer hold the movement together, and conflicts between members of the group undermined whatever claims to moral superiority the Third World thought it had. Moreover some decline in the intensity of the Cold War, as well as in foreign aid levels, vitiated the presumed tactical virtues of maneuvering between the Great Power blocs. Export pessimism about the prospects for primary products was also still prevalent, and import substitution had been in operation long enough to reveal its deficiencies. Domestic pressures to produce tangible results were rising at precisely the moment when opportunities to manipulate the international system were dissipating.

Historically the weak have had few weapons to use against the strong, except their ability to become unattractive targets (like Sweden or Switzerland) or effective economic competitors within the rules of the game (like Sweden or Switzerland). These weapons were unavailable to the LDCs, for they were unattractive targets only in the negative sense of reluctance to step into a "quagmire," and they were incapable of competing within any system in which they were treated as they ostensibly wanted to be treated—equally. What the LDCs did have—potentially—was their unity, their ability to act as an international pressure group against the rich. In the past this kind of tactic would have been unproductive, for it would have been ignored by the guardians of the system, even if it had occurred to the weak. But in the contemporary world perhaps more could be expected, for the decline in the utility of force and the slow and tenuous evolution of democratic and moral norms provided the weak with elements of strength they had not previously possessed. [19]

18. Quoted in Raymond Hopkins and Richard W. Mansbach, *Structure and Process in International Politics* (New York: Harper and Row, 1973), p. 149.

19. On the relationship between the role of the Small Power and various material and ideological developments, see Robert L. Rothstein, *Alliances and Small Powers* (New York: Columbia University Press, 1968), chapter 1.

Thus UNCTAD came to be described in a familiar metaphor: a trade union of the poor against the rich.[20] A trade union movement is not a nonaligned movement. In fact the very essence of the trade union movement was confrontation; alignment against all the rich, not maneuvering between the rich, was the primary goal. This clearly implied a class struggle, in which one economic order struggled against another to alter the distribution of benefits, and not a caste system, in which the lower orders accepted their fate as unalterable.

One point about trade unions needs to be stressed. The union and the employers are rarely truly equal. Ultimately the worker works for the employer; the employer manages for his own benefit. There is an asymmetry here that cannot be obscured. Unions, as Runciman points out, tend to be a permanent opposition, never destined to come to power.[21] This would be an inconsequential point, except that it has so often been forgotten by the LDCs: Trade union movements can improve the distribution of benefits within a society, but they cannot create a revolution within that society. That is to say, UNCTAD was a challenge to the leaders of the international system but a challenge to improve the terms for staying *within* the system.

What the LDCs sought through UNCTAD were improvements in their trading position—"trade, not aid," as the phrase (misleadingly) went. But demands for concessions that would permit the LDCs to increase their exports almost inevitably implied reform, not revolution. After all, the rich countries were hardly likely to be receptive to concessions that would overturn the system that had made them rich. Unfortunately form and procedure worked against substance and content. The LDCs at the first UNCTAD Conference in 1964, committed to the notion that only unanimity would provide sufficient leverage, caucused together to develop a common position on the issues. Split every conceivable way, the "Group of 77" could remain unified only by producing "maximum common

20. For example, Richard N. Gardner, "The United Nations Conference on Trade and Development," *International Organization* 22, no. 1 (Winter 1968):115.
21. W. G. Runciman, *Relative Deprivation and Social Justice* (London: Routledge and Kegan Paul, 1966), p. 42.

denominator" positions.[22] Compromise was difficult because any indication of flexibility threatened to unravel the unity the LDCs so desperately sought. Consequently the "we" versus "they" confrontation was doubly disabling: It lent an unhappy appearance of extremism versus extremism to the negotiations, although many countries in both groups shared important views and positions, and made it easier to reject reasonable demands that were mixed in with, and often obscured by, ideological posturing.

Most of the LDCs had been following inwardly oriented economic policies throughout the 1950s and early 1960s. The concessions they demanded at UNCTAD-I at Geneva were at least ostensibly much more outwardly oriented.[23] Prebisch, the first Secretary-General of UNCTAD, cautioned the LDCs about excessive degrees of import substitution, advocated serious efforts toward regional integration (although by an extension of import substitution), and emphasized the need to expand exports within the Third World and to both the socialist countries and the Western industrial countries. Since most LDC export earnings came from primary products, strong emphasis was placed on efforts to maintain and stabilize commodity earnings and to provide compensatory financing for emergencies (e.g., crop failures). But since Prebisch and his followers were still pessimistic about the prospects for primary products, even stronger stress was placed on the need to expand manufactured and semimanufactured exports. These exports faced quantitative restrictions, high tariffs, and special preferential agreements with particular groups of LDCs.[24] The LDCs thus demanded a generalized system of preferences (GSP) that would provide a guaranteed market (in effect the only kind of market most of them could compete in) for their manufactured exports.[25] Such demands

22. Branislav Gosovic, *UNCTAD: Conflict and Compromise* (London: A. W. Sijthoff, 1972), p. 290.
23. See Maddison, *Economic Progress and Policy in Developing Countries*, pp. 220 ff.
24. Many agricultural exports by the LDCs also confronted obstacles in the rich countries, especially tariffs and price support policies.
25. A good source for all of the foregoing issues, as well as for an analysis of the origins and operation of UNCTAD, is Gosovic, *UNCTAD: Conflict and Compromise*, *passim*. The underdeveloped countries that benefited from special preferential arrangements were not happy about the general system of preferences and agreed to

to reverse the system of protection in favor of the LDCs directly contradicted the efforts of the industrial countries to move toward a more liberal international trading system.

The demands that Prebisch and the Group of 77 laid out were designed to permit the LDCs to export more in order to import more. Chenery and Strout had already provided evidence that no country had been able to sustain a growth rate above its export growth rate for more than a short time.[26] And exports were necessary to earn foreign exchange to buy the imports necessary for industrialization. As Prebisch indicated,

> it should not be expected that, if the income of all developing countries is to rise at the minimum by 5 per cent every year, their imports can increase at a rate much less than 6 per cent.[27]

The foreign exchange constraint was thus central to the Group of 77's calculations, especially because they believed that foreign aid levels might be sinking.[28]

---

support the common position of the "77" only after inclusion of a resolution indicating that they were not to lose their benefits in the new scheme. Indeed, in the closed vote on the GSP at GATT, many of the LDCs that enjoyed preferential arrangements voted against the GSP.

26. Hollis B. Chenery and Alan M. Strout, "Foreign Assistance and Economic Development," *American Economic Review* 56, no. 4 (September 1966):679–733.

27. Quoted in David Wall, "Import Capacity, Imports and Economic Growth," *Economica* 35, no. 138 (May 1968):158.

28. A recent article raises a question about the practical significance of the foreign exchange constraint. Weisskopf argues that the savings constraint (or gap) was much more important and that only eight countries (including Brazil, Cyprus, Pakistan, Paraguay, and Peru) actually suffered severe foreign exchange constraints. See Thomas E. Weisskopf, "An Econometric Test of Alternative Constraints on the Growth of Underdeveloped Countries," *The Review of Economics and Statistics* 59, no. 1 (February 1972):67–78. If true, this has important implications for a number of things, including foreign aid policies. The foreign exchange gap was, however, perceived as crucial in the 1960s, whatever its real effects.

This finding may also explain why LDC exports to the advanced countries could grow at a rate of 6.3 percent per year from 1960 to 1965, while GNP growth rates in the same period—which were supposed to vary with export performance—decelerated. The figures are from the editor's introduction in Jagdish N. Bhagwati, ed., *Economics and World Order* (New York: Macmillan, 1972), p. 3. The point I am suggesting here is that internal factors dealing with attitudes, institutions, political will, and the like may be more important than either imports or exports, and it is a mistake to focus development policy on the foreign exchange nexus, for even sufficient foreign exchange cannot overcome other domestic obstacles.

The desire to reach a point where one can be competitive within a system is not really a fundamental threat to that system. In turning outward and seeking help from the major trading powers, the LDCs were moving in a direction sanctioned by both theory and practice. They might be moving too fast, or their methods might seem too radical, but their goal was essentially conservative. Indeed there were already a few commentators who questioned the wisdom of what the LDCs were trying to do. Guy Hunter, for example, writing in 1967, stated:.

> Through UNCTAD they insist that far more rich and powerful nations, whose policies they cannot control, should alter their pattern of trading and manufacturing in the interests of the developing world. By so doing they increase their dependence and multiply their risks; they narrow their choices of technology; and they distort their pattern of specialization to an external demand which is beyond their control. Nothing characterizes the developed market more than the high rate of obsolescence of capital and the rate of change in demand. . . . This is the most difficult field for countries short of capital and skills to enter.[29]

In 1964, however, the LDCs were not willing to contemplate the implications of this argument. Although they were intent on finding an alternative to import substitution, they sought it within the framework of prevailing notions about the need for rapid growth, fixed capital accumulation, and high rates of export growth.

The Group of 77's proposals were subjected to extensive criticism by a number of Western economists. Commodity agreements were attacked on two grounds. In the first place the historical record seemed to indicate that they were unworkable, for maintaining unity among (and within) both producers and consumers was necessary but also extraordinarily difficult. In the second place, commodity agreements obviously provided benefits only to particular groups within each LDC and to particular countries within the

29. Guy Hunter, *The Best of Both Worlds?* (London: Oxford University Press, 1967), p. 125. In effect, seeking to improve trade with the rich countries also meant dependence on patterns of demand and growth rates among the rich countries, as well as their tariff policies, the market control policies of their multinational corporations, and so forth. The point is that more is implied by accepting a particular trading system than is apparent from simply examining trade statistics.

Third World group.[30] These benefits bore no relationship to the country's need or to its economic performance. Since the benefits were really a disguised form of foreign aid—from consumers in the rich countries to groups of producers in the poor countries—it could reasonably be asked whether this was really an intelligent way to allocate the benefits the rich were willing to pass on to the poor. Giving aid directly to the government might be not only more efficient but also more equitable (on the assumption that the recipient government had efficiency and equity as goals.)

Preferences for exports of manufactures were also criticized. Pincus, for example, accused the LDCs of seeking to jump ahead of the "normal" (i.e., Western) process and export manufactures before they had a domestic industry. Preferences were "an escape hatch for premature industrialization" that could not be justified on economic grounds, for they merely transferred the costs of such industrialization to the rich countries.[31] Preferences would also create vested interests that would resist exposure to competition; they would discriminate in favor of the few LDCs that had the capacity to export manufactures and against domestic producers in the advanced countries; they would increase the dependence of the poor on the rich (note the Hunter comment quoted earlier); and, ultimately, they would force the rich countries to close off their markets.[32]

Exactly why the Group of 77 placed so much emphasis on the creation of a generalized system of preferences is somewhat unclear. The benefits from such a scheme were not likely to be high, and they were bound to be concentrated in a few relatively well-off LDCs. Nevertheless so much pressure was exerted that a number of advanced countries finally agreed to implement a generalized system of preferences; that agreement, after UNCTAD-II in 1968, was considered one of UNCTAD's major achievements.

The results, not surprisingly, have been meager. Cooper's anal-

30. Useful on this point is Colin Legum, *The First UN Development Decade and Its Lessons for the 1970s* (New York: Praeger, 1970), pp. 10–20.
31. John Pincus, *Trade, Aid and Development* (New York: McGraw-Hill, 1967), p. 230.
32. See *ibid.*, p. 205; and Harry G. Johnson, *Economic Policies Toward Less Developed Countries* (New York: Praeger, 1967), pp. 114 ff.

ysis of the European Economic Community's (EEC) preference system conclusively refutes the EEC's contention that its GSP is "both liberal-minded and outward-looking" and that it will stimulate exports or new investments.[33] Another study of the existing GSP agreements indicates why they are unlikely to have much impact. Slightly more than 61 percent of LDC exports to the countries that have established GSP arrangements are already admitted duty free and are thus outside the scope of any preferential tariff system. In addition the various schemes do not apply to dutiable agricultural and fishery products, which constitute another 16 percent of LDC exports. The GSP schemes are, therefore, limited to manufactured and semimanufactured products that constitute 23 percent of total LDC trade with the GSP countries. A little less than half of this 23 percent is accounted for by trade with the United States, which began to implement its scheme only in January 1976. Finally some of the remaining products have been specifically excluded from the GSP to protect domestic markets. The result is that only about 8 percent (including U.S. figures) of LDC trade qualifies for preferences under the implemented GSP arrangements.[34]

Part of the reason for the limited impact of the GSP is, of course, the nature of existing LDC trade, most of which is in duty-free areas. But of the 23 percent that might benefit from preferences, well over half has been excluded by special provisions. The central point is simple and clear: The rich countries would like to see the poor countries better off, but not at more than a marginal cost to themselves. Each of the implemented GSP schemes, for example, imposes ceilings on the amount of LDC exports that will be accepted; by 1970, EEC imports had already exceeded the ceiling limitations for most products. The notion that new investment in the LDCs will be stimulated by the prospects of large, protected markets in the GSP countries is thus a myth, for few exports beyond existing levels will be let in. The benefits from the existing GSP

33. Richard N. Cooper, "The European Community's System of Generalized Tariff Preferences: A Critique," *Journal of Development Studies* 8, no. 4 (July 1972). The quote is from p. 384. See also Mordechai E. Kreinin, *Trade Relations of the EEC* (New York: Praeger, 1974), pp. 10–13.

34. Tracy Murray, "How Helpful Is the Generalized System of Preferences to Developing Countries?", *The Economic Journal* (June 1973): 449–55.

schemes amount to less than $100 million from all the developed countries; such benefits have also been distributed inequitably (e.g., Hong Kong and Yugoslavia got more than 43 percent of the benefits in 1970).[35]

The narrower preferential arrangements between particular groups of underdeveloped countries and particular groups of rich countries have not been much more beneficial. The Commonwealth preference scheme and the agreement between the former French colonies in Africa and the EEC have been criticized for hindering industrial development and fostering continued dependence on primary product exports.[36] These criticisms are not especially convincing, for some of the Asian Commonwealth countries have managed to develop fairly significant manufacturing exports, and the former African colonies have raised their manufacturing exports to the EEC substantially from 1960 to the early 1970s.[37] And the reverse preferences that the Africans were forced to grant to the EEC members, while indeed providing captive markets, have not really been significant enough to warrant extensive complaint—at least if the benefits the Africans got in return were substantial.

There are other criticisms of these arrangements, however, that seem more convincing. In the first place some studies argue that the overall effect of the preferences has been negligible. Manufacturing exports may have risen by impressive percentages, but at the same time the LDC share of EEC trade has declined sharply (from 1958 to 1971, the LDC share of EEC exports dropped from 23 percent to 14 percent, and imports from 30 percent to 18 percent) and the African share of LDC trade with the EEC has also declined—even with pref-

35. *Ibid.*, p. 454.

36. See Reginald Green and Ann Seidman, *Unity or Poverty—The Economics of Pan-Africanism* (Baltimore, Md.: Penguin Books, 1968), pp. 165 ff.

37. Gerard and Victoria Curzon, "Neo-Colonialism and the European Economic Community," *The Yearbook of World Affairs, 1971* (London: Stevens, 1971), p. 135, indicate a 280 percent rise over the decade. These are surprising figures, to me at least, even given the very low initial base, and the extent to which many of the export firms are European owned. Lawrence B. Krause, *European Economic Integration and the United States* (Washington, D.C.: The Brookings Institution, 1968), 3 years earlier, had described the EEC relationship with the Africans as "stagnant," primarily because the Africans failed to increase supply sufficiently (pp. 183–85). A 280 percent rise would hardly be stagnant, nor is it likely that most of it took place after Krause wrote.

erences. And if a generalized system of preferences is widely implemented, or if the EEC tariff declines even further, the African share will decline again. One analyst has argued that the main effect of the agreement with the EEC has been in Europe: France has reduced its burden in subsidizing privileged markets for the Africans, so that the only real welfare shift has been within the EEC itself (that is, against France's partners).[38] In the second place the agreement has prevented the Africans from diversifying their trade patterns and seeking new markets—a disguised continuation of colonialism. Finally, and perhaps most significantly, particular preferential agreements divide the LDCs among themselves—as Nkrumah argued years ago—and impede both regional agreements (when some regional states are not in the arrangement) and unity at global conferences like UNCTAD. Since the LDCs need to cooperate among themselves, granting special rights to small groups of LDCs has come to seem, rightly or wrongly, as another effort on the part of the rich to perpetuate dependence among the poor.[39]

Cynicism about the generosity of the rich countries is probably not misplaced. Still, it is worth going back to our original question: Why did the LDCs exert so much pressure to get an agreement on a GSP when it was clear that it would yield so few benefits? There were indeed many critics who pointed out not only that few of their exports would be covered by such schemes but also that the LDCs would not always (or usually) be able to compete even when they

38. R. Lawrence, "Primary Products, Preferences, and Economic Welfare: the EEC and Africa," in P. Robson, ed., *International Economic Integration* (Harmondsworth, England: Penguin Books, 1971), pp. 383–84.

39. The Lomé Convention signed between the EEC and 46 Asian, Pacific, and Caribbean countries in February 1975, is much more forthcoming than the various GSP schemes: Lomé is not limited to tariff preferences but also includes financial assistance, a commodity stabilization fund, and a general attempt to increase industrial cooperation. Lomé is also a binding commitment, not a unilateral venture like the GSPs. Perhaps these changes reflect increased European fears of the effect of the new "poor power" in commodities. The problems with Lomé revolve around the fact that it is limited to 46 countries—which creates tensions with the other LDCs who want it generalized—and that it does not go far enough to meet all the LDC demands (e.g., by support prices for commodities, not merely compensatory financing). On tensions with other LDCs, note that the African countries, at the Group of 77 meeting in Manila in January 1976, adamantly refused to share their preferences with other LDCs; in response, the excluded groups were reluctant to support special measures for the least developed countries, the majority of whom are African.

received preferences.[40] Other critics argued that the quest for a GSP merely illustrated the tactical foolishness of the Group of 77: They sought concessions that not only had clear costs for powerful groups within the rich countries but also failed to offer any reciprocal benefits to the rich countries. What might have worked, according to this argument, is an appeal to the self-interest of the rich; what was attempted, conversely, was an appeal to the emotions, to feelings of guilt and expiation for past sins.

There is surely something to this argument, for the Group of 77's negotiating tactics left something to be desired. The splits within the Group were probably too profound for anything else to be expected. The richer LDCs opposed programs to aid the poorest LDCs, for they feared their own shares of aid would diminish.[41] Those with special preferential agreements opposed any efforts to generalize preferences, because they feared they would lose more by sharing their access than they would gain from access to new markets.[42] Beyond this, the LDCs were frequently contradictory—for example, in demanding more aid but arguing that repayment of debts was exploitation or in simultaneously demanding higher prices for natural products but an end to research on synthetics. In such circumstances the quest for unity probably did more harm than good; agreement to blame everything on the rich countries was the only position that won unanimous support.[43]

40. Malmgren, for example, notes: "Using the same techniques to produce the same product, the developing countries often find their own quality standards and labor productivity very low and thus find themselves to be uncompetitive." "Trade for Development," p. 465. Wall, "Import Capacity, Imports and Economic Growth," p. 159, makes the same point.

41. The Latin Americans thus complained that only 1 (Haiti) of the poorest 25 countries were from Latin America, and they feared preferential treatment for the 25 would reduce their own aid shares. See Heliodoro Gonzales, "UNCTAD-III—Beggar's Opera: The Bureaucrats Overreach," *Inter-American Economic Affairs* 25, no. 2 (Autumn 1972):62.

42. Reginald H. Green, "UNCTAD and After: Anatomy of a Failure," *Journal of Modern African Studies* 5, no. 2 (1967):251. Green also discusses various other splits among the LDCs themselves.

43. The fact that the rich countries were not united also made it more—not less—difficult for the LDCs to achieve gains, for they had no target they could aim at. For the splits among the rich, see Alfred S. Friedeberg, *The United Nations Conference on Trade and Development of 1964* (Rotterdam: Universitaire Press Rotterdam, 1968), pp. 99–101.

Some care has to be taken not to carry this argument too far. The Group of 77 may have negotiated badly, but was a good negotiating strategy really available? What could the poor offer the rich—except an agreement not to challenge the status quo? Even more critically, I believe, the Group of 77 was constrained by the intellectual framework within which they were working. Committed to rapid growth and industrialization, and thus the need for imports, they took as their central concern the acquisition of foreign exchange. Import substitution had not worked, and regional integration looked promising only if each state was willing to take risks and make sacrifices for the regional good. The only other alternative seemed to be pressure on the global system. So they sought as much aid as they could manage to extract, directly through grants and loans, and indirectly through trade measures that were actually another form of aid.

There was certainly nothing irrational about seeking more aid or even, necessarily, seeking it in a disguised form through preferences. After all, about 80 percent of the foreign exchange the LDCs earned came through trade, and better trading terms were obviously important. Where the LDCs went astray, I think, is in not realizing the limited impact that these trade concessions were likely to have.[44]

Why did the LDCs act as if trade preferences and commodity agreements were likely to be so much more beneficial than analysis suggested? Part of the answer, I believe, is that it was literally difficult to think of another alternative for small and weak states intent on industrialization. It was especially difficult to come to terms with the notion that what looked like the only alternative promised only slow and incremental benefits. In this sense, aid and trade prospects were exaggerated just because they were the only alternatives left. There was an element of wishful thinking here, of a reluctance to accept the fact that the poor normally have only an option between getting nothing and getting a little more, not a lot more. In addition many LDC elites were predisposed toward development

44. The notion that the LDCs were trying to hoodwink the rich by disguising aid as trade, which is frequently suggested, overlooks the fact that the issue was already being publicly discussed in these terms—that is, few were likely to be fooled.

policies that required the least possible amount of domestic change and turmoil. It was an easy step to move from blaming everything on the colonial system to blaming everything on the international system: In both cases, reparations for ancient and not so ancient sins might obviate the need to risk more unsettling alternatives. The international trading system became the new scapegoat for all the problems besetting the LDCs, and since the external world was the cause of these problems, so must it be the cure. It became an article of faith for many Third World elites that salvation had to come through transforming the international system, for otherwise domestic reforms were bound to fail.

I do not mean to deride the notion that the international system imposes some severe constraints on the options the LDCs have. I point out only that it was a mistake to argue and to act as if the international system was the only or even the dominant cause of LDC difficulties. Inflated expectations about what the international system would do for the LDCs were bound to be disappointed. Important benefits could be achieved by altering the way the industrial countries perceived and treated the problems of underdevelopment; those benefits were, however, likely to be significant only for those LDCs who were also willing to deal directly with their own domestic problems. It is indisputable, I think, that this meant that the LDCs were confronted with a crucial choice. They could attempt to achieve the best possible position for themselves within the system, an attempt clearly implying acceptance of a subsidiary, reactive role within that system, and policies that were conservative, reformist, and adaptive. Or they could attempt gradually to isolate themselves from the international system, stressing increasing self-reliance and an entirely different conception of growth and development. What the LDCs could not afford to do was to act as if accusations of guilt, demands for reparations, and disguised pleas for charity constituted a sensible policy.

One other reason is sometimes given for the particular proposals that UNCTAD sought to emphasize: the "Latin Americanization" of the organization. In this sense the intellectual influence of Prebisch and his familiarity with the problems of the Latin American countries presumably created a bias for proposals that reflected the problems of the relatively more developed countries of Latin America. Indeed many of the countries likely to benefit from the GSP and a number of other measures were in Latin America, and most of the least developed countries who were not likely to benefit very much were in Africa and Asia (except for Haiti). Nevertheless, while Prebisch was surely drawing on his own experiences, this argument also seems somewhat oversimplified to me. There were countries in Latin America that would not benefit very much, and there were countries elsewhere that might benefit substantially. Moreover the entire package of UNCTAD proposals did contain measures designed to help the whole range of developing countries. Consequently it seems more accurate to interpret the UNCTAD demands in terms of the prevailing intellectual frame of reference and the existence of a number of common problems throughout the Third World.

The demands of the Group of 77 at Geneva in 1964 were rejected (i.e., referred for "further study") by the developed countries. The LDCs became increasingly pessimistic thereafter about what they could expect from the external world. For example, a conference report by the Economic Commission for Africa in 1967 concluded that "African countries needed to aim at achieving national self-reliance and avoid drawing up pleas in which external assistance had a predominant share." [45] And UNCTAD-II in 1968 moved away from its emphasis on the foreign exchange constraint and argued that "external financial resources are not intended to play a dominant role in the growth process." [46] By 1970 self-reliance had become the new conventional wisdom. A group of radical economists thus responded to the Pearson Report by arguing:

> Poor countries should aim at self-reliance (not self-sufficiency). They should structure their economies so as to minimize the impact of influences from the developed world . . . export diversification and import substitution should be evaluated primarily in terms of their contributions to self-reliance . . .; aid would continue but the consequences of its

45. Quoted in A. F. Ewing, "Self-Reliance in Africa," *Journal of Modern African Studies* 6 no. 3 (1968):362.
46. Quoted in Wall, "Import Capacity, Imports and Economic Growth," p. 167.

volatility minimized and its political influence reduced—at the expense of lower rates in growth of GDP, if necessary.[47]

The response of the radical economists was also interesting in another way. Three years before the oil crisis and the outburst of enthusiasm among the LDCs for joint action against the rich countries, these economists advocated the following strategy: (1) repudiation of high-cost loans or repayment in local currency; (2) planned disruption of raw materials supplies, where demand is inelastic or supply controlled by the LDCs; (3) discrimination between suppliers of imports where the LDCs are a significant market; (4) coordinated expropriation of multinational corporations' investments; (5) and coordinated switching of reserves from currency to currency.[48] It is, of course, far from clear that such a strategy, even after the oil crisis, is either workable or wise. But in the present context the key point is that at least parts of the Third World were attempting to work out an alternative to conventional growth strategies and foreign exchange constraints. (I discuss this strategy in much greater detail in chapter 9.)

One last point about UNCTAD: The positions developed by the Group of 77 were extreme because the Group felt that unity was its most powerful weapon. Unity is obviously valuable, but it seems to me that too much of a premium was placed on it. In the first place the rich countries themselves were not unified, especially at UNCTAD-I, and LDC unity could not be applied with leverage against a single opposing position. Ironically the unity of the LDCs may be most valuable only when they confront a unified position, for otherwise they have nothing to manipulate. The other side of this coin is that the gains that the poor are likely to be able to extract from a united opposition are not likely to be large; small gains are probably the best that the LDCs can hope for.

Unity permitted the Group of 77 to pass a number of resolutions at UNCTAD-I that were unacceptable to the industrial countries and to offer policies on a take-it-or-leave-it basis. Since the in-

47. Their report is contained in Barbara Ward, J. D. Runnalls, and Lenore D'Anjou, eds., *The Widening Gap—Development in the 1970s* (New York: Columbia University Press, 1971), p. 277.
48. *Ibid.*

dustrial countries were not bound by policies they voted against or stated reservations to, such victories were exceedingly hollow. In terms of future strategies, to which I return in chapters 8 and 9, it seems to me arguable that the LDCs may actually have more meaningful power in organizations in which they have less formal power but in which all members are bound by a majority vote.[49] It is in organizations like the International Monetary Fund (IMF) that LDC unity may be most valuable, for there a unified minority can usually block actions until important concessions are granted.

---

UNCTAD has performed important services for the underdeveloped countries. The technical analyses of its secretariat and the experts that the secretariat has engaged have clarified some of the contentious issues between the rich and the poor countries; many of the ideas first broached or popularized at UNCTAD have now become practical negotiating issues of great significance; and UNCTAD itself has become an essential forum, not only for discussion and the quest for consensual agreement, but also for familiarizing many Third World countries with the problems and perspectives of their peers. Many criticisms may fairly be made of UNCTAD—the group voting system that forced too many divergent interests into a single package, the presentation of some positions that were not carefully thought through, the demand for concessions without sufficient effort to indicate why they were in the longrun interest of the rich countries, the tendency of the organization to become too identified with the rhetoric and the stance of the most radical countries, a rather astonishing lack of political sophistication on the part of some high-level staff, and a share of the responsibility for inflating expectations about what could be got from the international systems—but these criticisms ought not to be allowed to obscure the contributions that UNCTAD has made or to deflect an attempt to understand why UNCTAD has taken the form it has.

From the perspective of this book, however, the virtues or defects of UNCTAD itself have not been at issue. What I have been primarily criticizing are two interrelated aspects of the reaction of

49. For a similar suggestion, see Sidney Dell, "An Appraisal of UNCTAD III," *World Development* 1, no. 5 (May 1973):3.

many underdeveloped countries to the significance of UNCTAD for their own development programs. In the first place, despite the obvious importance of foreign trade for small countries, too much was expected from revisions in existing patterns of trade and aid, and too much hope was placed on what could be accomplished by poor countries with little power or influence in a forum that could not negotiate binding agreements. Expectations about the benefits that might be attained through UNCTAD were excessive for a number of reasons: A large number of underdeveloped countries would benefit not at all or in a marginal fashion from whatever concessions were granted; even those who could benefit substantially via increased exports were not always able or willing to distribute the gains equitably; and no serious effort was made to understand what or how positions could be made more attractive to the rich countries. In the second place improved trading conditions (and more aid) might be a necessary condition for growth, but they were not sufficient. The tendency to look abroad for salvation, to seek through UNCTAD alone gains that had to be sought jointly through domestic reform and international concessions, was an illustration of an increasing tendency on the part of many—not all—underdeveloped countries to lose sight of how much help could really be expected from abroad and to resist confronting their own domestic problems directly. Again, I am not asserting that domestic reform was sufficient and not merely necessary; I assert only that the balance of rhetoric and arguments veered too sharply toward the quest for external scapegoats and away from concern with what the underdeveloped countries could and had to do for themselves.

The attempt to extract more foreign aid from the rich countries was also a major theme of this period. But, as we shall see, this attempt also suffered from some of the ambiguities and problems associated with the quest for more trade—insofar as the two could be meaningfully separated.


## THE CHARITY OF THE RICH

Radical and conservative intellectuals have come to share a few central perceptions about foreign aid: They seem to agree not only that aid is not indispensable but also that it is frequently pernicious for any underdeveloped country intent on economic development. The American Congress has found these views congenial, even if they have not quite understood their implications. This happy consensus has not yet penetrated very far into the governments of the Third World, who are still operating with the no doubt naive and commonsensical view that foreign aid is necessary and beneficial. How we have arrived at this somewhat paradoxical state of affairs is our theme.

The debate on foreign aid has sometimes been carried on with such passion and ferocity that it has obscured the fact that our (and our allies') generosity has not been excessive. For example, after subtraction of military aid, repayable loans, and special programs (e.g, to stop drug imports into the United States or to support American hospitals abroad) from our 1968 aid commitment, $309 million was left over for grants (out of about $5 billion total): This was equivalent to the cost of 6 days of the Vietnam War.[50] During the Marshall Plan years, we gave about 2 percent of our GNP to our European friends; aid to the underdeveloped countries has never got above 0.7 percent of our GNP, and currently it is about 0.3 percent. We have given aid to more than 70 countries, but 8 countries have actually received about 75 percent of the total. All eight were military allies (South Korea, Taiwan, South Vietnam, Turkey, Pakistan, Brazil, Jordan), except for India (which actually was quite low on a per capita basis). Yugoslavia got more aid between 1945 and 1960 than all of Latin America. Between 1967 and 1969, of the 31 countries (of 127) who received the highest level of per capita aid, 24 were former colonies and 5 had military pacts with the West. The rest of the Third World got so little aid that it is difficult to see why aid became so controversial an issue: Even if the amount of aid had been doubled, surely unlikely at any particular time, by the time it had been divided among all the needy recipients it could not have amounted to much.

The need for aid was taken as axiomatic in the 1950s and 1960s. This meant that the debate centered on how aid could be extracted

50. In the same year the OECD countries spent $35 billion on liquor and $15 billion on cigarettes—at which time there was a sharp debate about adding $3 or $4 billion to total aid figures.

from the rich countries, not on whether it was necessary or useful. The "politics of foreign aid" usually referred to the domestic politics of the United States. Why we should give aid, when we should give aid, how we should give aid—and how much of it—were the critical questions. And when we looked at the recipients, it was primarily for technical reasons: to determine how much aid could be absorbed and to evaluate how it had been employed. The criteria for giving aid were never clearly established, and almost any range of behavior on the part of the recipient could be used to justify more aid—or no aid at all. If a country did well with our aid, that justified giving more aid, and if a country did badly with our aid, that justified giving more aid.

The needs for more aid and more trade were justified by the same set of beliefs about the need for rapid growth.[51] The Pearson Report, *Partners in Development*, commissioned by the World Bank because aid levels seemed to be falling, illustrates the point well, for it was the high-water mark of a set of beliefs that dominated the post-World War II debate about development: It restated the conventional wisdom just as it was becoming manifestly irrelevant.

The Pearson Report was obviously a committee product and thus unlikely to challenge what everyone took for granted. Since its function was clearly political anyway, this was not necessarily a disadvantage. Self-sustaining growth—a largely mythical beast, especially for small and weak states that cannot isolate themselves from external forces—was the goal. Capital accumulation via high rates of investment and savings was the means. Foreign aid was to fill whatever gaps existed, either the domestic savings gap or the foreign exchange gap. As a crucial supplement to domestic resources, foreign aid would be the catalyst that spurred growth forward.

The Pearson Report was optimistic, strangely so in retrospect.

51. It does not seem necessary in this context to debate exactly what is or is not aid. In general I would accept the argument that aid is not simply all foreign capital flows but those flows not provided by normal market forces (i.e., grants and the concessional parts of loans).

Although trade provided about three-fourths of the LDCs' foreign exchange and carried with it additional benefits (e.g., of learning, of self-help rather than charity), aid could still be useful, since the government could use it as it wished, whereas trade benefits tended to be concentrated in a particular group that could spend the benefits as it wished—and not necessarily on productive investments.

Provided aid commitments from the developed states reached the required levels (1 percent of GNP, 0.7 percent of which was to be in the form of public aid, another mystical notion), the need for aid would come to an end by the year 2000. This ignored the need to reduce income inequalities, although that was not a prominent question at the time. But if the growth rate of 6 percent prescribed by the Pearson Report were achieved, per capita income in Africa would rise to $107 by 1980, and by the year 2000 per capita income in India would reach $200 and that in the United States, $10,000.[52]

The Pearson Report did indicate that the correlation between aid and growth was quite low, which was attributed to the intrusion of various noneconomic factors (e.g., aid given for political or other reasons).[53] Indeed a few years later a study of the aid program in Latin America from 1957 to 1964 reported that "the general tendency . . . is that the greater the capital inflow from abroad, the lower the rate of growth of the receiving country."[54] Nevertheless the notion that aid was actually counterproductive was hard to accept; it did not seem to make much (common) sense. In addition there were studies that argued that aid had been very important. Jacoby, for example, maintained that "aid more than doubled the annual rate of growth of Taiwan's GNP, quadrupled the annual growth of per capita GNP, and cut thirty years from the time needed to attain 1964 living standards."[55] Of course the aid commitment for Taiwan was very large (34 percent of total gross investment), but the judgment that aid was useful if given in sufficiently

52. See G. K. Helleiner, "Beyond Growth Rates and Plan Volumes—Planning for Africa in the 1970s," *Journal of Modern African Studies* 10, no. 3 (1972):334.

53. Lester B. Pearson et al., *Partners in Development* (New York: Praeger, 1969), pp. 50 ff. It is unlikely that the effects of aid can ever be conclusively demonstrated, even with time series of flows of aid and changes in other variables, because it is impossible to say what would have happened without aid.

54. K. B. Griffin and J. L. Enos, "Foreign Assistance: Objectives and Consequences," *Economic Development and Cultural Change* 18, no. 3 (April 1970):318.

55. Neil H. Jacoby, *U.S. Aid to Taiwan* (New York: Praeger, 1966), p. 152. Irving Brecher and S. A. Abbas, *Foreign Aid and Industrial Development in Pakistan* (Cambridge: Cambridge University Press, 1972), also argue for the beneficial impact of aid on Pakistan's growth but do not make the kind of claims that Jacoby does. Edward S. Mason, *Economic Development in India and Pakistan* (Cambridge, Mass.: Harvard University, Center for International Affairs, Occasional Paper 13, 1966), p. 45, also attributes Pakistan's superior performance to Pakistan's getting double the aid per capita that India got.

large doses (roughly around 10 percent of GNP) seemed sensible.[56] Consequently Third World leaders who sought foreign aid were not acting irrationally: Available theories justified the quest for foreign capital, and available practice was at least ambiguous.

Foreign aid obviously could serve many purposes for both donor and recipient.[57] This may have been part of its charm, since failure at any particular purpose could always be obscured by reference to the fact that the end in sight was "really" something altogether different. In the 1960s the dominant purpose for both donor and recipient was, ostensibly, economic development. But even where economic development was a legitimate goal for either donor or recipient, it was never the only goal or necessarily the most important goal. Since relative priorities were not likely to be symmetrical very often, the grounds for misunderstanding were substantial.

We can see the effects of this asymmetry in priorities when we contrast the criticisms that have been made of the aid recipients with the perspectives of the elites to whom the aid has been granted. For the elites, aid is almost a free good, for even where aid has to be applied to particular programs, it releases other resources to be used in whatever way the elite chooses. In this sense aid simply increases the resources of the government, allowing it to invest more or consume more—with an unspecified effect on the growth rate, which is determined by how the funds are spent and by what other changes take place in attitudes and institutions.[58]

Aid's most salient purpose, from this perspective, is that it is a useful resource for an elite intent on staying in power. The case is self-evident for military assistance (if, of course, the elites use it to

56. Maddison, *Economic Progress and Policy in Developing Countries,* makes the point that those who got about 10 percent of their GDP in aid (Greece, Israel, South Korea, and Taiwan) grew about 8 percent per year, compared to 5 percent for other LDCs, "and most of the difference was due to bigger aid" (p. 274). However, overall the LDCs received only about 1.5 percent of their GDPs in aid.

57. The best treatment of aid from this perspective is, I believe, Samuel P. Huntington, "Foreign Aid for What and for Whom," *Foreign Policy,* no. 1 (Winter 1970–71):161–89; and "Does Foreign Aid Have a Future?," *Foreign Policy,* no. 2 (Spring 1971):114–34.

58. For the ambiguities of the effect of aid on growth, also interesting is Bauer, *Dissent on Development,* pp. 95 ff.

increase their own control over the military). But even development aid has primarily benefited industrialists and skilled workers, on the presumption that inequities are necessary to raise the level of domestic savings and investment sufficiently, and thus led to the bitter joke that aid is money taken from the poor in the rich countries (who pay the taxes from which aid is extracted and who subsidize the exporters who sell their "tied" goods at a good profit) and given to the rich in the poor countries. In any case the elites can direct this aid to their supporters and then control its profitability by judicious use of tariffs and import controls. This may account for the fact that the elites continue to seek high levels of foreign aid despite some evidence that it is not always very useful.

Development aid given in this fashion has not always increased the growth rate, at least in part because it has frequently been used to supplant rather than supplement domestic savings. As the Nultys' study of Pakistan indicates, some of the rich have used foreign aid for investment purposes but have used their own profits for consumption.[59] Griffin and Enos, after a statistical study of Latin American aid programs from 1962 to 1964, also argue that "an extra dollar of aid is associated with a rise in consumption of about seventy-five cents and a rise in investment of only about twenty-five cents."[60] Aid was associated with a proportionate decline in domestic savings, and in some cases the fall in savings was greater than the rise in aid so that the rate of investment actually declined.[61] (I discuss these arguments further shortly.)

59. Timothy and Leslie Nulty, "Pakistan: An Appraisal of Development Strategy," in Norman T. Uphoff and Warren F. Ilchman, eds., *The Political Economy of Development* (Berkeley: University of California Press, 1972), p. 139.

60. Griffin and Enos, "Foreign Assistance", p. 321. Although the donors might resist the argument, note that a 25 percent investment rate is actually much higher than the average savings rates in the poor countries. The donors would object that all the aid was meant to be invested to compensate for the low domestic savings rate and that they were not giving aid for consumption (an attitude that has now changed). Also, if the aid comes as a loan, which has been more and more true over the years, it has to be repaid. If only 25 percent of the loan is invested, the ability to repay may not rise as fast as the obligation to repay.

61. John White, *The Politics of Foreign Aid* (New York: St. Martin's Press, 1974), pp. 125–28, criticizes Griffin and Enos on various grounds, especially the quality of the data used. It seems to me especially true that they have not taken into sufficient account the possibility that aid did not cause the fall in the savings rate, but that both more aid and less savings were a consequence of other factors, particularly the

Conservatives have criticized aid on the sensible ground that it is not indispensable but that it is helpful if the other conditions for progress are present.[62] Aid is not really necessary where the country has the will to develop; where the will is absent, aid is irrelevant or pernicious. From this perspective, aid can be wasted on consumption or corruption or badly designed development plans, but used wisely, it can facilitate the fuller use of domestic resources: In sum the effect of aid depends on the way the recipient responds.[63] This is, of course, unassailable, for there is obviously no way that the impact of aid can be separated from the recipient's behavior. Nevertheless it is still a useful truism to emphasize, for too much of the aid literature, including the Pearson Report, appears to attribute virtually magical properties to small amounts of foreign capital.

Conservatives and radicals have come to share one argument about aid: Its impact on growth has been negligible, especially compared to the impact of the policies pursued by the government. Griffin, for example, has recently argued that Jacoby's estimate of the impact of aid on Taiwan's record growth rate was vastly overstated and that the decisive factor was the government's ability (and the people's willingness) to restrain private and public consumption. And Balassa has also concluded that foreign aid was not a significant factor in Taiwan's success.[64] This consensus is especially important when one recalls that foreign aid financed nearly 35 percent of gross investment in Taiwan and constituted almost 10 percent of its GNP.

(Before proceeding, it may be useful to highlight the contrast

rate of domestic inflation (which could lower savings but also require external aid to bring under control). At any rate from my point of view, the technical adequacy of the attack on aid is not as important as the fact that this kind of critique of the benefits of aid became increasingly popular, and not solely among radicals.

62. Bauer, *Dissent on Development*, pp. 95 ff.

63. See Chenery and Strout, "Foreign Assistance and Economic Development," pp. 701–3.

64. Keith Griffin, "An Assessment of Development in Taiwan," *World Development* 1, no. 6 (June 1973):34–35; Bela Balassa, "Industrial Policies in Taiwan and Korea," in Luis Eugenio DiMarco, ed., *International Economics and Development* (New York: The Academic Press, 1972), p. 75. Balassa points out that aid has had a positive effect on growth in Taiwan and Korea, but that aid levels dropped and growth still increased.

between "gap" theorists who argue the need for $250 billion a year in aid and various critics of the aid process who contend that aid exerts either a negative effect or a small but beneficial effect. That competent analysts can reach such divergent judgments illustrates how much of the debate reflects different values or different judgments about the future.)

The radical critique of foreign aid goes, however, far beyond the assertion that it is not indispensable. Two essential arguments have provided much of the basis for negative views of the aid process. The first, to which I have already alluded in passing, is that aid (and capital inflows in general) reduces domestic saving and may even lower aggregate growth rates. Presumably this happens either because aid permits a government to relax its tax efforts and increase its consumption expenditures or because private foreign investment usurps domestic investment opportunies (which would cut savings, to the extent that saving is determined by investment opportunities).[65] Both of these arguments have been empirically refuted by a number of careful UNCTAD studies concluding the data indicate that "capital inflows have a beneficial impact on the rate of growth of GDP, regardless of whether they are saved or consumed" and that "capital inflows have not been associated with lower tax revenue or increased government consumption."[66]

The second argument against aid is more political. Foreign aid programs have been accused of postponing the need for structural reforms and sustaining the existing structure of inequality and exploitation by giving arms, money, and political support to the ruling elites. Since the elites are presumed to be interested only in their own immediate survival, and surely not interested in any development program that threatened either instability or gains to potential enemies, aid from government to government merely perpetuates the status quo.

There are obviously many exceptions to a generalization such as this, for not all elites in all LDCs have behaved in a reactionary and corrupt fashion. It is also far from clear that aid itself is much of

65. See *Domestic Saving in Developing Countries* (Report by the UNCTAD Secretariat, TD/B/C.3/124/Supp. 1, September 12, 1975, p. 16).
66. *Ibid.*, pp. 21 and 27.

a factor in keeping a regime in power: As with economic growth, a regime that has the will to survive does not need foreign aid, and a regime without that will cannot be saved by foreign aid. Nevertheless, that aid has gone to many regimes whose first concern has been personal survival is surely true. I believe, however, that this is not all that needs to be said about this argument.

In the first place the western aid donors have been conservative states intent on stabilizing the existing configuration of power. It is difficult to see either how or why such states could run an aid program designed to destabilize the status quo. Nor is it easy to see how an aid program, even an international aid program, could avoid seeking the consent and support of the local government. But this has not meant that all aid has been given simply to freeze the status quo, to prevent any change at all—surely the programs for economic development attest to the fact that the developed countries sometimes sought more than simply buying off or bribing one or another colonel. Aid may be useful for those elites merely intent on staying in power, but it is also useful, I think, for elites who seek persistent and steady reform. The recipient elites may choose to take the money and run, or they may seek to establish a reasonable development policy, but the point is that what happens is not primarily a function of the aid process but rather of the elites. The radical critique of aid, that is to say, seems to me a critique of those to whom aid has been given, not of the utility or disutility of aid itself.

In the second place the radical critiques contain a number of unexamined premises. One such premise is that no aid is better than some aid, but Haiti and Burma have not got aid, and they are presumably not the kind of societies the radicals want to create. Another premise, perhaps the central one, is that only revolution can create an equitable society. This is obviously a statement of value, not fact. I think there are cases in which I would agree, but there are also many cases in which I would not. The poor have not always benefited from revolutions in the long run, but they have always paid the cost in the short run. What is involved here, of course, is the classic conflict between reform or revolution, to which no one has ever provided a definitive answer. It seems to me, in any case, that reform cannot be dismissed a priori on either moral or practical grounds. The case must rest, I believe, on an empirical judgment of whether aid recipients seek stability to implement reforms or merely to maintain the existing distribution of benefits. In the latter case, aid could be justified only in reference to the donor's severe shortrun needs; without such needs, aid would surely not be justified, and support for radical change might well be justified.

The arguments of the aid critics have also not always been consistent. For example, the radical contention that aid permits the government to maintain the status quo is in conflict with the conservative contention that aid is too frequently used by the government bureaucracy to intervene in matters that should be left to the play of market forces. Similarly the radical contention that aid has been used to sustain only conservative, anticommunist regimes is at odds with the conservative argument that too much aid has been wasted on unfriendly regimes. Moreover, some critics have asserted that aid encourages too much consumption, while others have asserted that it encourages too much investment (the wrong kind of investment). There are probably circumstances in which any or all of these criticisms are justified. Aid programs have gone on for so long and in so many different circumstances that an intrinsically ambiguous record is not surprising. Nevertheless what seems especially crucial is that all these arguments, conflicting or not, have created a new climate of doubt and apathy for the discussion of aid proposals. The fact that the liberal defenders of aid in the developed countries have become disenchanted has also been an important factor in the creation of the new climate. The optimism about the future, the faith in the beneficent effects of technologic progress, and the belief that rapid growth was the correct goal for any human society have all eroded. Consequently there is no longer an underlying belief structure that sustains the aid program in the face of the criticisms it has engendered.

The case against the effectiveness of aid does not seem to me to have been proved. Conversely the case for the effectiveness of aid is also not proved. What we can prudently say is not much more than a cliché. Aid is one factor in an extraordinarily complex situation, and what it accomplishes or fails to accomplish cannot be separated from the amount given, the form and the terms on which it is given, the behavior of the recipient, and the situation in which the recipient finds itself; nor can we ever know what would have happened if aid had not been given.

None of this argument justifies the conclusion that the issue of aid is likely to disappear from the agenda of discussion. There are at least three major reasons for this. The first, of course, is the oil crisis, which has had a devastating effect on many developing countries, and which will require substantial amounts of various kinds of aid. The second is that the aid programs, because of the increasing use of loans and export credits, have created one clear legacy: an enormous and mounting burden of debt on many recipients. The debt issue will be one of the major areas of likely contention between rich and poor in the next decade—it was a critical item on the agenda of UNCTAD-IV in 1976. Short of the extremes— outright repudiation by the poor or a complete refusal to renegotiate payment terms by the rich—some form of aid will have to be given to the countries that lack the means to meet interest or amortization payments. The discussion of this issue not only will ensure that the demand for aid will persist but also is likely to keep the current controversy about the wisdom of aid, both past and present, in full force.

Perhaps even more importantly, the commitment to rapid growth on the part of the governing elites, the increasingly desperate need to fill expanding resource gaps, and the diverse uses to which aid can be put by the government clearly imply that the criticisms of the aid process are not likely to be convincing to many potential recipients. There is no doubt that the elites who seek aid will have to be more circumspect in their demands, if only to deflect criticism of what Forbes Burnham of Guyana has called "selfish philanthropies" and the equivalence of "aid with raid." But the commonsensical proposition that getting external resources is better than not getting them is likely to outweigh fears of dependence and exploitation. As a result Third World pressures to extract more aid on better terms are not likely to dissipate, whatever the criticisms of radicals and conservatives and the disaffection of liberal aid supporters.

Both donor and recipient share an interest in this circumstance, I think, in not attributing too much or expecting too much—good or bad—from foreign aid. The evidence is quite convincing that, except for a few special cases (especially regimes facing a security threat), foreign aid (at any politically feasible level) is unlikely to be more than a marginal or residual factor in the fate of the Third World. Aid commitments will remain symbolically significant, as an affirmation that the rich do bear some responsibility toward the poor, but the donors ought to be careful that they do not promise (or expect) far more than they can deliver. Obviously the recipients will suffer even greater losses if they continue to act as if aid will be their salvation or as if accusations of guilt, however true, can convince the rich to transform the international system for the primary benefit of the poor.

Aid philosophy began to alter at the end of the decade. The arguments shifted away from aid as a catalyst in economic development to aid for the direct relief of human suffering. Aid for development went to those countries who could absorb it (which meant, more or less, to those with projects that promised reasonable returns on investment capital) or who had a foreign exchange shortfall.[67] As Wall points out, neither of these approaches were as "scientific" as their proponents implied, and the decision about who was to get aid was essentially a value judgment.[68] Switching the aid criterion from development to need did not, however, remove any of the problems in determining who was to get how much of what kind of aid.

In the abstract, aid for development was at least limited by the availability of profitable investment opportunities, but aid based on the needs of the bottom 40 percent of the population has limitations in neither time nor amount, for consumption could be subsidized

67. I have already noted in footnote 28 *supra* that there is now some evidence that the foreign exchange gap was less important than the savings gap. Ironically the oil crisis and the resulting balance of payments crisis may succeed in finally making the foreign exchange gap the critical gap—in the sense that domestic problems cannot be dealt with if there is no possibility of getting needed imports of fuel (and other things).

68. See David Wall, *The Charity of Nations—The Political Economy of Foreign Aid* (London: Macmillan, 1973), pp. 156–65.

indefinitely. Still, the need to abolish the extremes of poverty and to provide the destitute with a minimum standard of living is both morally and practically justified. What remains to be seen, as we shall see in chapter 9, is whether sufficient aid will be given on these grounds—for it is difficult to reconcile them with the political and security rationales that have heretofore extracted the most aid— and whether the governments through whom aid must still be dispensed will in fact use aid for these purposes and not see it as a potential threat to their own survival.

## THE LDCs IN THE INTERNATIONAL SYSTEM: FROM THE COLD WAR TO THE OIL WAR

The LDCs have entered the international system with a triple burden: They are poor and weak, they are underdeveloped, and they must deal with an international system that has itself become more complex and demanding. Underdevelopment makes it much more difficult to compensate for the disadvantages of size. Low levels of productivity, weak and inefficient political and economic systems, and little knowledge of the external world make it extraordinarily difficult for most (not all) LDCs to compete in the international system—even with trade preferences and foreign aid. In the international system itself, the gap between the developed and the underdeveloped countries has become much wider, the minimum requirements to achieve economies of scale have increased sharply in many industries, and the rapidity and costs of technologic change have made adapting to opportunity and obsolescence much more difficult.[69] All these things have made it harder for the LDCs to catch up (in the sense of achieving satisfactory levels of productivity and comparative advantage) and to become viable (nonchari-

69. Some of the difficulties of the LDCs in "catching up" become more apparent when we move away from simple connections between growth and fixed capital investment. Kuznets claims that we now see "the primary source of modern economic growth as a transnational stock of technological and social knowledge available for exploitation by any society that gears itself for this purpose." But it is here that the LDCs are most handicapped and are thus always consigned to activities with lower growth potential. See Simon Kuznets, "Notes on Stage of Economic Growth as a System Determinant," in Alexander Eckstein, ed., *Comparison of Economic Systems* (Berkeley: University of California Press, 1971), pp. 258–59.

table) members of the international system. These problems are compounded by the well-known fact that many of the industries in which the LDCs do become competitive are directly threatening to economically inefficient but politically powerful groups in the advanced countries.[70]

If the international system is so difficult for the LDCs, why try to compete within it at all? This question is now being debated and discussed by Third World intellectuals and some of their Western supporters, but it was not really raised in any fundamental way during the 1950s and 1960s.[71] There were, I think, two reasons for this. The first is that the LDCs were naive about the extent to which economic autonomy flowed from political independence. They thought that coping would be a good deal easier than it has turned out to be. In partial defense of this position, note that in political terms the LDCs were relatively more influential than earlier generations of new and weak states: They were not only more numerous but also likely to benefit from the increasing prominence of normative ideas about nonintervention, the right to be heard, and the range of acceptable state behavior. In effect, the LDCs, by virtue of sovereignty and increasing influence, might be more able to deal with economic intrusions and threats—if the LDCs had a clear sense of what they wanted from the external economic world and what they did not want. But the LDCs did not analyze the impact of the international systems in a serious fashion.

The other reason why the LDCs did not consider a wider range of alternatives is that they had neither the theorists nor the available theories to challenge the conventional wisdom. I am not arguing that the prevailing theories reflected a conspiracy to exploit the poor. On the contrary I think they were serious and sincere efforts to come to terms with the problems of economic development. Nev-

70. In addition, when multinational corporations (MNCs) do invest in the LDCs, they expect higher returns than from investment in rich countries (because of the "risk"); they tend to bring in capital-intensive technology and to concentrate in industries or activities (extraction or consumer goods) with little spillover into the rest of the society.

71. There have been many arguments about getting along without the system in recent years, and they have not all been confirmed to radical economists. See, for example, W. Arthur Lewis in *The Case for Development: Six Studies* (New York: Praeger, 1973), p. 63. I comment on this point again in chapter 9.

ertheless the theories not only were extrapolated from Western analogies that might not be appropriate but also featured a development strategy that made the LDCs dependent on the international system. As a result the flow of ideas from the rich countries to the poor may have exerted a more profound impact on what the Third World could or could not do than any tangible flow of goods or money.

The stress on rapid industrialization meant that imports, and thus the availability of foreign exchange, became the central LDC concern. In this sense all the strategies the LDCs pursued were attempts to deal with the foreign exchange dilemma, by import substitution or more aid and trade. The international system tended to become the dominant factor in domestic economic development, for there was no way rapid industrialization could take place without external support of various kinds. This focus was unfortunate, not because the international system was unimportant (for it was indeed very important), but because it created a bias against the most important part of the domestic economy (agriculture) and a bias toward a world that rewarded the kinds of strength the LDCs did not have. Perhaps worst of all, the theories created an impression, all too willingly seized upon by the LDCs, that development was a relatively easy task that could be accomplished without a fundamental transformation of domestic institutions.

The international systems did bear down heavily on the choices that the governing elites of the underdeveloped countries thought they had. This was inevitable, not only because of the size factor, which compels all small states into some degree of dependence on foreign trade, but also because the prevailing theories left few other alternatives open to the LDCs and because the LDCs were in so much need of external help. Nevertheless, in the majority of cases the decisions that the ruling elites made about their stance toward the external world seem to have been dominated by domestic concerns. This is hardly surprising, given the necessary priorities of insecure leaders in new and poor states, but it does suggest that the judgment that the underdeveloped countries were merely puppets manipulated by malign external forces is simplistic. The spectrum of behavior was much too wide to be encapsulated within a single proposition about the behavior of international capitalism: While there were corrupt elites intent only on replacing external colonial-ists with internal colonialists, there were also elites who adopted orientations toward the international systems that were not sanc-tioned by the experts or the governments of the industrial world,[72] or who accepted the prevailing wisdom but rejected it when the results were unsatisfactory, or who were simply ignored by the out-side world and left to do as they pleased.

The tendency to look abroad for salvation reflected a particular combination of domestic and external pressures. Bitterness at past deprivations seemed to justify the demand for reparations, and changes in the international system—bipolarity and the Cold War stalemate, the influence of the many new states, the competition in aid giving—seemed to provide the underdeveloped countries with a degree of flexibility in foreign affairs that was quite unique for small and poor countries. In addition the major powers in the inter-national system did not exert a perfectly consistent set of pressures, for some of their actions benefited the poor, while other actions were clearly harmful or indifferent. Nor were all the pressures dom-inant and profound, for some pressures were merely indicative or indirect; such pressures could be ignored, if at some cost. Even those LDCs who adopted choices sanctioned by one of the power blocs usually did so either because of a pressing security threat or because the elites happened to see that choice as directly in their in-terest. Domestic pressures, conversely, were of a different order: They required immediate, pragmatic responses, because failures could destroy the regime.

Pressures from abroad consequently did not always deprive the ruling elites of meaningful choices about the external orientations they wanted to adopt. The decision to concentrate attention on de-mands for change in the external environment was thus rarely a reflection only of either overwhelming external pressures or the changes in the international system that seemed to increase the in-

72. External policies such as nonalignment, ISI, and the particular kinds of trade preferences and the amount of aid demanded by the LDCs were sharply criticized by many Western analysts. That they were adopted anyway suggests a degree of choice for many developing countries that has been frequently denied by radical analysts.

fluence of the poor countries. That decision more frequently seemed to reflect elite perceptions of the benefits of concentrating on international changes and the dangers of attempting to transform domestic society. Also, the inadequate results achieved by the domestic policies that were pursued had an increasingly important effect: As domestic problems accumulated, and consequently as the means necessary to deal with them became more and more far reaching, the external systems—both as scapegoat and potential savior—became increasingly prominent.

I do not, of course, imply that this process went on in the same way or to the same degree in every developing country. And I clearly do not argue that either the domestic or the external system alone could provide a sufficient explanation for the increasingly desperate state in which many developing countries find themselves. These factors can be separated only as a matter of analytic convenience, and it is only an analytic judgment on my part—and no more—that the domestic factor generally tended to be *primus inter pares.* But failure in one realm exacerbated problems in the other; the adoption of an inappropriate development theory yielded meager results domestically but simultaneously got many developing countries prematurely and excessively involved with an international system that was too complex and not sufficiently responsive—or not aware of what the response ought to be. But because a workable alternative was hard to discern and because domestic resources for (acceptable) change seemed insufficient, even more demands had to be placed on a reluctant external world, and a dialectic of futility ensued in which domestic problems were highlighted only by a rhetorical ritual, and attention was focused on external demands that were not truly fundamental. Some countries avoided this dialectic; the majority did not.

Both domestic and international changes are necessary. Nevertheless the more fundamental change must come initially from the domestic realm. This is so because external changes cannot help a regime that cannot grasp new opportunities and because domestic failures engender demands upon the international systems that are not likely to be met and that undermine the stability of the systems

*[175]*

themselves. In any case, domestic changes are within the power of elites willing to take some risks, whereas the great majority of international changes are derived results for weak and poor states. In the next chapter, therefore, I discuss some of the factors that have made effective domestic policymaking so difficult.

## Part Three

## Domestic Politics
## and External Choices

# 6

## Politics and Policymaking: Problems and Prospects

The previous three chapters have attempted to illustrate something of the process by which the developing countries have come to blame more and more of their problems on the international systems and to place more and more demands on these systems for fundamental change. This was hardly a completely irrational development. The problems imposed by size alone virtually compel an abiding concern with external events, not only because of the limitations of small domestic markets, but also because of the dangers of external "shocks." Underdevelopment has also justified some stress on external change, for the poor countries inherited economic and social systems that made international competitiveness unlikely without special dispensations to overcome past inequities and present deficiencies. Imported doctrines of rapid growth and industrialization, and simplistic exhortations about the ease with which the conditions of underdevelopment could be overcome, also ensured that the developing countries would become increasingly involved with a complex international environment—and for this, the Western governments and Western experts must share some part of the responsibility.[1]

1. But not all of the responsibility, for some of the imported ideas that worked out badly came from Prebisch's ECLA and were in fact criticized by many Western economists.

But external change, even in the best circumstances, can do little for regimes unwilling to deal with their own domestic deficiencies. In a sense domestic and external failures have fed upon each other. Domestic elites, reluctant to risk fundamental domestic change, have followed misguided policies—or ineffectively implemented policies—and when the results were in, sought relief by raising the level of demand on the international systems. The response from abroad was never sufficient: too little aid given too erratically, too few trade concessions where it really mattered, and advice that was frequently wrong and that unwisely raised expectations about imminent benefits. Nevertheless the range of politically feasible response from abroad was never likely to reach a level where it could help countries who refused to face their own problems and sought only external scapegoats and/or external salvation. The Third World indictment of the international systems would always have been more compelling if the developing countries had been steadily reforming their own institutions and had been thwarted by a recalcitrant, selfish, and hypocritical external world; as it is, the limited and insufficient response from abroad was, in most cases, rarely decisive.

Apart from those countries already in such desperate straits that an international rescue operation is imperative, the first order of change—but not the only order—must be domestic. There are several reasons for this. First what opportunities there are within the international systems can be grasped only by developing countries with effective and flexible policymaking systems. Second the only consistent protection that the developing countries have against disabling and jarring external developments is in their own ability to cope. Third the level of aid and support that can be reasonably expected from the developed countries (both socialist and nonsocialist) is never likely to rise much beyond the point where it is most useful to those already capable of helping themselves. Finally, insofar as domestic failures continue to engender increasingly extreme demands on the international systems, some measure of domestic success is imperative to restore some balance between the pressures placed on weak international institutions and their capacity for response.

The difficulties of creating an effective domestic policymaking system are enormous. The gap between domestic needs and domestic resources has seemed so wide that only revolutionary options— or massive international charity—have seemed feasible. But not all the developing countries face problems that can be dealt with only in a revolutionary fashion, nor is it likely that many revolutions are probable or that revolutionary solutions are inherently more beneficial than efforts at more moderate change. And international charity is insufficient and degrading. But is there something in between revolution and charity? Are the political systems of the developing countries so hopeless, are the elites so corrupt, and are the demands of the masses so revolutionary that the quest for more effective policymaking is utopian and academic? I examine these questions in this chapter, and I suggest a revised approach to policymaking in the next chapter.

## POLITICS AND THE RESOURCE CONSTRAINT

One picture of the political process in developing countries began to emerge in much of the professional literature in the 1960s. This picture was inadequate for a number of reasons, which I shall note, but an outline of it is useful because of its effects on perceptions of the range of the possible in developing countries. In any case, we cannot develop a sense of how policymaking might be improved without understanding the political process—the style and the rules of the political game—within which policymaking operates.

Multiple cleavages—tribal, ethnic, regional, class—dominate many Third World countries. Since the state has frequently been created before the nation, citizen loyalties remain tied to narrow groups: There is only grudging identification with the new "nation," and the government itself has little legitimacy.[2] Moreover, there is little underlying consensus about either values or procedures to tie the groups together. What do exist are mistrust, fear,

2. One illustration of this is that local grievances, not national ones, tend to dominate citizen concerns at the time of independence.

and the dominance of a "constant pie" orientation—the notion that what one group gets must be taken away from, or is a threat to, the other groups.[3]

Mistrustful groups, committed to providing for their own interests above all, compete for the control of the few resources the state does have. Everything is politicized, for control of the state is also control of the economic and social marketplace. The state determines who is to benefit, not only from traditional sources of wealth (usually exporting and landholding), but also from whatever new economic structures are to be created. The struggle to control resources is also the struggle to control the whole internal order, for there are no autonomous realms; control the state or control nothing. The centrality of politics is thus a virtually universal proposition, for no other structures—except the military—are strong enough to contest the dominance of the machinery of state. Cleavages and conflicts unmediated by an underlying consensus also impart a particular character to the political struggle: It is winner take all, for the losers have few alternative power structures to which they can retreat, and, unsurprisingly, there is no perception on the part of either winners or losers of a loyal opposition. Distrust destroys the possibility of compromise, and conflicts merely reinforce one another—an economic or political conflict is also an ethnic or class or regional conflict.[4]

These are political systems that combine conflict and poverty. The usual result is an unstable equilibrium. The winner at any particular time lacks the power to do much more than concentrate on survival. Weakness frequently leads to a stalemate, a "politics of accommodation" in which controversial issues are avoided and policies are designed specifically to benefit whichever groups join the

3. For an interesting discussion of the "constant-pie" orientation, see James C. Scott, *Political Ideology in Malaysia—Reality and the Beliefs of an Elite* (New Haven, Conn.: Yale University Press, 1968).

4. This picture is a reflection of material in many places. I have found the following especially helpful: Aristide R. Zolberg, *Creating Political Order—The Party-States of West Africa* (Chicago: Rand McNally, 1966); Immanuel Wallerstein, *Africa, The Politics of Unity* (New York: Vintage Books, 1969); Norman T. Uphoff and Warren F. Ilchman, eds., *The Political Economy of Development* (Berkeley: University of California Press, 1972); and Scott, *Political Ideology of Malaysia*.

accommodation.[5] The government promises something to every group that has some power but as little as possible to those without power. As Genoud notes of Ghana, there is no one strong enough, or perhaps committed enough, to speak for a national future.[6] Even the emergence of a single, dominant leader, or an army takeover, does not change the calculus very much, for the leader or the army may be strong enough to retain control of the government but not strong enough to risk the dislocations of structural change.[7]

The most obvious effect of this kind of political system is that a concern for political stability always prevails over a concern for economic development. The ruling elites may disagree about many things, but they agree about the need for domestic order.[8] Order takes priority over the creation of national wealth, and policies aim at preserving the regime in power—not creating the conditions for long-term prosperity. In part this means a good deal of spending on arms and on symbols of national unity. More significantly, short-term consumption strategies, designed to reward supporters and bribe or pacify dissidents, diminish the possibility of raising the domestic rate of investment. Underdeveloped countries can rarely escape a large degree of dependence on the international system, but policies such as these ensure that the dependence will be extremely debilitating. Since no effort is being made to alter the socio-economic structure in any important way, few new capacities are developed—although there may be sharp alterations in which elite group benefits from traditional capacities.

5. The quoted phrase is from R. Crawford Pratt, "The Administration of Planning in a Newly Independent State: The Tanzanian Experience 1963–1966," *Journal of Commonwealth Political Studies* 5, no. 1 (March 1967):54.

6. Roger Genoud, *Nationalism and Economic Development in Ghana* (New York: Praeger, 1969), p. 194.

7. Latin American political systems clearly follow a somewhat different pattern than the one just described. But there are also some general similarities, particularly in terms of the existence of stalemated governments that do not function in pursuit of national goals but rather seek only to protect the self-interest of a few against the many. Herbert Goldhamer, *The Foreign Powers in Latin America* (Princeton, N.J.: Princeton University Press, 1972) explicitly stresses characteristics of Latin American political systems that parallel the discussion in the text above, especially the extent to which politics dominates all spheres of life and resolves all conflicts in society. See pp. 288–89.

8. See Zolberg, *Creating Political Order*, pp. 60–61.

Other effects are important but perhaps somewhat less apparent. The elites converge on the capital and struggle against each other for control of the state. Their common interests are protection against rising mass demands and against any attempt at major change. A significant by-product of this is a bias against rural areas and toward the urban areas where the elites live and carry out their activities. This puts a slightly different perspective on some of the arguments about relations between the capital and local areas, for it is clear that the elite may want to limit, not enhance, those ties, when more integration with local areas also implies more demands upon the center's scarce resources.

The style of policymaking that the elites have developed in these circumstances suffers a double burden. In the first place the need to survive distorts the process of choice toward shortrun projects and away from any serious attempt to support the public interest. Even more critically, decisionmaking tends to fall into a pattern of avoidances: Actions are chosen because they are likely to incur fewer costs or threaten fewer interests, and not because they have been evaluated in an objective framework.[9] The results are apparent in efforts to call upon the international system to rescue the elites from the consequences of having to make costly domestic choices. Alternatively, when domestic pressures begin to rise, inflationary financing can be used to try to create new resources quickly and cheaply. This is especially likely if the groups that bear the heaviest burden of rising prices, usually wage earners and agricultural interests, are also politically weak. (The rationale for inflation as a development policy rests on the doubtful notion that, if wages lag behind prices, inflation redistributes national income toward employers, who will then invest it wisely.) More aid, trade preferences, and inflationary financing all seem to share one characteristic—they are free goods in the short run. Finally, repression always remains an "easy" option, provided the army is under sufficient control.

9. John P. Lewis, for example, attacks Indian bureaucrats for their fear of making mistakes and observes that they are "dedicated to the prevention of wrongdoing rather than to the marshalling and energizing of 'right-doing.' " Quoted in Albert Waterston, *Development Planning: Lessons of Experience* (Baltimore: Johns Hopkins Press, 1965), pp. 258–59.

Such governments pose formidable obstacles to much beyond games of musical chairs. Many of the military coups that have occurred reflect these conditions, for the military by itself rarely can do more than ensure its own rule—if that. The military contempt for politicians in itself creates a predisposition to intervene that is usually activated when the government is overwhelmed by some crisis—for example, the fall in cocoa prices in Ghana—or when the government is imprudent enough to threaten military prerogatives in some manner. But if the army is a microcosm of the nation and mirrors national cleavages within its own ranks, the stalemate persists but within a new arena. And if the army represents only one national group against the others, there is no way it can unify the nation or establish any legitimacy for its rule. In addition the military usually lacks the knowledge and skills to devise effective development policies. One result has been the emergence of coalitions of expediency between the military and the civil service and the creation of an administrative state. The results thus far have not been encouraging, for the state continues to rest on force, and neither partner has seemed willing to risk the turbulence of structural transformations. Nevertheless this coalition of different kinds of expertise may become increasingly prominent in the next several decades.[10]

This interpretation of the political process is useful for several purposes. It illustrates, for example, why elite commitment to a national future or to some idea of the public interest is so difficult and problematic. Perhaps also it is a useful reminder of why domestic security is so pervasive a concern for ruling elites and of why policymaking so frequently is discontinuous and erratic. Finally, this sketch may also illustrate why there has been a growing sense of futility about the possibility of a meaningful reform strategy: What we are offered is something of an equivalent to the economist's notion of the "low-income equilibrium trap" but translated into political terms. Weak governments, compelled to expend most of their

10. On military coups, see Claude E. Welch, Jr., ed., *Soldier and State in Africa* (Evanston, Ill.: Northwestern University Press, 1970); Ruth First, *The Barrel of a Gun—Political Power in Africa and the Coup d'Etat* (London: Allan Lane, 1970); and Irving Leonard Markovitz, ed., *African Politics and Society* (New York: The Free Press, 1970), especially the Introduction.

energies on ensuring their own survival, cannot establish priorities and implement goals—except as an exercise in ritual—that would begin the process of creating a developed society.

There are also reasons, however, why this picture of the political process is either inadequate or overdrawn. One reason is that it is an inaccurate picture of some parts of the Third World, especially the more advanced states of Latin America, for not all developing countries are fragmented by multiple cleavages or without sufficient power of their own to begin getting out of the low-income equilibrium trap. In addition a new generation of elites may be emerging in some countries, and they may be animated by a different set of political perceptions—even the new military elites may have different priorities than their predecessors, especially if the higher ranks become increasingly middle class (events in Peru and Bolivia, and perhaps Portugal, are thus suggestive). Perhaps most critically, the sketch I have outlined takes insufficient account of the effects of external shocks and changes upon poor and exposed states. In this sense the picture is too static, for some kinds of change may be compelled by external events that the ruling elites can neither influence nor isolate—the effects of the oil crisis on the cost of food or fuel imports is merely an extreme illustration of the point. There are also less overwhelming but potentially critical external events that could induce a more progressive attitude toward change: for example, changes in development theories, or a more responsive attitude on the part of the developed countries, or even an increased confidence from joint efforts within the Third World at collective self-reliance. It goes without saying, of course, that some of the external changes might be pernicious, and all will engender asymmetrical effects, but the possibility of movement in desirable directions cannot be dismissed.

In these circumstances it seems to me that it is more useful to conceptualize the political process in terms of resource gaps or constraints. Since existing demands and available resources are rarely perfectly balanced, the central question for the government becomes how to deal with the gap between what its citizens want and what it can provide in response. This approach has two virtues. On the one hand it permits a more productive level of generalization, for all governments—irrespective of other differences—confront the need to deal with the problem of "rising demands and insufficient resources".[11] The political process is thus heavily influenced by basic resource constraints that narrow the range of choice, no matter what the intention or the ideology. On the other hand this approach also has the virtue of concentrating attention on specific tactics and strategies to reduce the gap; by contrast, sole emphasis on the "politics of accommodation" tends to foster an attitude of futility or a belief that only extreme solutions can make sense. What is crucial here is recognition of the fact that a resource constraint is not unalterable: The key questions become practical, not metaphysical.

Political leaders have a variety of methods to attempt to deal with resource gaps. They can, for example, attempt to expand the economy to stay ahead of rising demands, or they can attempt to transform the economy so that it is capable of higher levels of performance, or they can seek external aid to provide resources beyond their own means. They can also seek to control patterns of demand in various ways. At one extreme they can apply the numerous tactics of repression, silencing demand by threatening or applying force. At the other extreme they can attempt to persuade, to convince their citizens that belt tightening is the only feasible alternative and that the government is doing all it can with available resources. The government may also, in a time-honored formulation, attempt to divert attention to other matters by blaming its troubles on scapegoats or seeking to unify the nation against a real or imagined threat. Finally, if the gap between demands and resources cannot be eliminated, the government can attempt to alter its priorities and seek different goals: The current concern with measures of equity and redistribution is illustrative, for it implies less concern with rapid growth and more concern with a direct assault on poverty.

Why have the ruling elites so frequently seemed to choose a combination of domestic repression and external charity? Some-

11. For an interesting analysis of the range of possible responses to a resource gap, see Harold and Margaret Sprout, "The Dilemma of Rising Demands and Insufficient Resources," *World Politics* 20, no. 4 (July 1968):660–93.

*[187]*

times it may seem too dangerous to risk anything else. There are no spare resources to buy off the groups who benefit from the status quo and who would resist basic transformations of the socioeconomic structure. Dissident groups also cannot easily be integrated into the political system by promise of material benefits. And the army always lurks in the background, a menacing presence if discontent erupts into violence, or its own perquisites are threatened, or even if there is a "contagion of coups" in neighboring areas.

But what of the developing countries that have been the "success stories" of the past two decades? Many of these countries—like South Korea, Taiwan, Singapore, the Ivory Coast—were also poor and had to deal with serious domestic problems and did not possess mineral exports in high demand. They did have some unique assets, especially high levels of foreign aid and, in some cases, an external threat that helped to unify the country. But two factors in particular seem to set them apart: the choice of an outward orientation and a dedicated and committed ruling elite. I discuss the outward orientation in chapter 8 and the significance of elite attitudes and behavior in the rest of this chapter.

Two arguments have frequently been used as justification or explanation for the failure of a great many ruling elites to make a genuine commitment to national development. The first argument, no longer quite in fashion, is that they have not done so because effective policies are bound to be overwhelmed by a "revolution of rising expectations." I comment on this briefly in the next section, for in one sense it is still crucial. The second argument is that the elites have become so corrupt that they no longer have any interest in actually implementing a development policy, either because of greed, or fear, or class interests. I suggest a somewhat different interpretation of this argument in the concluding section.


## WHOSE "REVOLUTION OF RISING EXPECTATIONS"?

The potential for a revolution of rising expectations is surely present in the developing countries. There are clearly many ways in which demands upon a government can be fueled—from the demonstration effect, from the emergence of new sets of beliefs, from improvements in one set of values that create the desire for improvements in other values.[12] But whether the demands become truly revolutionary depends on a large number of situational variables.[13] In the developing countries, the elites themselves initially created some of the difficulty by stressing the ease and inevitability of prosperity once independence was achieved. The difficulties of paying off on easy promises were compounded by the quest for rapid growth, which seemed to require sacrifices, and inequitable sacrifices, rather than immediate gratifications. And if the government cannot give its citizens what they have come to think is properly theirs, the situation may become explosive.[14] Disappointed or unfulfilled economic expectations are especially critical, for economic values dominate the hierarchy of citizen concerns. Presumably this is one reason why there has been so much ambivalence about economic growth among ruling elites, for they feel the need for policies that provide immediate economic benefits, not merely the assurance of long-term growth.

Nonetheless, despite the potential for mass demands for continuous and massive gains, available evidence seems to indicate that aspirations and expectations have been sharply bounded by a strong sense of realism. The issue, of course, is not whether the masses have rising demands, for they do—as we all do—but whether they are also revolutionary demands. And in this regard there is little evidence to justify the notion of an explosion of what people hope for or what they expect is theirs by right.[15] The rele-

12. The ways in which expectations may be raised are discussed in Ted Robert Gurr, *Why Men Rebel* (Princeton, N.J.: Princeton University Press, 1970), p. 92 ff.

13. *Ibid.*, pp. 101 ff., discusses these variables at length.

14. *Ibid.*, pp. 41–50; and W. G. Runciman, *Relative Deprivation and Social Justice* (London: Routledge and Kegan Paul, 1966), p. 22.

15. Hirschman suggests that tolerance for inequality may be very high at the early stages of economic development "because advances of others supply information about a more benign external environment; receipt of this information produced gratification. . . ." Albert O. Hirschman, "The Changing Tolerance for Income Inequality in the Course of Economic Development," *Quarterly Journal of Economics* 87, no. 4 (November 1973): 546. He also remarks, however, that this tolerance is a credit "extended in the expectation that eventually the disparities will narrow again" (p. 545). This is a useful reminder that the absence of revolutionary expectations only gives the government the opportunity to respond to limited and realistic demands: Whether it will do so is another question.

vant reference group has been, not the affluent Western worker, but neighboring groups close by in both class and status. A gradualist framework seems to set limits to what is expected: Demands rise slowly and steadily but ultimately level off as people begin to achieve what they consider equitable within their own economic area.[16] There are few "rags to riches" myths among the poor.

The goals of the urban poor also seem modest and realistic. Nelson notes, for example, that they seem more intent on "getting by" than "getting ahead," and Cornelius provides additional evidence that the urban poor start with low aspirations and seek primarily to preserve whatever modest gains they have made.[17] As Apter has noted, the masses tend to be conservative and self-interested during modernization—hardly a revolutionary vanguard.[18] Even when the expectations that the poor have are frustrated, which is far from unlikely, the result need not be violence and instability: There are mechanisms, such as support from the family or the village, that provide both material and psychic support and make violence a last, desperate resort.[19]

The absence of revolutionary expectations is not equivalent to the absence of expectations: The government still faces the need to deal with rising demands as quickly and as equitably as possible. Moreover, whereas Hirschman has suggested some degree of tolerance for inequalities in the early stages of development, he has also

16. Evidence for the moderate and realistic nature of most demands can be found in Anthony R. Oberschall, "Rising Expectations and Political Turmoil," *Journal of Development Studies* 6, no. 1 (October 1969):5–22; Claudio J. Fuchs and Henry A. Landsberger, " 'Revolution of Rising Expectations' or 'Traditional Life Ways'? A Study of Income Aspirations in a Developing Country," *Economic Development and Cultural Change* 21, no. 2 (January 1973):212, 213; Hadley Cantril, *The Pattern of Human Concerns* (New Brunswick, N.J.: Rutgers University Press, 1965); and the previously cited works of Gurr and Runciman. For more impressionistic views of what the masses want, which also describe modest and realistic goals, see Robert J. Muscat, *Development Strategy in Thailand: A Study of Economic Growth* (New York: Praeger, 1966), p. 3; and Werner Levi, *The Challenge of World Politics in South and Southeast Asia* (Englewood Cliffs, N.J.: Prentice-Hall, 1968), p. 38.

17. Joan Nelson, "The Urban Poor—Disruption or Political Integration in Third World Cities," *World Politics* 22, no. 3 (April 1970):393–414; Wayne A. Cornelius, "The Cityward Movement: Some Political Implications," *Proceedings of the Academy of Political Science* 30, no. 4, pp. 27–41.

18. David E. Apter, *Choice and the Politics of Allocation: A Developmental Theory* (New Haven, Conn.: Yale University Press, 1971), pp. 49 ff.

19. See Oberschall, "Rising Expectations and Political Turmoil," pp. 8–9.

pointed out that such tolerance is less likely in divided societies—and many underdeveloped countries are very divided. Consequently tolerance that rests on the hope of emulating the success of others is likely to be sharply diluted if the "others" happen to be communal or tribal or ethnic enemies.[20] Although we need not visualize an inevitable explosion of expectations, we also must be careful not to assume that this is all that needs to be said about the pressures of mass expectations upon government performance.

There has been one kind of revolution of rising expectations in most of the Third World: by the elites. Many elites have demanded rapid growth, many have sought to emulate living standards in the developed world, and many have attempted to create states and institutions in imitation of the wealthy and the powerful. The consequences are by now well known and widespread: growth policies that increase inequities in income distribution and favor urban over rural areas; high import rates for luxuries, and distorted domestic investment policies; premature social welfare institutions that the state cannot afford, and extensive planning bodies that cannot plan; and massive corruption.

First priority for the masses has always been economic. Ensuring some minimal standard of existence and achieving some equity in the distribution of this world's goods take precedence over all other values.[21] The masses have not sought rapid economic growth, for they have not understood what it means and would probably reject it if they did understand it—because it has usually meant less for the many, and more for the favored few. The idea of rapid growth has been an elite import, since it is the elites who have found the "gap" between their societies and the advanced societies unacceptable and have sought to catch up as quickly as possible. And this is an essentially insatiable quest, because catching up is an unending process that simultaneously inflates expectations and ensures frustrations.

Cantril's surveys of Brazilian and Nigerian value hierarchies clearly illustrate the differences between elite and mass perspectives:

20. See Hirschman, "The Changing Tolerance for Income Inequality," pp. 552 ff.
21. See Gurr, *Why Men Rebel*, p. 66.

> Brazilian legislators are much more concerned than the pub-
> lic about Brazil's independent status and they want the
> country to become an important world power with techno-
> logical advances. . . . The Brazilian people as a whole are
> more worried about their economic problems and a greater
> proportion of them express a hope for economic stability.
> Members of the Nigerian Parliament are much more con-
> cerned than the public about achieving and maintaining the
> independent status of the country and having Nigeria
> achieve some regional leadership. . . . The Nigerian people,
> on the other hand, are more concerned than the legislators
> with public health and having modern amenities, and they
> are more fearful of the consequences of a lower standard of
> living and political instability.[22]

Adelman and Morris also argue that it is the strong elite desire for equality with other states that creates pressures for rapid growth and the desire to match foreign standards of living.[23]

There are, of course, wide variations within this theme. Not every member of the elite in every LDC gives status in foreign eyes the highest priority or is concerned only with catching up at all costs. The Burmese elite perhaps comes closest to rejecting external values altogether, although there has recently been some "opening" toward the outside world. And the Thai elite, as well as many other more or less traditional ruling groups, have sought rapid growth and the preservation of old values simultaneously.[24] Indeed, in many of the traditional cases, the quest for growth has been reluc- tantly accepted only because of the need to build a relatively mod- ern military establishment. Nevertheless, the general proposition still seems valid: Whatever revolution of rising expectations there is—or has been—in the underdeveloped countries has come pri- marily from the efforts of elite groups to imitate Western standards.

---

That the great mass of citizens appear to have realistic expecta- tions for the future is important, for it suggests, I believe, that not

22. Cantril, *The Pattern of Human Concerns*, pp. 286–87 and 289–90.
23. Irma Adelman and Cynthia Taft Morris, *Society, Politics and Economic Devel- opment—A Quantitative Approach* (Baltimore: Johns Hopkins Press, 1967), p. 182.
24. See Norman Jacobs, *Modernization Without Development: Thailand as an Asian Case Study* (New York: Praeger, 1971), p. 145.

all the policies open to the LDCs are necessarily futile or doomed to failure. Surely no government, especially a poor and weak government, can successfully deal with escalating and revolutionary demands. But even a weak and poor government can deal with moderate demands, if it makes a serious effort to do so, if it understands its own strengths and weaknesses, if its elites are not completely corrupt and inept, and if the international system manages to remain relatively benign. These are obviously important qualifications, but they are qualifications and not the central point. What is central is the argument that not all LDC governments need to be overwhelmed by the rising demands of their citizenry; blanket injunctions of total despair about the future of the Third World are, at least in this sense, misleading and pernicious.

The realism of the masses means that there is a potential for satisfying their demands. But there is no more than a potential, for it is apparent that this generation of elites is not likely to make much use of the potential. The elites, influenced by foreign standards and intent on pursuing their own interests, have been reluctant to attack the domestic socioeconomic structure from which they benefit and have usually also been too tied to foreign interests in the import–export sector to challenge the traditional way of doing business with the external world. Beyond this, their personal behavior has frequently been corrupt, licentious, and ostentatiously vulgar. This last point is important, because if the demonstration effect really works primarily on a face-to-face level, and not between widely separated societies, the behavior of the rich may quickly raise the level of discontent of its own population. Even when conditions are bad, the masses may not become violently discontented if they feel that the government is honestly seeking to do better and to act with justice.[25] Curbing its own excesses may be a necessary part of any elite effort to deal with the problems their countries face.

What then can we say about the argument that nothing can be accomplished in the developing countries until this generation of elites is ousted or destroyed?

25. See Cantril, *The Pattern of Human Concerns*, p. 305.

## DOMESTIC POLITICS AND EXTERNAL CHOICES

### THE FAILURE OF THE ELITES

Criticism of the ruling elites has mounted steadily in the past decade. They have been accused of an obsession with consumption (their own), of excessive corruption, and of sacrificing national interests for communal or local interests.[26] They have also been accused of artificially creating a revolution of rising expectations—for themselves and for their regimes—by attempting to emulate patterns of consumption and the range of state services provided in the advanced countries.[27] But these are only symptoms of a more profound charge: that the elites have been indifferent or hostile to the need to create a process of economic development.

Evidence for the failure to make a serious commitment to economic development takes many forms. For example, Griffin illustrates the low priority that development has for Latin American elites by pointing to their indifference to tax reform and their reluctance to increase the size of the public sector (which might permit some of the costs of development to be spread more equitably).[28] Latin American elites have also been accused of being opposed both to education for the masses (which might make them less tractable) and to birth control (for it would raise the price of labor).[29] Another charge frequently made, especially in Africa, is that the elites have been fundamentally conservative, compromising with foreign economic interests and their domestic counterparts against the masses. Capitalism in some of its least appetizing incarnations has thus survived, whatever the anticapitalist rhetoric, because the elites have wanted to enrich themselves. In this sense even "redistribution" may become a euphemism for altering the distribution of

26. In addition to Zolberg and First, see E. Wayne Nafziger, "The Political Economy of Disintegration in Nigeria," *Journal of Modern African Studies* 2, no. 4 (December 1973):505–36.

27. See the preceding discussion, pp. 191–92.

28. Keith Griffin, *Underdevelopment in Spanish America: An Interpretation* (Cambridge, Mass.: The M.I.T. Press, 1969), p. 278. Karl von Vorys, *Political Development in Pakistan* (Princeton, N.J.: Princeton University Press, 1965), p. 290, notes also that subscription to government bonds did not keep up with income growth rates in Pakistan: The elite preferred to invest their money elsewhere (or send it abroad).

29. R. Albert Berry, "Some Implications of Elitist Rule for Economic Development in Colombia," in Gustav Ranis, ed., *Government and Economic Development* (New Haven, Conn.: Yale University Press, 1971), pp. 12–25.

benefits between elite groups and a rationalization for expending scarce resources on jobs and projects that benefit only friends and supporters.[30]

Another aspect of elite indifference to economic development needs mention. It was particularly true for the first generation of elites that they frequently had little understanding of the implications of economic development. In part this surely reflected general unfamiliarity with the available theories of economic development and with the relationship between many of their immediate actions and the long-term prospects for increased prosperity. But, in part, it was also a failure to understand the political implications of different rates of economic growth and different decisions about the composition of production. Bienen illustrates the point well when he comments that the Tanzanian political elite did not know enough about how

> patterns of economy affect society to be able to determine whether their image of Tanganyika was being implemented by the planners' choices. Was *Ujamaa* being translated into economic policies by the planners? The political leaders could not tell.[31]

Indifference to economic matters and ignorance of the political implications of economic choices were obviously transient phenomena: Most soon learned how inextricably they were related. But indifference and ignorance did have a lasting effect, for they delayed a response to economic problems until a response was virtually compelled by internal discontent or external pressures.

This indictment of the elites on multiple grounds—narrow self-interest, corruption, conservatism, indifference, whatever else—cannot be dismissed, for there is much evidence to justify it. Nevertheless justice ought at least to be tempered with recognition of the hazardous choices the elites confronted. Conflict in the context of insufficient power or wealth is singularly difficult to resolve. Win-

30. See Dharam P. Ghai, "Concepts and Strategies of Economic Independence," *Journal of Modern African Studies* 2, no. 1 (1973):31–33; O. Aboyade, "The Economy of Nigeria," in P. Robson and D. A. Lury, eds., *The Economies of Africa* (Evanston, Ill.: Northwestern University Press, 1969), p. 192.

31. Henry Beinen, *Tanzania: Party Transformation and Economic Development* (Princeton, N.J.: Princeton University Press, 1967), p. 294.

ners can never be secure enough to risk thinking ahead; energies must be concentrated on either eliminating rivals, which is likely only to unify enemies, or coming to terms with all by promising something to everyone. Faced with no easy choices, any choice being bound to offend somebody, the easiest thing to do is to do as little as possible. This is, after all, a policy of procrastination that is hardly unfamiliar in industrial societies, although its costs are not usually as immediately apparent as they are in the underdeveloped world.

That we should have elites obsessed with order, control, and personal loyalty is not, in these circumstances, surprising.[32] More is at issue than that personal security dominates other concerns; it is also that all choices seem so uncertain and all results so ambiguous. Oscillation, as Eisenstadt reports, is one familiar result:

> . . . the policies undertaken by the rulers in these societies have been characterized by continuous oscillation between the attempts at controlling all the major power positions and groups in the society and monopolizing the positions of effective control, on the one hand, and a continuous giving in to the demands of various groups, on the other hand.[33]

Charisma, a rapidly depreciating asset, may provide some support, especially in a relatively symbolic arena like foreign policy—until foreign policy becomes substantively significant. Inevitably, whatever policy is made tends to be short range and *ad hoc,* "grand designs" being luxuries for the powerful and the secure.

Contemplation of the difficulties confronting the ruling elites and the futility of talking about long-range development plans to leaders who are unsure of what tomorrow may bring have engendered a number of studies of the tactics of elite survival. Presumably an elite assured of effective control can then be led to other concerns less self-interested. As Hopkins points out, this is a conservative, shortrun approach that aims, primarily, at regime building, not nation building.[34] But will the elite, even if they improve their control and ensure some degree of staying power, risk what-

32. See Zolberg, *Creating Political Order,* pp. 60–61.
33. S. N. Eisenstadt, "Breakdown of Modernization," *Economic Development and Cultural Change* 12 (July 1964): 361.
34. Raymond F. Hopkins, "Securing Authority: The View from the Top," *World Politics* 24, no. 2 (January 1972):275–76.

ever security they have established in pursuit of goals that will be achieved only long after they are gone—if then? Is this not a strategy that merely facilitates increased repression by the elite and its military supporters?

There are no clear and convincing answers to these questions. Some degree of elite security is surely a necessary—but not sufficient—prerequisite for a serious commitment to economic development. Whether even secure elites will be willing to support serious development policies is uncertain; the record of the past 30 years is no better than ambiguous. Perhaps what we need to ask is whether there are other factors at work that are propelling more and more elites toward a commitment to development or toward a perception that development policies are in their own interest.

Some external pressures may compel a serious concern for development. Envy and emulation of the record of neighbors and peers may have some influence. So, too, may the need to pay back earlier loans or credits or to earn enough foreign exchange to pay increasingly critical import bills. Foreign economic interests may also foster a degree of development by providing new knowledge, by inculcating new attitudes, and by creating linkages with other parts of the economy. Perhaps more critically a change in external economic conditions—a sharp drop in export earnings or another worldwide recession—could force concentration on internal development. This tendency might be accelerated if increasingly prominent discussions of national and collective self-reliance begin to be taken seriously.

What of changes in the elites themselves? The evidence that the second generation of postcolonial elites is much of an improvement over the first generation is inconclusive. Indeed Bienen has argued that the second generation of African elites has become increasingly deradicalized as it confronts the multiple problems of development. These elites cannot rely on the symbolic and psychic currencies their predecessors used; consequently they are less prone to seek large changes.[35] Perhaps this implies the beginning of a "Latin Americanization" of African political systems in which the elites

35. Henry Bienen, "Political Parties and Political Machines in Africa," in Michael F. Lofchie, ed., *The State of the Nations: Constraints on Development in Independent Africa* (Berkeley: University of California Press, 1971), p. 211.

cooperate with each other, against the masses, to divide up the spoils.[36]

There are, however, some countervailing trends. For example, the need to provide jobs as a result of population growth or of the growth of aspirations as educational levels rise may engender more concern with development—if only to avoid internal conflict.[37] Generational changes may also be important, since elites who have matured in an age of television, nuclear weapons, and moon landings may be more open to the need for change and more influenced by the values of industrial society.

Whether this fragmentary and contradictory evidence will lead to more corrupt and repressive elites, or to more committed and modernizing elites, or—as is probably most likely—to a shifting and confused mixture of the two must remain an open question. At a minimum this at least suggests that the possibility of meaningful change cannot be foreclosed: Not all the elites are completely corrupt or indifferent to the fate of their citizens, not all the elites can resist external pressures for change, and not all the differences between the newer and the older elites are necessarily antithetical to a genuine commitment to development. These are statements that ought to be taken for granted, but they have been obscured by the pervasively unfavorable image of the elite that dominates much of the recent literature on developing countries.

I think a more useful perspective on elite corruption may emerge if we examine the problem in the context of the resource constraints that they confront. The degree of corruption in the developing world seems (and is) excessive because, almost literally, it takes food from the mouths of the starving; in contrast, corruption in industrial societies seems several degrees less debilitating be-

36. Myron Weiner, "Political Participation: Crisis of the Political Process," in Leonard Binder et al., *Crises and Sequences in Political Development* (Princeton, N.J.: Princeton University Press, 1971), p. 185, also provides some evidence from Ceylon and Turkey that the newer elites are less educated than the older elites and more likely to represent rural areas. If true, this might suggest a reduced commitment to social transformation.

37. There is some discussion of this in P. C. Lloyd, ed., *The New Elites of Tropical Africa* (London: Oxford University Press, 1966), pp. 60–62, but primarily in terms of the lack of bureaucratic jobs for university graduates, given the already inflated (and youthful) numbers in "official" jobs.

cause it works at the margin of generally prosperous societies. But it is at least possible to argue (or hypothesize) that the elites in developing countries are not intrinsically any more corrupt than their counterparts in developed societies; in effect the range of elite motives for behavior is likely to be as mixed as it is in other societies.

Why then is corruption apparently so much more pervasive? One answer, I believe, is that the elites, who recognize the enormous gaps between their countries and the developed countries, do not really believe that the policymaking systems they operate can produce persistent, steady, and satisfactory results. This leads to a large gap between rhetoric and actual beliefs and to psychologic uncertainties and doubts about the possibility of meaningful change—beyond their own expulsion from power, a fear exacerbated by the absence of a role for "opposition" elites in single-party states. The sense of futility about results and the lack of faith in future progress engender not only rhetorical hypocrisy but also a feeling of the need to "take the money and run"—or take the money and hide behind the army or the police.

Each failure to produce results acts as a self-fulfilling prophecy. This pattern can be broken—if it can be broken at all—only if a policymaking process can be created that has the capacity of producing consistent and steady, and not massive and revolutionary, gains. Indeed the very claim that a particular approach or a particular set of policies is designed to achieve quick and fundamental change may only induce even more cynicism and hypocrisy among elites who are well aware of the limitations of the societies they control. Seeking more change than is either feasible or likely may induce apathy, or appear to be fakery, and destroy the possibility for smaller but still meaningful gains. Perhaps seeking more moderate goals and establishing more moderate expectations about the policymaking system will engender sufficient faith that measurable progress is possible and that pervasive corruption is not the only guarantee of a decent future. In the next chapter I examine the possibility of creating a policymaking system that might be able to produce these gains.

# 7

## Policymaking in the Context of Underdevelopment

Powerful constraints on the political process in the developing countries clearly limit the results that can reasonably be expected from any system of policymaking. Nevertheless these constraints do not necessarily justify the contention that only revolutionary policies make sense. It is at least arguable that many developing countries—as yet—face problems that are potentially manageable by more moderate means. Moreover the demand for revolutionary solutions also overstates the likelihood of vast numbers of revolutions or the prospect that revolution will either overcome the deficiencies of underdevelopment or yield the successes foreseen.

In these circumstances it seems useful to ask whether and how more effective policymaking strategies can be devised for those developing countries for whom a reform strategy still seems feasible. But the constraints already cited set the limits within which this quest must operate. For example, no policymaking system that threatens the security of the existing regime or that promises only long-term benefits is likely to win elite support. The initial point, then, is the need to devise a policymaking system that takes account of elite fears but also attempts to go beyond obsessions with security and self-interest. That suggests a system that does not seem too radical, that does not promise to transform society massively and rapidly, and that seeks steady and persistent change in a desired direction. No doubt this seems unexciting, but it has the virtue of realism, not only in reflecting existing conditions, but also in suggesting how far and how quickly they can be changed.

Another constraint reflects the fact that everything of significance seems to happen in the capital between elites. Commitment to the state on the part of outlying areas, or of groups that are not within the ruling groups, is bound to be minimal. They can hardly feel that their interests are being fairly considered. Efforts to bring local areas and groups within the political process are thus imperative. A simple plea for decentralization is insufficient, for the ruling elites are not about to disperse willingly the little power they do have. What seems necessary is a serious attempt to bring local elites and groups into the planning process so that they can feel their interests are being given a hearing and so that they can see how they fit into a picture of the nation's future. Also necessary, however, is a careful effort to ensure that local interests do not dominate national interests.

Weak governments have enormous difficulty in controlling or altering policies once made. Procrastination, altering as little as possible, becomes a political way of life. This is a warning about the need to be careful in making large-scale policy commitments that, once begun, simply persist. In addition it is a warning about assuming that choosing a policy is sufficient and that implementation can be safely left to administrators and bureaucrats. Taken together, these points imply small-scale pilot projects carefully monitored and evaluated; more than this is too much until a record of feasibility exists and a corps of competent personnel have been established.

Finally, if everything is political, nothing is technical. What is best in weak and inefficient political systems in which distrust and self-interest dominate most calculations is not necessarily what is best in political systems that can presume an underlying consensus on values. What is best in this context is what begins to engender commitment to the nation, what convinces the elite that meaningful results are within reach, and what promises to meet the immediate needs of all groups—and not what is technically "sweetest." Moderate expectations reflect the limits set by underdevelopment; immoderate expectations are the enemy of the good that can be and needs to be done.

These comments provide an introduction and a justification for the analysis of planning, "muddling through," and the other policymaking approaches discussed in the remainder of this chapter.

## APPROACHES TO POLICYMAKING

### PLANS, PLANNERS, AND PLANNING

Nothing has been more fashionable among the LDCs than "plans." And nothing has become more fashionable than criticizing the plans—and the planners—for a variety of sins. The necessity of planning has seemed self-evident: What else could introduce an element of control into an environment of risk and uncertainty? But planning has also seemed impossible: How could one devise rational plans for governments that could not think beyond tomorrow and were more concerned with self-interest than the national interest?

Indeed, why should any small, underdeveloped country attempt to plan? Was it not bound to be at the mercy of external forces that it could neither control nor influence? As Wriggins notes of Ceylon,

> Systematic planning was hampered by a widespread feeling that, as a small island vulnerable to all manner of outside influences, Ceylon was at the mercy of economic and other forces that could never be controlled. Many felt that planning exercises would prove illusory, that good times should be used to accumulate large liquid reserves for the unpredicatable but inescapable hard times that were bound to come again.[1]

Yet it was just these conditions that put a premium on planning, for only the very rich and the very powerful could afford to stumble into the future blindly.[2]

1. W. Howard Wriggins, *Ceylon, Dilemmas of a New Nation* (Princeton, N.J.: Princeton University Press, 1960), p. 314.
2. One needs only to note how badly the failure to plan has hurt Ceylon, which is now in desperate straits, though initial conditions after independence were reasonably favorable. I do not argue the failure to plan "caused" what ensued in Ceylon (vast overspending on consumption and public services, underspending on investment), for many factors played a part, but clearly some of the consequences of many

## Policymaking and Underdevelopment

Planning thus created a dilemma for most of the LDC governments. They were pressed on all sides to prepare plans as an indication of the seriousness with which they approached the development task, but they were politically too weak and administratively too inefficient to risk implementing the plans their planners devised. Obviously many LDCs resolved the dilemma by simply ignoring the plan, perhaps occasionally taking it out of the back drawer for a visiting foreign aid mission. Conversely several strong governments that did make a serious commitment to economic development—Pakistan, South Korea, Taiwan—signaled their intention of doing so by giving their planning staffs new attention and new power.[3] Burma, which sought to end foreign dependence by nationalizing virtually all industries, had no planning staff at all.[4]

None of these decisions prove or disprove the contention that planning and underdeveloped economies—and polities—are incompatible. Part of the problem, familiar to anyone who has studied the planning process, is that no one defines what is meant by planning—in the abstract a meaningless term—and consequently the debate is dominated by preconceived stereotypes of what planning is and against what standards it is to be judged.[5]

short-range decisions were foreseeable (and foreseen). The critical question is whether—or what kind of—planning is possible for a political system like Ceylon's.

3. Pakistan is a classic example. Thus one of the planners, Mahbub-ul-Haq, notes that "the Planning Commission was isolated from the political process—its only mandate being to devise policy for yet a faster growth rate." "Pakistan's Economic Choices for the 1970's" (unpublished paper, 1971). Davis C. Cole and Princeton N. Lyman, *Korean Development: The Interplay of Politics and Economics* (Cambridge, Mass.: Harvard University Press, 1971), p. 219, make the same point about the role of the planners in the new Park Government.

4. See Mya Maung, *Burma and Pakistan: A Comparative Study of Development* (New York: Praeger, 1971), p. 59. As in the Ceylonese case, the disasters that ensued could not be attributed solely to the absence of planning, but it was surely a factor.

5. For extended comments on this point, see Robert L. Rothstein, *Planning, Prediction and Policymaking in Foreign Affairs* (Boston: Little, Brown, 1972), pp. 89 ff. The point is that planning need not be defined in terms of controlling the future or of producing optimal outcomes in a technical sense. I use the term to refer simply to purposeful activity in relation to a predetermined goal, or as a relatively systematic effort to solve problems. The key elements in the planning process from this perspective are (1) efforts to estimate the future as a basis for present choices, (2) explicit formulation of general goals, and (3) coordinated action to achieve the goals. For another approach to the planning issue, see John Friedmann, "A Conceptual Model for the Analysis of Planning Behavior," *Administrative Science Quarterly* 12, no. 2 (1967):225–52. Friedmann lists a number of different forms that planning can take.

And the contention that planning and politics are incompatible rests on the premise that planning must always be comprehensive and that politics is always a form of incremental bargaining among groups, which would make any commitment to the future problematic or irrelevant. For the most part the LDCs have indeed attempted to adopt the most complex and far-reaching form of planning: centrally controlled, comprehensive four- or five-year plans designed to reach a set of predetermined goals. Inevitably they have failed to achieve their goals. I examine why this has been so and whether other forms of planning may be more useful for the LDCs.

Any plan can be impeded by all sorts of "surprises"—for example, unplanned decisions, unanticipated needs, events that cannot be controlled, or failures of skill or implementation in the plan itself. Administrative weaknesses in the machinery of government are especially important: The lack of connection between the capital and local areas, deficiencies in information and expertise, and the lack of coordination and consultation within the government itself make it extraordinarily difficult to devise sensible plans and to convert them into policy actions. Weak and poor governments also lack the resources to build hedges against either internal or external uncertainty into their plans or to seek safety in "redundant" capacities. These factors complicate an already complex situation, for they suggest that even an LDC government genuinely committed to implementing a plan would have great difficult in doing so.

Plans are ventures into clarity about the allocation of benefits in the near future. This is not necessarily a virtue for weak governments, since making clear who is to gain and who is to lose is bound to create more conflict. Plans have been made, nevertheless, because they also serve some useful purposes. Many observers have stressed the extent to which plans respond primarily to external pressures, particularly the need to satisfy the technical requirements of the World Bank and the foreign aid agencies.[6] This is surely true but also insufficient, since planning also serves some

6. See Raymond Vernon, "Comprehensive Model-Building in the Planning Process: The Case of the Less-Developed Economies," *The Economic Journal* 76, no. 301 (March 1966):59. Further evidence, mostly from Latin America, is in Keith Griffin and John L. Enos, *Planning Development* (London: Addison-Wesley, 1970), pp. 201–4.

important domestic functions. Planning and plans have become a symbol of intent to move forward and to achieve a *national* future. (By underlining national here and in later references, I suggest a contrast with efforts designed primarily to benefit only the ruling elite or some segment of the society; such efforts, sometimes incorporated in "national" plans, have been all too frequent in countries sharply divided between different class, or ethnic, or regional groups and help to explain the distrust and cynicism with which many plans are greeted.) Planning has also reflected elite ideologies that have been dominated by anticapitalist rhetoric and a commitment to central control and public enterprise.[7]

The plans that emerged from this set of contrary pressures were hardly textbook models of the state of the art. As Binder notes of Iran,

> The present goals of the plan organization have been determined by the immediate desirability of certain projects, from a political point of view, and by an arbitrary balance between agriculture, industry, communications, and social welfare projects. Balance, here, means spending about the same under each head. Balance has been sought in order to avoid political accusations of bias. . . .[8]

At best, then, the plan became a rather vague statement of good intentions and a shopping list of things that it might be nice to have. Adedeji, a Nigerian planner, makes the point well:

> . . .the Plan, a compromise document that it is, is honoured more in the breach than in the observance. . . there is little discernible relation between what is contained in a Plan and what in fact gets done. Thus it would be a mistake to regard a Plan as a blueprint for action. Rather. . .a Plan [is] a document assessing a country's problems, stating broad conclusions about the scale and direction of development efforts and indicating some of the main projects, programmes, and policies to be executed. . . .[9]

7. On the impact of the ideological baggage of the first generation of elites, see A. H. Hanson, *The Process of Planning—A Study of India's Five-Year Plans, 1950–1964* (London: Oxford University Press, 1966), pp. 18–19.

8. Leonard Binder, *Iran—Political Development in a Changing Society* (Berkeley: University of California Press, 1962), p. 314.

9. Quoted in Reginald H. Green, "Four African Development Plans: Ghana, Kenya, Nigeria, and Tanzania," *Journal of Modern African Studies* 3, no. 2 (1965):250.

The failure of such plans is to be expected, for they were never meant to succeed—at least as plans. The leaders were more concerned with political unity than with economic development and with responding to events as they arose, not following a blueprint into the future. The plans themselves were thus meant to change as little as possible. In Tanzania, for example,

> The decision to finance the [1964–1969] *Plan* through foreign investment and loans rather than through a program which would necessitate sharply rising taxation, involuntary savings, or a vast program of mobilized "voluntary" labor meant that the planners and politicians were trying to achieve *Plan* goals without making major transformations in *TANU's* operation.[10]

Moreover, most of the plans tended to be unrealistic, usually being created by a few intellectuals—some of them foreign—who were isolated and alienated from the outlying areas of the country.[11]

Plans never meant to be seriously implemented cannot be faulted for failing to achieve their ostensible goals. But what of plans meant to be taken seriously? Could they achieve their goals or perform any other useful functions? Some part of the answer must be unclear, because it is impossible to specify what would have happened if the plan did not exist and whether or not the plan was—by itself—responsible for any particular outcome. Wildavsky "solves" the problems by defining planning as "the ability to control the future by current acts"; since no state, let alone a poor and weak LDC, can control the future, planning, virtually by definition, is impossible.[12] Suppose we ask, however, whether there are other, more modest goals (more modest than seeking to control the future)

Wolfgang F. Stolper, *Planning Without Facts—Lessons in Resource Application from Nigeria's Development* (Cambridge, Mass.: Harvard University Press, 1966), notes that the Nigerian plans did at least have the virtue of giving the ministries some sense of the direction the country was meant to follow and some notion of how the ministries were meant to approach their tasks (p. 43). These are indirect, but not irrelevant, virtues.

10. Henry Bienen, *Tanzania; Party Transformation and Economic Development* (Princeton, N.J.: Princeton University Press, 1967), p. 305.

11. See Hanson, *The Process of Planning*, pp. 353 ff., for some of the reasons why so many plans were unrealistic.

12. Aaron Wildavsky, "If Planning Is Everything, Maybe It's Nothing," *Policy Sciences* 4, no. 2 (1973):128.

that might be set through the process of formulating and adapting a long-range national plan and that would not have been sought if the plan did not exist? Such goals would involve a commitment on the part of the government to move steadily in a preferred direction within a particular time frame: for example, to begin to emphasize redistributive measures rather than growth, to make an effort to begin controlling foreign investment, or to seek to favor local areas at the expense of the capital. Two questions need to be asked about these kinds of goals. First, is it possible for developing countries to achieve these goals by central planning? And second, is a national plan alone sufficient to implement such goals?

No clear or completely satisfactory answers to these questions are available. Surely an unqualified yes is not justified by the record. Too many incompatibilities exist between the requirements for long-range planning and the nature of underdeveloped countries to make for a very good fit. Many observers, for example, have commented on the difficulties that any underdeveloped country has in developing enough trained people to run a centralized system or in providing them with the necessary information or administrative help.[13] Government controls also provide fertile grounds for corruption, especially if the civil service is not well paid. In addition, insofar as centralized control creates a bias toward large, mechanized farms, agricultural development may suffer.[14] The bureaucratic and administrative regulations that tend to grow up around central control may also make it difficult for an LDC to compete effectively in foreign trade, there being a premium on quick responsiveness and knowledge of the market in international competition—and these are not the virtues planning systems usually have. Finally we can never forget we are dealing with segmented, distrustful societies in which the government is not seen as a neutral actor. In these circumstances government planning is likely to be interpreted as in

13. See Gustav F. Papanek, *Pakistan's Development, Social Goals and Private Incentives* (Cambridge, Mass.: Harvard University Press, 1967), pp. 228–29; and Elliot J. Berg, "Socialism and Economic Development in Tropical Africa," *Quarterly Journal of Economics* 78, no. 4 (November 1964):549–73.

14. Berg, "Socialism and Economic Development in Tropical Africa," pp. 562–66. Note that large, mechanized farms are not always inefficient—this is an empirical question, not an ideological one.

the interest of only a particular segment of society. Still, none of these criticisms are completely decisive: Trained people may be becoming less scarce; large, mechanized farms are not always inappropriate; not all the LDCs export the kind of products (or very many of them) that require a quick and skilled response to a fluid market; and we may be able to suggest methods to make planning and local interest more compatible.

Planning may be extremely difficult, but some of its virtues are important enough to make the effort worthwhile. One problem with market societies is that savings and investment behavior are essentially unpredictable. This is a particular problem for underdeveloped countries with few resources to waste on luxuries or with resources dispersed without effect on too many projects; presumably planning would avoid these kinds of waste.[15] More significantly the market does not effectively represent the social values of the community; conversely planning may impose a whole range of social decisions and worry about a whole range of social costs that are ignored by individual decisionmakers in the market. These decisions may involve such things as determining the rate of saving, or attempting to increase the growth rate, or raising tariffs on luxury goods, or attempting to change the distribution of income. Finally the distribution of income seems to be more equitable in countries that have a large public sector.[16]

How these balances between the advantages and disadvantages of planning work out probably ought to be left to individual cases. Nevertheless I would venture the opinion that the more elaborate forms of planning require too much skill and commitment to be very helpful to LDC governments. For true central control, as Wildavsky argues, the "nation's rulers must be able to commit its existing resources to the accomplishment of future objectives."[17] This is almost impossible for most LDCs to do, because they have too few resources to be able to expend many to ensure a better future. In addition the weakness of the political system may have a number of

15. Papanek, *Pakistan's Development*, pp. 231–33, has a good discussion of some of the inefficiencies and imperfections of market systems, especially in underdeveloped countries.

16. Irma Adelman and Cynthia Taft Morris, *Economic Growth and Social Equity in Developing Countries* (Stanford, Calif.: Stanford University Press, 1973), pp. 165 ff.

17. Wildavsky, "If Planning Is Everything, Maybe It's Nothing," p. 133.

different, but equally debilitating, effects on the plan and its implementation. Full-scale, centrally controlled plans may be dangerous. They demand a commitment of all available resources to a vision of the future that may be inappropriate or may be based on inadequate knowledge or data; once committed, however, it may be especially difficult for a weak and relatively inflexible society to change course. Inflexibility may be particularly severe when the plan has simply stitched together the demands of different power groups whose support is necessary to keep the whole package from unraveling.

It is equally possible, however, that weakness will compel, not rigid and inflexible implementation, but no implementation of the plan at all. Few governments are likely to be strong enough to impose many shortrun sacrifices on the population. This is especially likely when consensus is too low to permit agreement on the shape of a common future and when any sacrifice is unacceptable (or may appear unfair) to a group whose support for the plan is based solely on its own gains. As a result the plan is likely to be only a ceremonial device to satisfy external aid agencies or to bear witness to the government's "commitment" to alter the status quo.

In these circumstances the only detailed planning likely to be useful is decentralized, local planning that responds to the needs and desires of the different groups within the society. This planning is likely to be successful just because local grievances have usually been at the root of citizen protest against the government—whether the colonial government or the postcolonial government. Local planning scales down the resources needed to plan well, and such plans are likely to be able to set proximate goals that can be satisfied in a reasonably short period. Accurate information may also be more easily acquired, and feedback as the plan is implemented may be more readily available. What evidence there is also tends to indicate that the most successful plans in the LDCs have been local plans that required control over only a relatively narrow base.[18] Local planning may also show results quickly and thus responds to the desire of the elites for prestige and political

18. Peter Kilby, *Industrialization in an Open Economy: Nigeria 1945–1966* (Cambridge: Cambridge University Press, 1969), p. 363; and Karl von Vorys, *Political Development in Pakistan* (Princeton, N.J.: Princeton University Press, 1965), p. 293.

*[209]*

capital. Such planning responds to a double imperative: It is politically acceptable, for it deals only with a particular group and does not commit vast amounts of resources, and it is more likely to fall within the range of available knowledge, skills, and needs. We cannot sensibly expect the government to adjust to the needs of planning; rather, planning must be adjusted to the capacities of weak governments and insecure elites. What I am suggesting here is that it must be recognized that local groups do not trust central plans, that some effort must be made to bring them into the political system, and that this goal merely recognizes that planning is never entirely a technical function, for it is always part of the political process.

A stress on local planning is a useful response to some of the political problems associated with planning, especially the need for integration of outlying areas and for quick, tangible results. But local planning, or indeed any planning, takes place within a political system dominated by sharp conflicts over limited resources. The planners are simply one group among many in these conflicts (unless, as in Pakistan and South Korea at different times, they are given unusual power by the ruler). What cannot be forgotten in these circumstances is that the local planners cannot succeed unless the ruling elite is committed to planning and unless the plans themselves are sufficiently supported by local power centers. This is not to deny the importance of local planning but only to insist that it too can become an exercise in ritual unless it achieves the necessary political support.

Modest, decentralized local planning makes a good deal of sense in terms of the "art of the possible." It is less attractive in terms of what is necessary. It is not likely to do much more than scratch the surface of the policymaking problems of the LDCs who face massive and immediate problems—the Indias, the Bangladeshs, the Ceylons. For these countries and for other LDCs overwhelmed by rising food and fuel costs, help must come from abroad. There are no magical methods by which weak and moribund political systems can deal with revolutionary problems.

But even the LDCs whose problems appear potentially manageable need more than local planning. The problem with such efforts is that they lack cumulative direction. Local plans may also be insufficient because they do not always take external effects into account. They are a first step toward doing something productive and provide the populace with some sense that the government is trying to respond to its needs. But such efforts are more likely to be politically useful in the short run than economically useful in the long run. What seems necessary is some mechanism by which the local plans are joined to a larger vision of national development. Part of this vision can be supplied by national planners who have some notion of the general directions the country ought to be heading in and some influence—at least indicatively—over local efforts. National planning may also be the only level of decision at which the costs of external effects can be thoroughly evaluated. Citizen participation at the local level must be joined to government counseling at the national level: Local planning without a national input will probably lead only to drift and inertia, but central planning without local efforts will probably lead only to conflict and failure.

The central or national planning I am advocating here is a good deal less elaborate or comprehensive than, say, a full-scale five-year plan. There may be something of an analogy, in intent if not in detail, with what the French have called "indicative" planning, that is, a nondirective but influential effort to set general guidelines and to ensure that national goals and purposes are carefully articulated and considered. This is, at best, a loose analogy, for not all of the institutional devices by which indicative planning in France has been implemented are likely to be available to the governments of developing countries (especially financial resources to induce compliance with indicative goals). Consequently "indicative" here should be taken in a limited sense: as an effort by the government to establish national goals that provide guidance for local plans and an element of coherence so that the local plans are more than a random collection of specific needs. This effort is likely to be successful only if the government has some elements of both the carrot and the stick—in the form of some financial resources and some legislative authority over local planners—to elicit cooperation and coordination.

The national plan could also be conceived (or reconceived away from elegant but irrelevant comprehensive plans) as an effort to achieve shortrun goals that promise quick results, not longrun goals that promise much better results—someday. As Waterston observes, this approach, which urges the necessity of accepting sufficiently good solutions within the context of existing economic, social, and political realities, aims primarily at improving the quality of immediate decisionmaking.[19] Whereas this seems eminently sensible to me, it may be inadequate if it is not animated by some notion of the general goals the nation is seeking: Immediate improvements may lead nowhere if they are not in response to a consistent perspective on longer run goals. By "general goals" I mean simply a governmental commitment to broad aims such as rapid growth and industrialization or to redistribution via land reform and other measures directly designed to help the poorest segments of society.

Planning is not by itself enough to constitute an effective policymaking system. Planning has virtues in setting directions and in ensuring that questions of social costs and national interests are (or can be) raised. Planning does not, however, provide much guidance about how daily decisions to implement a plan are to be made. What policymaking system offers some hope of providing the decisions necessary once a plan or a series of plans have been adopted? One suggestion that has become increasingly fashionable is that the LDCs ought to adopt the modest and prudent policymaking style that corresponds to "incrementalism" or "mudddling through." Normally incrementalism has been perceived as a sharp alternative to any form of planning. I ask whether this needs to be so.

"MUDDLING THROUGH"—VARIATIONS ON AN ANCIENT THEME

The political system of the United States has often been described as pluralist. Pluralist political systems, composed of large numbers of competing groups, have been forced to devise subtle operating rules to avoid complete stalemate. The groups compete, but since no group is strong enough to dominate the others, alli-

19. See Albert Waterston, "An Operational Approach to Development Planning," in Mike Faber and Dudley Seers, eds., *The Crisis in Planning*, Vol. II: *The Experience* (London: Chatto and Windus, 1972), p. 103.

ances must be formed on each issue to reach agreement. Bargaining and negotiation provide the momentum by which the system moves from decision to decision. Indeed agreement to settle issues by bargaining is an essential prerequisite for the system to function at all. Without such an agreement the rather singular mixture of conflict and cooperation among the groups might easily be tipped in the direction of unmitigated conflict.

Central to the pluralist idea, then, is not simply group conflict but conflict within the context of an underlying consensus on values. Consensus keeps conflict from going "too far," for all groups share some overlapping interests and accept the need to agree to the rules of the game, the proper range of policy decisions, and the legitimate arbiter of disagreements. Thus a normative consensus about the need to limit conflict, and the means of doing so (bargaining), provide the glue that keeps a structure of dispersed and fragmented power from flying apart.

This is a complex system—"a flux of restless alterations"—and even consensus and dispersed power may be insufficient to keep it together. The system probably also has to provide easy access into the political arena for new groups, and sufficient resources to make agreement on each issue more acceptable to all the groups than continued conflict. Groups denied legitimate access may be forced into violating the norm of not going "too far"—by sit-ins, demonstrations, or even terrorism. And insufficient resources may simply make the lowest common denominator of agreement too low. Together these norms provide a classic picture of a relatively satisfied, unrevolutionary political system, a system that all participants want to persist so long as they continue to receive an adequate and fair share of the benefits.

A large and complex political system with many competing groups obviously faces great dangers of stalemate or chaos. Dispersed power is difficult to aggregate into decisions that have majority support. This means that the emphasis within the system is procedural, not substantive. A "good" decision is simply one accepted by all the groups that have power on a particular issue. There is an "ethical laissez-faire" at work in this process, for the resolution of a conflict takes precedence over the rightness or wrongness of the outcome itself.[20] There are two dangers in this situation: that the common good or the public interest will be sacrificed to particular interests and that the interest of the weak—those who do not have sufficient power to get into the game—will be ignored or exploited.

What are the characteristics of the decisions negotiated by the competing groups? Perhaps the most salient one is that they are incremental decisions; that is, they only marginally alter whatever has previously been accepted. With so many groups and values in conflict, with information about the present imperfect, and with the consequences of action unforeseeable, it is easiest to go on doing pretty much what has been done in the past. As a result a conservative bias is built into the system, for agreement on doing something, which usually means agreement on doing very little, is more important than change. Change threatens, because no one knows where it will lead; for those already doing reasonably well within the status quo, there is a premium on moving slowly and limiting conflict—and discussion—to familiar issues.[21]

The incremental decisionmaking style that characterizes pluralsit systems has come under sharp attack in the past decade. Some of the costs implicit in the system have begun to outweigh the benefits. Minorities excluded from power and denied access to the decisionmaking arena have had to resort to extreme tactics to be heard. Neither the political nor the economic marketplace have worked well, as social costs and the public interest have been ignored or thwarted by the monopoly power of large corporations and unions. Resource margins have begun to shrink, so that it has become increasingly difficult to buy off the losers in any conflict—the surplus has diminished too far, and we have begun to worry about an economics of scarcity, not affluence. The ethical neutrality of incrementalism has thus come to seem suspect, questions of distribution

20. The quoted phrase is from Charles E. Lindblom, "The Handling of Norms in Policy Analysis," in Moses Abramovitz et al., The Allocation of Economic Resources (Stanford, Calif.: Stanford University Press, 1959), p. 171.

21. In addition to various works by Lindblom, also useful is Andrew S. McFarland, Power and Leadership in Pluralist Systems (Stanford, Calif.: Stanford University Press, 1969). There are, of course, vast numbers of comments on pluralism and so forth, and my analysis attempts to synthesize some of this literature.

having come to dominate debate. Finally incrementalism has created a tendency toward drift and inertia, with many policies simply floating around in equilibrium, going no place, apparently coming from no place. Cumulative progress in many areas has been nonexistent; conversely, in other areas, persistent incremental additions to base programs, without thought about direction and purpose, have created enormous financial burdens.[22]

Despite these problems several analysts have argued that incrementalism could be useful for the LDCs. R. S. Milne, for example, notes:

> If the culture is indeed resistant to large, sudden changes, the incremental strategy would be appropriate. The strategy would also take account of the need to conserve the scarce resources in a developing country by committing them gradually to projects instead of staking them all on a single throw. Use of the strategy would also be consonant with the lack of information about resources and possibilities of implementation which exists in developing countries. . . . It also takes account of the impossibility of setting comprehensive objectives in developing countries where the environment changes rapidly, for example, because of the dependence on the export of a few primary products. . . . Finally, it would be compatible with the idea of the "beachhead strategy," "pilot projects," or the "nuclei approach," methods which seem promising for promoting innovational decision-making in developing countries.[23]

There is much to be said for this approach to decisionmaking in underdeveloped countries, for the notion of gradual and limited decisions, slowly building on previous successes, seems to be a

22. For some of the criticisms, see the essays in William E. Connolly, ed., *The Bias of Pluralism* (New York: Atherton, 1969); and Shin ya Ono, "The Limits of Bourgeois Pluralism," in Charles A. McCoy and John Playford, eds., *Apolitical Politics* (New York: Thomas Y. Crowell, 1967). On the last point in the paragraph in the text, note that the Social Security Act used to be described as one of the best illustrations of incremental policymaking. But now, with the costs of that program rising rapidly to astonishing parts of the Federal Budget, it no longer appears so wise to have avoided an effort to think through long-range consequences.

23. R. S. Milne, "Decision-Making in Developing Countries," *Journal of Comparative Administration* 3, no. 4 (February 1972):394. Another argument for incrementalism can be found in Robert P. Clark, Jr., *Development and Instability* (Hinsdale, Ill.: Dryden Press, 1974), pp. 228–40.

sensible and pragmatic response to a universe of uncertainty, imperfect knowledge, and limited resources.[24] But incrementalism is more than just a procedural response to an environment of dispersed power and insufficient knowledge of how to get where we want to go. Incrementalism presupposes an underlying consensus on values, access to the decisionmaking arena for all groups, and sufficient resources to make a commitment to the system attractive even to the (relative) losers in any conflict. The difficulty of successfully meeting all these conditions explains a good deal of criticism of incrementalism in recent years. What is especially striking, and what makes a commitment to incrementalism in the context of underdevelopment more problematic than it first appears, is that few LDCs are likely to be able even to approximate these conditions.

The political systems of many LDCs are split by sharp conflicts over scarce resources between groups that mistrust each other and share only the desire to control the state for their own benefit. There is little consensus, there are insufficient resources to satisfy all groups, and the losers fear (with much justification) that they will be permanently denied access to the political arena and to their fair share of the benefits. Procedural agreement is thus virtually impossible, since there is no agreement on the rules of the game. And ethical indifference is dangerous and unsupportable, because it not only justifies whatever behavior the winner adopts but also rationalizes an indifference to questions dealing with distribution, social costs, and the public interest.

In many underdeveloped countries the group structure is rudimentary. This tends to mean that the conflict is really between the elites themselves, rather than between groups representing carefully defined interests. This creates a double problem: Only the views of the elite, not all the relevant views in society, are considered, and there is little feedback to the elites, once a policy has been adopted, there being no interest group to provide some organized response to policy implementation.[25] Whatever adjustments an in-

24. It is also, of course, similar to Hirschman's familiar arguments about the need to call forth innovative decisionmaking in underdeveloped countries. See especially Albert O. Hirschman, *The Strategy of Economic Development* (New Haven, Conn.: Yale University Press, 1958).

25. See Milne, "Decision-Making in Developing Countries," p. 395.

cremental system can make through the response network of groups is thereby lost.

Additional problems arise from incrementalism in political systems dominated by a small number of elites. In one sense it is ironic even to discuss incrementalism and elite dominance together, since they have usually been regarded as alternative approaches to decisionmaking; indeed many of the pluralist models were constructed in direct opposition to notions of the hegemony of a "power elite." Nevertheless elite domination and incrementalism are not necessarily incompatible, for the ruling elites can choose to act in an incremental fashion. Failure to underscore this point probably reflects a tendency to extrapolate the experiences of the Western countries, in which incrementalism has been associated with a condition of dispersed power. Thus we need not presume that incrementalism is impossible simply because of elite dominance. There is another reason, however, why elite dominance may make a choice of incrementalism unlikely. Incrementalism is not written in the language of centralized power and the dominance of the central institutions of government. Beyond the problems this may create in terms of social costs, it may also be antithetical to elites who have been attracted to an ideology that favors public over private control and who themselves are intent on building state power as rapidly as possible. Incrementalism may also not seem "grand" enough to elites who want quick and dramatic results. As Hirschman commented several years ago,

> man may simply be unable to conceive of the strictly limited, yet satisfactory advances, replete with compromises and concessions to opposing forces which are the very stuff of "incremental politics." [26]

Incrementalism frequently tends toward drift and inertia. Marginal adjustments in familiar ways of doing things are not always sufficient in the face of new or major problems and may not even deal successfully with traditional problems over a period of time. Incrementalism also tends to favor short-term policies, be-

26. Albert O. Hirschman, *Development Projects Observed* (Washington, D.C.: The Brookings Institution, 1967), p. 33.

cause uncertainty about the future implies the need for prudence in committing resources much beyond a year or so. These characteristics of incrementalism create fundamental problems for many LDCs. Marginal adjustments without cumulative progress in a clear direction are obviously inadequate for countries that need major change. Piecemeal reform mongering is useful, but only if it is sustained and purposeful. In addition the short horizon of incrementalism may create a bias for consumption strategies that, once initiated, may be difficult to reverse.

Keehn's case study of Bolivian politics provides an interesting illustration of the limitations of pluralism within an underdeveloped country. Bolivia has a great deal of group conflict, but the result has been stalemate, not bargaining and compromise. There are no underlying consensus and no loyalty to the government: Consequently no group is willing to sacrifice to help another group or even to sustain the government. The central government is too weak to impose solutions and governs by promising something to everyone. Concessions, once granted, cannot be revoked. The government survives by heavy spending on consumption and sharp sacrifices in investment.[27]

With the political process in stalemate, and consumption demands rising, the options for the Bolivian government began to narrow. The government sought to expand its resources through additional foreign aid and foreign trade but was not sufficiently successful. It then tried deliberate inflationary policies by expanding the money supply, but this soon ran into a negative reaction from the International Monetary Fund (IMF). But the deflationary policies that the IMF imposed meant that the competition among groups now revolved around a smaller economic pie. The only other option seemed to be repression, tempered by occasional bouts of concession. The Bolivian case is almost a paradigm of the problems the LDCs have had and of the interaction between a weak domestic

27. Norman H. Keehn, "Building Authority: A Return to Fundamentals," *World Politics* 26, no. 3 (April 1974):331–52. The Bolivian case discussed by Keehn has some striking parallels with the Ceylonese case. See Robert N. Kearney, *The Politics of Ceylon (Sri Lanka)* (Ithaca, N.Y.: Cornell University Press, 1973).

political system and a difficult—but not completely hostile—international environment.

Kenworthy provides another perspective on the limitations of pluralism in underdeveloped societies. In Latin America, as development proceeds, there is sharp conflict between elites with different interests. Nevertheless the governments are incremental: They do not change much, not even the faces of the ruling elites. Governmental continuity is a result of an elite coalition in which competing or new elites are brought in, provided they are willing to play by the rules of the game. What goes on, then, is something of an oddity: competition between the elites that is limited by an agreement not to challenge too much of the status quo and that is ultimately a coalition of the elites against the masses. This coalition can last as long as it can hang together, as long as the masses do not perceive an alternative to submission, as long as the international system does not become actively hostile (as it may as a result of the oil crisis), and as long as a Castro does not emerge. Meanwhile the political systems stagnate and the economic systems are used for exploitation and corruption.[28]

These cases illustrate some of the problems implicit in incrementalism within the LDCs. Prudence, gradualism, building on what has been done, risking as little as possible—all these things seem sensible, especially in contrast to exaggerated notions of how the LDCs can improve their performances. But for the LDCs the central question is this: Can they achieve the procedural virtues of incrementalism if they cannot fulfill the underlying conditions that have made it a reasonable approach to decisionmaking—or to some kinds of decisions[29]—in complex, modern societies? Or, without these conditions, will incrementalism succeed only in sustaining structures of privilege and in rationalizing a commitment to do as

28. Eldon Kenworthy, "Coalitions in the Political Development of Latin America," in Sven Groennings, ed., *The Study of Coalition Behavior* (New York: Holt, Rhinehart and Winston, 1970), pp. 103–40. Kenworthy builds on the work of Charles W. Anderson, *Politics and Economic Change in Latin America* (Princeton, N.J.: Van Nostrand, 1967).

29. For a discussion of the kinds of decisions for which incrementalism might or might not be appropriate, see Rothstein, *Planning, Prediction and Policymaking in Foreign Affairs*, pp. 30–32.

little as possible? Finally, even if all the conditions of incrementalism could be met, would it be an adequate decisionmaking approach for countries that need rapid change?

I believe that no definitive answer to these questions is possible. It does seem clear, however, that a simple transfer of the surface aspects of incrementalism—its commitment to procedural agreement and to marginal adjustments in the status quo—is likely to be inadequate. The context of decision in the underdeveloped world is too frequently dominated by conflict, basic mistrust, and sharp resource scarcity to make the adoption of an incremental style much more than a facade for keeping the elite safely in power. Wildavsky's justification for "muddling through"—". . . one does the best one can at the time and hopes that future information will enable one to do better as circumstances change"[30]—is a "best" strategy likely to be insufficient when operated by insecure elites with insufficient resources.

Much of the earlier literature on development was so optimistic and oversimplified that it tended to obscure the need for modest and pragmatic decisionmaking approaches. In these circumstances it may be worthwhile to ask whether some of the more useful aspects of incrementalism can be salvaged or adapted to the needs of policymaking within the context of underdevelopment.

GETTING THERE FROM HERE

I am discussing a decisionmaking style appropriate only for routine or "normal" decisions. Crisis decisions must be dealt with in another fashion, probably by some form of intra-elite consultation. Fundamental decisions about the direction a society is to take or decisions that require the creation, acquisition, or application of massive resources are also likely to be well beyond the capacity of an incremental approach. Still, limiting the comments that follow to routine or normal decisions is not as restrictive as it might appear. Such decisions are obviously critical for states that do not confront

30. Aaron Wildavsky, "If Planning Is Everything, Maybe It's Nothing," p. 135. Wildavsky's criterion for decisionmaking is broad enough to encompass virtually any action, since one presumes not too many policymakers—beyond the stupid and the corrupt—seek to do less than the best they can.

an immediate and major crisis; performing the routine decisions well may be necessary to keep a crisis from developing. Moreover, even states with massive problems, like India or Bangladesh, are likely to have at least some areas of their political process in which a modest and pragmatic approach still makes a good deal of sense.

The necessity of beginning with elite needs and elite perceptions should be clear. The question is, what would make the more modest and procedural aspects of incrementalism attractive to the ruling elites? The answer for elites merely intent on staying in power in the present and increasing the probabilities for future tenure is that incrementalism may be a good coping strategy. In this sense, incrementalism may have a significant, though generally unappreciated, virtue: It avoids the inflation of expectations that has accompanied the initiation of other policies and may thus avoid the disappointment attendant upon policies modestly or partially successful. How effective incrementalism would be in these circumstances would probably be a function of how long "normal" politics, doing only what is good enough, could persist: whether, for example, the population growth rate undermined the ability even to run in place, or the revolution of rising expectations became truly revolutionary as a result of the demonstration effect or, worse yet, a decline in living standards sharpened the sense of relative deprivation. The fact that these developments are far from unlikely is one indication why merely coping, of seeking to be effective at staying in power, is not enough.

Whether the ruling elite must do more than concern itself with its own survival is a function of a number of variables. One variable is, of course, how secure the elite perceives itself. Insecure elites, however much other pressures may suggest the need for new approaches, are unlikely to be able or willing to be "distracted" by larger matters. Another variable is personal, for the Duvaliers and the Somozas are too corrupt for much more to be expected than an obsession with repression and self-interest. But other elites—the Nyereres and the Castros—are much more likely to seek some vision of the public interest. Probably most elites fall somewhere in between: Self-interest and the community interest are likely to be mixed together in complex ways. Finally the demonstration effect on the elites—the need to acquire status by growth and development—and external developments are likely to compel increasing attention to something beyond survival (or, perhaps, merely in order to survive). There is a paradox of being poor at work. Poorness implies dependence on the international system; conventionally the only way to reduce dependence (or to ease its costs) is rapid development, but development increases dependence, for it means more imports and more involvement with foreign technology and foreign patterns of behavior. For the leader who does not give up the struggle—either through isolation and self-reliance or through capitulation to an enclave economy dominated by foreigners—moving forward is the only alternative.[31] That means an increased concern with inducing change and with building the institutions to direct and control it.

The point at which the elite attempts to expand its concerns beyond self-survival is also the point at which incrementalism becomes increasingly problematic. This is especially true in an underdeveloped country where the adaptive and remedial responses that keep incremental policies functioning in developed countries may not exist. Two deficiencies are particularly acute: the absence of groups and institutions to provide signals about the success or failure of implementation and the tendency of incremental policies to "muddle around" (not "through") and not go anyplace in particular. In addition, if pervasive distrust exists among tribes or regions or classes, incrementalism (in the form of promises of even shares to all) may keep the pot from boiling over for a while, but it cannot work at removing the grievances that create the fire. Finally the process of change may have a momentum of its own, but it is apt to be discontinuous, erratic, and unfocused within an incremental system.

The tendency in underdeveloped political systems dominated by a few elites or a single leader is for policies to be imposed by the center on outlying areas. Incrementalism without strong groups or institutions is unlikely to alter this perspective. The only way to

31. The general unattractiveness of all the conventional strategies open to the elites is one reason why strategies of self-reliance and redistribution—which imply leaving the international system—have become so prominent.

preserve the useful virtues of incrementalism in these circumstances is by a deliberate effort to consult with local groups and have many policies originate in and under the control of local or regional interests. What this suggests, I believe, is the need to bring together planning and incrementalism.

This effort to tie together two different approaches to policymaking may seem inherently contradictory. I believe this to be true, however, only if we define planning and incrementalism in a fashion that predetermines the issue. If we are reasonably precise about the meanings to be ascribed to the terms, a large part of the contradiction disappears. In fact I believe there is no necessary contradiction at all between some forms of planning and some aspects of incrementalism, for I see no reason why a planning group cannot be a useful part of an incremental system.[32]

Centralized, long-range planning is virtually impossible for political systems with sharp cleavages and low levels of technical competence. I have suggested the need for more modest, decentralized forms of planning that are more likely to be politically acceptable and technically feasible. These local efforts are, however, unlikely to lead to cumulative progress unless they are joined to an effort by the national government to establish and implement more general goals for the society: not merely goals that choose between, say, rapid growth or redistribution, but also goals that attempt to provide benefits not limited to particular groups. The national plan and the local plans need not be tightly integrated; what is necessary—or possible—is an indicative national plan that provides guidance and direction for the local planners, not control. But the possibilities of conflict between the two sets of goals are likely to be diminished if the government disposes of enough resources to induce compliance on the part of local planners—and if, of course, its commitment to benefit all groups is credible and sustained. Given existing levels of distrust between the capital and outlying areas, this may mean that in the short run the balance will have to be tipped in favor of local interests until the central government is perceived as authoritative and not merely powerful. It might also be useful to consider central

32. I have argued this in the context of the American political system in *Planning, Prediction and Policymaking in Foreign Affairs*.

control of what used to be called the "commanding heights" of the economy to ensure that the national and local plans are not merely exercises in rhetoric, with real power exercised by the owners of a few critical industries.

There is a resemblance—and one would not want to suggest more—between my suggestions and what has been called "concertation" in Europe. Coombes notes that *concertation*

> is a method of making the exercise of the power of government to manage the national economy more representative by obliging government to consult the main "economic forces" . . . before taking economic decisions. However, the process of consultation is also seen as a means whereby the power of government over the national economy can be extended. . . . Thus *concertation* may be said to give an extra arm to government to act in the public interest. . . .[33]

More specifically *concertation* also includes the ideas that economic decisions "should be coordinated in the light of some set of overall national economic objectives"; "that the individual objectives of corporations and groups should be set in terms of some general view of the common good"; and that "a form of public direction of the national economy is adopted which is intended to preserve individual freedom and de-centralization of economic decision-making by relying either on centralized forecasting without direct intervention, or on what have become known as 'soft' techniques of direct intervention (mainly consultation with those directly affected)." [34]

*Concertation* is an attempt to provide some of the advantages of a publicly controlled economy without a number of its disadvantages: excessive centralization, a lack of responsiveness, diminished entrepreneurial initiatives, and so forth. Quite clearly the elaborate forms of *concertation* that have developed in Europe are well beyond the capacities of the underdeveloped countries. Nevertheless, even in a more rudimentary form, *concertation* goes some way toward

33. David Coombes, " 'Concertation' in the Nation-State and in the European Community," in G. Ionescu, ed., *Between Sovereignty and Integration* (New York: Halsted Press, 1974), p. 87.
34. *Ibid.*, pp. 87–88.

correcting the deficiencies not only of centralized planning but also of the "muddling through" ethos of incrementalism. The way-wardness and drift, the loss of cumulative progress, that so frequently characterize incremental policymaking is here compen-sated by the existence of a national plan that provides direction and guidance for each policy decision. Rather than the automatic, "hid-den hand" incrementalism to which we are accustomed, we have a deliberate and conscious effort to take small and modest steps *per-sistently in a defined direction.* In addition, to compensate for the weakness of group structures in underdeveloped countries and for the exclusion of many groups from the decision process, we have an effort on the part of the national planners to consult with all groups, to indicate where the nation is heading, and to illustrate how local or regional plans fit into the national plan. This also means that some idea of the public interest will always be present against which to evaluate the efforts of different groups. Finally, to com-pensate for the distrust and fear of competing groups, much of the detailed planning must be left to local or regional areas.

The attempt to combine a loose and indicative national plan-ning, more detailed local plans, and a modest, pragmatic, and ex-periential style of implementation is neither easy nor, even in the best of circumstances, a panacea for policymaking deficiencies in underdeveloped countries. But some combination of approaches such as this is virtually compelled by the context of decision in poor, weak, and divided countries. This is especially so because such countries must still be able to respond to citizen demands that are inevitably rising, though probably not at a revolutionary pace. An incremental response seems to me the only viable way to make policy in these circumstances, but only if it is also joined to a na-tional vision of some sort, and only if the elite is itself committed to creating a better future for their fellow citizens. The point, I think, is that this incremental system with planning has a reasonable chance of effective policymaking. But effectiveness is only one of the values that the elite must seek; they must also seek to legitimize their rule not only by functioning competently but also by receiving the loyalty and support of the masses. They can do this only by con-vincing the masses that the government is actively seeking the public good and by evincing some reciprocity in their own behavior—by attacking corruption, by refusing to govern for the benefit of special interests, and by living in a style that is neither luxurious nor decadent.

Laying out the conditions for success of the policymaking approach we have been discussing illuminates the difficulties of the task before the LDCs. The approach itself, however wise or sensible it may be, does not "solve" the decisionmaker's problems: The decision to choose one action rather than another in the practical world must rest on individual judgment, not the application of one or another conceptual scheme. Beyond this, even if by some sleight of hand the scheme could be applied directly to the practical realm, a perfectly functioning policymaking system still could not protect an underdeveloped country against unfavorable external developments. At best the policymaking system could lessen whatever costs have to be paid and perhaps speed the time of recovery—but no more. And, of course, we have been talking only about the range of "normal" decisions, not crisis decisions.

None of these qualifications should be taken to imply that conceptual schemes are useless. What such schemes do is to affect the ways in which we perceive and think about particular issues and to limit the range of alternatives considered. These are powerful influences, even if they do not permit us to choose A rather than B. Furthermore, for the LDCs confronted with new and complex problems, and with neither adequate knowledge nor useful experience, even thinking about the problems of policymaking in a coherent fashion may be useful, for discussion and analysis of these issues is surely preferable to stumbling along from one crisis to another.

Apart from the impact of the international system, the factor most likely to affect the success or failure of any LDC political system is the vision and commitment of its elites. They must want to do more than cope with their own problems of survival, and they must not be deluded into the belief that there are magical methods by which the problems of the present can be quickly and painlessly overcome. For elites with a proper sense of what can and needs to be done, this means some attempt to balance costs and benefits and not simply, as has been true in the past, an attempt to minimize costs, whatever the benefits.[35]

One final point. Both implicitly and explicitly, the foregoing comments have rested on an assumption about the possibility of reform. It seems to me that, when the "Third World" is disaggregated into more specific groups, there are a substantial number of countries for whom slow and steady progress is both a real possibility and a reasonably satisfactory response to the demands placed upon the government. At any rate, most of these countries ought to be exerting some effort to ensure that they at least get this much progress, for they are not likely to get much more (except, for a while anyway, a few mineral and fuel producers). It also seems true to me that there are countries with elites too corrupt or inefficient to make reform a sensible option—it is more a euphemism for inaction—or countries whose problems, for a variety of reasons, have got well beyond the range of normal policy action. For these two groups of states, revolution or some form of radical socioeconomic change may be likely. No one familiar with the record of revolutions can view this prospect with much enthusiasm; however, compared to perpetuation of a repressive and degrading status quo, the revolutionary impulse is not only understandable but also arguably justified. The developed countries ought at least to be willing to be agnostic about whether revolution in these circumstances is necessarily bad (or good) and about whether it is or is not in their national interest.

---

We shall now see what relevance these general comments on politics and policymaking have for the external orientations open to the developing countries. The decision to choose one orientation rather than another must rest on more than a single judgment about

35. The fact that military coups are likely to continue to be prominent parts of the Third World landscape is one reason why the system I have described may never be tested: The military seem to be psychologically averse to the kinds of consultation and bargaining I have discussed; they are predisposed toward central control; and repression is simply too salient an alternative for those who control the available force.

its relationship to existing policymaking capacities. Nevertheless the ability to implement a particular choice is a critical variable, not simply because it determines the range of likely results, but also because it has a significant effect on which groups will gain most (or lose most) in which time period.

# 8

## Taking a Stand: Orientations toward the External World

Choosing an external orientation is a critical and complex decision for poor and weak countries. It is critical because the external world seems to provide poor countries simultaneously with opportunities to diminish their disadvantages and enhance their advantages and with risks of losing even more autonomy or distributing national income (and national tastes) in even more inappropriate ways. And it is complex because the decision must balance all the considerations we have discussed: the security of the ruling elites and their attitudes toward the international systems, the economic assets and level of development of each country, the capabilities of the policy-making system, and some judgments about the results that various policies have achieved in the past and their prospects in the future.

One illustration of the complexities involved may be useful. A number of analysts have underscored the significance of one basic point: Given the intimate connections between internal and external policies, a sensible external policy is not possible unless the ruling elites have a clear conception of what results they want to achieve from the performance of the domestic economy. The consequences of failing to make this judgment are readily apparent in the almost reflex decision to concentrate on rapid growth and industrialization. There was little understanding that this decision was bound to create more dependence on the industrial countries. If the trade-off between rapid industrialization and dependence had been more clearly perceived, perhaps efforts to improve the terms of the trade-off by diversification might have been attempted. Instead, apparently surprised at increasing degrees of dependence, the ruling elites jumped from strategy to strategy, frequently seeking incompatible ends, or gave up and accepted unnecessarily large degrees of dependence.

From this perspective there is a range of goals that the ruling elites must choose between. Rapid industrialization might make sense for some. For others, raising per capita consumption rates might be more imperative. Equity in income distribution might be a parallel but not identical goal. Or the government might seek transformation of the socioeconomic structure it has inherited. There is some possibility that any or all of these goals might establish better grounds in the long run for reduced dependence than the quest for rapid growth does. But even this is not completely clear, for only theories of autarky take the reduction of dependence as the central goal, and other costs or trade-offs are associated with autarky. More advanced economies may use entirely different criteria of judgment and seek primarily national strength, full employment and price stability, or a balance in international transactions.

The need to establish priorities among such divergent goals, and to do so before an orientation toward the international division of labor is established, seems virtually self-evident—in the abstract. In practice, however, the difficulties are enormous, for a variety of reasons. For example, much of the country's external policy may already be determined by inherited patterns of interaction, and change to new patterns can only be slow and costly for countries with few resources and minimal flexibility. Priorities may also be difficult to establish, not simply because goals cannot easily be disentangled—not only economic goals but also political and social goals—but also because many of the trade-offs cannot be calculated at all and because the pressures of the present are frequently so overwhelming that taking a quick gain against potentially larger longrun costs may seem imperative.

I have made these points to highlight the extent to which any analysis of the factors affecting particular orientations toward the external world is bound to oversimplify the process of choice: Even a narrow discussion of a single decision cannot definitively isolate and weigh all the factors in play. Consequently the three major orientations I discuss in this and the next chapter—closed, open, and a more recent orientation toward redistribution and self-reliance— must be understood as ideal types. I doubt the existence of a "pure" case of any type (although perhaps China or Burma are or have been close), which is hardly surprising for weak states exposed to so many different pressures. More critically, I suggest adaptations in which the open orientation becomes more influenced by redistributive concerns and in which the emphasis on redistribution and self-reliance is sharply modified to take account of possible external gains. Nevertheless it is useful for analytic purposes, and perhaps even for more practical efforts to establish relative priorities, to remember that there are important "more or less" distinctions between each of these choices and that they provide some guidance in efforts to develop coherent and consistent approaches to the external world.

In what follows I comment on the economic arguments usually raised for or against each choice, on the results that have ensued from each choice, on the political factors that have affected elite decisions in each case, and on the relationship of each choice to the policymaking system I advocated in the last chapter. I reserve for chapter 10 more detailed forecasts of which countries might actually choose which orientation.

## THE CLOSED, INWARD ORIENTATION

Large numbers of developing countries adopted policies of import substitution industrialization in the 1950s. Pessimism about the export prospects for primary products, fluctuations in export prices, the impact of World War II shortages, and the presumed "linkage" superiority of manufacturing over primary products all played some part in popularizing this version of the closed orientation.[1] Perhaps

1. See Barend A. DeVries, *The Export Experience of Developing Countries* (Washington, D.C.: World Bank Staff Occasional Papers, No. 3, n.d.).

even more important were the psychologic and political aspects of the decision. Industrialization, especially symbolic industrialization (steel plants, auto industries, etc.), was much in fashion, and industries could be built only behind heavy tariff protection. Nationalism also provided support for acquisition of the current symbols of status and prestige in economic development. Finally, as I have already argued in chapter 3, import substitution was a relatively easy choice to make for weak and insecure governments: It appeared to attack primarily foreign interests (all the while allowing them in through another gate), and it provided the ruling elite with a reasonably short-term possibility of developing resources that it controlled and could dispense to friends and allies.

The inward orientation means that production must be aimed at the domestic market. Since this market is obviously smaller than the market that could be provided by the international division of labor, a closed economy, by definition, is a second-best choice. The first goal of this strategy is to cut imports as sharply as possible. The means to do so include high tariffs, import quotas, and multiple exchange rates. Centralized control of the economy is also normally necessary to ensure that only critical imports are allowed into the country and that the domestic price structure is manipulated in favor of urban manufacturing interests.

Economic costs are attached to all of these policies, but there are also a few economic benefits. Streeten, for example, stresses the learning effects of doing for oneself by doing without; moreover domestic, not external, demand determines the structure of production, and indigenous, not foreign, technology must be developed and applied.[2] Consequently, at some future date, import substitution might actually increase the possibility of export expansion, since an industrial base may have been created, and also provide technical support for the expansion of agricultural productivity. Seers observes that an inward orientation necessitates fewer outside experts and *may* also succeed in attracting better terms from the few

2. Paul Streeten, "Trade Strategies for Development: Some Themes for the Seventies," in Paul Streeten, ed., *Trade Strategies for Development* (London: Macmillan, 1973), p. 3.

foreign investors allowed in.[3] Still, these are not impressive benefits (or they are benefits not achieved by the policies followed) when they are arrayed against the costs and disabilities.

Sachs has argued that the developing countries have never really had a choice between an inward and outward orientation, but rather only a choice between an inward orientation and no growth at all—for the rich countries have closed their markets to manufactured exports from the poor.[4] This is both partially wrong, for some LDCs have managed to do quite well with manufactured exports, and oversimplified, for import substitution was not the result of any single development—external or internal. I have already pointed out the interaction between pessimism about export prospects and the political attractiveness of a strategy that seemed to be aimed at foreign economic interests. But one other factor behind the popularity of import substitution ought to be isolated. The ruling elites were intent on industrialization, irrespective of domestic economic circumstances, as a symbol of independence. Investment funds for *rapid* industrialization could not come from an industrial sector that did not exist, and foreign investment was either unacceptable or insufficient.[5] Thus the necessary funds had to be obtained from other sectors of the economy, which could be done only by a variety of unpleasant tactics—taxing rural interests unfairly, turning the terms of trade against agriculture, forcing the peasants to be a captive market for high-priced domestic products, and so on—all of which were part of a strategy of import substitution. In effect, if industrialization was the preeminent goal, and if it had to be accomplished quickly and without much external support, only a closed domestic market could be compelled to buy products likely to be overpriced and low in quality.

The results were unfortunate. The goods produced behind pro-

3. Dudley Seers, "The Other Road," *International Development Review* 9, no. 4 (December 1967):2–4.

4. Ignacy Sachs, "Outward-Looking Strategies: A Dangerous Illusion?" in Streeten, ed., *Trade Strategies for Development*, pp. 51–61.

5. I have underlined rapid because I do not imply that industralization is an unwise policy—in general. The central issue really concerns timing, that is, whether industrialization should have been delayed until more of the prerequisites for success were present.

tective walls frequently tended to cost a good deal more than the imports they replaced. The higher consumer prices might have been justified if the new industries created more employment opportunities or generated "spread effects" in other areas. These supplementary effects did not occur, because much of the new industry was capital intensive and inefficient. Exports of both new and traditional products were also hurt. The new products were too costly, and technology and quality control were not sufficient to penetrate foreign markets. Traditional exports were hurt by the high cost of inputs and overvalued exchange rates. Consequently, as soon as the small domestic market was saturated, the closed strategy was in trouble—stuck with inefficient, high-cost domestic industries, unable to export, burdened by corrupt and/or inefficient administrative structures, and, above all, still dependent on ever more necessary imports to operate the new industries.[6]

Regional cooperation seemed to be a rational response to these problems. For example, a number of radical analysts of African development problems argued for a continental or Pan-African closed strategy of industrialization.[7] But these and other efforts foundered for a variety of political and economic reasons. In any case, given the limitations of the economies that were supposed to cooperate, regionalism was not likely to create enough prosperity to overcome the deficiencies of closed, national economies. Regionalism did not, moreover, necessarily diminish the area's degree of dependence, since the prime beneficiaries were frequently foreign companies. Carefully and prudently negotiated, regionalism can play a meaningful role in economic development; it cannot save the members of an agreement from the need to solve their own problems.

There is also a difference between regionalism in conjunction

6. Bela Balassa has a number of important critiques of the inward orientation, from which I have benefited. See, for example, "Development Strategies in Semi-Industrial Countries," (Washington, D.C.: World Bank, Economics Department Working Paper No. 34, June 1969).

7. See especially Reginald Green and Ann Seidman, *Unity or Poverty—The Economics of Pan-Africanism* (Baltimore: Penguin Books, 1968); and Samir Amin, "Development or Structural Change: The African Experience, 1950–1970," *Journal of International Affairs* 24, no. 2 (1970):203–23.

with a closed strategy and in conjunction with an open strategy. An inwardly oriented strategy, even at the regional level, may not create a sufficiently large market, if only because the individual national markets are so badly integrated. Thus the regional market may also be "stuck" below the most advanced levels of industrial development. Perhaps more critically, at least in the long run, it is not clear that a world of autarchic or near-autarchic regions will create a workable international order. Beyond obvious losses in welfare, the potential for conflict over resources and markets both within and between regions may rise rather sharply. In effect a closed form of regionalism may not only provide few economic benefits but also generate potentially dangerous global economic conflicts. But it has not yet been possible to negotiate a more open form of regionalism, because few industries have really wanted to face international competition, and harmonization agreements (about which countries are to get what industries) have not been very successful.

The popularity of an economic strategy that promised so little and produced even less cannot be understood in wholly objective terms. Ultimately, I think, a good part of the explanation must lie with the fact that most of the LDCs wanted something more than economic growth—and perhaps even something more, though never anything less, than elite security. What they especially wanted was a reduction in external dependence. This is surely an understandable goal for a group of new and weak states that had just emerged from a period of colonial subjugation. Within limits, it was also a reasonable goal, since diversification and a reduction of market concentration were both possible and sensible. But most of the elites also wanted a rapid and tangible indication of autonomy and equality. This was an impossible goal. If it had to be sought, however, the only means to do so was industrialization. Once rapid industrialization was perceived as a means to end dependence, or to appear to do so, whatever economic policies the LDCs adopted were asked to square the circle—to perform tasks they were incapable of doing. The reasons for this, simply stated, were that industrialization required more (and more critical) imports, which meant more dependence.

*[235]*

I do not mean to suggest that industrialization was an inherently wrong goal. The correlations between wealth and industrialization are too strong to suggest that the LDCs should have remained content with exporting primary products.[8] The real issue was not whether to industrialize but how and when. This was especially true given elite commitments to rapid growth, which suggests that industrialization would have been favored even if the correlations with wealth were nonexistent. The LDCs, by moving rapidly and prematurely, could only create an industrial base that was inefficient, dominated by foreign interests, and injurious and inequitable to the other sectors of the economy. They were also compelled to use capital-intensive technology and were too much in a hurry to worry about whether the industries they developed had any long-term comparative advantages. They never made any serious attempt to consider whether they would need to devise a new pattern of industrialization because of their own special circumstances and the existence of so many more advanced countries; they plunged in and hoped for the best. Unfortunately, whereas more developed political and economic systems might have got enough early warning signals to slow the process before it got out of hand, the LDCs were forced to operate with systems that found stumbling forward the easiest option—for a while.

By the early 1960s many of the LDCs that adopted some form of the closed strategy began to move toward an outwardly oriented strategy.[9] The failures of the closed strategy *as it has been practiced*

8. Specializing entirely in agriculture (and thus importing all industrial needs) is not really possible, because, among other things, as incomes rise a smaller proportion of income is spent on food and a larger proportion on industrial goods and services. Also, all the working population could not be employed in agriculture; note, for example, that advanced countries that have specialized in agricultural exports (Australia, Denmark) have only a low proportion of the labor force in agriculture (10–20 percent, as against 70–80 percent in the LDCs). In fact, industrialization and an increase in agricultural productivity (which provides surplus food for industrial workers and increases demand for industrial products) have tended to complement each other in the past. These complex connections were never adequately analyzed by the LDCs, primarily because the elites were interested in industrialization as a symbol of autonomy and modernity.

9. See Benjamin J. Cohen and Gustav Ranis, "The Second Postwar Restructuring," in Gustav Ranis, ed., *Government and Economic Development* (New Haven, Conn.: Yale University Press, 1971), p. 440.

*thus far* have been too salient to make it a likely choice for more than a handful of LDCs in the future, most of whom are likely to be large. Nevertheless several points are worth keeping in mind. First the psychologic pressures that made the reduction of dependence so critical a goal are still present; they only seek new forms. Second, the results that ensued again illustrate the dangers of overcommitting what resources a poor country has to a single policy, for the policymaking system has too little flexibility (or power) to alter course easily. Finally the decisionmaking style of the closed orientation stands in direct contradiction with the suggestions I have made in the last chapter. The almost exclusive emphasis on central control, the deliberate effort to benefit one group of citizens to the (presumed short-term) detriment of others, and the stress on physical rather than human capital at least provide illustrations of where we do not want to go in the years ahead.

## LOOKING OUTWARD

Stolper has argued that a small country never really has a choice between open or closed economies but only a choice of how open to be.[10] Certainly this seems true for any small country that is intent on rapid growth and that must remain within the international trading system. From this perspective the LDCs that did badly in the last 25 years did so because they followed incorrect policies (import substitution, multiple exchange rates, high tariffs, etc.), and not because of exploitation or dependence on the policies of the rich countries, or of multinational corporations, or of technology developed by and for the rich.[11]

Myint, for example, argues that Thailand, Malaysia, and the Philippines were more successful than Burma and Indonesia because they managed to achieve much higher rates of export growth

10. Wolfgang F. Stolper, *Planning Without Facts—Lessons in Resource Application from Nigeria's Development* (Cambridge, Mass.: Harvard University Press, 1966), p. 59.

11. For example, see H. Myint, "Economic Theory and Development Policy," *Economica* 34, no. 134 (May 1967):117–30.

and that their export performance was a direct reflection of outwardly oriented domestic economic policies.[12] The argument gains in force because the two groups of countries were exporting essentially the same set of primary products. In a similar fashion Berg attributes the success of the Ivory Coast to the open policies followed, and the failures of Ghana to its attempt to reduce dependence, move away from the market system, and adopt an inward orientation.[13] The Ivory Coast, presumably recognizing its limitations, concentrated on export promotion, private capital, and the market system. And, in contrast to some critics who have maintained that the Ivory Coast has achieved "growth without development" by selling out to foreign interests and their domestic allies and by sharply increasing income inequities, Berg argues that the Ivory Coast has actually become less dependent by accepting the inevitability of its dependence: It has diversified its exports, opened new markets, and begun to spread the benefits of growth around.[14]

The policies associated with an outward orientation are, in a sense, simply the obverse of those associated with an inward orientation. Tariffs or other restrictions on trade are reduced or eliminated, orthodox monetary and fiscal policies are followed (e.g., devaluation rather than multiple exchange rates), domestic competition is encouraged, exports are promoted (usually by subsidies), and foreign capital, foreign aid, and foreign experts are encouraged and accepted.[15] No distinction is made between domestic

12. *Ibid.*, p. 121. See also Bela Balassa, "Industrial Policies in Taiwan and Korea," in Luis Eugenio Di Marco, ed., *International Economics and Development* (New York: Academic Press, 1972). Balassa notes that Taiwan and South Korea had export growth rates of more than 9 percent per annum in the 1960s and that per capita incomes rose 6.5 percent per year compared to slightly more than 2 percent for non-oil-producing developing countries (p. 75).

13. See Elliot J. Berg, "Structural Transformation versus Gradualism: Recent Economic Development in Ghana and the Ivory Coast," in Philip Foster and Aristide R. Zolberg, eds., *Ghana and the Ivory Coast: Perspectives on Modernization* (Chicago: University of Chicago Press, 1971), pp. 187–230.

14. *Ibid.*, p. 222. But the statistics on which some of these judgments are based do not appear very reliable. In addition a number of critics contend that the Ivory Coast's prosperity is misleading and bound to be short-lived. Thus value judgments are once again in conflict here.

15. Oscar Braun, "The External Economic Strategy: Outward or Inward Looking?" in Dudley Seers and Leonard Joy, eds., *Development in a Divided World* (Harmondsworth: Penguin Books, 1970), pp. 151–73.

and foreign producers: Nationalism is a luxury, so the argument goes, that the LDCs cannot afford. The outward orientation presumably also engenders benefits from the indirect socioeconomic effects of openness. There are potential educational effects from imitating and learning how the successful operate.[16]

The countries that adopted outwardly oriented strategies constituted a rather unusual group. Some, like Singapore and Hong Kong (and Puerto Rico), really had no choice. Others, like Taiwan, South Korea, and Israel, confronted external threats that required tacit or real alliances with the United States; they had no prospects of regional integration, they possessed labor forces that were highly educated and motivated, and they had strong leadership. Finally, others, like the Ivory Coast and Senegal, had leaders who were strongly pro-West, were very much aware of the distance between their own societies and Western societies, and consequently seemed willing to accept a continuing period of external dependence. In political terms, for a variety of reasons, most of these leaders were in strong control of their countries and were not confronted with powerful vested interests intent on monopolizing a protected domestic market.

Few other LDCs have many of these advantages. The absence of serious external threats, vested interests reluctant to face competition, unskilled labor forces, and insecure ruling elites prevent an easy conversion to an open economy. Little, Scitovsky, and Scott make the point that the switch is easiest when output and income are on the rise.[17] This may not be true, however, for rising income may only confirm the elites' commitment to the status quo. There are also enormous difficulties in turning full-scale policy commitments around in policymaking systems that have insufficient power or resources to adapt to new circumstances or to compensate potential losers. In any case, since few LDCs who have followed closed strategies have achieved much prosperity, the point may be moot: The closed strategy may create conditions only for its own perpetuation, at least until the situation becomes desperate. By then, of

16. Streeten, "Trade Strategies for Development," p. 3.
17. Ian Little, Tibor Scitovsky, and Maurice Scott, *Industry and Trade in Some Developing Countries* (London: Oxford University Press, 1970), p. 390.

course, matters may have got beyond rescue by any shift in domestic policy.

The critics of the outward orientation have gone much beyond the argument that few developing countries have the power, the stability, or the skills to risk exposure to the international environment. The critics have also asserted that the results would be bad even if the LDCs could make the switch. Helleiner, for example, argues that joining the international division of labor can have a whole range of potential costs: the "backwash" effect, in which the LDCs become appendages of the more developed economies; an export bias that hinders the creation of an integrated, national economy; socioeconomic stratification as the gains from trade are inequitably distributed; the destruction of indigenous entrepreneurs by an influx of imports; a lowered savings rate as a result of the demonstration effect; overrapid use of exhaustible resources; and a decline in the terms of trade.[18] Others have also argued that the effort to promote exports has a negative distributional effect, for the same two groups benefit as in import substitution: entrepreneurs and elite workers.[19] There are also problems on the supply side of the equation. As Streeten has pointed out, the LDCs have few entrepreneurs to respond to international market signals, their governments are administratively weak, and nationalist sentiments still strongly oppose foreign capital and free trade.[20]

Others have argued that it is impossible for the LDCs to deal equitably with an external market in which there is a high rate of change in demand and a high rate of obsolescence for capital investments. To adopt a policy of export promotion in these circumstances is difficult, because even if the developing countries manage to promote exports with good elasticities of demand—"export substitution"—comparative advantage is likely to be very dynamic.

18. G. K. Helleiner, *International Trade and Economic Development* (Baltimore: Penguin Books, 1972), p. 18. A slightly different list of the costs of belonging to the system can be found in Thomas E. Weisskopf, *Capitalism, Underdevelopment and the Future of the Poor Countries* (New York: World Law Fund Occasional Papers, 1972).

19. This point is not everywhere accepted, for some have argued that an export orientation is superior on income distributional grounds to the extent that the exports are labor intensive. I comment on this point later.

20. Streeten, "Trade Strategies for Development," pp. 18 ff.

This means that the LDCs would have continually to adjust their production structure in response to changes in demand, and the costs could be high. Frances Stewart has argued that each change is also likely to be more capital intensive and to continue patterns of dependence on foreign technology. Export promotion is thus doubly bad: It is inappropriate for production, because the processes are capital and skill intensive and reflect the size of the industrial economies, and it is inappropriate for consumption, because the products created and consumed reflect the taste of consumers (or advertisers) in rich countries.[21]

These criticisms fall into two patterns. One set points to the intrinsic weaknesses of underdeveloped countries that make it extremely difficult for such countries to compete effectively in a free trading system. These are not, however, either/or weaknesses: That is, there are sharp differences in capacity between different underdeveloped countries, and there are also significant prospects of improvement through learning for many LDCs that follow open economic policies. The second set of criticisms is more fundamental, asserting that an LDC should not participate in the international system, even where it might be able to do so effectively, for the result is bound to be increased dependence, an inequitable distribution of income, and an inappropriate structure of production.[22] The result is a production structure keyed to foreign demand—and perhaps owned by foreign capital—and the absence of much domestic motivation to change the internal socioeconomic system. Few meeting grounds exist between these two sets of criticisms, for success in overcoming the first set of weaknesses—as, say, in the Ivory Coast or South Korea—does not dilute the charge that the success rests on false grounds, that it is merely "growth without development." A value conflict could be deflected over time, if it could be shown that the values are not actually in conflict; it cannot be

21. Frances Stewart, "Trade and Technology," in Streeten, ed., *Trade Strategies for Development*, pp. 252–53.

22. Guy Hunter, *The Best of Both Worlds?"* (London: Oxford University Press, 1967), notes that the industrial sector in Africa has been isolated from the rest of the economy, has been capital intensive, and has had little multiplier effect on the rest of the economy (pp. 30–32).

deflected by showing improved performance on variables perceived as irrelevant or pernicious.[23]

Other criticisms of the outward orientation could make the debate on its domestic consequences essentially irrelevant. If the underdeveloped countries all adopted an outward orientation and began rapidly increasing their exports to the rich countries, how long would it be before the rich countries responded by closing their markets? We have already seen in chapter 5 the limited generosity and the escape clauses written into the preferential schemes negotiated between the rich and the poor countries. And many critics have asserted that the rich countries will react negatively when—and if—the growth rate of LDC manufactured exports goes much above 10–15 percent per year.[24] Moreover, most of the LDC manufactured exports have been concentrated in a few areas of labor-intensive production that compete with strongly entrenched politicoeconomic interests in the developed countries. Optimism about the prospect for manufactured exports by the LDCs has thus rested, not only on the hope of diversification to products with better elasticities of demand, but also on the hope that the developed countries would gradually move out of areas in which they were no longer competitive. But declining growth rates in the industrial countries, much predicted of late, may make it much more difficult to convince labor unions and their political supporters of the necessity of ceding some areas of production to more competitive foreign workers.

Several LDCs have done reasonably well by increasing exports of primary products that happen to be in high demand. Most LDCs have not possessed such favorable prospects for their primary product exports and have also faced heavy population pressures in the agricultural sector. Only the export of manufactured products has seemed a way out of this bind, both in the sense of providing nec-

23. This may make the issue of income distribution even more important, for it is a value in both orientations—although at different time periods. Unfortunately the data remain too ambiguous to convince minds not already made up. See note 33 below.

24. See Thomas Patrick Melady and R. B. Suharto, *Development—Lessons for the Future* (Maryknoll, N.Y.: Orbis Books, 1973), pp. 16 ff.; see also Mahbub ul Haq, "Developing Country Alternatives" and Ignacy Sachs, "Outward-Looking Strategies" in Streeten, *Trade Strategies for Development*.

essary foreign exchange and in providing jobs for new workers and migrants from rural areas. A small group of relatively advanced developing countries—some of whom, like Argentina, Mexico, Brazil, and Taiwan, are now described as "semi-industrial"—have done very well with such exports (at least in terms of growth rates, if generally much less in terms of income distribution). The great majority of LDCs have, however, manufacturing sectors that constitute a small part of their GNP. In addition what manufactures they do have tend to be in simple products, to be foreign owned (which means their primary effect is only on local wages), and in many cases to be above world market prices (and thus sellable only to partners in protected regional arrangements).[25]

Obviously these LDCs have only a minute share of the international market for manufacturing exports. In terms of future prospects, this is not necessarily bad. Apart from the handful of LDCs with large domestic markets and a small share of any international market—which means that they can try either an inward or outward orientation—most LDCs must export to enjoy any substantial degree of prosperity. But an orientation to the external world reflects something more than economic size and economic attitudes; a country's international trading position is also important. In this sense small countries with a small share of an international market may have more change to improve their own export performance than a small country with a large share of an international market.[26] Ceylon in tea, Malaysia in tin and rubber, Chile and Zambia in copper, and Chana in cocoa are already so important in their markets that efforts to expand production and sales are likely to meet instant resistance. This seems to imply that the LDCs with small shares of the market for manufactured goods have some potential for increasing their exports before, so to speak, anyone notices. This brings us, however, to the final argument used against the outward orientation, for it is clear that this potential for expanded exports rests not only on the receptivity of the rich countries but also on the willingness and ability of the LDCs themselves to avoid duplicating each other's efforts.

25. See especially Haq, "Developing Country Alternatives."
26. See DeVries, *The Export Experience of Developing Countries*, pp. 56–57.

The need for coordination among the LDCs rests on the fact that they tend to have comparative advantage in the same labor-intensive goods. This could easily lead to oversupply and a consequent fall in the terms of trade for these exports (unless the industrial countries get out of labor-intensive production quickly, which is uncertain).[27] There is some evidence of a tendency among the LDCs to copy each other's successes, which considerably exacerbates the problem: Not only are the same products manufactured, but also agreements to harmonize production are politically difficult because of the discontent of the workers and employers in industries that have to be ceded to other poor countries.[28] At any rate, production for domestic consumption under import substitution, concentration on the same simple products (textiles, plastic goods, shoes, cement), and the need to feature industries that do not require much capital investment lead to similar patterns of output.

In the last decade there has been a great deal of discussion of the possibility of new, labor-intensive manufactured exports of a particular kind: process and component specialization within vertically integrated international manufacturing firms (e.g., electronics assembling processes). The internationalization of production and marketing means that the LDCs, because of low wage scales and other advantages, could do more than supply necessary raw materials; they would provide the part of an international manufacturing process that rested on unskilled, labor-intensive technology. Note for example, that 27 percent of the increase of United States' imports from the LDCs in the last few years has come from such component specialization.[29]

This is an important development, but it does not eliminate the problems we have been discussing. Helleiner notes:

> There may exist unexploited opportunities for small countries to enter these markets in what, for the world market, is a

27. This may provide grounds for another conspiracy theory argument for radical intellectuals: The advanced countries give up only industries that many LDC's can develop and thus drive prices down even further.

28. See the "Introduction" in Theodore Morgan and Nyle Spoelstra, eds., *Economic Interdependence in Southeast Asia* (Madison: University of Wisconsin Press, 1969), pp. 19–20.

29. G. K. Helleiner, "Manufactured Exports from Less-Developed Countries and Multinational Firms," *The Economic Journal* (March 1973):30.

modest way but for them may be a quite significant degree
. . . if all small countries adopt such policies on the assumption that their individual impact upon the world market for
labour-intensive manufactures will be small, the total impact
may nevertheless be large and may generate the market barriers which each alone could successfully have avoided.[30]

The internationalization of production also does not mean that nationalist reactions by the developed countries will not occur. Lowered growth rates may engender protests by labor unions and labor-
intensive industries that they are being impoverished by "run-
away" factories and substandard wage rates in the poor countries.
In addition developing countries concerned with reducing dependence and improving the distribution of income may not welcome
industries that usually form an isolated enclave within their economies, that make them even more dependent on a production and
marketing process they do not control, and that tend to reward a
small group of entrepreneurs and their workers disproportionately.
Whether these considerations are true or not now, or whether they
are necessarily true in the future, may not be as important as that
they are likely to be perceived as true by many LDC leaders.

Multinational corporations (MNCs) are obviously not charitable
institutions. They will invest abroad only where certain economic
factors are present: low labor costs, limited economic distances from
important markets, and special concessions from the host governments. This means that only a limited number of LDCs are likely to
benefit from the internationalization of production and that competition among the LDCs who want to attract such investment is likely
to force increasingly onerous concessions. It should also be clear
that the decision by an MNC to invest is not entirely economic, for
political factors play a major role. The MNC investment is concen-

30: *Ibid.*, p. 27. In response to the last sentence in the quotation, and to similar
fears expressed by numerous other writers (see footnote 24 above), note that they
may be overemphasizing the dangers of a massive reaction from the rich countries: If
LDC manufacturing exports to the industrial countries expanded by 15 percent per
year, one group of experts has estimated this would still amount to only $28 billion
by 1980, or around 7 percent of manufactured imports by the industrial countries.
*Reassessing North–South Economic Relations* (Washington, D.C.: Brookings, 1972),
p. 13. The central point is that, even with high growth rates, the magnitude of the
change would not be overwhelming. Still what is probably critical here is that the
fear of a negative reaction by the rich countries is strong.

trated not only in a limited number of LDCs (about 20 countries get almost 80 percent of the total) but also in countries that are—or seem to be—politically stable and "reliable": for example, South Korea, Taiwan, Mexico, a number of Caribbean islands, Brazil, Venezuela, and Argentina.[31] This is likely to be particularly true in the context of component processing, for interruption of any part of the process may endanger production of the final product.

---

The argument between defenders and critics of the outward orientation seems inconclusive to me. One reason is that the arguments reflect different values, time horizons, and judgments about the future. In the abstract the proponents of an open economy and export promotion make a good deal of sense. Weak and poor states that want to establish high rates of growth and to industrialize as rapidly as possible must concentrate on the international market. Careful specialization in products for which there is some possibility of dynamic comparative advantage offers the prospect, not only of earning necessary foreign exchange, but also of establishing industries large enough to enjoy economies of scale. Rapid growth and industrialization require escape from the constraints of a small market; only competition in the international market place provides that escape.

One of the central issues in this discussion is the distribution of gains from the outward orientation. Are the profits from the export sector being used to help other sectors of society, or are they being wasted on luxuries? Some analysts have recently argued that an open economy is likely to promote more equitable income distribution because of the labor intensiveness of most Third World manufacturing exports. South Korea and Taiwan are usually cited in illustration. For example, the income of the lowest 40 percent of the population in South Korea increased 7–8 percent per year from 1964 to 1970 by concentrating on such exports. Yet these may be decep-

31. For breakdowns of the figures on MNC investment, see *Multinational Corporations in World Development* (United Nations: Department of Economic and Social Affairs, ST/ECA/190, 1973), p. 19. Note also that the MNCs usually demand higher returns on investments in the Third World than they do in Europe or the United States.

tive statistics, and not merely on technical grounds: One recent report from South Korea has argued that 7-day, 84-hour workweeks are common, that pay averages 22 cents an hour, and that Korea's growth has been based on exploitation of its labor force.[32] Income may have gone up, but not in proportion to hours worked or in sufficient compensation for brutal working conditions. But beyond this, there are other cases in which the income distribution figures themselves are a convincing indictment of the greed and corruption of the elites that dominate the export–import sector.

Immediate efforts to improve the quality of income distribution are relatively recent additions to the arguments for an open economy. Indeed until recently the emphasis has been on the necessity of shortrun inequality to enhance the possibilities of longrun equality. Consequently, since the new emphasis on redistribution is very much concerned with immediate efforts to improve the quality of life of the bottom 40 percent of the population, full-scale commitment to an open-economy, export orientation is unlikely unless the evidence that it is a superior redistributive approach becomes much more convincing—empirically and psychologically.[33]

I have already presented the other arguments that make an outward orientation seem dangerous. The domestic weaknesses that make international competitiveness improbable have to be eliminated: weak and corrupt administration, few entrepreneurs, vested interests intent on maintaining the profits protection brings, and so on. There has to be some optimism among the elites about how the developed countries will respond to expanded exports from the LDCs, and there has to be some willingness to accept *increasing* degrees of dependence on the international trading system. And there has to be some optimism about the possibility of agreement

32. See John Saar in the *International Herald Tribune,* February 13, 1976. I discuss other data on the distribution question in the next chapter. To be fair, one ought to note that the Taiwan case seems much stronger for the advocates of an open economy. But then the Chinese and the Japanese seem to be special cases for a variety of cultural and other reasons.

33. One recent study thus notes "that no reliable conclusions can yet be reached in the area of income distribution, and this applies equally to the relationship between income distribution and foreign trade strategy." Jagdish N. Bhagwati, "Protection, Industrialization, Export Performance and Economic Development" (Geneva: UNCTAD/MD/80, May 19, 1976), p. 31.

among the developing countries themselves not to duplicate each other's efforts.

I discuss the states most likely to adopt the outward orientation, despite its risks, in chapter 10. Here I note only that the most likely candidates will be the "success stories" of the past 10 to 15 years, that small group of developing countries who achieved high rates of growth by exporting manufactured goods to the rich countries. I believe some of the larger semiindustrial countries of Latin America—Chile, Argentina, Venezuela—will also slowly abandon some elements of the closed economy and begin moving toward an export orientation. Perhaps also some of the commodity exporters that have small domestic markets but large trading positions in a particular commodity will also be forced to become even more outwardly oriented: Since it will be difficult to expand traditional exports any further, some degree of industrialization (beginning with increased processing of commodity exports) is likely to become necessary. This industrialization program may be outwardly oriented, if only because of existing patterns of economic and political behavior.

How much a developing country benefits from an open strategy is likely to depend on its size and level of development. There is also, however, some potential benefit from an escalator process: As the most advanced LDCs move out of a market for a product (perhaps, like Japan, to a higher level of technology), the next most developed countries may move into the vacuum (say, Mexico and Brazil), and thus vacate a market for the next level down, more or less *ad infinitum*.[34] At any rate these countries have two hopes: that they can find (or continue) a pattern of industrialization viable in terms of their own limitations, whether by component specialization or some other means,[35] and that they will be the major benefi-

34. The problem with this rational picture of a linear game of musical chairs is that it is likely to get more difficult over time as the number of countries who join the game grow larger and similar in what they can produce. It is also implicitly optimistic about the adjustment behavior not only of the rich countries but also of the more advanced LDCs who will have to vacate industries in which they are losing comparative advantage.

35. Note that Little, Scitovsky, and Scott, *Industry and Trade in Some Developing Countries*, p. 390, admit that, even for the large LDCs they have studied, "Success has depended heavily on factors outside the control of the countries themselves"

ciaries of most of the reforms in trade, aid, and finance currently on the international agenda.

In terms of the analysis of policymaking in the last chapter, the outward orientation is problematic. Insofar as it avoids the centralized, detailed administrative control of the economy associated with the inward orientation, it also avoids the consequent inefficiencies, unresponsiveness, and corruption of overgrown and overwhelmed bureaucracies. Nevertheless the outward orientation also suffers from the defects of its virtues: There is no satisfactory mechanism by which to ensure that entrepreneurs invest wisely, or that weak or disaffected groups receive a fair share of national wealth, or that social costs and the public interest are properly weighed. Failure on the part of the ruling elites to seek to control private interests by articulating and implementing public goals is a good prima facie case against their commitment to development: Providing an outlet for the avarice of only the exporting classes is not sufficient.

The outward approach is essentially conservative. For some developing countries, whose problems have not yet reached the unmanageable stage, a slow and conservative, step-by-step approach is not necessarily inappropriate. Nor is it always necessarily wrong to welcome foreign capital or to give substantial leeway to private entrepreneurs. But this is also an approach that may be congenial to deradicalized elites who have more or less given up any hope of creating a national development strategy. The line between a moderate, step-by-step policy and a more corrupt posture in which merely staying in power and accommodating other domestic elites and foreign economic interests becomes the real goal is easily breached—especially by insecure elites who do not really believe their policymaking systems can be made to work effectively.

As a result I believe that an outward orientation cannot be justified in the unfettered way it has usually been implemented. Quick and fundamental change of such regimes does not seem possible to

(e.g., weather or the availability of enough foreign aid). The question for the LDCs is whether this risk is more or less acceptable in either economic or psychologic terms than the risks of self-reliance. And, apart from ideologies, there is no single, clear answer.

*[249]*

me, for they lack the power, the will, and the flexibility. But I think there are two directions in which such regimes can move, slowly but persistently, that might spread the economic benefits of the outward orientation more widely and deeply.

The first direction is toward a policymaking system that attempts to balance the necessary freedom for entrepreneurs against the need to establish national priorities and to incorporate local areas into the policymaking process. This was the theme of the last chapter. A policymaking system that lets entrepreneurs and foreign interests do what they will—on the ostensible presumption that someday everyone will benefit—is as pernicious as a system that relies only on central planning from the capital. No "pure" policymaking system is likely ever to be feasible in a developing country, and the attempt to create a mixed system that might be able to produce quick and steady gains may be more important than the attempt to create a system that produces large gains for only a limited number.

The second direction is toward more explicit concentration on redistribution. In a sense this is a mirror image of a suggestion I make in the next chapter. But here I believe it is necessary for the advocates of an open approach to go beyond a concern for the employment possibilities of labor-intensive exports. They must also indicate just how they intend to control the behavior of individual entrepreneurs so that benefits are widely shared. One might have more confidence in the virtues of the outward orientation if its supporters were also in the forefront of efforts to control corruption, to reform regressive tax systems, to control the behavior of multinational corporations, and to prevent domestic capital from disappearing into Swiss bank accounts.

———◆•••◆———

For a variety of reasons I doubt that the great majority of LDCs will adopt an outward orientation. Objectively many will be reluctant to do so because they lack the entrepreneurs and the other domestic requisites for successful international competition. Some of these states, among them perhaps the middle level of Latin American countries and some of the Southeast Asian states that have had a degree of success with primary product exports, may adopt a halfway house posture—controlled contact with the external world, careful selection of production possibilities with good elasticities of demand, and perhaps regional agreements on who is to specialize in what.[36] This is an extrapolation of the infant industry argument, in which temporary withdrawal from the system is justified until an industry becomes competitive. It is also only a partially closed system, not a complete attempt at import substitution.[37]

Criticism of the outward approach has tended to be too ideological and unbalanced. Even countries that adopt some form of the closed orientation will need imports to begin creating a relatively self-sufficient society—and that means they must improve their export prospects. In addition, for some of the more advanced developing countries that have already created a reasonably large manufacturing sector—and with many interests dependent on it—the outward orientation may be the most effective road not only to rapid growth but also to more equitable income distribution. At any rate, given the limitations of these societies, massive change

36. This implies a concern with comparative advantage, not between the LDCs and all the other states in the international system, but rather between the LDCs themselves who are in a regional system.

37. There is another factor that might make even the "success stories" somewhat doubtful about the risks of an outward orientation. This is that the fast-growing exporters of manufactures have been the biggest losers from the sharp rise in petroleum prices, primarily because many of the industries they have established depend on imported (cheap) oil. And they have also suffered heavily from the fall in demand for their exports (and not benefited from the short-lived commodity boom in 1973–74). Note the following table (adapted from various UNCTAD estimates):

| | Terms of Trade | | Trade Balance | | |
|---|---|---|---|---|---|
| | 1970–73 | 1973–74 | 1970 | 1973 | 1974 |
| | (percentage change per annum) | | (billions of dollars) | | |
| Major petroleum exporters | 10.4 | 160.6 | 6.7 | 17.4 | 107.0 |
| Other developing countries | 1.7 | −2.1 | −8.9 | −11.8 | −20.0 |
| Of which: | | | | | |
| Fast-growing exporters of manufactures | −2.4 | −13.4 | −4.7 | −7.1 | −13.9 |
| Others: | | | | | |
| GNP per capita more than $250 | 3.5 | 1.2 | −2.0 | −2.2 | −2.1 |
| GNP per capita less than $250 | 0.8 | 0.1 | −2.2 | −2.4 | −4.0 |

toward a different economic strategy may be improbable because of the strength of opposition forces and because of the inability of developing countries to alter policy commitments easily and painlessly. Consequently, in these cases, it may be more appropriate to seek to diminish the faults of the outward orientation, not to destroy it.[38]

I doubt that the poorer LDCs will move in an outward direction. They obviously lack the skills to compete effectively, and any attempt to do so among so many similarly situated countries is not likely to lead to much success. In any case, many of these countries have begun to reevaluate their economic strategies and to think about new economic goals. These new goals place much greater stress on an immediate improvement of living standards for the poorest citizens, on a more equitable distribution of income, and on sharp increases in agricultural productivity. In this new doctrine, which I discuss in the next chapter, growth and industrialization yield to equity and agriculture. And from this new perspective, both the inward and outward orientation are inadequate, for, whatever their other differences, they are still concerned with improving the rate of growth and achieving the optimal allocation of resources. Worse yet, both may increase the degree of inequality, the inward orientation by reducing demand for labor-intensive products, and the outward orientation by rewarding the factors of production that are most scarce, skills and capital.[39]

38. After writing this I read an important technical argument that corresponds very closely to what I have in mind here. Bela Balassa, *Reforming the System of Incentives in Developing Countries* (Washington: World Bank Staff Working Paper No. 203, 1975) argues convincingly for a series of changes in countries that have established an industrial base behind high protective barriers that would not only accelerate economic growth but also increase employment and improve the distribution of incomes. These changes would include the elimination of credit practices that favored large capital-intensive import-substitution projects, subsidies for the use of unskilled labor, reforms in the structure of protection, and other measures. Balassa also emphasizes the need to proceed gradually because of the opposition of vested interests and the dangers of industrial dislocation, both points with which I agree. One notes that this approach to redistribution differs from the more direct strategies discussed in the next chapter, but may well be the only politically feasible approach in relatively advanced developing countries.

39. See Streeten, "Trade Strategies for Development," p. 7 f. It should be noted, however, that a change toward labor-intensive component specialization might change this if the benefits were not limited to small industrial enclaves.

# 9

Revisioning Development—Redistribution,
Growth, and Self-Reliance

## THE VIEW FROM THE BOTTOM

The debate about the future of the underdeveloped countries began
to shift its ground in the late 1960s. What had been at issue in the
1960s were questions of success or failure: which countries had succeeded and which had failed, and why. But succeeded or failed at
what? The obvious answer was achieving satisfactory rates of economic growth and industrialization. So long as these were the
goals, the acquisition of sufficient foreign exchange to pay for necessary imports was imperative. Thus all of the strategies the LDCs
pursued—opening or closing their economies, seeking regional cooperation, demanding more aid and trade preferences—were variations on a single theme, for all the strategies were designed to provide the means by which rapid industrialization could be achieved.
And this also meant that relationships with the dominant members
of the international system, and the patterns of interaction they had
created, sharply affected the fate of the domestic economic policies
the underdeveloped countries sought to implement.

Conventional theory assumed that progress in the rich countries would be diffused to the poor countries. As long as demand
remained high in the rich countries, and as long as they did not
suffer high rates of unemployment, the demand for low-cost re-

sources and labor-intensive manufactures from the poor countries was bound to rise. Small amounts of foreign aid, as well as the skills and knowledge of foreign investors, would be the necessary catalysts to begin to fit the LDCs into the system. All of this, of course, rested on the assumption that the LDCs would follow outwardly oriented policies, for the wealth of the rich presumably could not be diffused through tariff barriers and overvalued exchange rates. Questions of income distribution and employment rarely arose, since they would be dealt with in the process of growth itself.[1]

There have always been critics who have asserted the irrelevance or inaccuracy of these views. But the critics never received much of a hearing from the audiences they needed to persuade—Western academics and policymakers, and the ruling elites of the LDCs themselves (with, of course, some notable exceptions like Nkrumah). Part of the reason was that those who benefit from the status quo are unlikely to see the need of altering conventional ways of behaving; the powerful do not establish patterns of behavior for either aesthetic or charitable reasons. Part of the reason also, I think, had to do with the fact that the LDCs had not been independent long enough to test the accuracy of either the conventional theory or its critics. Moreover, the critics tended to concentrate on imperialism—that is, on how the rich countries had behaved or must behave toward the poor countries—and thus lacked a development theory of their own. Certainly Marxism was something of an alternative but a problematic one. After all, Marxism had been tried only in a very large country, which cut the costs of self-sufficiency sharply; in any case, the Soviets sought the same goal, rapid industrialization, by the same means, capital accumulation, as the conventional theories. All of these conditions have now changed.

The rich countries themselves have begun to question the wis-

1. Thus Mahbub ul Haq, "Pakistan's Economic Choices for the 1970's" (unpublished paper, 1971), reports that, when Ayub came to power, the decision was made to devote "all the energies of the system towards a faster pace of economic development and to forget about the issues of more equitable distribution or a more democratic system of economic organization. The first priority was growth; the other questions will come later" (p. 2).

dom of "growthmanship." Environmental and ecologic costs of growth—"externalities"—are only part of the story. So, too, are rising fears of resource depletion and a declining faith in virtually automatic technologic fixes. Perhaps also a growing concern for the "quality of life," however ambiguous, or at least rising discontent with what affluence has provided, played a part. These factors, among others, have made it increasingly legitimate to question the conventional wisdom of growth.

The most significant change was, however, simply the condition of many underdeveloped countries after a decade or more in quest of rapid rates of growth. Surely some countries had done well, by some standards. Others obviously had done badly, and the immediate prospects of doing much better were not good—even before the oil crisis. Certainly the defenders of the conventional dogma about free trade, the international division of labor, and the diffusion of wealth had a reasonable response: So long as the LDCs wanted rapid growth, many of them had pursued policies that were inappropriate and misguided. And, they argued, the international trading system offered small states opportunities and advantages, direct and indirect, that they could not get anyplace else. Finally, they argued that rapid growth had led to more equitable income distribution in some countries and that what was really at issue was the trade-off between present and future employment.

The critics were not convinced, for they could argue that, even if the LDCs followed "correct" policies, the results could be—or were bound to be—disastrous. It was impossible to prove that the rich countries would continue to liberalize their trading system or increase (or even maintain) their generosity to the poor. It was also impossible to prove that very many LDCs could capitalize on whatever opportunities the international system provided, since it was a system constructed to reward virtues and skills that the LDCs did not possess (or possessed minimally) and that anyway required a degree of coordination and harmony among the LDCs themselves that was improbable. Still worse, the conventional growth theories were long-range theories; whatever the ultimate benefits, in the short run most of the gains were likely to be limited to a small group of Westernized elites and a small number of skilled workers.

## DOMESTIC POLITICS AND EXTERNAL CHOICES

The debate between advocates of inward and outward orientations thus seemed, from this perspective, to be increasingly irrelevant and to be a struggle within the small group of entrepreneurs and skilled workers who benefit from growth policies over the division of spoils. For the mass of peasants and urban unemployed the prognosis was increasing "marginalization." Income inequalities would increase, unemployment would surely continue to rise (especially because population growth rates were still astronomical in some countries and because so many of the industries already created were capital intensive), and a minimal and decent standard of life would be an ever-receding goal for too many people in too many places. The gains from growth were likely to be too small and too distant and pocketed by the wrong groups; the costs of growth, in contrast, were immediate and overwhelming.

Rational discussion, even recitation of one or another set of facts, is unlikely to settle the conflict between defenders and critics of what the international system can do for the poor, since the conflict is, in part, about conflicting values, and, in part, about divergent judgments of future behavior. Enough of the past record is reasonably clear, however, to indicate why growing numbers of development intellectuals began questioning the wisdom of doing either more of the same or more of what orthodox development theory ordains. This is not to say that the critics are necessarily right or wrong or that they have a reasoned alternative to the dogmas they now attack. It is only to insist that the reaction of the critics is neither irrational nor merely rhetorical posturing; it is also to say, as we shall see, that much of what they are saying makes a great deal of sense for at least some LDCs in some circumstances.

Whether any policy could have provided enough jobs to keep up with population growth rates of 2.5 percent per annum, or worse, is far from clear. At any rate, by the early 1970s expert analysts estimated that 25–30 percent of the labor force in the undeveloped world was underemployed or unemployed.[2] Even the success stories were not immune. Haq, for example, indicates that

2. See David A. Morse, "Employment and Development," in Andrew E. Rice, ed., *Development Targets for the 70's: Jobs and Justice* (Dobbs Ferry, N.Y.: Oceana, 1972), pp. 2–14.

Pakistan had a 6 percent per year growth rate in the 1960s, and unemployment still increased.[3] He also estimates that the LDCs will need growth rates on the order of 10 percent or more per year to bring unemployment problems under control. These and many other estimates give some hint of the direction a new development theory was likely to take: If high growth rates did not increase employment, perhaps concentrating on employment as the first priority might increase growth—or anyway diffuse discontent.

Inequities in the distribution of income in the underdeveloped countries also became an important issue in the early 1970s. Conventional growth theories justified the necessity of inequities on the presumption that the middle and upper classes had a higher propensity to save than the lower classes. It was, in any case, a doctrine that the elites could appreciate. Other developments were, furthermore, associated with initiating a process of growth that tended to reduce the income of the lowest 40 percent of the population. As Adelman and Morris have demonstrated, inflation, population growth, technologic change, and urbanization—among other things—increased the degree of inequality.[4] Moreover, it did not seem to matter very much whether the institutional approach was socialist, capitalist, or mixed. India adopted generally socialist policies deliberately designed to reduce inequality, and Pakistan adopted a generally free market policy that accepted the short-range necessity of growing inequality; both have emerged from more than 20 years of effort with more inequality.[5] The absence of a clear correlation between open and closed policies and the degree of in-

3. See Haq's contribution to the symposium in *Ibid.*, p. 62.
4. Irma Adelman and Cynthia Taft Morris, *Economic Growth and Social Equity* (Stanford, Calif.: Stanford University Press, 1973), pp. 182, 183. The authors argue that income shifts to the middle and upper classes and that the poor lose both relatively and absolutely—there is no "trickle down" below the middle classes.

The views of Adelman and Morris have been attacked by a number of respected economists at the World Bank, with the general thrust that they have not sufficiently proved their case and that different policies could yield better results. I have no position on this dispute, except to point out that there are enough other interpretations of unemployment and distributional inequities to suggest that Adelman and Morris can hardly be completely wrong.

5. Angus Maddison, *Class Structure and Economic Growth* (New York: Norton, 1971). See also Montek Ahluwalia, "Dimensions of the Problem," in Hollis Chenery, John Duloy, and Richard Jolly, *Redistribution With Growth: An Approach to Policy* (Washington, D.C.: World Bank, 1973), chapter 2, p. 5.

equality was, of course, only part of the problem: More critically the argument that high rates of growth would take care of the problem of inequality no longer seemed valid, for empirical studies could not detect "any connection between the growth rate of GNP and the degree of income inequality." [6]

The evidence that the distribution of income in the underdeveloped countries became noticeably worse in the past decade is far from clear.[7] This is probably misleading, however, for whether income was more or less unequally distributed is not as important as the actual incomes of the bottom 40 percent of the population (that is, how much income the poorest people actually have is more critical than whether their share of national income is 10 percent or 30 percent). One careful study reports, for example, that, for a group of countries that have half the total population of the Third World, "almost 30% of the population live below the poverty line defined by U.S. $50 per capita and about 55% are below the poverty line defined by U.S. $75 per capita." [8] This is enough by itself to account for rising concern with directly diminishing the poverty of the great mass of citizens.

With a quarter or more of the labor force unemployed, with rising birth rates, and with almost a third of the population living below any minimally acceptable standard, the only interesting question may be, how did the conventional wisdom hold on for so long? External circumstances were not much better. Aid levels had fallen, debt service payments were rising (eating up increasing amounts of foreign exchange), trade preferences were not yielding much benefit, and the prospects of a more benevolent response from the rich countries were growing dimmer as the rich began to turn more and more inward. Of course, not all the LDCs were so badly off; even some of those who were badly off were unwilling to contemplate change, preferring repression, indifference, or bread

6. Hans Singer and Richard Jolly, "Unemployment in an African Setting: Lesson of the Employment Strategy Mission to Kenya," in *The Pilot Employment Missions; and Lessons of the Kenya Mission* (Brighton, England: Institute of Development Studies at the University of Sussex, 1973), p. 9.

7. David J. Turnham, "Income Distribution: Measurement and Problems," in Rice, ed., *Development Targets for the 70's,* p. 42.

8. Ahluwalia, "Dimensions of the Problem," p. 6.

and circuses plus a Swiss bank account. Nevertheless, enough intellectuals and experts, and even a number of ruling elites, did begin to cast about for a new approach, and we shall examine some of the results in what follows.

Before we do so, a brief comment about the effects of the oil crisis may be useful. In the short term, the efforts to create cartels of raw materials producers and a new international economic order are likely to dominate the thoughts and actions of the LDCs. During this period the attempt to devise new approaches to development are unlikely to attract much interest or support. OPEC's success has simply been too hallucinatory. Nevertheless I think the new approaches will become increasingly attractive within the next 5 years just because the oil crisis has made rapid growth increasingly problematic for the majority of the LDCs and might not even do very much for the raw materials producers if their cartels do not function well. In the meanwhile both groups of LDCs will have to pay sharply higher prices for fuel, fertilizer, and food imports (and perhaps other commodities); when (and if) they do begin thinking about new approaches, most will do so from an appreciably worse position.

There are two reasons for this pessimistic judgment about the effects of the oil crisis. The first reason concerns the fact that the economies of the developing countries are not very flexible and are not likely to be able to adjust easily to the problems created by higher import prices. The LDCs will find it harder to attract OPEC investment dollars, to develop new sources of energy, to cut their own energy consumption, to increase agricultural productivity, or to cut their own import levels (without increasing unemployment levels or the threat of starvation). The other reason, related of course to the first, is that slower growth in the industrial countries will decrease their demand for LDC exports, while higher commodity prices will increase the cost of the exports that the rich countries sell to the LDCs. Aid levels are also likely to decline, perhaps even below current levels of about 0.3 percent to 0.4 percent of GNP.

The movement on the part of the LDCs to overturn the existing economic order is thus unlikely to succeed. Nevertheless I think it represents a radical extension of what the LDCs have been seeking for the past 25 years, rather than a thoroughly new approach to the problems of development. In this sense it is an attempt to stay within the international system, except an international system rigged in behalf of the have-nots. Even efforts at "collective self-reliance," which we shall shortly examine, do not contradict this judgment, for basically they seek better bargaining power for the poor countries within an international order that is being progressively adapted to benefit the Third World.

The new approaches to development we shall examine, conversely, seek to move away from—perhaps even entirely out of—the international system. They do so, in the first instance, by attempting to deal directly and immediately with the incredible human problems the LDCs confront—poverty, starvation, unemployment, disease—rather than wait for them to be dealt with by the progress that growth theory promises at some future date. But expending time and funds on shortrun consumption needs may make it even more difficult for the LDCs to achieve a degree of competitiveness within the international system. Thus the LDCs have also begun to talk about self-reliance and self-sufficiency, about putting the means of dealing with their problems in their own hands. The "great debates" about foreign aid and foreign trade (presumably) fade away and are replaced by an overriding concern with agricultural cooperatives, land reform, labor-intensive technology, vocational education, and a more equitable distribution of income.

This is, as Mahbub ul Haq has observed, a closed strategy with a difference: What is being substituted here is not the domestic production of consumer goods but an entire way of life.[9] The emotional appeal of this is particularly strong for Western intellectuals horrified at what the quest for growth has done to their own societies. But these are not ideas that can be taken on faith: Agreement that conventional development doctrines have not worked (or worked well enough) is not equivalent to agreement that the new approaches are likely to do much better. In addition the underdeveloped countries have already been victimized by one generation of imported development theories; great caution ought to be exer-

9. Mahbub ul Haq, "Developing Country Alternatives," in Paul Streeten, ed., *Trade Strategies for Development* (London: Macmillan, 1973), pp. 134 ff.

cised to avoid another repetition of the past in which theories and doctrines are uncritically grasped simply because they are the latest fashion. We should like to know more about the details of this strategy and about what results—if any—it has produced. We should also like to know how it relates to our discussion in the previous chapter: Is it too much to expect this generation of governing elites to implement so potentially revolutionary a strategy, or will they use the strategy merely as a device to buy off the discontented and to stay in power? What is the relationship between this strategy and the policymaking systems that the LDCs must operate? And what meaning can there be to discussions of self-reliance within small and weak states?

---

Before attempting to answer these questions I comment on the new emphasis within the Third World on collective self-reliance. Heretofore the underdeveloped countries have concentrated on seeking increased benefits from the industrial countries but have not paid much attention to the possibilities of increasing cooperation among themselves—except, of course, on the regional level, with less than satisfactory results. But collective self-reliance seeks more than regional cooperation, for the aim is to improve cooperation at all levels: global, regional, and among countries having the same level of development, or having common commodities to sell, or having complementary products to exchange. In effect the goal is to increase the level of interdependence within the Third World, not only to achieve immediate welfare gains from increased trade and specialization, but also to improve the quality and credibility of common bargaining positions against the industrial countries.

An improved bargaining position would presumably emerge from the fact that more collective self-reliance would gradually provide the Third World with a feasible alternative in any confrontation with the rich countries. But even apart from this, there is no doubt that efforts to increase cooperation make a great deal of sense: The immediate gains might not be large, and the gains might not be equitably distributed, but the longrun significance of such actions could surely be important. This is particularly true if the industrial countries remain in a recession, or if they turn inward, or if they begin actively to seek substitutes for many of the Third World's commodity exports.

Some danger is, however, associated with the outburst of enthusiasm for collective self-reliance. One danger is familiar: inflated expectations about how much can reasonably be expected from such efforts. Collective self-reliance faces many of the same problems that have impeded regional integration, except in a more extreme form—the lack of transportation and communications infrastructure, a reluctance to expose new industries to competition, the difficulties of harmonization, equity problems, and so on. Even with OPEC's support, upon which most of the inflated expectations for collective self-reliance rest, substantial short-term gains are unlikely—and faith in OPEC's charity is also beginning to decline. In these circumstances some of the proponents of collective self-reliance seem dangerously unrealistic when they argue, as Surendra Patel has, that top priority ought to be given "to economic co-operation among developing countries themselves and lip-service to international co-operation." [10]

Inflated expectations about the immediate effects of collective self-reliance may also have been engendered by some recent visions of what the underdeveloped world might be in the year 2000. W. Arthur Lewis, for example, has commented:

> Actually, taking developing countries as a whole, there is no reason why they must in the long-run depend on trade with the industrial countries. They have enough land to feed each

10. Surendra J. Patel, "Collective Self-Reliance and Developing Countries," (WFUNA Background Paper 8, 1974), pp. 13, 14. The actual politicies that would be part of a strategy of collective self-reliance include a trade preference scheme among the developing countries themselves (including payments arrangements), joint action on exports and imports, technologic cooperation, and various institutional arrangements for research and investment. For a discussion of these and other measures, see "Trade Expansion, Economic Cooperation and Regional Integration Among Developing Countries," (Geneva: United Nations Conference on Trade and Development, TD/B/557, June 1975). The most significant problem may be the need for very general commitment to collective self-reliance; without this, the LDCs would have to compete with the products of the developed countries in the markets of the LDCs who remained outside any agreement. See Frances Stewart, "The Direction of International Trade-Gains and Losses for the Third World," in G. K. Helleiner, ed. A World Divided (Cambridge: Cambridge University Press, 1976), p. 102.

other; they are surplus producers of most of the agricultural raw materials, metals, and fuels; and they should within the next two or three decades be in a position to finance rapid growth entirely through their own savings. So if, in the year A. D. 2000, all the countries now industrialized were to sink under the sea, this should make little difference to the potential growth of the countries that are now less developed.[11]

This seems to justify manipulating the international system to achieve only shortrun gains—for the rich, so the argument goes, will not be needed in the future. But the rich definitely will be needed in the shortrun, and I believe they will still be needed in the long run; consequently arguments such as these may succeed only in creating a *folie de grandeur*.[12]

## REDISTRIBUTION AND SELF-RELIANCE: TURNING THE CONVENTIONAL WISDOM ON ITS HEAD

The new approaches to development are quite diverse, but they share a number of perspectives and aspirations. Domestically they feature policies aimed directly at reducing the poverty of the bottom 40 percent of the population, improving the distribution of income, increasing employment (even at the cost of accepting second-best technology), and improving the productivity per acre of agriculture

11. W. Arthur Lewis, "The Development Process," in *The Case for Development: Six Studies* (New York: Praeger, 1972), p. 63. Note also Paul Streeten, *Aid to Africa: A Policy Outline for the 1970's* (New York: Praeger, 1972), pp. 101–2: "Developing countries have the land, the raw materials, the fuel, and the ability to acquire the skills and raise the savings and finance to dispense very largely with dependence on the industrial countries."

12. The same might be said in reference to a recent comment by a radical economist: "One therefore comes to wonder whether, in order to rebuild the world system—for this will, I think, have to be done one day—one should not begin by destroying it (i.e., pulling out of it) . . ." Samir Amin, "Should We Dump the Present Economic Systems and Start Again from Scratch?" *The UNESCO Courier*, October 1976, p. 11. One needs to ask whether pulling out by some or even all the developing countries is more than a romantic fantasy, whether (if possible) it would achieve the desired ends, whether the costs—especially to the poor who would be the first casualties—would outweigh the benefits, and whether such comments are irresponsible insofar as they raise false hopes and distract attention from the quest for solutions to immediate and emerging problems.

so that more food for domestic consumption can be produced.[13] Externally they emphasize increasing self-reliance: Central to this notion are not only the dangers and limitations of depending on world markets but also the desire to meet domestic demands from domestic sources (and, as with Soviet foreign trade theory, trading only when absolutely necessary and/or to dispose of surpluses). Domestic and external policies are integrally related. A domestic concentration on redistributing income, which may slow the rate of growth by forcing concentration on second-best, labor-intensive technology to deal with rising levels of unemployment, may also compel an external emphasis on self-reliance, for the domestic policies may (not will, as we shall see) make exports increasingly uncompetitive. In addition, apart from the possible effects of an employment-oriented domestic technology, the new approaches (in their less radical forms) stress a much more selective and discriminating contact with the external world in which inappropriate technology, unfair bargains, and misconceived ideas and institutions are resisted. A generation of development theory is being stood on its head here, for the impossibility of self-reliance, the welfare gains from international trade, the need to concentrate on industrialization, and the virtues of inequality have been part of the conventional wisdom for more than 25 years.

On the surface some similarities exist between these views and

13. See the discussion in Edgar Owens and Robert Shaw, *Development Reconsidered* (Lexington, Mass.: D. C. Heath and Co., 1972); and Patricia W. Blair, ed., *Political and Social Realities of Development: Recognition and Response* (Washington, D.C.: Society for International Development, 1973), which lists the premises of the new approach as an emphasis on employment, decentralization, the need for market towns, faith in the efficiency of small farmers, and faith that the poor can save enough to pay for their investments (pp. 35–37). Another recent source on this approach is Robert L. Ayres, "Development Policy and the Possibility of a 'Livable' Future for Latin America," *The American Political Science Review* 69, no. 2 (June 1975):507–25.
    Agriculture is central to the new approaches because, when the domestic economy is the only source of supply in a low-income country, agriculture must be by far the largest sector, since most income must be spent on food and other necessities, that is, on household consumption. Only resource-lucky countries can pay for imported food. But LDC agricultural productivity is very low, much lower than in the rich countries, and also difficult to upgrade. So it is a central area of concern for both redistribution and self-reliance. See Simon Kuznets, *Modern Economic Growth* (New Haven, Conn.: Yale University Press, 1966), pp. 409 ff. The emphasis on agriculture and rural development inevitably raises the complex issue of land reform, with its attendant political and economic conflicts.

*[264]*

earlier arguments for the creation of an independent national economy. Green and Seidman, for example, argued that independence required production for national needs, control of the economy in national hands, and increasing diversification of foreign ties.[14] Many of the specific policies implicit in the quest for economic independence are also similar to the policies currently advocated: rural development, improving income distribution, mobilization of the population, and government control of large parts of the economy. As Green claimed some years ago, the goal was a closed economy, publicly owned.[15] I think, however, that the new strategy incorporates much of the earlier argument, especially in the sense that self-reliance presupposes growth generated by internal forces and internal needs but also goes appreciably further in design and direction.

Some of the differences are in detail. The new approach is, for example, much more concerned with a direct assault on the human problems most of the LDCs confront, perhaps because these problems have got noticeably worse in the past few years. There is also much more concentration on decentralized decisionmaking and consequently much less on government control of the economy (although, as I argue shortly, this may indeed be necessary). The main difference is, however, that the earlier arguments were really arguments for a more extended (geographically) and more extensive (economically) closed economy. Rapid growth via industrialization remained the goal: Capital imports remained imperative, and autarky was specifically foresworn. The newer approach is more radical, for it contemplates not only increasing degrees of autarky—at least among some of its proponents—but also the creation of an entirely new life-style, a "bicycle culture" for the "Madison Avenue culture" of the industrial states. This necessarily implies massive social reforms and a movement away from the market economy.[16]

14. Reginald H. Green and Ann Seidman, *Unity or Poverty—The Economics of Pan-Africanism* (Baltimore, Md.: Penguin, 1968), p. 79.

15. Reginald H. Green, "Political Independence and the National Economy: An Essay on the Political Economy of Decolonization," in Christopher Allen and R. W. Johnson, eds., *African Perspectives* (Cambridge: Cambridge University Press, 1970), p. 284.

16. Haq, "Developing Country Alternatives," talks of the need for a "poverty curtain" between the rich and the poor, accompanied by massive domestic reforms. Haq's proposals were sharply criticized in this symposium. Some attacked on the

The policies implicit in a strategy of redistribution and self-reliance are obviously different from those implicit in a growth strategy. In the first instance the two approaches have different time frames and different attitudes toward inequality. Growth theories stress immediate sacrifice and long-term gratifications; the new strategy stresses immediate gratifications and different kinds of gratifications in the long term. Growth theories also emphasize the necessity of inequality; the new strategy underscores the imperative need of reducing existing inequalities. Adelman and Morris also claim that the specific policies implemented are different. Growth strategies concentrate on savings and investment rates, increasing exports, raising productivity, and improving the quality of fiscal and monetary institutions. Distribution strategies, conversely, emphasize the condition of the individual, human resources, agriculture, the control or limitation of foreign intervention, the structure of foreign trade, and an increased role for the government.[17]

The views implicit and explicit in the new strategy still float pretty much above the battle. They have not penetrated very far into the actual policymaking process in more than a few LDCs, nor have many ruling elites been obviously converted to a new vision of the good life. Immediate problems of survival have become too grim to permit much contemplation of new patterns of behavior, especially when the new patterns are both untried and potentially revolutionary. Nevertheless, I believe that a number of pressures, domestic and external, may make new approaches increasingly attractive—to some, but not all, of the LDCs.

---

ground that it was an inappropriate application of the "Chinese Strategy" (p. 140), and David Wall accused Haq of "irresponsible defeatism" that would commit the poor to perpetual poverty (p. 264).

Paul G. Clark, *American Aid for Development* (New York: Praeger, 1972), pp. 67–68, provides a more technical critique of Haq, arguing that "assisting the national economies to develop more rapidly is much more effective than assisting people directly. External assistance is fairly typically on the order of 2 to 3 percent of a recipient country's national product, so that if used directly to raise living standards it could at best make a small once-for-all contribution. . . . On the other hand, external assistance is often on the order of 15 to 20 percent of investment, and this marginal supplement can greatly facilitate the recipient government's efforts. . . ." The problem with this is, of course, that it misses the thrust of an argument that is primarily concerned with employment, equity, and human capital—not growth.

17. Adelman and Morris, *Economic Growth and Social Equity*, p. 165, provide evidence that there is substantially more equity where there is a large public sector.

The developing countries for whom the new approaches seem particularly appropriate—that is, both feasible and necessary—are the large number of very poor countries variously described as "least developed" or as having per capita incomes below, say, $200. These are loose and shifting designations, but they encapsulate well over 60 countries. Three factors are especially critical about these countries: They are usually the first victims of major "shocks" in the international system and have fewer means to protect themselves against such shocks, they have been doing less well than the developing countries as a whole on a number of important variables, and they do not benefit very much from most of the external measures designed to help the developing countries.

I believe that much of this discussion is also relevant for some of the other developing countries that already have reasonably advanced manufacturing export sectors or a commodity export in high demand. This presupposes that these countries want to alter the existing distribution of benefits more rapidly and more directly than traditional growth theory has prescribed. The approach clearly must be somewhat different, but the ultimate aim is the same, and some of the policies are also identical.

## LESSONS FROM EXPERIENCE: TANZANIA AND CEYLON

The one country that has made a serious attempt to implement a program containing many of the elements of the new strategy is Tanzania. Unfortunately the program has not been in existence long enough for us to get a good reading on how well it is doing, and data are bound to remain sparse because of the Tanzanian government's reluctance to allow foreign researchers to evaluate government policies. Moreover, the oil crisis has hit Tanzania very hard—it is on the UN list of countries "most severely affected"—and the strategy may thus fail because of external developments over which the Tanzanians have no control—a sad and ironic illustration, once again, of the limits of independence for poor and weak states. Recent World Bank estimates, for example, indicate that Tanzania will need at least 50 percent more gross capital inflow for the next 3 years than the figure for 1973 and that a shift in investment strategy toward directly productive activities and away from human capital investments will also probably be necessary.

It may be too early to establish a meaningful balance sheet for the Tanzanian experience, but the government's intention to break new ground is at least clear. It may be easier to see this by noting what is not in the Tanzanian program: rapid industrialization or heavy industry, exports of manufactured products, and central control and planning. In the program are public ownership of major industries and infrastructure, a decrease in foreign investment and aid, an emphasis on agricultural productivity, vocational education, equity in the distribution of income, sharp conflict of interest rules for government officials and a general effort to control corruption, and nonalignment in foreign policy.[18] The attempt to limit contact with the external world is apparent; so, too, is the effort to establish goals and policies that take account of Tanzania's limited natural resources, the absence of a stock of capital or skills and knowledge necessary for an industrial economy, and the limited demand for Tanzania's likely exports. Whether all the elite, and not just President Nyerere, are committed to this vision, or will remain committed once their own interests are threatened, is far from clear. Nor is it clear that the government has the capacity to carry out all of these policies or that it will receive the necessary support from the great mass of citizens. Nonetheless this program cannot be dismissed, for it surely seems to make as much or more sense than a desperate effort to industrialize before the conditions of industrialization are present. And, I think, it is much more likely to attract the support of the people at large—though perhaps not the elite—and begin the slow process of constructing a national economy.

Two countries, Ceylon and Uruguay, have attempted to implement redistribution policies in the last two decades (although not policies of self-reliance). The Ceylonese case is especially interesting, illustrating some of the difficulties that confront weak governments intent on using their resources to improve current comsump-

18. G. K. Helleiner, "Socialism and Economic Development in Tanzania," *Journal of Development Studies* 8, no. 2 (January 1972):183–204.

tion levels. Ceylon deliberately sacrificed economic growth for large amounts of social welfare spending in the late 1950s. The results have been disastrous, and Ceylon is one of the few small LDCs who risk becoming an immediate disaster area. The Ceylonese government guaranteed free education through the university level, free medical services, and government subsidies to keep the price of staple foods and transportation down. The level of current consumption was very high: During the 1950s it went up from 90 percent to 94 percent of disposable income. The results of these policies in the 1960s were a sharp rise in both inflation and unemployment, an increase in food deficits that had to be met by imports (which became difficult as tea and rubber prices fell), and a consequent decline in living standards for all classes, but especially the middle class.

The political pressures for consumption spending far outweighed the pressures for investment spending. Once the commitment to extensive social services was made, the government lacked the power or the will to risk taking away what the population now considered theirs by right. Ceylon, like Uruguay, was a relatively advanced LDC in terms of political and social development (it was nominally a democracy and had high rates of literacy and a reasonable supply of trained personnel, etc.), but the citizens of Ceylon were no more willing to sacrifice their subsidies than the citizens of any other state. The redistribution policies were also badly implemented, although even well-implemented policies would have strained government resources badly.[19] The Ceylonese case is a useful warning about the limits of effective performance for poor and weak governments. The government was obviously a victim of the demonstration effect in its premature efforts to institute social welfare programs that come late in the development of industrial societies. Effective central planning was also beyond the capacity of the Ceylonese government. And politically, weak governments lack the flexibility to alter their commitments when they grow too on-

19. My discussion of Ceylon rests on Donald R. Snodgrass, *Ceylon: An Export Economy in Transition* (Homewood, Ill.: Richard D. Irwin, Inc., 1966); and Robert N. Kearney, *The Politics of Ceylon (Sri Lanka)* (Ithaca, N.Y.: Cornell University Press, 1973).

erous. Finally, growth rates eventually did decline, especially after export receipts fell, and the results were an increase in dependence on the external world and a decline in the reduction of income inequalities.

Both the Ceylonese and Uruguayan welfare programs required a great deal of central government control and intervention. Many of the arguments for a new approach to development stress the virtue and necessity of decentralization. Certainly there is something to be said for decentralization, for central control of any process as complex as economic development surely strains the competence of LDC governments (not to say any modern government). It seems to me, however, that any serious attempt to redistribute societal income, let alone create a "bicycle culture," may compel centralization, not decentralization. The empirical evidence to justify this contention is admittedly sparse and difficult to interpret. Nevertheless there are two reasons why I doubt that genuine decentralization is likely in many instances. First, to most of the elites currently in power, redistribution is bound to look much more threatening than maintenance of the status quo. Insofar as they are pushed and pulled into redistribution policies, whether because of mounting domestic problems or whatever, elite fears of losing control of the process—especially to dissident elites or disloyal local areas—may mean that any redistribution will have to be monitored by the central government. Perhaps this will be less true if the elites can be convinced that redistribution is not always revolutionary (as we shall shortly see). Second, in a good many cases the local structures necessary to implement redistribution policies may not exist, or there may be resistance to some elements of redistribution, or local elites may act in a narrow and antinational perspective. In these circumstances the central government may have to generate its own "devolutionary" groups and attitudes. This is clearly likely to be done only by a government genuinely committed to redistribution; merely rhetorical commitments are unlikely to engender efforts to create alternate centers of power and influence.

If centralization does become the norm, it creates a double problem: Effective (i.e., more than repressive) central control is beyond the capacity of poor and weak governments, and the mere effort to centralize in societies divided by multiple cleavages is likely to increase the distrust and uncooperativeness of local groups. But the remedy is not simply decentralization—even where the elites accept it—for no program as far-reaching as redistribution and self-reliance can be established and implemented without strong elements of national guidance. I discuss how the balance between these potentially divergent pressures might be set in a later section.

---

Existing evidence is inevitably inconclusive, since the new approach has barely been tested and could not survive the massive external shock reflected in the oil crisis and recession in the industrial countries. Its appeal clearly reflects something more than, or something different from, a record of practical successes. On the one hand, rejection of prevailing patterns of development, and of the risks and uncertainties implicit in remaining within the international system, have played a part. On the other hand the ultimate justification for redistribution and self-reliance is clearly moral, not practical. The conviction has grown that no goal that entails impoverishing the already impoverished—no matter what potential benefits it promises—can be worth the costs. Two streams of thought come together here: practical doubts about what the international system can offer and how well the developing countries can respond and moral doubts about a set of priorities that values growth more than the immediate relief of suffering.

Redistribution and self-reliance are not simply economic doctrines, for they also include critical political and psychologic dimensions. Some judgment of the economic consequences of these doctrines is indispensable. But we also need to seek answers to two other questions. First what meaning are these doctrines likely to have for the distribution of domestic economic and political power and how are they likely to appear to the ruling elites? And second, does the implementation of these doctrines require policymaking capacities that do not and cannot exist in the context of underdevelopment? I discuss the first question in the next section, but I delay a response to the second question until we have examined the economic implications of these doctrines.

## REDISTRIBUTION AND SELF-RELIANCE: ELITE PERSPECTIVES

The governing elites of most underdeveloped countries have come to power at a time when the achievement of rapidly rising rates of growth imparts great status and prestige in the external world. Cantril's study of differences between elite and mass attitudes in Brazil, Nigeria, and India clearly demonstrates the extent to which the elites are more concerned with their country's international and regional status—which means how their countries are doing in terms of rising or falling growth rates.[20] The elites are also more concerned with, or aware of, the notorious "gap" between the rich and the poor countries and are also likely to object to any policies that might make the gap increase. These objections may persist even if the new policies succeed in raising the absolute levels of income for the bottom 40 percent of the population. President Suharto of Indonesia, for example, has indicated great doubts about the wisdom of concentrating efforts on the poorest members of society:

> This may be a new form of imperialism. If the West contributes only to small-scale grassroots projects, our plight may be somewhat alleviated, but we will never grow.[21]

Note also the implicit suspicion that one reason why Western governments favor this policy is that it will allow aid levels to be diminished.[22]

Redistribution would definitely require some sacrifice from the elite. The new policies would probably lead to a reduction of ser-

20. Hadley Cantril, *The Pattern of Human Concerns* (New Brunswick, N.J.: Rutgers University Press, 1965), pp. 286–90.
21. Quoted in Joseph Lelyveld, "A Case Study in Disillusion: U.S. Aid Effort in India," *New York Times*, June 25, 1974.
22. But see below, p. 295.

vices for the urban areas in which most of the elites live, as well as some restrictions on the unfettered acquisition of wealth.[23] Tanzania, for example, has passed a law limiting the disparity of income between officials and workers to a maximum of 6:1. Potential political costs are also implicit in the new approach, for some amount of political power and influence would undoubtedly begin to flow to new rural and working-class groups and away from the small group of urban elites who have usually dominated LDC governments. The extraordinary difficulty of implementing effective land reform policies in many developing countries, which are a critical part of a number of efforts to improve agricultural productivity, may illustrate the difficulty of overcoming elite resistance to any measures that threaten their power.[24]

The ruling elites are also likely to be frightened by the notion that redistribution and self-reliance are revolutionary strategies. And, indeed, it has been argued in this fashion by a number of analysts. But redistribution may not in fact be as revolutionary as a good deal of current rhetoric suggests. Some understanding of why this is so might make the new approach less frightening to insecure elites.

A number of commentators have indicated some doubt about the revolutionary potential of the new approach. Charles Anderson, for example, has argued that the effort to create a "counter-culture" of development may well be conservative in its implications. He has argued that there has been a shift to coping with problems and adapting to what is possible that is essentially antirevolutionary.[25] Providing a minimal standard of living for the very poor and seeking to establish a society that is "merely" decent and workable are surely likely to fall short of creating a revolutionary dynamic. Anderson doubts that this vision of the future would be acceptable to many Latin Americans, who may assert contempt for the material-

23. G. K. Helleiner, "Beyond Growth Rates and Plan Volumes—Planning for Africa in the 1970's," *Journal of Modern African Studies* 10, no. 3 (1972):354.

24. If self-reliance was also the goal, elite losses would be even sharper, for they would have to forego foreign aid, which is under their control, and support for the export–import sector, from which many elites benefit.

25. Charles W. Anderson, "The Changing International Environment of Development and Latin America in the 1970's," *Inter-American Economic Affairs* 24, no. 2 (Autumn 1970):80–84.

istic values of the United States but also want more for themselves at the same time.[26] But this is still less than a revolutionary ethos. And for the less advanced LDCs a decent but unrevolutionary future may be eminently desirable—if possible.

The conservative implications of concentrating on making the life of the poor more bearable have not escaped some radicals. An Indian radical political weekly, for example, responded to Robert McNamara's efforts to concentrate the World Bank's aid programs on the lower 40 percent of the population in this way: "Mr. McNamara is trying to prescribe a course, which, while keeping up neo-colonial exploitation, will bring down the danger of revolution in the starved countryside of the third world." [27] If the poor react to even marginal improvements in their condition by becoming selfish and conservative, the likelihood of a radical revolution will surely decline—although the possibility of a fascist or populist revolution cannot be discounted. The fact that the urban masses in many underdeveloped countries, despite many forecasts of revolutionary explosions, have not (yet) acted in a destabilizing fashion is one indication that the relationship between inequality and discontent or violence is complex.[28]

Radical intellectuals are suspicious of the motives of Western governments and aid agencies that support redistribution policies for another reason. From the environmental point of view a development strategy that emphasizes redistribution rather than growth is particularly attractive. It would slow the worldwide depletion of resources, and it would not increase the level of global pollution.[29]

26. *Ibid.*, p. 83.
27. Quoted in Lelyveld, *The New York Times*, June 25, 1974.
28. Jack Nagel, "Inequality and Discontent: a Nonlinear Hypothesis," *World Politics* 26, no. 4 (July 1974):453–72.
29. In the past 20 years the rate of use of natural resources was greater than the growth rate of the GNP. This was even more true for the LDCs than for the rich countries, and it is likely that this trend will continue: The LDC share of nonrenewable materials use will grow even larger because modernization increases the intensity of use of raw materials (up to a certain point). But while the share of resources of the poor countries may go up 50 percent by the year 2000 and the share of the rich may decline, the LDCs as a whole will move from only 10 percent of world demand for nonrenewable materials now to about 15 percent by 2000. See *Materials Requirements in the United States and Abroad in the Year 2000* (Washington, D.C.: National Commission on Materials Policy, 1972).

There may be room for one country that uses resources as prodigally as the United States; many more would be a worldwide disaster. This means that if the rich countries are going to maintain high rates of growth, the rich have some serious reasons to delay and impede the use of scarce resources by the poor—unless the rich countries move rapidly and efficiently out of many industries that have high intensity of use ratios for raw materials. At any rate what holds the poor back in present circumstances, according to this argument, is the overdevelopment of the rich, not their own underdevelopment. The stress on redistribution, which means a movement away from rapid industrialization, thus begins to appear counterrevolutionary—at least to some radical intellectuals. In addition one sees another traditional argument being stood on its head here: The argument that LDC growth is good for the rich also, because the LDCs will become more profitable markets, may seem problematic, for rapid LDC growth rates are likely to deplete resources that the rich need for their own growth.

Suspicion of the motives of Western advocates of redistribution is particularly acute when the LDCs are simultaneously urged to cut their population growth rates. After all a citizen of the United States consumes 30 to 60 times more of the world's resources than a citizen of an LDC. Who then should cut birth rates—or consumption of resources? An Asian delegate to the Population Conference in Bucharest made the point rather starkly: "What they're saying is that it's O.K. to breed if you're a Californian but we must stop having any more little piccaninies." [30]

I do not support the notion that a concentration on redistribution and population control is part of a Western conspiracy against the poor. It is necessary to understand, however, how such fears could arise and why they are not completely irrational. Japan has, for example, indicated that henceforth some part of its foreign aid grants must be used for family planning. Why have the Japanese suddenly adopted this policy? According to former Prime Minister Kishi, "It's a question of food and natural resources," for even if Japan holds its own population at zero growth, ". . . its supplies

30. Quoted in the *Manchester Guardian*, September 1, 1974.

will be endangered by the massive growth in India and else-where." [31] Sentiments such as these from influential circles make the contention that birth control is in the interest of the LDCs seem hypocritical or cynical. It is not surprising that many LDC officials see the population problem as a Western invention designed to shift attention away from the "real" source of the problem. This is at best a half-truth, for fears of resource scarcity are obviously a recent phenomenon in industrial societies, and the belief that the rich can prosper in the future only by exploiting the poor is doubt-ful (one would have said absurd until recent years, but no longer); meanwhile such beliefs do deflect some of the LDCs from a proper concern with an issue that is critical irrespective of the behavior of the rich countries.

The question of whether the new approaches are truly revolu-tionary or not obviously cannot be settled in any definitive manner. We do not have enough experience in actually implementing such policies to permit any simple conclusions. In any event the results would probably vary widely between individual cases. Nonethe-less, if I had to make an educated guess—and it is no more than that—I would venture the opinion that this strategy might not be very revolutionary; indeed, effectively implemented, it might suc-ceed in allaying more popular discontent (by direct spending on immediately felt consumption needs and human capital invest-ments) than a standard growth policy that succeeded only in in-creasing disparities of income between the various social classes. This is especially true in light of the evidence that the expectations of the poor are not revolutionary but rather moderate and realistic. Thus, in contrast to what some of its advocates believe, the new strategy may be a more effective reform strategy than a revolu-tionary strategy. This could be conceived as a criticism only by those dogmatically committed to revolution, or unaware of the doubtful results of most revolutions for the poor, or simply indiffer-ent to policies whose most salient virtue is that they respond imme-diately to the extraordinary human needs of the great mass of the citizens. Finally, perceived in this fashion, redistribution ought not

31. *Ibid.*, p. 9.

to be a policy that elites reject because they fear they will not be able to control its effects—they may be able to retain control and implement a serious development strategy more easily this way than by following any other set of policies. Unfortunately it is probably doubtful that many elites will make the calculations necessary to arrive at this judgment.

## REDISTRIBUTION, GROWTH, AND THE TIME PERSPECTIVE

The discussion thus far has suggested that the elites are unlikely to favor the new approach because of the prestige associated with high rates of growth, because of potential losses in elite welfare as gains are shifted to new groups, and because of possible fears that they will be overwhelmed by revolutionary turmoil. It seems to me that all these factors are variations on one central theme in the discussion of redistribution and self-reliance: that commitment to such policies must inevitably lower the rate of growth by lowering the rate of domestic saving or by reallocating investment in second-best technologies that reduce unemployment but also raise costs well above world market levels or increase inefficiency (by increasing the labor/capital ratio at the cost of raising the capital/output ratio).[32] There is also likely to be some anxiety among the ruling elites that the redistribution of land could lower agricultural productivity for food consumption.[33] Moreover, the fear that the new approach must inevitably lower the rate of growth and thus increase the dangers of domestic conflict and the magnitude of the gap between rich and poor countries has been compounded by the tendency of many advocates of redistribution and self-reliance to ignore or dismiss the problems of redistribution without growth and to fail to establish priorities of their own between redistri-

32. I owe the last point to a communication from Paul Streeten.
33. Land reform may also, of course, increase productivity per acre, provided that appropriate institutions are created, so that the apparent conflict between equality and output disappears. At any rate the fact that agricultural productivity for domestic consumption has declined recently in some of the poorest countries and has not kept up with population growth rates might make the elites more open to the need for land reform and other structural changes.

bution and self-reliance. I attempt to clarify these issues in this section; doing so should permit more sensible judgments about the implications of a commitment to redistribution and self-reliance.

In the following discussion I am primarily concerned with how redistribution policies are likely to be perceived by key elite groups. This inevitably oversimplifies some of the complexities of redistribution, for, as Streeten and Stewart note, the objectives of redistribution "are rarely clearly defined . . . but normally simply refer to giving more weight to distributional objectives." [34] Consequently some of the potential conflicts between reducing poverty and reducing inequality, or between shortrun and longrun gains, have been ignored in the public debate. [35] Elite perspectives are, I believe, likely to be dominated (to the extent that they begin to take redistribution seriously) by the need to reduce poverty—because of its salience and because of the desire to defuse discontent—and by a short time horizon, because poor and insecure governments are bound to work with a high discount rate on the future. As we shall see, however, the other objectives of reducing inequality and evincing some concern for long-range prospects cannot be ignored, for they are likely to have a significant impact on the general workability of a commitment to redistribution.

The classic argument against redistribution is simply put: Redistribution in favor of lower income groups is apt to reduce the level of domestic saving, for such groups save a lower portion of incremental income than higher income groups. Consequently the governments of poor countries confront a painful trade-off, because more shortrun equity may mean slower growth over the long run, but a concentration on high rates of saving may lower the immediate welfare of the already poorer groups. Recent empirical studies have, however, cast some doubt on the validity of the equity versus growth trade-off. An UNCTAD study of the relationship between income distribution and savings rates in 59 countries found, for ex-

34. Frances Stewart and Paul Streeten, "New Strategies of Development: A Comment," (unpublished paper), p. 9. I should like to thank Professor Streeten for sending me this paper, from which I have greatly benefited.
35. See *ibid.* for a sophisticated discussion of these issues.

ample, that the evidence supported the "hypothesis that savings performance is positively related to the equality of the distribution of personal income." [36]

These results may not be as surprising as they first appear. For example, perceptions of living in a more equitable society may lead to a more effective tax system, either because burden sharing is easier when many contribute a fair share or because there is less incentive or desire to avoid taxation in an equitable society. At any rate, although these results must be treated with some caution, they virtually stand the traditional trade-off on its head: They suggest that long-term growth may be much easier if it rests on improved short-run equity. Evidence that investment in human capital, which is normally classified as consumption expenditure, is the major factor in growth reinforces the argument that a diversion of spending from investment to consumption is not always bad, even from the growth standpoint. [37] And even if these results are wrong and the traditional trade-off still holds, this is not decisive for those who believe that meeting immediate human needs must always take first priority. For the elites, however, the discovery that equity facilitates growth (especially by increasing government tax revenues) could be important.

Conventional growth theories demand great sacrifices in immediate consumption from both government and people. Such sacrifices are doubly difficult for weak and unstable governments and for people already living in or near the subsistence level. One of the more attractive aspects of the emphasis on the direct reduction of poverty and distributional equity is that it seems to justify immediate gratifications—and without any loss in long-term potentials for growth. This conclusion masks, however, one fundamental difference between traditional approaches to growth and the new approach: The groups who benefit in the short run (and perhaps over the longer term also, if the aim of creating a "bicycle culture" is

36. *Domestic Saving in Developing Countries* (Geneva: United Nations Conference on Trade and Development, TD/B/C3/124/Supp. 1, September 1975):31.
37. See Theodore Morgan, "Investment *versus* Economic Growth," *Economic Development and Cultural Change* 17, no. 3 (1969):392–414.

maintained) will be very different, for entrepreneurs and skilled workers will no longer receive special privileges, and the gains from growth will be directed toward the mass of the population.

This argument seems to suggest that the choice at issue is not really between a growth and a no-growth strategy, but rather between a different vision of what growth is to bring (the consumer society vs. the "bicycle culture") and a different distribution of the benefits of growth between the social classes. The elites (broadly defined here to include both the middle class and the ruling elite itself) are not likely to find this acceptable, not only because they must sacrifice some gains, but also because a loss of status is implicit in foregoing efforts to match the record and the institutions of the industrial countries. But even if a ruling elite is committed to the creation of a new socioeconomic order, major short-term problems are likely to arise—even if domestic savings levels are not cut—if other effects are associated with redistribution policies that cut the growth rate. In particular two such effects must be dealt with before even a committed elite is likely to be able to implement sensible redistribution policies.

In the first place most of the advocates of redistribution also favor efforts to increase the degree of self-reliance. Self-reliance presumably means less foreign aid and foreign investment, either because of deliberate decision or because of the reactions of foreign governments and investors. These connections between domestic and foreign behavior are obviously salient for small states. Now self-reliance need not necessarily cut the growth rate (if aid has been used as a substitute for, not a supplement to, domestic savings).[38] But it is quite clear that the absence of foreign support

38. The key issue in the trade-off between growth and self-reliance is likely to be the time frame: In the short run, self-reliance may cut the growth rate, but in the long run it may help the growth rate by diminishing debt payments and by increasing the ability of the country to fend for itself (if it has really "learned by doing"). In any event, it should also in the long run help to establish a more appropriate pattern of development. The decision on which value to sacrifice when may depend, in turn, on whether self-reliance is seen as an end in itself—which means immediate sacrifices of aid and investment—or whether it is seen as one important value among others (including growth). In the latter case the decision on immediate sacrifices is much more likely to be moderate and prudent. Thus far, most Third World governments have had neither the inclination nor the capacity to see self-reliance as an im-

means that immediate consumption levels must be cut unless the government has given up any intention to increase growth rates—a dangerous policy, not to say suicidal, as we shall shortly see. What this means is, of course, that either the effort to help the poor directly must cease or the funds to do so must come from other sectors of the economy. This is an explosive situation for a weak government, and it begins to suggest that only governments that are very strong or have earned windfall profits are likely to take the risk of redistribution and self-reliance. The point is, I think, that the two policies may conflict unless some way can be found to maintain adequate growth rates without excessive domestic conflict. It also begins to raise questions about the need to tie the two policies together, a point to which we shall return.

A small country can turn away from the opportunities that foreign trade provides only if its government can meet domestic demand pressures from resources under its own control. Alternatively the government may be forced to turn inward if it is convinced that it cannot survive in open (or even preferential) competition or if it is unwilling to risk the policies implied by an open economy. The latter reasons are more likely to prevail in present circumstances, but this does not make the first reason—the government's ability to meet demand pressures—any less important. Self-reliance may make redistribution much more difficult by cutting the size of the available economic pie. In these circumstances redistribution will create a great deal of social conflict unless the growth rate is sufficiently high to buy off or pacify the discontented.

Economists have generally regarded distribution as a political issue. Consequently the relationship between growth and distribution is not very clear. It is clear that there are potential conflicts over issues like tax policy and government expenditures, although they might be avoided or ameliorated if there was convincing evidence that the upper classes did not invest surplus income or squandered it on luxury investments. But the evidence on this point is far from

---

mediate goal, but a good deal of radical rhetoric seems to be trying to push them in this direction.

clear; the fact that the poor will save, given proper incentives, does not mean that the upper classes will not save more.

The conflict between redistribution and growth might also be avoided if redistribution policies were designed to put claims only on future income.[39] This would be possible, however, only if the growth rate continued to rise in the future (perhaps even at a faster rate to compensate for two sets of demands for more: from the haves and the have-nots). If growth slowed as a result of redistribution, conflict would be inevitable. Historically, in the context of rapidly growing economies, the relative share of the upper classes could be left alone, while the absolute incomes of all groups increased: The poor were still at the bottom of the ladder, but the height of the lower ranges was consistently raised. Obviously this diminished the costs of helping the poor, for all groups were rewarded, although some were rewarded more. But if the growth rate slows, or comes to a halt, there is a smaller (or no) increment to divide. The poor then cannot improve their position or can do so only at the expense of (and not jointly with) the rich. Unless the rich are altruistic, or a new source of funds is discovered (e.g., raising prices sharply on irreplaceable resources), or old forms of spending are reduced (e.g., from the military budget, although this surely raises the likelihood of a coup [40]), the ruling elite is unlikely to take the risks of redistribution. In these circumstances, if the elite confronts rising levels of mass discontent, repression is the probable outcome. Caught between the already discontented poor and the about-to-be discontented rich (if growth is slowed or they fear

39. For brief mention of this possibility, see Shane Hunt, "Distribution, Growth and Government Economic Behavior in Peru," pp. 375, 376, in Gustav Ranis, ed., *Government and Economic Development* (New Haven, Conn.: Yale University Press, 1971). Actually there are probably only three ways in which a government can try to redistribute income: The traditional approach, now in some disrepute, has emphasized rapid rates of growth, with the poor gradually getting a greater share (or enough of a share) of the growth increments; alternatively, a government can attempt to redistribute through fiscal or pricing methods (e.g., subsidies for food or health for the poor) or, as is now the central focus, by a direct assault on the problems of poverty, unemployment, malnutrition, regional inequities, and so forth.

40. The point is that political interference with the army correlates very highly with coups. See Claude E. Welch, Jr. "The Roots and Implications of Military Intervention," in Claude E. Welch, Jr., *Soldier and State in Africa* (Evanston, Ill.: Northwestern University Press, 1970), p. 34. Anyway there has been a general upward trend in military budgets among the LDCs in the past few years.

efforts at redistribution), what alternative is there—especially if the international system does not respond? [41]

These complexities have been more or less ignored by many of the advocates of the new approaches to development, for they seem to feel that any concern with growth is indecent since it implies dependence on the international system—on foreign aid, investment, and values. But distributional equity without economic growth merely impoverishes everybody. The contention that the choice is between distribution or growth is thus dangerously simplistic, because what is properly at stake here is what the composition of growth ought to be—the bicycle culture versus the Madison Avenue culture—and what the society feels must be the principle by which the results are distributed. And these are political questions about who gets what and when, not a debater's question about how to get one without the other.

One of the primary ways that the poor can really be helped, especially in economies that cannot afford massive social welfare programs, is by providing remunerative employment for the unemployed or the unproductively employed. That is, where the redistribution of existing income would succeed only in making everyone poor, redistribution can work only by increasing the income-earning opportunities of the labor force. It is difficult to see how this can be done without a high growth rate. Indeed Chenery cites evidence that the condition of the poor is relatively best in societies that have increased employment as a result of high rates of growth (and high rates of export growth).[42] Unfortunately, as critics like Haq have pointed out, it is unlikely that these "success stories" can be repeated *ad infinitum:* There are only so many cheap exports that the rich countries will take before closing the gates. Moreover, not all the success stories have done much for their own poor, or decreased inequities in income distribution, or stopped exploiting

41. Perhaps this implies that redistribution may be easiest where the elite itself has little (e.g., if foreign investment has not created domestic cliques whose members are both wealthy and dependent on foreign support), and thus a sharp gap between elite and mass does not exist, or where the elite itself is already committed to equalitarian ideas.

42. Hollis B. Chenery, "Growth and Structural Change," *Finance and Development* 8, no. 3 (September 1971):27.

the workers who do have jobs: "Successes" like Taiwan, South Korea, and the Ivory Coast must be matched against "failures" like Brazil, Mexico, Venezuela, and Senegal.[43] Finally, since providing sufficiently remunerative employment for enough workers is unlikely without major structural reforms of the existing economy—away from capital-intensive, high-technology inputs—we move here from a concern solely with reducing poverty to a concern also with the reduction of inequalities. This raises in severe form the question of how willing existing elites are likely to be to see their own gains threatened.

This brings us to the second way in which redistribution may slow the rate of growth. If one of the key elements of redistribution is the effort to cut unemployment, and if this can be done only by using labor-intensive technologies that also raise production costs above world market levels, the result may be increased employment but only at the cost of much slower growth (since the potential of the world market will be lost). And if such technologies are inefficient, they will waste scarce resources. Myrdal and others have argued that the excess labor force must be absorbed by the agricultural sector, which must then, in turn, increase its productivity. This may be a contradiction in terms, for many of the advances in agriculture have come through capital-intensive technology. Nevertheless it does seem clear that some improvement in the employment situation can be achieved by more careful and selective use of labor-intensive techniques, land redistribution, and the provision of other services for the agricultural sector.[44] But this sector is unlikely to be able to deal with the whole range of the employment problem, and at present rates of population growth in many underdeveloped countries, even a rapid growth rate in the nonagricul-

43. See the tables in Ahluwalia, "Dimension of the Problem," pp. 5 and 7.

44. There is much debate about this issue in the technical literature, but it is clear that some possibilities of increasing agricultural employment do exist. See *An Assessment of Constraints to Development and the Role of External Assistance in the Least Developed Countries* (Geneva: Report by the UNCTAD Secretariat, TD/B/AC.17/Misc.1, July 1975):13; and John Cole, *The Poor of the Earth* (London: Macmillan, 1976). E. F. Schumacher, *Small Is Beautiful* (London: Abacus, 1974), pp. 148–59, is optimistic about the potential for intermediate technology in local areas, but it seems questionable to me that enough such technology will be available soon to really "solve" the employment problem.

tural sectors of the economy can probably deal only with a part of the problem. This suggests that redistribution in the form of increased income-earning opportunities may not by itself be a sufficient employment strategy. External support may still be necessary, especially over the next 10 to 20 years. Self-reliance in these circumstances may be an impossible luxury for the vast majority of underdeveloped countries, and redistribution policies that force these countries out of the international system may not make much sense *as long as reasonable amounts of help from the external world are forthcoming.*

What is at issue here is another version of a classic principle of social science: Everything is connected to everything else. A small and poor country cannot afford to concentrate on an employment strategy that cuts it off from the external world and forces it to rely on its own resources.[45] The shortrun costs will be especially severe because they are likely to cut growth rates sharply (decreasing employment opportunities over time) and increase the dangers of domestic unrest. Is it absolutely certain that an employment strategy must force these countries into a closed economy and increasing degrees of self-reliance? Or can the new approach be redefined to take advantage of the benefits of redistribution without incurring all its costs?

## REDISTRIBUTION REDEFINED

Redistribution policies seem to me to make eminently good sense. They are obviously justified on purely humanitarian grounds, but they may also exert a beneficial impact on birth control (where living standards have gone up, the population growth rate has frequently gone down), on the productivity of the working force, and on incentives to save and to invest—and thus ultimately on the rate of growth itself. But if it is inevitable that such policies

45. P. N. Rosenstein-Rodan has stressed the extent to which employment strategies emphasizing second-best techniques may make it impossible to integrate the LDCs into the world economy: "The Have's and the Have Not's Around the Year 2000," in Jagdish W. Bhagwati, ed., *Economics and World Order* (New York: Macmillan, 1972), pp. 35–36.

will have to rest on uncompetitive, protected industries, the beneficial results are likely to be short term and limited. The government will have to forego whatever resources it might have extracted from competitive exports, a carefully controlled foreign investment policy, and foreign aid. Perhaps more significantly, redistribution in the context of declining or stagnant growth rates is bound to create a great deal of domestic conflict, especially in societies already divided by profound social cleavages. This means that some concern for growth is still imperative, for it can help to reduce income differentials through the provision of jobs and may help to defuse some degree of domestic conflict.[46] It seems useful to ask, then, whether the new strategy could be modified to retain the benefits of redistribution policies without necessarily returning to traditional growth policies. That is, is there a redistribution policy that does not necessarily compel a departure from the international system and thus a sharp cut in growth rates? The key point to keep in mind is, I believe, that redistribution policies may have a beneficial impact on growth over the medium and long term, but in the short run such policies are either less helpful for growth or are taken to be so by conventional theory. What is necessary is a way to get to the long run at least cost.

This revised strategy might not be acceptable to radical intellectuals and elites who feel that any contact with the international system—even a controlled and limited one—is evil. The answer to these questions also must be entirely hypothetical, for neither the original strategy nor a modified strategy have been adequately tested. Nevertheless speculation about the possibility of a revised strategy may be helpful, since the benefits of redistribution seem important enough to impel one to seek ways to avoid or dilute the attendant disadvantages. The comments that follow must, of course, be taken as merely suggestive.

46. Chenery, "Growth and Structural Change," argues that the growth-versus-redistribution problem can be handled easily by simply shifting the benefits of growth to different groups within society. But it is, of course, the question of just how to do this in poor and weak societies that is at issue—as well as the costs of shifting the benefits to groups that may not (or may) be as productive as the groups from whom benefits are taken. I believe Chenery also oversimplifies the problem by failing to note the extent to which the shift of benefits also implies a corresponding shift in the composition of benefits.

De Vries has noted:

It is extremely unlikely that full employment policies will mean a slowing of growth. How would improved utilization of human resources throughout the economy and society reduce output below the production levels of an economy in which 30% of urban labor is unemployed and needs public support and there is widespread rural under-employment? [47]

But what is implied by the "improved utilization of human resources"? The usual answer is a switch to labor-intensive technology to take advantage of existing domestic factor endowments. The problem with this is that it can or might make the structure of production increasingly inefficient and uncompetitive. This means that the new strategy will work only in conjunction with a more general strategy to alter the composition and methods of production. Labor-intensive technology ought to be used to produce the simplest and most unsophisticated products for mass consumption. But where exports or intermediate domestic goods can be produced most efficiently by capital-intensive technology—and perhaps even by some foreign companies—such technology ought to be adopted.[48] Labor-intensive technology ought not to be used in areas of production where it succeeds only in making the goods (especially export goods) produced uncompetitive. The government is simply too poor to give up doing the few things it can do well: It needs the money too desperately. There are, however, two important qualifications to this argument. I am suggesting, in effect, a partially open "bicycle culture," rather than a completely closed strategy. This necessarily implies that the industrial countries will remain open to these exports, will provide foreign aid to help the other sectors of the economy, and will not respond as if this

47. Barend de Vries, "Jobs," in Rice, ed., *Developments Targets for the 70's: Jobs and Justice*, p. 97.
48. *Ibid.*, pp. 100–1. In any event even a strategy oriented toward self-reliance and an effort to meet the needs of the mass of the populace will still require some export growth—at least for a reasonably long period of transition—to buy the necessary imports that permit increasing self-reliance. Obviously exports would become less critical over time in the new approaches, for presumably the need for imports would gradually decline. In my revision of these approaches, however, the issue would be stated or perceived differently: What creates a profit that can be used for the benefit of the whole society—whether exports or not—will be pursued.

strategy was subversive or a threat to their own interests. Even more critically the LDC governments themselves must be willing and able to use the profits from the more competitive, capital-intensive production to help subsidize the other sectors of the economy. Private entrepreneurs in the export sector must be given a reasonable return for their efforts, but they must not be allowed to invest in whatever they choose or to spend as they see fit.

Once an economy is created, particular patterns of demand are also created, vested interests exist to resist change, and particular kinds of skills and knowledge develop. Thus altering the structure of production away from products created primarily for the urban middle and upper classes, and with large inputs of foreign capital and skilled labor, is likely to be enormously difficult. It is easy to say that what is needed is an economy that produces less sophisticated, more labor-intensive goods designed to meet the needs of poor, rural societies. But doing it overnight by a massive revolutionary effort seems to me a romantic illusion. What I am arguing for here is reform, not revolution, which is to say, not throwing away whatever benefits can be got from the external world by a radically inward turn, creating so much domestic conflict that no consistent policies at all can be implemented. This is a strategy that deliberately seeks to make redistribution less threatening to the elites—at least to those elites who are concerned with their own security but also concerned with decent standards of living for the mass of the populace. I am also arguing, in the short run, for a combination of some aspects of the two growth strategies: redistribution for long-term growth and as a short-range response to the needs of the great mass of the population and retention of those aspects of the more conventional growth theories that have enabled competitive industries to be established and that may keep the middle and upper classes from discontent and confrontation. The compromise I am advocating implies more than redistribution with growth (although it does imply that); it also implies redistribution without self-reliance.

A degree of openness toward the external world must, of course, rest on selectivity. Openness does not imply the need to accept any or all of the restrictive business practices employed by many multinational corporations. Nor does it imply the need to continue importing luxury goods or highly capital-intensive production processes that benefit primarily only those already rich. In this sense the controls now being sought through codes of conduct for the transfer of technology and the behavior of multinational corporations, even if such codes of conduct are not legally binding, provide useful guidance on what is or is not permissible. Moreover, there is no necessary conflict between openness and an increasing degree of collective self-reliance within the Third World.

In the shortrun period with which we are concerned, however, neither collective self-reliance nor controls on foreign business practices are likely to exert a major practical effect. This is so because of the difficulties of negotiating such agreements, because of the weakness of existing ties within the Third World (and the difficulty of reorienting elite perspectives), because of the lack of flexibility within poor economies, and because of the condition of many of the poorest countries, which remain in serious need of external support. Some tension is thus inevitable between long-range objectives and short-range needs, and it would be imprudent to act as if the long range were close at hand or could be telescoped forward by some magic means. The results, as with import substitution, might be perverse: more severe dependence as a consequence of premature assumptions about increased power and autonomy and willingness to cooperate within the Third World. In these circumstances a two-track strategy may be imperative: on the one hand, efforts to establish the practical grounds for self-reliance and to control the behavior of foreign companies (and governments) and, on the other hand, recognition of the need for short-term compromises to ensure whatever foreign support remains necessary.

Radicals may object that this is an antirevolutionary strategy that does not immediately overturn the existing socioeconomic structures and does not eliminate corrupt and self-interested elites. This is true but not decisive. Where the elites are totally corrupt or inept, there is no possibility that a new approach to development will be seriously considered. As a result the policies we have been discussing cannot be treated sensibly apart from a preliminary judgment that a ruling elite exists that is able to understand and make a genuine commitment to a new development strategy—that we have in power a Nyerere, not a Pinochet.

Conservatives will object that any attempt to reduce income differentials is mistaken because such policies create a disincentive to work hard, save, and invest and a positive incentive to conceal wealth, to send it abroad, or even to emigrate.[49] One response to this is that the modified strategy still permits entrepreneurs and skilled workers some amount of leeway, although considerably less than they normally get in an open market economy. In any case these groups hardly have a consistent record in support of the public interest—they have not always worked hard or saved and invested wisely, and they have managed to conceal wealth or send it abroad or emigrate even in systems favorable to their interests.[50]

Streeten and Stewart have argued that conversion to "investment in small-scale activities, and production of investment and consumption goods for the worst off . . . would thus almost certainly reduce the rate of growth measured in conventional terms, at least for a time."[51] This would cut the available resources to redistribute; perhaps even more critically, it would undermine elite support, especially if that support rested on the notion that elite gains would not be suddenly or radically threatened. I am in general agreement with this argument, for I believe that elite fear about the shortrun effects of a slower growth rate is one of the critical obstacles inhibiting the adoption of redistribution policies. I have argued for a moderate approach to redistribution and to a continuing concern with growth, not because I believe it guarantees success or is likely to be sufficient in all cases, but because there is no other redistribution policy that seems to stand any chance of gaining more than random or occasional elite support. But in addition I believe that the only other way in which the negative effects of slower growth might be attenuated is by substantial external sup-

49. See P. T. Bauer and B. S. Yamey, "The Pearson Report: A Review," in T. J. Byres, ed., *Foreign Resources and Economic Development* (London: Frank Cass, 1972), p. 67.

50. For example, Karl von Vorys, *Political Development in Pakistan* (Princeton, N.J.: Princeton University Press, 1965), p. 294, reports that private subscriptions to government bonds or yields from broadly based taxes did not keep pace with the growth of national income in Pakistan.

51. Stewart and Streeten, "New Strategies of Development," p. 19.

port for a new approach to development; this is why I have argued for a partially open orientation. More than this may be necessary in many cases, however, including a new concept of aid, new attitudes toward technology transfer, and more understanding among Western political leaders that redistribution is not in conflict with the interests of the developing countries—or, *a fortiori*, with developed country interests.[52] There is some evidence that these changes are at least fermenting, but it is fragmentary, and the results may be too long delayed.

## REDISTRIBUTION: OTHER VIRTUES

What does the preceding discussion suggest about the likelihood that the ruling elites of many underdeveloped countries will adopt policies of redistribution and self-reliance? Many reasons make such a decision unlikely. The sacrifices demanded from the elite in terms of their own opportunities to amass wealth, the loss of ties with an external world that serves as a point of reference for many elites, continued fascination with the status aspects of economic growth, potential political threats from newly powerful interests, the difficulties of transforming economic institutions and patterns of behavior, and the doubts that some—not all—radical intellectuals have about the wisdom of these policies certainly suggest that genuine commitments to redistribution (and self-reliance) are likely to be limited.

This argument implies, I believe, that if a number of LDCs begin adopting strategies of redistribution and self-reliance, they are likely to do so reluctantly and by the force of events. A combination of desperate domestic problems and an insufficiently respon-

52. This indicates, I believe, one salient but unnoticed connection between the more or less traditional demands on the UNCTAD agenda—more aid, commodity agreements, preferences, technology transfer—and the newer emphasis on redistribution. In addition it may be another reason to question the demand for radical efforts at redistribution: Beyond the facts that it frightens the elites and that the conditions to make it work successfully are not present in many developing countries, radical redistribution is also likely to engender a negative reaction from the developed countries whose support in the short run could be important. This, of course, presumes that there is some possibility that this support could be forthcoming.

sive international system may simply force not only a sharp inward turn but also a direct assault on a range of extraordinary human problems. This provides another perspective on the question of whether these strategies are revolutionary or not. Where the ruling elites are committed to both redistribution and self-reliance, an attempt to transform the domestic socioeconomic structure in a revolutionary fashion may be the result. It is of some interest, I think, that a number of military regimes have recently come to power that at least ostensibly seek such radical goals (e.g., Peru, Bolivia, even Portugal), which may be one of the primary ways in which self-reliance and redistribution become more popular among the elites in the years ahead—especially if the officer class increasingly comes from the middle and lower middle class. (This is an odd inversion of the once fashionable notion that the military would lead the way in development and anticommunism; now they may lead the way to self-reliance and anti-Westernism.) Whether such an attempt at revolution by either the military or other elites can be successful is another matter.

Where the commitment to a new approach more closely parallels the revisions I have discussed, the most likely result may be a sustained effort at reform. But where the elites adopt the new approach without much personal conviction, but only to buy off the discontented, a fundamental transformation of the socioeconomic structure is improbable. The most likely result in this circumstance is a piecemeal application of some of the policies associated with redistribution—for example, as in Ceylon with subsidies for food and transportation—but no effort to begin creating an integrated national economy. But buying off the discontented cannot survive the next foreign exchange crisis, because nothing much will have been done in the interim to remove or alleviate the causes of discontent.

There is another way in which redistribution might become increasingly fashionable among Third World ruling elites: by the demonstration effect. One needs only to recall that most of the prevailing ideas within the Third World—rapid growth, industrialization, long-term planning, and so on—were imported by the elites from external sources. Redistribution may shortly become the dominant doctrine in enough institutions to be passed along in the same fashion. Indeed it already is a central element in the programs of the World Bank and the Agency for International Development. Perhaps the effects of this intellectual import will be more beneficial than some of its predecessors. Nevertheless the impact of the new approach to development may not be profound (or prolonged) if it is accepted only because it is in fashion, or because it has been accepted by peers, or because it is a good gambit in efforts to extract more aid.

The new approach constitutes an important addition to the debate on development. But does it make any difference to the industrial countries? After all, apart from the relatively small group of LDCs who possess important resources, it probably makes little tangible difference to the industrial states if large numbers of LDCs turn inward and cut or limit their ties with the external world. Indeed, if conditions in a number of LDCs continue to deteriorate and the prospect of much external support erodes any further, the rich countries might well advocate such inward orientations as an alternative to desperate measures like terrorism, obstructionism, and nuclear threats, all designed to blackmail the rich states into some compensatory charity. Such tactics would probably hurt the poor far more than the rich; nevertheless the rich might be willing to pay some blackmail to avoid whatever inconveniences might result. From this perspective, withdrawal from the system by potential charity cases might be an even more preferable alternative than paying the costs of blackmail. But I have not, of course, laid out the premises of a revised redistribution strategy simply to make it easier for the rich countries to ignore a particularly troublesome group of underdeveloped countries. Quite to the contrary, I believe the new approach in no way threatens the legitimate interests of the rich countries and is a fundamentally sound orientation for large numbers of developing countries.

There are other reasons why the new approaches to development are worth some consideration. Perhaps the most important reason is the contrast between most of the development strategies of the past 25 years and the new approaches that have begun to appear in the past 5 years. The older strategies were offered with inflated expectations about how easy it would be to establish a process of self-sustaining growth and to reduce the degree of dependence on the external world. When the old strategies failed or, more accurately, were not sufficiently successful, they were dropped, and the quest for a new "key" to development was begun again.

The new approaches seem especially important to me because they have, for the first time, rejected more or less desperate efforts to mold the economies of the developing countries into the latest set of theoretical abstractions and have begun to move toward indigenous responses that reflect an attempt to deal with real and immediate problems. Inflated expectations are less likely to arise, and policies are not likely to be discarded when they fail to solve all problems. These are not small virtues. They do not guarantee success or provide a magic formula by which Niger can become a Denmark or Paraguay a Switzerland. What concentration on problems does do, I think, is to increase the possibility that the LDCs will be able to live with their problems at a more bearable level in the near future and perhaps even learn how to contain or ameliorate them by themselves.

Another virtue of the new approaches ought to be noted. Most advocates of redistribution and self-reliance share the belief that the international system is primarily responsible for their poverty and underdevelopment, which is surely at least partially wrong—one needs only to consider that some countries relatively untouched by outside forces (Haiti, Ethiopia, Thailand) are still very backward and that some countries that were under foreign control (Ivory Coast, Malaysia, Kenya) have done reasonably well. In any case, whereas the attribution of guilt may or may not be justified, the proponents of the new approach have also argued that the solution to the problems of underdevelopment cannot be found in or from the international system. Isolation from the rich, perhaps some limited cooperation with other poor countries, and an emphasis on the need for fundamental national change—toward a "bicycle culture"—are the leitmotifs of the new doctrines. This is surely salutary, for even in the best of circumstances the international system could not help national states that have made no effort to cope with their own problems. There are asymmetries in the relationship between system pressures and the LDCs: A malign and conflicted international system can do more harm to the LDCs than a benign international system (which means something much less than an altruistic system) can do good, for in the latter case the LDC must still be able to take advantage of the opportunities proffered. In both cases, therefore, concern for the quality of national institutions and capabilities must be the first priority.

The context and meaning of foreign aid would be significantly altered within this approach. The major economic rationale for aid has been its function in filling the "savings gap" or the "foreign exchange gap." Aid was thus designed to provide the difference between needed investment funds and available investment funds in a growth process. The advocates of redistribution and self-reliance have rejected aid on these grounds, arguing that it has been ineffective or disruptive (or, for radicals, that it has been insufficiently disruptive). At best, aid would presumably be limited to technical assistance from international organizations or to immediate relief efforts in case of a disaster of some sort. This might require aid levels below the Pearson Report target of 1 percent of GNP (and 0.7 percent in public aid), and perhaps even below current levels of giving, which partially explains radical suspicions about the motives of some Western analysts who have expressed support for redistribution and self-reliance. Aid could also be given to finance some investments in human capital. If aid was also given to relieve current consumption problems, the total could mount substantially. Nevertheless, even in this case, unpublished estimates by reputable experts suggest a top figure of $30 billion per year, which is not much beyond the current level of resource transfers. In any event, political constraints would ensure that the level would not rise appreciably.

Foreign aid for these three purposes—technical assistance, emergency relief, and investment in human capital—is consistent with redistribution policies but inconsistent in an important degree with a quest for self-reliance. This seems to me another argument for a revision of the new approach, with immediate emphasis on redistribution. There seems to me no reason at all for external aid agencies to reject this approach, except for attachment to ancient doctrines that badly need revision or to the shortsighted realpolitik vision that we owe support only to those who support us and, worse yet, seek to emulate us.

## REDISTRIBUTION AND THE POLICYMAKING SYSTEM

A sensible policymaking system for developing countries must take account of the context of poverty, weakness, and inefficiency within which it must operate. A fully coordinated, centrally planned economy is obviously out of the question. A market economy, conversely, is unlikely to function very well where the entrepreneurs are in short supply, where social costs and the public interest are likely to be ignored, and where the market itself suffers from many deficiencies. As a result it might make sense to consider creating a policymaking system that attempts to combine less elaborate forms of national planning—which are necessary to give overall guidance to the economy and to maintain some responsibility for the public interest—with a more extensive effort at local planning—to give each segment of society some sense of control over its own interests—and with a more modified and limited market system, to take advantage of whatever entrepreneurial and export skills do exist. This model of a policymaking system is intended not simply to facilitate agreement on particular policies but also to make sure that the agreements move the country in desirable and consistent directions. One seeks here also mechanisms by which to avoid one of the most salient weaknesses of many policymaking systems: the tendency to adopt a policy and then let it drift out of control through inertia or ignorance. Feedback from local areas is a critical variable in systems characterized by low levels of information and sharp discontinuities between urban and rural areas. This is also an argument against overcommitment of resources at the inception of a program.

The advocates of redistribution and self-reliance have emphasized decentralization and local planning, but they have underestimated the need for some form of central guidance and have totally rejected the market system in either its domestic or international forms. The modification I have proposed in the new approach, in which redistribution measures are emphasized and self-reliance measures are deemphasized or delayed (unless the international system becomes so hostile that there is no alternative to self-reliance except submission), seems to me much more consonant with the policymaking system I have advocated. Clearly a need exists for central guidance and government intervention in devising and implementing programs to redistribute income and improve the quality of human capital, but there is also a great need for local participation in planning and implementation, for these are policies that grant priority to individual welfare. Finally, there is also some room for entrepreneurial activity where comparative advantage exists and there is some willingness to risk contact with the world at large in exchange for needed benefits.

Redistribution combined with a careful degree of openness toward the external world might also succeed in allaying some elite fears about the dangers of direct redistribution. Exporting and importing interests, to which many of the ruling elite are connected, would be controlled but not eliminated. Foreign investors would be limited to certain areas and to certain practices, but this is less likely to engender hostile reactions than outright expulsion. And the fact that imports are sought, not simply to begin the process of creating an economy that could ultimately withdraw from the international trading system, but rather to operate industries that can become competitive with imports or to help in implementing redistribution policies (e.g., via food or technical assistance) might also diminish the opposition of many conventional economic theorists.[53] Finally the approach I have outlined does not attempt to jump quickly from stagnation to revolution, for this may well be beyond the capacity of more than a handful of underdeveloped countries. Making steady and tangible progress in a consistent direction may be the most that can legitimately be expected, and this is the aim also of the policymaking approach I have described.

53. Albert O. Hirschman, *A Bias for Hope: Essays on Development and Latin America* (New Haven, Conn.: Yale University Press, 1971), pp. 25–26, suggests that the LDCs should alternate contact with and insulation from the developed countries, first learning from the rich and then withdrawing to digest the learning. This is an interesting idea, but I expect that an LDC that could manage so complex a process might also be at the stage where it could deal adequately with the system without an in-and-out strategy.

## REDISTRIBUTION: IN CONCLUSION

I emphasize, in conclusion, not only the provisional nature of these observations, but also the fact that they are not completely irrelevant for the small group of underdeveloped countries who are able and willing to compete in the international system. There are three areas of activity—and one attitude—that may determine the success of a redistribution policy (beyond, of course, a thoroughly malign international system) and that may also serve as indicators of the seriousness of the government's commitment. The first area is agricultural productivity, for no such policy can work unless the country frees itself from the need to import large amounts of necessary foods. This is self-evident for LDCs that also seek self-reliance, for food imports must be paid for through export receipts or foreign aid. Tanzania's recent difficulties have been compounded, for example, by the fact that she had to import 40 percent of her food needs in 1974. Since an increasing number of LDCs are running into food deficits, this makes a more modified turn away from the international system sensible, if not imperative. Increasing agricultural productivity will still be necessary, however, to begin the slow process of industrialization.

The second critical area is population policy, for it is unlikely that gains in agricultural productivity can keep up with a population that doubles every 20 or 25 years.[54] Any government that asserts its commitment to redistribution but denies the need for population control is either naive or willfully lying about its intentions. About 30 LDCs have adopted family planning as official policy, and

54. It was generally true, I believe, that agricultural productivity kept up with population growth in the Third World in the 1960s. But there are ominous signs that this is no longer so, especially for the least developed countries. Note the following table:

|  | Agricultural Production | | Food Production | | Population |
|---|---|---|---|---|---|
|  | 1960–70 | 1970–74 | 1960–70 | 1970–74 | 1960–73 |
| All developing countries | 2.9 | 1.5 | 3.0 | 1.5 | 2.5 |
| Least developed countries | 2.7 | 0.6 | 2.5 | 0.9 | 2.6 |

SOURCE: *Review of Progress in the Implementation of Special Measures In Favour of the Least Developed Among Developing Countries* (UNCTAD, TD/B/AC.17/3 (Parts I and II), June 1975):5.

in another 20 countries the state allows voluntary agencies to support family planning efforts. Family planning is heavily supported in Asia (covering 90 percent of the population), but only about 20 percent of the governments in Africa and 20–25 percent in Latin America support it.[55] This is at least somewhat indicative of the seriousness of a government's commitment to slowing population growth, although many experts doubt that family planning (as distinct from more extensive population control strategies) can or will achieve its goals. Still, for many of the smaller LDCs, population growth is a manageable problem, and family planning programs are not likely to be useless or irrelevant.

The last area of concern, which appears without fail in any discussion of the problems and prospects of the LDCs, is elite behavior and elite commitment. Unless the government elite accepts the need for personal austerity, limits the salaries and perquisites of official life, reforms the tax structure to remove its most regressive features, and attacks corruption directly, the population at large is hardly likely to believe that the elite is sincere or that its commitment is more than another rhetorical bow to the latest fashions among development intellectuals. Obviously the ruling elite is unlikely to take the risks implicit in redistribution unless it feels personally secure—or desperate. How does one move the elites past an obsession with personal security (and gain) to a willingness to take risks to achieve a national future? Waiting on the accidents of personality seems insufficient, for there seem to be as many Idi Amins as Julius Nyereres. Perhaps the demonstration effect among peers will help, especially if there are a few "success stories" to contemplate. It is more likely, however, especially among states so exposed to every storm within the international system, that only the pressure of events may finally compel acceptance of anything as threatening as redistribution, let alone self-reliance.

Finally one attitude or belief that is increasingly prevalent among many advocates of redistribution may be dangerous. This is the presumption that redistribution has the power of achieving a

55. See Theodore K. Ruprecht and Carl Wahren, *Population Programmes and Economic and Social Development* (Paris: Organization for Economic Co-operation and Development, 1974).

rapid and profound transformation of the developing countries. I believe this is not so, because there is too little to redistribute, because the weight of past attitudes and past mistakes is too heavy, because elite opposition may be too strong (and mass attitudes initially too hostile or too indifferent), and because external shocks in the short and medium term may still be too overwhelming. The enormous moral and practical virtues of redistribution may well be lost if its advocates inflate expectations beyond reasonable bounds and if they are naive about the ease with which they can overcome obstacles or produce beneficial results.

----◄••►----

I think that no one who has become familiar with the problems confronting the underdeveloped countries can escape a large amount of intellectual and moral sympathy for the argument that what these countries need is a revolutionary transformation of their socioeconomic structures. But the reality of the moment is insecure elites and weak and inefficient governments. These governments may not have much power, but they are likely to have enough to repress revolutionary movements. If they do not have that much power, the likely results are a long period of internal warfare and an even sharper drop in immediate living standards. Even if the revolutionary movement wins, it will still face the problem of creating a revolution in a society that remains poor, weak, and badly integrated. As the historical record attests, revolutionary élan may rapidly degenerate into a struggle for survival within the movement, and the goals of the revolution may recede into the ever more distant future.

I do not argue that revolutions in the underdeveloped countries must always fail (except in the sense that a new ruling elite may emerge). Nevertheless it seems to me that the problem of overcoming all the deficiencies that call forth the revolutionary movement may well be beyond a revolutionary solution; that is, deficiencies that are so profound and pervasive may be eliminated only by a gradual, evolutionary attempt to create the human and institutional infrastructure of a developed society. In any case it seems to me that the arguments for the necessity of revolution may be more a reaction against past policies and a romanticism about future policies than a carefully considered evaluation of what revolution is likely to bring to an underdeveloped country.

Uncertainties about the possibility of revolution in the present, and doubts about the wholly beneficient effects of revolution in the future, have underlain this argument. I confess to uncertainties of my own that the reform strategy I have advocated will be sufficient—even in the countries to which I have limited its application. On balance—and no more than that—I think that the risks of gambling that a committed reform strategy will work are slightly less than the risks implicit in a revolutionary strategy. Ultimately, I think, this decision rests on the fact that the reform strategy I have proposed aims at improving the quality of life as quickly as possible for the great mass of poor people. It is, after all, the well-being of these people that the revolutionary theorists are willing to sacrifice to their vision of an even more beneficial future.

## Part Four

---

# The International Systems: Responding to the Third World

# 10

## Emerging Patterns:
## The Third World in Evolution

### ON THE UTILITY OF FORECASTING

Ten years ago Bertrand de Jouvenel wrote that ". . . forecasting would be an absurd enterprise, were it not inevitable." [1] This catches the dilemma of all attempts at futurology very well. On the one hand the absence of social theories makes formal efforts at prediction futile, for there are no lawful generalizations about relationships between events that permit the judgment that, if A happens, B will always follow. Even statements of probability must be treated with great caution, since there is no way of knowing whether all the factors that might affect future events have been included in the analysis that established the original set of probabilities. Moreover, in many cases the data on which hypotheses have been established may be inadequate or inaccurate. On the other hand, whatever the difficulties of deriving accurate forecasts, all of us—individuals, organizations, governments—are implicit or explicit forecasters when we decide what actions we are going to take. The alternative, then, seems to be either to do the best we can with whatever means we have in peering ahead or simply to stumble into the future blindly.

1. Bertrand de Jouvenel, *The Art of Conjecture* (New York: Basic Books, 1967), p. 248.

We can avoid some of the dangers of this situation if we are careful about acknowledging the limitations of our efforts to forecast. This means that we must emphasize that no model of the future is a precise and accurate blueprint of what will actually happen. Despite the practitioner's demand for specific predictions about what must happen in the future, the social scientist—unless he is pretentious or foolish—must accept the fact that he cannot meet the demand. The social scientist can also respond, however, that this does not necessarily mean that his forecasts are useless: By using available trends, data, and insights—and even intuitions—the social scientist can provide a range of plausible outcomes of current developments that educates and sensitizes the practitioner to the long-range consequences of present actions. This emphasis should clarify what I think is an indispensable point in any effort to forecast in the social sciences: What such efforts do is to help us make reasoned choices now about where we would like to be some years hence and what we should think about doing to get there. The visionary and speculative nature of forecasting should never be allowed to obscure the fact that it is a practical enterprise designed to help us make better choices in the immediate present.[2]

The climate of opinion for such ventures into futurology has altered markedly in the past few years: The assumption that we are in the midst of fundamental change has risen sharply, but expectations that the changes will be beneficial have fallen sharply. We no longer fear instability without change—what one observer called "agitated immobility" a few years ago—but rather the loss of control over events that can decisively affect our fate. Pessimism about our ability to manage the future has also been encouraged by a loss of faith in the workability of the rules by which we run our economic and political systems and by the failure to devise generally acceptable substitutes.

These uncertainties intensify the already extraordinarily difficult task of forecasting a set of plausible futures. Nevertheless we need to make the effort, not only because the alternative of drifting

2. This is a major theme in chapter 4 of Robert L. Rothstein, *Planning, Prediction and Policy Making in Foreign Affairs* (Boston: Little, Brown, 1972).

or "muddling through" is too dangerous, but also because there is no other way of establishing a sensible long-term policy toward the developing countries. There are, however, a number of specific limitations to the forecasts that follow that must be understood. In the first place they do not refer to the immediate future, but rather to a mid-term period approximately 5 to 10 years hence. In the second place a number of critical issues that could have a major long-term impact on relations between rich and poor are not discussed: for example, nuclear proliferation, persistent inflationary biases in the economies of the industrial countries, the problem of converging comparative cost structures among the industrial countries, the related problem of devising a new industrial geography for the world, and, finally, increasing efforts to enhance the degree of collective self-reliance within the Third World. I presume that none of these issues are likely to exert a major impact in the period with which we are concerned. Finally I presume that the current confrontation between the rich and the poor does not end in the creation of a "new international economic order"—as I have already argued in chapter 1. I do not mean that important changes in the international systems will not occur in the next few years; rather, I mean only that, even with those changes, the existing hierarchy between rich and poor and the existing needs of the poor for some external support will not have changed very much. Indeed too much concern with the possibilities of radical transformation within the international order and too little concern with domestic transformation may make the needs of a good many developing countries for external support even more salient in the next decade.

I do not outline a whole range of alternative futures in the next section. Most such efforts seem to consist of statements that things will remain pretty much the same or that they will get slightly or more than slightly better or worse. To simplify the task at hand, I discuss only a single, plausible set of developments. These developments are likely to create an international system in the period around 1980 that is more tense and more conflict oriented than the present system but also that has not deteriorated into open conflict—one in which the sense that shared and mutually beneficial solutions are still necessary and possible has not completely disappeared. The primary justification for focusing on this outcome is simply that a system more benign than the one I discuss is not likely to have much difficulty in establishing cooperative norms, and a worse system is not likely to have any possibility of establishing such norms. Finally it should be clear that the forecasts in the next section are not meant to be normative. I seek only to outline a set of choices that I think might be made in the years ahead, not choices that I think necessarily ought to be made.

## THE EMERGING INTERNATIONAL SYSTEM: PATTERNS AND PROPHECIES

One issue, combining practical and metaphysical concerns in a complex fashion, may exert a profound impact on the way the relationship between rich and poor is perceived or dealt with in the next decade. The vector of two divergent trends—the rising or continuing strength of nationalism and the rising and increasingly felt strength of interdependence—is likely to provide the terms of the intellectual debate within which rich–poor issues are negotiated.

Nationalism, in terms both of ideology and of increased citizen demands on national governments, is neither a wholly malevolent nor benevolent trend, but it may create demands for insulation against the pressures of the international system or, among the strongest powers, a demand for order and control to ensure access to needed resources or to contain deliberately disruptive behavior. This would imply a system in which the values of order and control, but also certainty and power, prevailed over the values of justice. Intervention by the strong, in the name of stability, could become the operative norm.

Rising levels of interdependence threaten national control and an order dominated by traditional notions of hierarchy. In some cases it may be necessary to seek to limit or control the immediate effects of interdependence until national perceptions of the need for global bargains become more powerful. But there are also very few longrun national solutions to most of the major problems (and opportunities) created by interdependence; there are only questions of how much more it will cost to thwart cooperative solutions that also have some shortrun national costs. Part of the problem of resolving or ameliorating these complex issues is a reflection of the inability or unwillingness of weak governments to take a sufficiently long-range perspective. Another part of the problem, however, reflects uncertainties about the significance and meaning of interdependence itself: Is it issues or countries or both that are interdependent; are solutions that increase interdependence always better (for whom?) than those that enhance national control; what are the areas of choice, and what are the areas in which efforts to control interdependence are likely only to decrease everyone's welfare? Perceptions of interdependence as a major political issue (in contrast, say, to perceptions of it in the classic economic sense as an argument for specialization) are perhaps too new for much more than *ad hoc* and fragmentary efforts to come to terms with these uncertainties to be expected. This is especially true so long as we remain committed to economic and political doctrines that take it as an unexamined premise that interdependent solutions must be evaluated in terms of the shortrun costs they impose to acquire other shortrun national benefits. At any rate, in an international system in which interdependence began to prevail over nationalism, there might be more openness to change and more tangible concern for equity. In this context, intervention would still persist, but not to enhance the power of the strong or to maintain control over the weak. I do not imply that interdependence ought to be sought as an end in itself (which would anyway be a politically futile injunction), but rather that the potential conflicts between nationalism and rising levels of interdependence cannot be satisfactorily resolved within a horizon dominated by the next election.

From the perspective of the underdeveloped countries, interdependence has generally seemed to be a euphemism for dependence. They have never been powerful enough to protect themselves against some of the most negative effects of interdependence. Consequently, while the attempt to resolve the conflict between interdependence and nationalism may be the overarching issue that determines the relationship between the underdeveloped countries and the industrial countries in the next decades, two supplementary themes will probably also be of great importance. One, reflected in UNCTAD and the demands for a New International Economic Order, will be an attempt to alter the rules of the existing order so that the benefits of interdependence are distributed more equitably. But the other theme will reflect an effort to increase the degree of interdependence within the Third World—the main area in which interdependence has lagged, if not actually decreased—by collective self-reliance.[3] Such an effort seeks not only to increase bargaining leverage against the industrial countries but also to provide some protection against the possibility of increased inwardness and disinterest in the Third World by the industrial countries.

---

I now turn to my effort to indicate the kind of group system that I think may emerge roughly around 1980. What are the salient characteristics of each of the Third World groups? Elite perceptions of stability, elite commitments to economic development, and elite attitudes toward the international division of labor will clearly remain significant. Nevertheless, as domestic problems become increasingly intractable, the need for some kind of leverage against the international system to extract more aid and trade will probably become a dominant consideration. So, too, will more objective consideration of what assets each country has to manipulate. These narrower national concerns are bound to become increasingly important as (or if) efforts to use the group pressure of the Third World—the trade unions strategy—fail, or if cartel pressures cannot maintain artificially high prices—the monopolist's strategy. Insofar as a unified Third World strategy continues to exist, I expect it will shift toward moral pressures to move the international system in the direction of the welfare state (e.g., with a progressive tax to fi-

3. Many factors may impede this development, not only economic ones (e.g., different levels of development, a lack of infrastructure, and the need for widespread agreement to avoid competition with exports from the developed countries) but also political ones (the need for OPEC support for self-reliance to be more than a marginal factor). Nevertheless there is a real emotional commitment behind collective self-reliance, as well as sensible practical judgments, and over time—even without OPEC support—it could be important.

nance foreign aid levies)—that is, to a vision of a more just order—
and to efforts to improve ties within the Third World.

In the interim the LDCs will have to make the best of whatever
they do best or of whatever they possess that remains in high demand. This could be a grim outcome, although much depends on
the particular asset and the likely reaction of the industrial states.
Small and weak countries do not "invent their futures"; with skill
and good fortune they can influence the terms and quality of their
dependence, but only in exceptional circumstances more than that.
And what the LDCs may have to bargain with in the years ahead—
basic commodities that are likely to fluctuate a good deal, but not
even to approximate the oil explosion, and weak or low-level manufacturing sectors—will not provide much leverage against the rest of
the world. At any rate I divide our groups according to the assets
that will probably strongly affect the positions they take toward the
external world.

THE RESOURCE RICH

High commodity prices in the last few years have increased the
share of LDC exports from 17 percent to 27 percent of the world's
exports. Most of the gains have gone, of course, to a relatively small
group of countries, preeminently the oil producers, but also to the
lucky possessors of minerals like copper, bauxite, rubber, tin, and
fluorospar. Less fortunate but reasonably well off were the exporters
of a number of products, like beef, cotton, iron ore, lead, rice, and
wheat, that were also exported by the industrial countries but were
still in high demand.

Nothing in particular ties the resource rich together except
being resource rich. There are enormous ironies, which may also be
the source of a great deal of local conflict in the years ahead, in the
disposition of resources. Zambia, for example, by geologic accident
sits on a fortune in copper: more than 90 percent of its foreign
exchange earnings have come from that one export since Zambian
independence. But neighbors like Uganda and Tanzania are not so
blessed and can only observe in envy. In Latin America, Chile,
Peru, and Venezuela have been blessed; Paraguay, Colombia, and

Uruguay, not so. In Asia, Indonesia and Malaysia have been lucky, but Pakistan and India, in desperate need, have been unlucky. And note Egypt (and Israel) without oil, in contrast to Kuwait and Saudi Arabia.

In the abstract, as has been repeatedly argued, it is unlikely that any of the new mineral cartels will be able to repeat OPEC's successes. Indeed, if demand for oil is cut, and if the oil consumers begin to produce substitutes for foreign oil, OPEC itself may begin to crumble by 1980—but those are problematic "ifs." In any event, for many of the important minerals crucial reserve positions are held by the United States, Canada, Australia, and New Zealand, all of whom presumably would resist efforts to overturn the existing international economic system (which is not to say they will not seek higher prices for their minerals).[4] Substitutes, synthetics, and improved conservation methods also give the major consumers a good deal of leverage, except in the case of oil. In addition the dominance of the industrial countries does not rest on their use of resources: It rests on superior technology, management skills, the control of information, and the marketing skills of large corporations. Consequently expropriation and the control of domestic resources are not likely to be sufficient to guarantee increasing returns for a particular mineral. This is obviously why so many raw materials producers have been intent on processing more of their resources domestically and improving distribution and marketing capacities, but they will still remain dependent on access to foreign markets.

4. The Western countries produce about 66 percent of total world minerals but consume about 90 percent, and so imports are necessary. For the breakdowns in different minerals, see Alexander Sutulov, *Minerals in World Affairs*, (Salt Lake City: University of Utah, 1972). On reserve positions, Canada has the world's largest reserves in tar sands, nickel, potash, and asbestos; is the largest producer of silver, zinc, and sulphur; and is important in copper, gold, iron ore, molybdenum, lead, titanium, uranium, and platinum. Australia has the largest reserves of bauxite and is very strong in iron ore (pp. 108–20). I cite these figures only to indicate some of the difficulties the cartels could have in achieving sufficient leverage, especially in the short and medium term. For technical discussions of the difficulty of constructing commodity cartels, see Marian Radetzki, "The Potential for Monopolistic Commodity Pricing by Developing Countries," in G. K. Helleiner, ed., *A World Divided: The Less Developed Countries in the International Economy* (London: Cambridge University Press, 1976) and Anthony Edwards, *The Potential for New Commodity Cartels* (London: The Economist Intelligence Unit, 1975).

For the cartel strategy to work, either super cartels of more than one material would have to be formed or OPEC would have to use its surplus funds to finance aggressive actions. The political and economic difficulties of constructing a super cartel are enormous, and there is little evidence that such an entity could function successfully. As for OPEC, there is a small group within it—Kuwait, Saudi Arabia, the United Arab Emirates—that may have problems in investing all its returns domestically; such funds could be used to support other cartels. But such conservative regimes also have a strong vested interest in maintaining an international system from which they clearly benefit; it is also unclear why they should favor higher prices for raw materials that they do not possess and that raise the prices of the manufactured goods they must import.[5]

Presumably the radicalization of OPEC could alter this judgment. The replacement, say, of the Shah of Iran and the King of Saudi Arabia by radical leaders might create the necessary ideological support for an alliance of raw materials producers against the consumers. The ideological emphasis is important, for only broad agreement on long-range values and goals would probably justify actions on OPEC's part that might not be in its own interest either in the short or the long term. I doubt this outcome, however, even if OPEC is radicalized, because most of the OPEC members cannot afford to sacrifice their own immediate gains in pursuit of a vision of an entirely different international order—and one in which they might be worse off.

Almost all the producer countries, including most of the OPEC states, cannot afford to be very charitable, for they have many domestic uses for their gains. This suggests, I think, that OPEC's support for other cartels probably will not be sufficient to "fuel" a major assault on the system. But OPEC, willingly or not, will continue to provide some support to Third World demands for change,

5. Our reaction to the OPEC threat has jumped from hysteria (invasion, occupation, etc.) to apathy. But we ought not to become overconfident now, when OPEC is having problems with excess production, because demand will soon rise—and we have been irresponsible in failing to take measures to reduce future leverage (or blackmail) against ourselves. In addition, we ought not to count too much on support of the conservative OPEC countries, since they share some of the attitudes of the radical countries and are under great pressure to support challenges to the existing order.

in part because some of the demands reflect shared grievances and in part because of fears of being isolated from and attacked by some states or groups in and out of the Third World. In any event, short-run gains are surely likely, the resource producers having strong incentives to cooperate with each other and to limit opportunities to break their control by divisive tactics. As long as they do not act intemperately in the next few years by raising prices arbitrarily or employing discriminatory embargoes—and thus making substitutes economical or intervention possible—they will probably be able to maintain reasonable rates of growth. Whether this will be sufficient to avoid domestic turmoil is unclear, much depending on other factors like the population growth rate, the degree of dependency on oil imports, and the costs of other imports. But some of the oil countries have also begun to inflame the expectations of their citizens, and some have invested their earnings unwisely, and a sharp drop in export earnings (or perhaps insufficient growth in earnings) could create a great deal of instability.

Prospects for this group of countries (both OPEC and the other resource rich) may begin to deteriorate in the late 1970s and early 1980s, at least in terms of maintaining rapidly rising prices. A number of forecasts by reputable experts suggest that commodity prices in the early 1980s will begin to fall to their 1960 levels.[6] By then, also, many of the efforts of the rich countries and of their large corporations to devise substitutes, to improve conservation, to develop new extraction technology, to invest in safe areas, and to stockpile against shortrun emergencies may sharply reduce the leverage of the resource producers.

Many of the resource producers are currently making long-range plans based on the assumption that they can sustain high prices for their commodities well into the future. If prices fall, these producers may be hurt particularly badly, because they are overextending themselves in the present and ignoring some of the necessary precautions against fluctuations in export earnings. Since

6. See, in particular, *Prospects for the Developing Countries* (Washington, D.C.: IBRD, Report No. 477, July 8, 1974), p. 10. There are some exceptions to this generalization, for the prices for timber, sugar, beef, fishmeal, and bauxite are expected to remain high.

many of these countries are trying to industrialize rapidly to reduce resource dependency, foreign exchange losses may be painful because they endanger newly created industries that need to import capital equipment (and sometimes raw materials). The list of the resource rich is also filled with large numbers of LDCs that have substantial domestic conflicts, either class or ethnic, that will be exacerbated by any slowing of growth. One needs only to note the following to illustrate the point: Chile, Peru, Malaysia, Philippines, Thailand, Nigeria, and Indonesia. Finally these countries may not find much support for higher prices from the rest of the LDCs: The LDCs who are attempting to industrialize and who must import raw materials to do so are especially vulnerable to higher prices, since they lack the capital or technology to develop substitutes.[7] And the LDCs who face higher costs for food and fertilizer imports or are the first victims of system-wide inflationary pressures may become increasingly hostile (fear of offending OPEC and OPEC's friends may dissipate if costs continue to mount and benefits remain promises).

What foreign policy will these countries adopt? Aggressive rhetoric is apt to persist for the next few years, and substantive efforts are likely to be directed toward creating effective resource cartels or to gaining consumer support for higher prices and a fairer commodity trading environment. These efforts probably will not provide much support for regional cooperation, the cartel members rarely falling into one geographic area. By the late 1970s the rhetoric may be considerably cooled, and major efforts may be directed primarily at getting consumer cooperation rather than at imposing producer demands. This may be especially true, not only if the rich countries become less dependent on foreign suppliers, but also if they are forced to compete with the Soviet Union (which may also be trying to sell raw materials in return for advanced industrial

7. One can see this already in the reluctance of some developing countries to support UNCTAD's integrated commodity program. The doubtful countries tend to be those who are net import losers because of the higher prices that might result from the integrated program or whose commodities are not included in the program. Also, there are a substantial number of developing countries who are not likely either to gain or to lose much from commodity agreements; they are likely to demand compensation for continued support.

products). Still, the resource rich have important assets that the industrial economies are likely to want; this gives them a degree of reciprocity that does not exist for exporters of cheap manufactured items. But the resource rich will be walking a thin line between pushing just enough to ensure high prices and pushing too far to ensure intervention (disguised or otherwise) and conflict.

In sum my forecast for this group is not optimistic. I believe that many of the resource rich are overestimating how much and for how long they will be able to sustain very high prices for their resources. By not preparing for trouble, they are liable to make it worse when it comes. Domestically the likelihood of conflict is high. Externally they are liable to end even more dependent than in the past on the charity of a Great Power patron, and they may also confront a number of serious local conflicts with other LDCs who covet their assets. Local wars, arms races, and constant problems with interventions and border skirmishes may be the result.

### MANUFACTURING EXPORTERS

The "success stories" among the LDCs in the last two decades included a number of small countries that developed a capacity to export manufactures.[8] The most prominent members of this group included South Korea, Taiwan, Pakistan (for a period in the 1960s), Hong Kong, Singapore, Israel, Puerto Rico, and Mexico. They are, or may be, joined by a few medium and small semi-industrial Latin American countries that may be compelled to emphasize export promotion policies after import substitution comes grinding to a halt.

The shortrun impact of the oil crisis and the rise in commodity prices have been particularly severe for this group of countries.[9] The recent experience of South Korea may be illustrative. For the past decade South Korea has had an extraordinary growth rate of more than 10 percent per year. Essentially the Koreans prospered by importing raw materials and converting them into finished goods for reexport. Cheap labor was a critical part of this process.

8. Hollis B. Chenery, "Growth and Structural Change," *Finance and Development* 8, no. 3 (September 1971).
9. See the table in chapter 8, p. 251.

Recent events illustrate why the open-economy, outward orientation can be so risky for small countries. Increased commodity prices raised the import bill sharply, and the slowdown in the economies of the major industrial states cut export receipts sharply; as a result, in the 6 months from June to December 1974, industrial production declined more than 9 percent, unemployment increased, the wholesale price index went up 37.4 percent, and the government was forced to devalue the currency by 20 percent.[10] South Korea was caught in what now almost seems to be the conventional bind between recession and inflation, and whatever the government did to relieve one problem—for example, devaluation as an antirecessionary policy—seemed likely to exacerbate the other. But this bind was much worse for a small country heavily dependent on foreign trade, for the Koreans could not sell their exports domestically, and they could not cut their imports sharply or whole industries would collapse.

The manufacturing exporters are making a series of bets about the future. They are gambling that they can remain competitive by keeping wages down or by developing enough flexibility to move on to higher levels of technology when new competitors enter the market. New competitors are especially threatening when the market itself is not expanding rapidly: Severe competition is likely because the prospect for any single country's expanding its exports is usually much higher than the prospects for the group as a whole. This is true because most of these countries tend to produce a similar range of products and because any large, across-the-board increase in exports will probably be met by market restrictions in the rich countries or by excess production that drives demand down.[11] Each suffers by seeking to maximize its own interests. And agree-

10. For the figures, see *The New York Times*, December 26, 1971. But there is also a paradox at work here. Part of the cost of the outward orientation is more exposure to external "shocks" but the learning process presumably ought also to provide the South Koreans with more ability to recover quickly by responding to new opportunities: in effect, hurt worst, recover first. Whether this will be true in fact is uncertain, in part because of other factors associated with the South Korean case.

11. On the differing prospects for single countries and a group of countries exporting the same commodity, see Ian Little, Tibor Scitovsky, and Maurice Scott, *Industry and Trade in Some Developing Countries* (London: Oxford University Press, 1970), pp. 234 ff.

ment on prices, market shares, and the restriction of production are difficult for poor countries that need revenue badly and have few other options.

The manufacturing exporters are also gambling that increasing dependence on the rich countries will be productive. Most of the manufacturing exporters need not only to export larger amounts of goods to the industrial countries but also to import more and more crucial goods (both raw materials and capital imports) to run their industries. The industrial countries can, however, obviously survive a drop in manufactured imports from these countries more readily than early and semi-industrializers can do without imports from the industrial world—the elements of reciprocity that have begun to appear between the resource-rich and the industrial countries are not nearly as apparent here. If the industrial countries feel threatened by cheap manufactured imports (as their labor unions and some industries already do), or if they slow their growth rates (e.g., by spending marginal dollars on leisure or services or by experiencing problems of adjusting to resource scarcity), the outward orientation may begin to look like a bad gamble. The general trend toward liberalizing the international trading system may not be able to survive the trend toward increasing governmental responsibility for national economic welfare—particularly when the two trends appear to be on a collision course.

Many of the manufacturing exporters chose an outward orientation, either because they had no other choice (Hong Kong, Singapore, Puerto Rico) or because they faced a major military threat and thus received (and needed) special treatment from the rich countries by way of foreign aid and trade benefits (South Korea, Taiwan, Pakistan). Military regimes confronting a threat can control domestic demand and impose the necessary sacrifices for growth. But if the military threat declines, and if aid levels are cut, and if growth begins to slow, domestic dissent may begin to rise rapidly. The many challenges to the regime of General Park in South Korea are indicative; some part of Pakistan's instability, beginning with the fall of Ayub Khan, may also be illustrative; and future problems in Taiwan, unless it becomes part of China, are predictable.

These states, as a group, have a strong interest in liberalizing trade among themselves, as well as with the group of raw materials exporters. Since they are competitive but frequently have different underlying cost structures, some welfare gains could be expected. In practical terms, however, they are not likely to be achieved: These countries do not fall into clear regional patterns, trade patterns have been established with the rich countries, transportation and marketing difficulties are enormous, nationalism makes it difficult to give up certain industries, and agreement on who is to specialize in what has been impossible. In addition it will be difficult for the manufacturing exporters to reach agreement with the LDCs who have not yet established much of a manufacturing capacity: The latter object to opening their markets to the products of neighbors, for they are frequently costlier and less efficient than products from the rich countries. Still, the potential for more intra-LDC trade is there—although it actually dropped as a percentage of total LDC trade in the last decade—and a series of efforts to increase such trade is likely to be a major theme of the next decade. As long as expectations are not raised to unreasonable levels, these efforts are likely to yield some important minor successes. And they may become more than marginally important if the rich countries turn inward or slow their growth rates.[12]

Both the resource-rich and the manufacturing exporters remain committed to rapid growth, which means continued high levels of dependence on the international economic system. But the manufacturing exporters have less leverage against the industrial countries, for what they have to offer is not indispensable, and the advantages they possess—cheap labor costs—are widely shared with other underdeveloped countries. Specific forecasts for this group of countries are problematic, for much depends on the behavior of the rich. Unless the rich countries grow very rapidly in the years ahead, one forecast could be for a great deal of economic conflict within the group of manufacturing exporters, each vying with the others to establish preferential agreements, to keep competitors out, and to

12. But the LDCs themselves must be willing to make some real, and not merely rhetorical, sacrifices for each other to make this work. Thus far they have not done so, primarily because it is so difficult for a poor country to give up whatever slim advantage it may have (e.g., a preference agreement) for longer run benefits.

offer more and more concessions to private foreign capital to invest in protected enclaves. As for foreign policy orientations toward the industrial world, I expect that these countries will be much more moderate than the resource rich and that they will seek to maintain close alignments with the industrial countries. This will probably ensure a disproportionate share of whatever foreign aid the Western countries give, as well as preferential access to Western markets. Western investors may also continue to favor these countries, so long as they seem secure and stable; indeed alignment may increase at least the shortrun probability of stability, for domestic elites threatened by radical groups may receive a good deal of foreign support—as with the current military regime in Chile, which has received a surprising amount of "unpolitical" aid from the World Bank and the United States.

### TURNING INWARD: OTHER ROADS TO DEVELOPMENT

The oil crisis and its attendant effects have devastated the immediate growth prospects of the "Fourth World," or what the U.N. calls the "most severely affected" states. For the next few years these countries will be in a desperate race to stay afloat—not to grow rapidly but to grow at all. A number of surveys have actually predicted negative growth rates for many of these countries in the next 5 years. Although these forecasts must be taken with great caution, they do indicate something of the dimension of the problem the poorest of the poor confront.

Even before the recent crisis few of the underdeveloped countries were actively challenging the conventional wisdom about theories of economic growth. Arguments in favor of turning inward, of emphasizing redistribution to benefit the poor directly and self-reliance to escape exploitation by the rich countries, were limited to a small number of development intellectuals and an even smaller number of governing elites. In the context of the present crisis neither growth nor redistribution look promising: Charity, more sacrifice, and a few lucky harvests may be all that the "most severely affected" can legitimately expect. Nevertheless, as I have already argued in chapter 9, I believe that redistribution may become an increasingly compelling choice to a large number of LDCs in the 1980s. The small countries that move in this direction are liable to be without much prospect of earning enough foreign exchange to sustain a program of industrialization and rapid growth: They are "have-nots" in natural resources or a manufacturing capacity.

What impact this group will have on the international system depends on how seriously they take their commitments to redistribution and self-reliance. Obviously any serious attempt to become more self-reliant would gradually remove these states from any significant contact with the international system. This would be far from splendid isolation, but it would nonetheless represent a clear movement away from the demands and pressures the LDCs have attempted to exert on the industrial powers for the past 25 years. These countries (presumably) would not seek as much foreign aid or would seek (or accept) only limited amounts of technical assistance; they would not actively seek foreign investment and would control whatever investments they felt it necessary to accept; and they would trade only for absolutely necessary items or to dispose of unusable surpluses.

This image of a relatively clear separation between the "bicycle culture" of the South and the Madison Avenue culture of the North is appealing to many of the advocates of redistribution and self-reliance. As I indicated in the last chapter, however, I doubt the ability of many LDCs to implement any significant degree of redistribution and self-reliance simultaneously. Redistribution, especially by means of a direct assault on the problems of poverty, malnutrition, and disease, is by far the most critical and most immediate task—except to ideologues who simply assert that nothing, not even the relief of suffering, can be accomplished until all ties with the capitalist world are cut. In any case self-reliance is likely to be a futile goal or at least an extraordinarily costly one. Redistribution itself will be inordinately difficult, and I believe that a good number of the LDCs who set out to achieve it will be compelled to seek whatever external support they can get—provided the rich countries decide that redistribution with a partial opening to the external world is not subversive.

The underdeveloped countries that follow this modified form of the "other road" to development will remain something of a charge on the international system. They will not need trade preferences, although they might benefit somewhat from improved access for what exports they do have, and they probably will not seek much foreign investment, but they will need aid in the form of technical assistance and for the relief of deficiencies in current consumption. In general I believe the external behavior of this group is likely to be reasonably moderate, with most energies concentrated on internal tasks that can be accomplished only by a genuine domestic commitment to improving the standard of living for all. The one qualification to this argument, which is likely to hold for any kind of attempt to redistribute, is that rising expectations may exceed available resources, and domestic turmoil may be the result. If the government is not strong enough to maintain control or if a populist leader emerges, domestic discontent may spill over into the international system.

Redistribution policies can also be used illegitimately, merely as a device to keep the ruling elites in power by periodically buying off the discontented—a new version of "bread and circuses." This possibility explains much of the radical suspicion of redistribution policies, for policies designed primarily to raise immediate consumption levels may succeed in diminishing the probability of immediate revolution. From this perspective, creating a satisfied peasant or worker is also creating a conservative peasant or worker. Suspicion that this is the real goal of redistribution is especially strong when such policies are advocated by foreign aid agencies or the World Bank. At any rate, when redistribution becomes the ostensible goal of the Somozas and the Duvaliers, the effects on the international system are likely to be minimal: The elites who seek only to remain in power will probably remain tied to the international system and are unlikely to sanction a great deal of deliberately disruptive behavior.

In sum the group of states who adopt redistribution policies are unlikely to exert a single, consistent impact on the international system. Too many variables cannot be accounted for—the intentions of the elites, the response of the external world, the rate of population growth, the food situation, and the play of events themselves. Nevertheless, on balance, I think this movement inward is sensible and justified and that it will create fewer problems for the emerging international system than any of the other orientations that could be adopted by this particular group of developing countries. In part this may reflect my own bias that the proper task for the underdeveloped countries in the immediate future is to launch a full-scale assault on the human problems they confront: Rather than justice and jobs emerging as a by-product of growth, let growth emerge as a by-product of improved conditions of life.

### THE LARGE LDCS

This group contains all the LDCs with large enough domestic markets to make import substitution and the closed economy feasible. These countries can also benefit from foreign trade, but they can survive the loss of export markets provided that they can meet domestic demand from domestic output. In contrast to the small LDCs, these countries are not likely to face a permanent foreign exchange constraint or the need to gamble always on the openness of foreign markets. This does not necessarily mean that the large LDCs will be less dependent on the international system in the years ahead, since they still need foreign aid and investment to run the domestic economy. What is at issue here is the range of choice: The large LDCs have wider choices, for they can more sensibly choose either an inward or outward orientation and can work with different assumptions about what can be done in the future.

These countries are so large and prominent that whatever happens to them tends to be identified with whatever happens to the whole of the underdeveloped world. This is particularly true for India, but also somewhat true for Nigeria, Indonesia, Brazil, Pakistan, and Bangladesh. The situations of these countries are so different that a single pattern of future behavior is improbable. Still, all of these countries have profound domestic problems and needs, and they are unlikely to be generous to their neighbors or willing to pay a price to keep regional agreements working. One persistent fear in these circumstances is imperialist or aggressive behavior against weaker neighbors, however irrational such a policy may be for states that cannot control their own territories.

If population and food pressures continue to rise, which is likely to be true even for oil producers like Indonesia and Nigeria (especially if oil prices and other commodity prices drop), domestic turmoil is probable. So, too, perhaps is the emergence of populist leaders espousing the need for revolutionary domestic changes. This behavior may spill over into the international arena, with alternating patterns of supplication and threat (of terrorism, nuclear blackmail, etc.). Unless the Great Powers take immediate measures to relieve the distress of some of these countries, which I think is unlikely, the large LDCs are liable to become the most destabilizing factor in the international system by the early 1980s. They may find willing support among disaffected members of the other LDC groups we have discussed.

### REGIONAL GROUPS

Predictions about the rise in regionalism have become increasingly fashionable in recent years. If the rich countries turn inward, presumably the underdeveloped countries—by inclination or by necessity—will turn toward each other. Regionalism has also become a residual category: When the rich countries find the poor countries increasingly tiresome, suggestions that the poor countries ought to deal with each other more often inevitably appear. I expect that the regional motif will remain strong in the years ahead but that the practical effects of regionalism are unlikely to be significant.

I have already outlined the reasons for my doubts about regionalism in chapter 3. The probability that weak and intensely nationalistic governments beset by enormous domestic problems will turn their attention to regional cooperation is not great. After all, what help can they get from their neighbors—except a hands-off policy? Moreover both the raw materials exporters and the manufacturing exporters have superior and absolutely necessary ties outside their own regions. In fact, competition for external markets and foreign investment is more likely than cooperation. The facts that most of these countries have already created similar low-level consumer goods industries by import substitution and that these industries have become relatively powerful vested interests also mean that co-operation will probably have to be limited to agreements on sharing new industries. In the short and medium run the impact of these agreements is likely to be minimal.

The four groups of LDCs I have already discussed do not fall into a regional pattern. The only exception might be the large group of LDCs who turn inward and concentrate on redistribution, but even here I expect that cooperation will be primarily rhetorical: Turning inward and concentrating on agricultural development means that these countries are not going to be able to do much for each other. An enforced regionalism might develop as a result of imperialist actions by regional "Great Powers" like Brazil, Nigeria, India, or Indonesia, but I think such ventures (or adventures) may succeed only in creating the grounds for cooperation among the threatened small countries—as the Andean Pact was a response to fears of Brazilian dominance.

Many of the issues on which the industrial countries need the cooperation of the underdeveloped countries—pollution, nuclear proliferation, the oceans, and so on—are global, and the pattern of cooperation that the underdeveloped countries need to extract concessions is also likely to be global. At this level, efforts to construct a Third World position, like the "Group of 77" at UNCTAD, are likely to continue. Finally, the support of the rich countries for regional cooperation among the LDCs may become increasingly rhetorical. The rich countries are unlikely to persist in support for regional groups that will then cooperate against the rich countries. The major exception to this would occur if the rich countries began to create a bloc system, dividing up the world among themselves, but this would hardly be the regional "cooperation" that the poor countries advocate. Doubts about regionalism can also be extended and extrapolated to recent efforts to enhance "collective self-reliance," which implies not only regional but also global and functional cooperation. In any case, support for collective self-reliance partly reflects disappointment with the results of regionalism—as well as the hope that OPEC will (or can) support wider efforts of collaboration. Finally, I am not arguing that such efforts at cooperation are misguided or ultimately futile: Rather, they are not likely to have a fundamental effect in the period with which we are concerned.

———◆•••◆———

In the remainder of this section I comment briefly about likely patterns of behavior among the industrial countries (including the Soviet bloc). These comments refer only to patterns of behavior that will directly affect the underdeveloped countries.

### THE SOVIET BLOC

The Soviet bloc economies seem more complementary with LDC needs and capabilities than the economies of most Western states do.[13] The socialist countries might import some food, especially tropical products, in exchange for capital goods of various kinds. Foreign exchange problems could be avoided by payment in local currencies (in effect, goods exchanged for goods). In addition, since many LDCs are now seeking less advanced but more labor-intensive technology, the Soviets might be even more useful trading partners. Some degree of ideological compatibility, if only agreement on anticapitalism, may also facilitate cooperation, but only in helping each side discover what common interests they might share.

The effort to increase trade (or barter) between the socialist countries and the LDCs is thus likely to be a major theme for the next decade—at least for the LDCs. Existing trade is very low, and the percentage increases may look quite spectacular. Nevertheless it would be premature to presume that the Soviets will replace the Western states as the dominant market for the LDCs or, indeed, that the Soviets themselves will make any major effort to construct important trading relationships with many underdeveloped countries.

Soviet imports of most raw materials are quite limited, except for tropical products, and it is difficult to see much prospect for improvement over the short or medium term. The Soviet Union is also

13. For a good, brief discussion, see Lloyd G. Reynolds, *The Three Worlds of Economics* (New Haven, Conn.: Yale University Press, 1971), pp. 120 ff.

likely to concentrate on satisfying excess demand domestically, and this may limit willingness to export large amounts of capital goods. Perhaps most significantly, what the Soviets apparently want from the external world is high-level technology, which can be got only from the Western countries. Even agreements between the Soviets and the LDC manufacturing exporters may be problematic: The Soviets can produce the same manufacturing products, and they are likely to want either to save their natural resources or to sell them only in exchange for advanced technology. What we may see happen, then, is competition between the Soviets and many LDC exporters in attempting to sell raw materials and some cheap consumer goods in exchange for more advanced goods. Competition for shares of the Western market could be avoided if the "Second" and the "Third" Worlds decided to join together to form a separate international subsystem, but this is unlikely unless the Western countries themselves turn sharply inward and try to function as a self-contained bloc. (Dependence on outside resources alone makes this a dubious possibility, but it could happen if the Western countries get angry enough with the rest of the world—and technology provides sufficient substitutes for foreign resources.) Conflict between the Soviets and the LDCs who adopt redistributive policies is unlikely, for they would have few grounds for disagreement.

At any rate, if the Soviet Union continues to seek advanced technology, and if it offers to trade raw materials in exchange (or even its hoard of gold), the prospects for cooperation between the LDCs and the socialist bloc do not look promising. In effect East and West could more or less ignore the underdeveloped world. I believe that this will not happen, since there are too many conflicts between East and West and too much residual ideological antipathy for peaceful coexistence to go quite that far. But the fact that it is even possible to discuss the outlines of such an arrangement illustrates the limited leverage that the LDCs can exert on the international system. Only OPEC has something that is indispensable, and even OPEC's leverage may begin to decline rapidly after 1980.

The shortrun position of the Soviet Union has improved markedly as a result of the general rise in commodity prices. Perhaps above all, in Soviet (and Chinese) eyes the current crisis may seem to have clearly justified the policies of self-sufficiency that have been followed since 1917. Such policies have given the Soviets a degree of maneuverability and choice that none of the other Great Powers, all of whom are dependent on foreign resources in some important ways, have or are likely to have in the next 5 years. The foreign exchange windfall that the Soviets have got as a result of rising prices for their own commodity exports may also mean that the Soviets have somewhat less need for credits from foreign governments and less need to barter their resources in exchange for advanced technology—as long as commodity prices remain high, the Soviets may be able to pay cash for a good portion of what they need. But they are also likely to need and to seek Western credits and loans—if primarily to preserve their own resources. And they are not likely to find it difficult to develop willing trading partners in the West, although rising debt may slow the pace at which future loans are granted.

This picture could change, however, by the early 1980's if commodity prices fall, if the Soviets decide for political reasons that they must continue to provide oil and a few other resources to their East European allies at prices below the world market, and if the growth rate of the Soviet economy remains high (since resource use will probably grow faster than the growth of national income for some time). The Soviets will then have considerably less flexibility, because they will need most of their own resources and will not be able to get as much for whatever resources they do export. Consequently my forecast of potential conflict between the Soviets and LDC exporters of raw materials (and some manufactures) rests on a double assumption: that many commodity prices will fall and that domestic demand pressures in the Soviet Union will continue to rise. I expect this will put the Soviet leadership under great pressure, because the quest for advanced technology may require some sacrifice of practical and ideological ties with parts of the Third World.

Potential clashes between the socialist countries of Eastern Europe and the underdeveloped countries are not entirely hypothetical. They have already appeared at UNCTAD, for the socialist countries have been disturbed at the low priority that the expansion of "East–South" trade has had on the UNCTAD agenda, and the underdeveloped countries have been unhappy with the unwillingness of the socialist countries to break much new ground in their proposals (e.g., by offering convertible credits). But even more critically, almost all the proposals within the New International Economic Order (and, *a fortiori*, on UNCTAD's agenda)—for an integrated commodity program, for more access for manufactures and processed agricultural products, for a code of conduct for the transfer of technology, for renegotiation of debts—are "within-system" proposals. Provided that the Western countries do not reject this package *in toto*, which would be a mistake, since there are many elements in it that promise mutual benefits, the socialist countries are confronted with a difficult choice. If they do not want to be frozen out of whatever patterns of accommodation begin to emerge, they must join a number of institutions (like the World Bank and the IMF) and participate in a number of processes (like multilateral aid, or the negotiation of commodity agreements) that they have heretofore ignored or dealt with in a different fashion. But moving toward accommodation with these within-system demands could also impose substantial ideological and practical costs. In the interim I expect that the socialist countries will follow a waiting policy, yielding as little as possible to Third World demands (except to ideological partners); the result, I think, is that the developing countries probably will not get much more from this direction than they have in the past.

THE WESTERN INDUSTRIAL COUNTRIES

The industrial countries could cooperate with each other to create an international economic order that functioned to maintain their own prosperity. This is something short of saying that they will do very much for the poor countries. Cooperation to liberalize trade further and to control the uncertainties of the international financial system would probably not help the poor very much: The LDCs capable of taking advantage of competitive opportunities would clearly benefit, but the great majority of LDCs need more direct and persisting help. Nevertheless, since the rich countries themselves have an obvious shared interest in this level of cooperation, it may be the most probable outcome of the present difficulties. Such a solution has the apparent virtue of not breaking sharply with the past and of leaving each rich country free to insulate itself or protect itself against disturbances from the Third World.

This is a forecast of a patched-up world in which the rich countries have regained control of the resource situation by decreasing domestic demand and increasing domestic supply (conservation, better extraction techniques, etc.) and by dividing the resource producers against themselves. The "new" economic order will be familiar, and perhaps stabilized, in part, by fears of the effects of disunity between the resource consumers—as the nineteenth century was partially stabilized by fears of revolution if any country sought too much for itself. This would be a reasonably good world for the LDCs who exported manufactures; it would be a very bad world for the resource producers; and it would not be a very relevant or important world for the LDCs who turned inward.

Fears of impending disaster could compel more profound forms of cooperation. Conversely these fears could engender increasingly nationalist responses to the dangers of interdependence. More positive outcomes are unlikely to emerge automatically: No "hidden hand" is going to be strong enough to control the forces at work in the present international system. The leading states must make a deliberate effort to engender cooperative action, perhaps even by sacrificing some of their own shortrun gains. But the poor countries can also contribute, for they are not negligible factors in an era of resource scarcity (or fears of it) and interdependence. Thus an intense and persistent effort on the part of the poor countries to repeat OPEC's successes will probably force the rich countries either toward increasing self-reliance or toward tightly controlled satellite systems. The point I emphasize here is that, in the context of escalating domestic inflation, the demise of internationalism among labor unions fearing "run-away" plants, and a general disillusion with the costs of dealing with the external world, the moderately pessimistic outcome I discussed in the preceding paragraph may be the most that can be expected from the rich countries in the next 5 to 10 years. Consequently the poor countries ought to recognize the risks of demanding too much in these circumstances or of threatening continually disruptive actions. The outcome is apt to be worse for all sides.

There have been a number of discussions of the possibility that a bloc system or a sphere of interest system, with each bloc seeking self-sufficiency and controlling its international trade extensively, will emerge from the current crisis.[14] This is surely a possibility, for the desire to insulate domestic economies against the "shocks" they have recently had to endure remains strong in most of the developed countries. And a bloc system would provide the insured access to essential supplies that may seem necessary. I believe, however, that a bloc system is not an immediately likely outcome, for too many other needs and ties cut across any set of spheres of interest to make easy agreement possible. Note, for example, the extent to which Japanese and European interests have already penetrated "our" sphere in Latin America. The sharp resistance of many of the LDCs incorporated in such spheres might also make it a costly strategy, although some of the LDCs currently following an outwardly oriented policy would not resist too desperately. The governing elites in the latter groups would ensure their own prosperity and probably also receive substantial help in controlling domestic discontent. In any case, in the short and medium term the costs and difficulties of creating a bloc system—especially the extent to which it contradicts the liberalizing values of the postwar generation of industrial country leaders—may make efforts to patch up the old system the most probable direction of effort for the next decade.

———————◆◆◆◆————————

This forecast of essentially moderate changes in existing patterns of behavior presumes, of course, the absence of massive external shocks—a depression, an escalating Middle East war, and so on. Whether such a pattern of change is sufficient to deal with the problems that both developed and developing worlds confront is unclear, but it does seem that the political systems of the developed countries are not ready for or capable of much more. This judgment sets the limits within which the developing countries are liable to

14. See, for example, Ernest H. Preeg, "Economic Blocs and U.S. Foreign Policy," *International Organization* 28, no. 2 (Spring 1974): 233–46.

have to operate and within which the norms I discuss in the next chapter must be established.

Some mitigating factors appear in this rather bleak forecast. I have argued that the industrial countries are likely to agree on a minimal level of cooperation among themselves but that they are also likely to remain too preoccupied with their own problems to offer the poor much beyond previous levels of support.[15] But this is not an entirely negative conclusion, for a number of reasons. First, for some developing countries this level of support may be sufficient. Second, to the extent that the developing countries begin to realize the limits of what they can expect from external sources, they may thus finally be willing to treat the problems of domestic change more seriously—which ought to be, in any case, the first order of business. Finally I have not argued that any of the extreme policies toward the Third World that have been discussed by various publicists—military intervention, autarky, spheres of interest, "benign neglect"—are likely to achieve widespread support. There are, in my judgment, simply too many factors in operation that suggest that an abiding, if fluctuating, level of concern for the developing countries is likely to remain part of the political agenda in the industrial countries. These factors, which must exist in tension with persistent irritation at the rhetoric and ingratitude of the Third World (and with theories that advocate separation), include a new perception of mutual needs, fears of disruptive action, increased bargaining power by the poor, and a genuine moral commitment to help those in need.

The potential for instability in the world I have described will be extraordinarily high. Value conflicts abound and will exacerbate the difficulties of resolving conflicts of interest. What can be done to prevent this world from exploding into more virulent forms of instability, terrorism, and war? Put somewhat differently, many LDCs now see a positive interest in disrupting the international system, for they feel that the system is either deliberately or unconsciously unjust. Can actions be taken that alter their perception of an in-

15. If the present confrontation strategy gets out of hand, even this level of support might dissipate, and some of the rich might become involved with more aggressive or reactionary policies—autarky, invasion, and so on.

herently exploitive system, actions that do not simultaneously undermine the structure of the system itself? Can we begin constructing an international system in which cooperation is based on
influence, not force, and authority, not manipulation? I suggest a
few precepts in the next chapter that may move us in this direction.[16]

16. The economic issues we have been discussing do not have any "neutral"
economic solutions: Virtually all these issues can be resolved only through the political process, domestic or international. This is especially true in the international context, since the conflict between efficiency and distributional criteria is complex and
ambiguous—and may be made more so if a criterion of redistribution becomes increasingly salient. Rising levels of uncertainty about the validity of our prevailing
doctrines and beliefs, which seem to produce more and more unforeseen consequences, makes the resolution of this conflict exceedingly difficult: when in doubt
about what we want to do or how to achieve what we want, the tendency to do or
risk as little as possible rises. But this exacerbates tensions with the developing
countries who demand major changes quickly.

# 11

## Inequality, Exploitation, and Justice in the International System: Reconciling Divergent Expectations

An attempt to improve the quality of the relationship between the rich and the poor countries cannot be concerned only with changes within the poor countries themselves. Such changes are necessary, perhaps even preeminent, for they provide the only means by which the poor countries can respond effectively to external opportunities, to protect themselves against adverse external developments, and to raise demands upon the external systems that are not disruptive and are more likely to be feasible. But such changes are not sufficient, for there are external developments that can unfairly overwhelm even poor countries following sensible domestic policies, and there are obligations incumbent upon the rich countries to help the poor countries for both moral and practical reasons. An improved relationship must consequently seek changes in both domestic and international policies, since failure in one realm can engender failure in the other.

Our concern in this chapter with external changes thus does not imply that domestic change is unnecessary or that external change is sufficient. But it does imply that we cannot rationalize refusal to accept substantial external change by arguing that the failures of the developing countries are always their own responsibility or that badly conceived domestic policies are always responsible for the difficulties in which the developing countries find themselves. On one level we are at least obligated to provide them with protection and support against adverse external developments for which the poor countries are neither responsible nor capable of insulating themselves—for example, against worldwide inflation or recession. On another level we are also obligated to remove hindrances and obstacles that violate our own doctrines and that prevent even policies we favor from working well—for example, tariff and nontariff barriers against developing country exports or monopolistic behavior by our corporations. We also share some responsibility for repairing the effects of misguided or simplistic economic doctrines that we strongly advocated and that succeeded in enmeshing the poor countries prematurely in a complex international economic system—for example, doctrines of rapid industrialization or the necessity of inequality.[1] Finally we have a simple moral obligation to help those in need, irrespective of why they are in need, and a practical obligation, in our own interest, to seek to create an international system less dominated by distrust, bitterness, and poverty.

We seek norms and precepts that take account of these obligations and interests in this chapter. But we seek them within the limits of existing notions of political feasibility—and moral commitment. This will surely seem insufficient to the poor countries who want to create an entirely new international order, and it will surely seem excessive to the rich countries who seek primarily to protect and refurbish established patterns of behavior. But it is in the intersection between these sets of divergent expectations that we must begin the process of creating a more just and stable international order.

## NORMS AND PRACTICES FOR
## A FRAGMENTED AND DANGEROUS WORLD

Normative suggestions about what behavior ought to be inevitably have a hollow ring, for such norms need not be asserted if the

1. The emphasis should be on shared responsibility—not all of the doctrines passed on were incorrect, and not all originated in the developed countries.

predisposition to obey them already exists. If the predisposition does not exist, the assertion of norms often seems a self-righteous or self-interested moral cheerleading, of the order of "we will all benefit if we all behave better." This is probably interesting only if untrue.

Norms—rules by which behavior is judged—may be more important in a world in which consensus on values and beliefs is low than they would be in a world in which consensus was high and the meaning of desirable behavior could be left implicit. A deliberate attempt to articulate norms may also be critical when degrees of uncertainty about the future have risen sharply, when faith in a progressive and beneficent future has dropped sharply, and when belief in the viability of traditional doctrines and standard operating procedures is strikingly limited. Norms cannot resolve these problems, but they may be able to provide some guidance in the quest for solutions. And when substantive agreement to remove the grounds for conflict is unlikely, procedural norms on how to coexist may become imperative—as, for example, with nuclear weapons, where all the antagonists share an interest in not blowing each other up inadvertently.

Conflict in such a world is always prevalent, but it need not be unmediated. Areas of mutual interest do exist and can be enlarged. But in an unstable system with a high degree of unpredictable behavior the propensity to use power arbitrarily or capriciously may rise. Perhaps the psychologic pressures of living with so much uncertainty and so many traditional benchmarks in question in themselves create a pressure toward the preemptive use of violence. This could very well destroy the international system we are discussing, either more or less literally or by compelling the Great Powers to transform the system into a series of rigid, satellite blocs. The need for order and for justice are not likely to be compatible, and the use of force may tilt the balance rather sharply toward order.

In the best of all possible worlds, the first principle in such an international system ought to proscribe the use of force except in carefully defined circumstances. But this is obviously utopian unless one manages simultaneously to remove the cause of conflict. The same objection can be made to another version of this principle: Everything must be negotiable; bargaining and compromise must be the norm. The agreement to bargain must itself rest upon prior agreement about the rules of the game and upon some shared sentiments that the game will be played fairly. The norms we seek must, therefore, be more practical and immediate: They must seek to establish more desirable patterns of behavior within a system dominated by high levels of conflict and uncertainty. Such norms must establish some balance between what is good and wise—for example, avoiding conflict, allocating resources efficiently—and what is acceptable and prudent—for example, keeping elites in power, measures of reform, not revolution.

Are the propositions that follow meant to improve the quality of the results achieved within the existing pattern of institutions and beliefs or to create an entirely new international system? [2] The answer is both, but in a special sense. Quite clearly the effort to establish an entirely new system is neither politically feasible nor intellectually sensible (because we do not yet understand how to do so or what the precise elements of such a system ought to be). But also an effort simply to patch up the existing system is not likely to be adequate, because the random, *ad hoc* responses that could result may not resolve problems that are essentially interdependent, and because patchwork is unlikely to be sufficient to deal with the severe problems of some Third World countries—who may as a consequence be forced into desperate behavior or into efforts to thwart otherwise useful measures of reform.

In the long term, a major reform of the international system may be necessary. But that reform cannot be achieved all at once—even if we were certain of both direction and substance—and we have no choice but to work slowly and steadily on two interacting levels. On one level, practical and immediate measures that stand some chance of improving the quality and equity of the relationship between rich and poor in the next decade must be pursued. But on another level we need to work simultaneously to establish new atti-

2. It would also be possible to phrase this question in terms of the distinction between a process level and a structural level of analysis, more or less reflecting a distinction between the short and the long term. See C. Fred Bergsten, Robert O. Keohane, and Joseph S. Nye, "International Economics and International Politics: A Framework for Analysis," *International Organization* 29, no. 1 (Winter 1975):5.

tudes and perceptions about the way in which the international system ought to be managed. Without this effort, improvements on the first level are not likely to lead in any consistent or persistent fashion in the direction we would like to go. This is why I make an effort in the first two principles to deal with what may seem to be abstract issues of morality and justice. I have no illusions, of course, that immediate conversion to the principles I enunciate is either imminent or probable, but I hope that discussion of such issues will alert us to the need to gauge immediate actions by more general standards and perhaps even slowly begin to alter the way in which we perceive and think about our relationship to the developing countries.

## A NORM OF COMMITMENT

Rightly or wrongly the great majority of underdeveloped countries believe that the international systems are inherently exploitative. From this perspective even apparently charitable programs like foreign aid can be interpreted as disguised forms of imperialism, and even normal commercial exchange can be interpreted as unfair. For the more radical exponents of these views, responsibility for the poverty of the poor countries is itself attributed to the rich countries, and since the rich countries will not accept their responsibility, the poor countries must leave the international system altogether. More moderate exponents of these views are content simply to assert an inclusive moral principle: Those responsible for causing an injury are also responsible for repairing it.

Are the rich indeed guilty of impoverishing the poor? Determining causation and responsibility in the historical record is incredibly difficult, and it is not always much easier when the case is directly before us. The quest for a consensus between rich and poor on this issue is bound to fail—even if one disagrees with this judgment, the time lost in debate cannot be spared. If our domestic social welfare system had to wait upon a determination of why the poor are poor, we probably would not yet have a social welfare system.

It seems to me that nothing useful can be accomplished as long as we continue to debate questions of guilt and responsibility. What we need, I believe, is an initial commitment on the part of the rich countries that is tangible and significant enough to begin to undermine the belief that no relationship between a poor country and the international system can be fair or charitable. But the commitment itself, if it is to survive transient shocks, must rest on an acceptance of the responsibility to help the poor, insofar as we can, because the alternative of letting the consequences of actions fall where they may is morally unacceptable. This is a commitment that ought to reflect not only our values but also the fact that we share some of the responsibility for establishing and sustaining a division of labor that has made it increasingly difficult for the poor countries to diminish their poverty. The wealth of the rich is obviously immoral if it entails the poverty of others; here we accept the additional argument that the wealth of the rich can become immoral if it merely coexists with the poverty of others and is not used to help those in need. One does not have to be guilty of creating poverty to feel the moral imperative of reducing its consequences.[3]

In an international system dominated by high levels of distrust and sharp conflicts of interest, the mere assertion of moral obligations is insufficient. The poor countries are hardly likely to have much faith in the depths of our moral commitment or in its persistence over time. If the moral commitment is not credible, it is not likely to avert deliberately disruptive actions or to begin to establish more cooperative patterns of behavior. Indeed there is little evidence that support for such a commitment is growing or that the existing level of support can be sustained in the face of difficult domestic economic conditions or increasing disenchantment with the behavior of various Third World governments. Nevertheless economic conditions may improve, and not all of the Third World is likely to engage in actions that consistently seem to us to be deliberately provocative. More critically the revival of more liberal atti-

3. One also does not have to resolve the interminable—and probably insoluble—debate about who is responsible for the poverty of the developing countries. The attempt to resolve the issue is not irrelevant, for it clearly has implications for practical policy choices. But we do not have time to wait for the debate to be settled or even clarified.

tudes toward the Third World may be accelerated by practical trends that seem to enhance the need for cooperation.

In the interim, and along the way, we need to make our commitment as credible as possible by a series of small but cumulative—and politically feasible—steps that point in a consistent direction. In the abstract, to do so consistently, and to provide guidance for specific decisions, we would need a principle of allocation—or justice—that explains how the goods of society ought to be distributed. But the creation of an acceptable theory of justice is beyond my means. Perhaps more critically, time is too pressing: If what we are going to do must wait not only upon the articulation of a theory of justice but also upon its acceptance by a world sharply divided in values and perceptions, we would lose time that we may not be able to afford to lose. We must, therefore, take the risk of acting, not upon a theory of justice, but upon a loose sense of what we now believe is just—and this is a real risk, for which evidence surely exists in sharp changes over the years in what we have thought we ought to do for the developing countries and in sharp divergences now between different groups over the nature of our obligations. Nevertheless I see no alternative to taking the risk—and hoping that a consensus on justice emerges along the way to guide our actions, or to correct our mistakes. As a result what follows attempts to respond to popular and felt conceptions of justice that currently prevail within the international system and that are manifested in the demands that each group of countries feels it has the right to place upon the others.


## A PRINCIPLE OF JUSTICE:
## PRACTICAL RESPONSES TO FELT INEQUITIES


Justice and equality are not equivalent terms: A just order is not simply one in which all are treated equally or even one in which similar cases are treated equally. Justice refers to some principle of allocation, and that principle need not assert the absolute necessity of equal treatment. What it must do, however, is justify any deviations from equal treatment by reference to generally acceptable principles—to principles that do not violate the notion of justice. Thus unequal treatment is usually considered just if it is based on need, or different degrees of contribution, or merit, or the nature of work. Freely negotiated agreements may also sanction some unequal treatment. Which principle is chosen in what circumstances is a matter of societal choice.[4]

Historically the Great Powers have been granted superior rights (e.g., in both the League of Nations and the United Nations), presumably in reflection of the principle that different degrees of contribution justify different degrees of equality. Inequality in responsibility for the operation of the international system is not going to disappear, nor is it clear that it should. The poor countries now seek some adjustments in this situation, not primarily because they reject the need for inequality on some matters, but because inequality has frequently been used to exclude the poor countries from decisions that decisively affect their fate. As a result they seek more voice on issues of direct concern—but not a return to a pure principle of equality.

There is no doubt, of course, that the poor countries have attempted to use the voting power engendered by equality to further their own interests—as we have used our superior voting power in smaller arenas, where voting reflects criteria of wealth and power, to further our own interests. But what the poor countries have been seeking has not usually been the establishment of a simple principle of equality—which is neither feasible nor necessarily in their interests—but rather an adjustment in the way that the large countries have used their superior rights in various arenas and the simultaneous establishment of a different principle of unequal treatment in some areas of direct concern for the poor countries. If the Great Powers have been justly granted special privileges in reflection of the contribution they can make to security and prosperity, the poor countries seek special privileges justly as a reflection of special needs. To seek to use what power they have to establish this justification for inequality is completely legitimate, for it is neither

4. There are interesting discussions of justice in Richard B. Brandt, ed., *Social Justice* (Englewood Cliffs, N.J.: Prentice-Hall, 1962).

more nor less just to discriminate on the basis of contribution or need—in both cases, it is a social decision.

The different principles on which a just order can be based are frequently in conflict, particularly in the international arena, where divergent values and multiple needs inhibit the possibility of clear or simple choices. For example, an emphasis on merit—by, say, providing support to those who can use it most effectively—can easily conflict with an emphasis on need—by, say, providing support to those who seek domestic redistribution.[5] The recipients would change, the forms of support would change, and expectations about present versus future benefits would change.[6] Choosing a single principle of allocation is not mandatory. Consequently, so long as we realize that we are acting according to different principles, and so long as there are sufficient resources to allocate to different purposes, the use of more than one principle of allocation creates complexities, but not necessarily contradictions.[7]

Perhaps we can gain some perspective on this argument by briefly examining the history of the evolution of social welfare programs in the industrial states. Experience within the international system obviously will not exactly parallel experiences within the nation-state. Still, taken with caution, some of the similarities (and differences) may be instructive.[8]

We can visualize the state as roughly two generations ahead of the international system. After the state gradually solidified control

5. And there are, of course, difficult practical problems within each choice: for example, in the emphasis on merit, in determining how much support a country can "absorb." Or, in the case of need, problems exist in determining what constitutes a minimally acceptable level of existence. See the discussion in N. N. Franklin, "Minimum Living Standards," in Richard Symonds, ed., *International Targets for Development* (New York: Harper, 1970).

6. Redistribution, for example, would imply more emphasis on immediate consumption needs and less emphasis on physical capital, and more emphasis on present benefits and less emphasis on long term benefits.

7. The possibility of employing a combination of need and merit is discussed below.

8. They will be less so if we give up the idea of seeking a positive principle of justice. Jack N. Behrman, *Toward a New International Economic Order* (Paris: The Atlantic Institute for International Affairs, 1974), pp. 10 ff., argues that we can agree only on what is unjust, but I do not find defining injustice any easier than defining justice. In addition a negative principle does not provide much guidance for practical choices.

over the central institutions of war, finance, and justice, it began to expand its functions into more and more areas. And with the rise of the welfare state, the central government has become the dominant factor in the national economy—protecting workers, aiding consumers, contesting monopolies, providing credit, and accepting responsibility for stability, employment, and equity.

The central government has also been compelled (with decreasing difficulty as both prosperity and the suffrage have widened) to become a critical instrument of redistribution. The creation of trade unions provided an important element of group support for mass demands—helped along by wars that made the denial of equality difficult. Social welfare programs were at first narrowly conceived (e.g., against accidents) but then broadened (e.g., to cover widows or orphans). Taxes became an important redistributive element also, especially as many services were provided to the public below cost (e.g., education). And in times of crisis (like wars or depressions), wage freezes and price controls have been used as direct measures of redistribution.

The international system has not been able to achieve commensurate progress, because the security issue has remained both dominant and unsettled: Whatever institutions emerged within the international system were always peripheral or residual responses to convenience and were not built upon a previous political and security settlement. The increasing importance of nonsecurity issues, as well as the declining utility of force, may perhaps alter this calculus, and the new institutions and procedures that need to be created in response to new problems and pressures may begin to achieve a degree of autonomy from the security issue that has not previously been possible. If so, the grounds upon which domestic social welfare programs have rested may provide a few useful insights about the directions in which we ought to head.

Benefits have been given for a wide variety of reasons in domestic welfare systems. They can provide partial compensation for disservices directly caused by society (e.g., pollution, unemployment) or even for less identifiable disservices (e.g., urban blight). Benefits can also be used as a means of overcoming unmerited handicaps (e.g., blindness, retardation), or as an investment in the society's future collective good (e.g., educational aid), or simply as an increment to immediate personal welfare (e.g., health care). Most of these benefits, which are passed on without any attempt to determine initial responsibility, reflect the moral judgment that a society should provide benefits to those who bear part of the cost of everyone else's progress.[9] Some of the benefits are also provided for programs that do not reflect social problems, but rather social needs or social goods—for example, for education or health.

Welfare programs did not evolve out of a single logical plan, and consequently the rationale for many programs has altered or is multidimensional.[10] Nevertheless it remains possible to distinguish two separate conceptual approaches to the welfare problem. In the first approach welfare policies are essentially devices to reduce social conflict and to protect private property against the depredations of the poor. The social pathologies that result from poverty and its attendant affects are envisaged as a threat to social stability, and welfare programs become a means of adjusting people more equably to existing social norms—by buying off disruptive behavior.[11] In this sense, foreign aid, trade preferences, and whatever other benefits are provided to the poor countries in the international system could be interpreted as the price the rich countries are willing to pay to avoid subversive behavior on the part of the poor.

The price that the rich countries have been willing to pay has been a small price, for the damage the poor countries have been able to inflict has usually also been small. It seems to me true that a welfare system based on this approach is almost inherently unstable, for the poor must constantly remain a menace to extract any concessions at all from the rich. This is especially true in the international system, where the commitment to a welfare system will be weaker, where national demands always threaten international

9. My comments draw upon Richard N. Titmuss, *Commitment to Welfare* (London: George Allen and Unwin, Ltd., 1968), pp. 130 ff.

10. There is also an argument very fashionable among market enthusiasts that social welfare institutions are not necessary, for social problems will be resolved by economic growth. Whatever its relevance in domestic systems, the argument is decidedly premature and misleading in the international system. At any rate millions would die or survive in degradation if they had to wait for the benefits of growth to "trickle down" from the rich.

11. See Richard M. Titmuss, *Social Policy* (New York: Pantheon, 1974) p. 48.

charity, and where the immediate evidence of mutual welfare gains will be less apparent. What we have is a zero-sum conflict situation, in which what the poor get has to be subtracted from what the rich have. If, however, we are moving toward an international system in which cooperation is essential, the welfare benefits in that system must be based on something more than blackmail and conflict between class enemies.

The other approach to welfare rests on the notion of need and on the argument that help ought to be given by right, regardless of whether those in need constitute immediate social problems. This is also essentially a redistributive argument, for it seeks to raise the living standards of the poorest, even if it must come at some expense to the richest. It is a commitment to this kind of support that the poor countries now seek to extract from the rich countries.[12]

The reluctance of the rich countries to accept this commitment has usually reflected considerations of political feasibility. But beyond this, there are critics in both the developing and the developed countries who assert that such a commitment would be detrimental to the developing countries, for it would keep them more or less permanently on the dole—always expecting to be rescued by international charity. I discuss these and other criticisms shortly. Before doing so, however, I indicate more specifically how the emphasis on the criterion of need has become increasingly salient and what implications its acceptance might have in terms of measures currently on the international agenda.

The parallel between the evolution of domestic and international welfare measures in the post-World War II period is rough and approximate, and one clearly risks seeing more than is there— but it may also be a parallel that is more than an hallucination of misguided idealists. During the height of the Cold War period, our shortrun political needs dominated "welfare" considerations. The underlying principle of support began to shift in the early 1960s, and perceptions of merit began to dominate calculations: Aid to

12. Some developing countries, or some spokesmen (real and self-styled) of the Third World, demand more—not a sustained commitment from the rich, but revolution or reparations or isolation. But I deal with what is, I believe, the central, practical focus of most current Third World efforts.

those who could use it most effectively for rapid growth and efforts to reform the international trading system to help those countries that could compete (with a little help via preferences or the reduction of trade barriers) were increasingly conspicuous. These measures were perceived as *mutually* beneficial; welfare was still heavily tinged with narrow and short-range notions of self-interest. Tacitly the operating principle reflected the possibility of creating a reformed order in which differential treatment (e.g., nonreciprocal preferences) for the developing countries was acceptable, provided that any agreement offered mutual benefits or did not injure the interests of the developed countries.

A third stage in the evolution of the international welfare system began to emerge in the late 1960s and gained increasing force after the oil crisis of 1973. Direct conflicts between rich and poor became increasingly sharp and pervasive, for much more has been at stake than marginal revisions in the distribution of benefits—or even the quest for mutual benefits. The poor clearly seek a radical restructuring of the entire system, and new rules, not merely revised rules, of the game. Bitterness toward the past, increased desperation in the face of mounting problems, and a new sense of resource power have engendered an effort to establish a new and inclusive welfare principle: Those in need must be helped, irrespective of merit, and if necessary at direct and substantial cost to the rich countries.

The relationship between this principle and specific measures of practical support has been difficult to establish: "Need" has simply been extended or inflated to cover virtually any demand by any member of the Third World in good standing. If the developed countries decided, however, to accept the legitimacy of the need criterion, or at least to begin to move toward it, by what actions could they express their commitment?

The most popular welfare measure currently on the international agenda is the attempt to persuade the developed countries to achieve an overall aid level of 1 percent of their GNPs. This is a figure without analytic significance, but it has acquired a symbolic importance among the developing countries; consequently it ought not to be dismissed simply because it was not chosen by completely scientific methods (which, in any case, do not really exist in the context of aid programs). [13]

A number of problems exist, however, with this approach. Neither the 1 percent target, nor the 0.7 percent target for official development assistance—which is the more important figure because of some of the ambiguities surrounding private resource transfers—have been approximated in the aggregate, and current levels are below the levels reached in 1960–61. The OECD countries, for example, averaged 0.92 percent of their combined GNPs in total resource transfers in 1960, but the figure has dropped by about 20 percent; official development assistance has declined even further, from 0.53 percent in 1960–61 to 0.32 percent in 1973. [14] Recent estimates by the OECD secretariat suggest even sharper drops in the next 5 years, in part because of economic conditions, and in part because of the continuing difficulties that aid appropriations confront in national legislatures. Both the 1 percent and the 0.7 percent figures are, of course, regressive, for they do not distinguish per capita income from national income; a more progressive standard would attempt to establish aid commitments as a proportion of per capita income, but this is clearly not politically feasible. [15] At any rate the decline in aid levels is unfortunate for a number of reasons: It would provide a tangible indication of a sustained commitment on our part (and for very little cost), and if we insisted that the aid be employed for purposes of domestic redistribution, there would be much less likelihood that it would disappear into the pockets of a few corrupt leaders.

There are other measures, perhaps fortunately, that could also reflect the commitment of the developed countries to a more just order. Furthermore, since many of the developed countries are still acting on perceptions derived from earlier periods, these measures

13. On the influence of values on the choice of recipients in aid programs, see David Wall, *The Charity of Nations—The Political Economy of Foreign Aid* (London: Macmillan, 1973), p. 156; ". . . there is no objective basis for criticisms of the existing distribution of aid: the donors pay their money and they take their choice."

14. The figures are in *The Concepts of the Present Aid and Flow Targets* (Report by the Secretary-General of UNCTAD, TD/B/493/Rev. 1, 1975).

15. Using GNP would be regressive because, for example, Japan would have to pay much more than West Germany, although per capita income in West Germany is much higher.

reflect some degree of mutual benefit and seek primarily to redistribute from new areas of activity. We could be more sensitive to LDC demands for shared control of the oceans, not only because the issue is so crucial to raw materials exporters, but also because we are likely to need their cooperation on many other matters before anyone can benefit very much from the riches of the oceans. (But the developed countries also have a right to protect their interests in the seabed, especially as a hedge against hostile action by resource cartels.) The tension here between the need to help the developing countries and the need to ensure protection or leverage against some developing country threats well reflects the complexities and uncertainties of the current relationship between rich and poor. A tax on income derived from seabed resources might be devised so that most of the benefits went to the poor countries. A tax on exports of nonrenewable resources, especially when the main exporters are developing countries and when demand is generally price inelastic, might also be useful. Perhaps also a more serious concern with the creation of a new industrial geography in response to shifts in comparative advantage should also be included here. This would involve an effort to move the developed countries out of areas in which they were clearly losing a competitive edge—and easing the process by adjustment assistance—and also, perhaps most critically, to remove some potential problems before they reach an acute stage.

More controversially, over the longer run we might indicate some willingness to examine indexation proposals more sympathetically—or at least less emotionally. Indexation seeks to prevent a further deterioration in the terms of trade of the underdeveloped countries, in effect maintaining the real purchasing power of their commodity exports against their manufactured imports. Indexation involves many problems, particularly the direct forms that would require strong market intervention to control prices and supplies. The more indirect forms are less problematic, for they substitute *ex post facto* compensation payments for direct market intervention, but a combination of ideology, self-interest, and technical disagreements inhibit the chances of agreement.[16] In addition two groups of

16. For a useful treatment of the whole indexation issue, see *The Indexation of Prices* (Geneva: Study by the UNCTAD Secretariat, TD/B/503/Supp. 1, July 1974). If

underdeveloped countries are also unenthusiastic: those whose commodity is not covered by indexation and those who are net importers of indexed commodities. Indexation proposals would also have to be carefully devised, not only to limit the potential costs to some developing countries, but also to ensure that many of the benefits did not go primarily to a few developed countries (who export the relevant commodities).

Nevertheless indexation has some virtues as a welfare measure. In particular it limits the impact of price inflation in manufactured goods; that is, it provides some protection against a circumstance that the underdeveloped countries are not responsible for, and against which they have few defenses. The rich countries have few objections to such proposals domestically: via price support for agricultural products, cost of living adjustments in wage settlements, and adjustments for inflation in loan agreements. These proposals are acceptable domestically because our notions of equity justify protection for weak sectors of the economic community and efforts to eliminate handicaps imposed by history, nature, or technology. We are a long way from agreement on such measures internationally. Still, recent efforts to increase and improve compensatory finance mechanisms (e.g., in the IMF) to provide support against unexpected export shortfalls indicate that the possibility of movement is slowly improving. In the short run, however, or at least until the technical and political difficulties of indexation have been resolved, the most that is likely to be acceptable is a general commitment to review prices regularly to permit adjustments that take account of inflation or other adverse trends.

Finally, one ought also to stress the need to extend efforts already begun to remove external impediments that reduce Third World trading opportunities, or to provide protection against adverse developments for which the Third World is not responsible. For example, increased funds and more liberal access conditions for a financial mechanism to deal with balance of payments deficits that result from general trends in the world economy would be useful to

---

the terms of trade turned in favor of resource exports, indexation might begin to benefit the developed countries—at which point it would have to be adjusted again. At any rate, the current opposition of the developed countries has more to do with the impact of indexation on oil prices than any other factor.

many developing countries. A more favorable attitude toward commodity agreements that not only stabilized prices but also ensured that prices were equitable and that financing for diversification was available would also be useful—and mutually beneficial if it engendered a better investment climate and guaranteed access to resources. Many other small but important measures could be included here: extending the coverage and duration of the GSP, support for research on Third World technologic needs, restraints on some aspects of the behavior of our transnational corporations, and so on.

———————◆◆◆◆◆▶———————

As an ideal, or as an indication of the direction in which we may be heading, an international welfare system based on the principle of need is useful and suggestive. Only acceptance of such a principle, or substantial movement toward it, is likely to meet our need to create an international system in which the developing countries are not compelled to use strategies of deliberate disruption or efforts to blackmail the developed countries by inhibiting global bargains that are in everyone's interest. In addition a principle of need guarantees support when the other principles fail, which would respond to the fears of many developing countries that they will not be helped steadily or sufficiently—the other (but still just) principles of merit or contribution may leave too many developing countries aside or may exacerbate the fear that the developed countries will retreat into selfishness and self-interest once (or if) they regain control of the resource environment.

Nevertheless, in the short and medium term, acceptance of the principle of need is neither politically feasible nor necessarily more just than a system based on a combination of different allocation principles. In part this reflects the fact that the developed countries may have to act on different grounds for justifiable political reasons—in the Middle East, or southern Africa, or in an effort to bribe potential nuclear powers. More significantly it reflects the difficulty of implementing a principle of need—or, indeed, any principle that is to be applied universally—in a world in which many recipient governments are corrupt, indifferent to mass welfare, or guilty of aggressive or irresponsible behavior.

The dilemma thus arises, not merely because the rich countries have too many interests to be easily accommodated within a single principle, but also because the principle of need refers to the needs of citizens at large, but benefits must be passed on through or by governments that do not always share the donors' values, or interests, or perceptions. This means that we shall need to combine the principle of need with a principle of merit—that is, a judgment about the competence and willingness of particular governments to provide for the basic needs of the populace. For this reason I have not emphasized universal measures such as a "development tax" on incomes in the industrial countries. Such a measure would help all the developing countries, and it would also increase with the growth of incomes in the developed countries. But, beyond the facts that it is not politically feasible and that it may not be wise to attempt to "trick" the legislators in developed countries into commitments for which otherwise they lack the will or desire, resources would also automatically be transferred to countries that we do not want to help or that do not deserve help.

There are other difficulties with the need criterion. Most of the specific proposals we have discussed are likely to help primarily the most advanced developing countries (and the most advanced sectors within them) or the most geologically fortunate developing countries—those who are in a position to benefit from trading advantages or who happen to possess the right raw materials. Moreover, however valuable these measures may be, few are so designed that they are likely to provide immediate and tangible benefits to the great mass of citizens. On the one hand this implies that some measures ought to be explicitly designed to benefit primarily the poorest countries (e.g., a tax on seabed resources) and other measures ought to be reserved primarily for these countries (e.g., food aid, most of the "pure" grant aid, technical assistance). On the other hand, to ensure that the governments who receive these benefits actually pass them on to their citizens, perhaps we should offer (or continue to offer) external benefits and concessions only to those governments who actively promote domestic reform. This is justified on both moral and practical grounds, for only domestic reform will permit external measures to achieve a substantial degree of effectiveness.

[351]

It might also be argued that the measures we have discussed are not sufficient to begin the massive international redistribution of resources demanded by many observers (e.g., as in the most recent "Club of Rome" proposals). This is true but not decisive. These proposals reflect current limits of political feasibility, not romantic notions of massive redistribution efforts. In any case one doubts that the developing countries could absorb massive redistribution quickly or effectively or that they would benefit from measures that simultaneously endangered the prosperity of the developed countries. In this sense these proposals are not primarily concerned with closing the gap between rich and poor—which is unlikely anyway in any foreseeable period—but rather with improving existing levels of existence. These proposals would seek to do as much as we can (and to push steadily on those limits), and to indicate clearly to the developing countries that we will accept a persisting commitment to provide support in meeting minimal human needs, and to remove or dilute external impediments that hinder their efforts to help themselves. It is not a commitment that we shall provide support for, say, a 6 percent or a 10 percent growth rate or that we will narrow the gap between the rich and poor by sharply decreasing our own levels of prosperity (which would probably simply make everyone poorer). And it is not a commitment to help any government, irrespective of its behavior. If we do not accept this qualified commitment—and there is little indication that we are yet willing to do so—the probability of dangerously disruptive behavior by the poor countries will surely rise. We can protect ourselves against such actions, although at some cost; the question we ought to ask is which set of costs we want to pay when.[17]

————◆•••▶————

There is another range of criticism that is not directed at the specific content of the proposals I have outlined but that challenges the wisdom of offering the developing countries help via a series of

17. There are other possible criticisms that do not appear worth extended comment. One such criticism would assert the priority of efforts to help our own poor. This is true, but we are not dealing with a single sum to be divided between our poor and the poor elsewhere. After we have helped our poor, we then have a choice between helping others or building bigger missiles and so on.

moderate and incremental measures. These criticisms rest on the notion either that such help succeeds only in enabling the elites to avoid necessary domestic changes or that it is positively harmful by virtue of the demonstration effect or the importation of the wrong kinds of technology or products. Some sympathy for these arguments is surely justified, for there have been many cases in which they are true. Nevertheless I believe they cannot be sustained as a general proposition.

A number of arguments can be raised against these criticisms. Presumably since revolutionary amounts of aid are not likely to be forthcoming—and would anyway merely reinforce the denigrated effects—the alternative would be to give no help at all (except possibly limited humanitarian aid). A simple response to this would be that, however right or wrong it might be, complete dissociation is not going to happen, because the developed countries have too many interests in the Third World to break off contact and because the elites in the developing countries want external support badly enough to continue to exert pressure to get it. In the circumstances the best approach would seem to be to attempt to ensure that whatever aid is given is used as productively as possible. In addition the criticism itself suffers from the familiar vice of aggregation: Not all the recipients of aid or trade benefits have used such support corruptly or unwisely. Again this would suggest care and discrimination in whom we support, not a complete cessation of support.

On a more specific level other problems arise from these criticisms. As I have already argued in chapter 5, the empirical evidence that foreign aid has always been associated with a cut in domestic savings or that it has led to overspending or a reluctance on the part of the government to reform tax systems has not been confirmed. That is, aid has not always had negative effects.[18] The same response is justified for the argument that trade has had only negative effects: Some countries have done well with an export orientation (in some cases, even in terms of income distribution).[19] In addition even countries that want to turn inward cannot do so quickly and

18. In addition to chapter 4, see *Domestic Saving in Developing Countries* (Report by the UNCTAD Secretariat, TD/B/C.3/124/Supp. 1, Sept. 12, 1975).
19. See the discussion in chapter 8.

without a stream of necessary imports for quite some time: Self-sufficiency is a myth, especially for developing countries, and there is no way that poor countries who have become so enmeshed in the international system—wisely or not—can suddenly close the gates without a great deal of suffering.

The contention that external support has succeeded only in keeping the ruling elites in power and enabling them to avoid difficult domestic choices like population control is also dubious. Aid surely has been used to keep elites in power, but the desire to use whatever means are available to remain in power prevails whether aid is given or not given and whether the elites are conservative, moderate, or radical. At any rate there is no clear correlation between aid giving and elite stability, for some elites have received no aid and retained power, and others have received much aid and been overthrown. In any event the great majority of aid has gone to a small number of countries, most of whom have faced external threats, and the evidence is thus bound to be inconclusive. There is also little clear evidence that foreign support has been a decisive factor in decisions to support population control measures: The "success stories" here (e.g., Taiwan, Singapore, South Korea) seem to reflect primarily cultural differences. In general these criticisms seem to me to overrate the influence of external support or nonsupport on domestic decisions: It is far from clear that conditions would be markedly better if the industrial countries had done nothing at all.

I make three points in conclusion. We are partially responsible for the doctrines that have got many of the developing countries so involved with the external world and for some of the negative effects that have ensued domestically (e.g., overemphasizing rapid industrialization) and thus have some responsibility for the results. But, second, development doctrines are changing in important ways, and there is no necessary reason why some of the admittedly bad effects of the past need to be repeated. Finally, there is also no reason why we cannot discriminate sensibly between those using external support corruptly and those using it to meet real needs.

This discussion has rested on a rough and informal conception of justice: We have worked with measures currently perceived as elements in a more fair treatment of the developing countries but not with a completely articulated theory of justice. Developing a widely accepted theory of justice in the international arena is extraordinarily difficult because of value conflicts, the absence of legislative institutions to implement any agreement (or other institutions to enforce or interpret it authoritatively), and the dominance of traditional notions of international relations (especially security and sovereignty) that tend to delimit obligations to others by boundaries. Thus efforts to extrapolate the principles used in domestic discussions of justice—like merit or need— must be made with great caution; at best, they give us some general insights about directions we might pursue and perhaps some sense of the distance between what we feel is acceptable domestically and internationally, but they cannot be used to argue that obligations in both realms are always or necessarily identical. This is another way of saying that international relations is a distinct realm and that conflicts over security and different values are not imaginary. Nor can it be argued (nor is it generally accepted) that obligations to others can take priority over obligations to citizens.

But this is hardly all that needs to be said about the issue of justice within the international arena, because we do have obligations to help others as much as we can and because we have interests that make an effort to fulfill those obligations more imperative. In addition the increasingly felt perception of living in an interdependent world *may* make it increasingly appropriate and acceptable to extend domestic conceptions of justice into a wider realm. (I emphasize *may* because felt perceptions of interdependence have also engendered some strongly nationalistic and realpolitik reactions). In this sense we might be slowly moving toward a new standard by which to evaluate policy choices: Those in need must be helped first and must receive a disproportionate share of any of the future benefits of growth (and a redistribution of existing benefits if the growth increments are insufficient). This will be a loose and (necessarily) imperfect criterion in which what is good will be evaluated by the immediate benefits passed on to the poorest individuals and countries, at the least cost to the already rich. In the interim, however, we cannot escape the obligation to dilute the principle of need by a clear concern with the merits of the governments with which we must deal.

It is highly unlikely that there will be quick acceptance within the international system of this or any other conception of justice. What we are more likely to see is a slow, episodic, and perhaps almost uncalculated movement toward a new (and tacit) notion of what is just. We can, however, facilitate this movement—shortening its length, moderating its gyrations—if we are more conscious of the need for a new international conception of justice and if we begin to realize that the policy responses we make are not merely responses to particular opportunities or problems but also part of a longer term effort to move consistently in a preferred direction. Particular choices must also be seen as part of an effort to establish new rules and principles of order.

## THE DISCOUNT RATE ON THE FUTURE—
### TIMING PROBLEMS

One of the most difficult tasks confronting any political system is to give long-range costs and benefits their proper weight. The pressure of the present is enormous, and by its nature the future has a small constituency with which to assert concern for issues that have not yet arisen and may indeed never arise. Paying present costs to avoid what are only potential dangers is difficult, especially if the dangers will fall upon another generation—if they fall at all.[20] And if, as Robert Solow has noted, "the accumulation of technological knowledge will probably make our great-grandchildren better off than we are, even if we make no great effort in that direction," sacrifices of current consumption for those who will be even better off than we are may seem unnecessary or irrelevant.[21] Ironically the

20. For a discussion of some of the difficulties in making even a developed political system take the future seriously, see Robert L. Rothstein, *Planning, Prediction and Policymaking in Foreign Affairs* (Boston: Little, Brown, 1972).

21. Robert M. Solow, "Is the End of the World at Hand?," in Andrew Weintraub, Eli Schwartz, and J. Richard Aronson, eds., *The Economic Growth Controversy* (White Plains, N.Y.: International Arts and Sciences Press, Inc., 1973), p. 46.

idea of inevitable progress could justify indifference to the future and its claims.

Advanced, industrialized societies have obviously managed to ignore this implication of the idea of progress: They have invested massively in roads, dams, and factories, which will benefit future generations who have contributed nothing to their cost. Why they have made these sacrifices in current consumption is unclear, but one reason may be that it is not much of a sacrifice for a country with per capital income around $7,000. But the industrial countries have not treated future generations as completely equal partners, for some sacrifices for the future have not been made or not been understood. Profligate use of resources, indifference to the environment, and *ad hoc* decisions about programs (like nuclear power) that could have devastating long-run consequences testify to the difficulties that even industrialized states have in lowering the rate of discount on investments for the future.

The pressures of the present are obviously even more overwhelming for countries that are small, poor, and unstable. This has not prevented representatives of the industrial world from freely offering their less fortunate brethren advice about the need to sacrifice now and the need to take a longrun perspective in order for future generations to prosper. I do not suggest that the advice to make present sacrifices for future goods is entirely wrong or pernicious. The need for high rates of investment is self-evident, for even a redistribution policy does not make sense unless the economic pie is growing larger. But it does frequently seem hypocritical for those who have much to lecture those who have little on the virtues of sacrifice.

What outside observers have not sufficiently appreciated is the meaning the burden of sacrifice has in the context of underdevelopment. Putting off some amount of current consumption is not difficult in rich countries, but cutting (or not increasing) consumption for those living near subsistence is another matter entirely. Worse yet, not only are investment rates likely to have to be higher than they are in developed countries (especially if the incremental capital output rate is higher), but also it may take much longer for results to begin to show. The wisdom of sacrifice is thus not likely to be immediately apparent to the masses. And the ruling elites are unlikely to take the risk of treating the claims of the future seriously if doing so could endanger their own claims in the present.

A sustained diet of sacrifice is clearly insufficient and unrealistic. Economic policies that do not provide any shortrun gains or that provide gains only to groups that threaten the government will never be seriously implemented. A sensible political economy must take account not only of economic limitations but also of the nature of the government that exists, its need to survive in the face of "rising demands and insufficient resources," and the necessity of repression if it has no other means to deal with present discontents. We have a choice only between inefficient and weak authoritarian governments that are completely indifferent to the claims of the future and inefficient and weak authoritarian governments that are willing to make some sacrifices for the future once assured of their own security. The paradox is only apparent, for no one can take the long range seriously—when we are all dead, which may be one of the last Keynesian propositions to fall—until assured of the present.

What happens when sensible programs with only long-range effects are proposed may be inferred from elite reaction to population programs in many underdeveloped countries. The studies that have attempted to analyze the effect of reduced fertility on per capita income agree that it raises income about 3–5 percent after 10 years, 15–25 percent after 20 years, and 25–50 percent after 30 years.[22] This means that such programs contribute nothing toward immediate elite survival and in fact impede survival if population programs themselves become objects of controversy. The long lead time of population programs also indicates how they tend to be overlooked in many planning exercises, which usually run in 4- or 5-year cycles—the accumulative effect of such programs is easily ignored, and the immediate effect of ignoring the problem does not seem significant. Unless we understand how these time problems affect elite perceptions, we will not be able to understand why some policies and programs are more interesting and important to outside observers than they are to the elites themselves.

22. See Theodore K. Ruprecht and Carl Wahren, *Population Programmes and Economic and Social Development* (Paris: Organization for Economic Cooperation and Development, 1970), pp. 20–21.

There is no clear and simple solution to these difficulties. Nor is there any obvious way in which to establish what the precise trade-off between a better present and a better future ought to be. In any case it is something of an advance to note at least that we are dealing with a trade-off and that there are two values involved, neither of which is necessarily always superior. The priority between present and future must be reordered so that one set of claims is not always the victim of the other. In current circumstances the claims of the present have too easily been sacrificed to the claims of the future (the doubtful results of many longrun investment policies, especially in terms of distribution issues, may suggest the sacrifice was much too easy). We have not been sufficiently sympathetic to the elites whom we have been asking to take the risks of our theories of economic growth.

What makes the greatest sense in these circumstances are aid programs that serve a double purpose: providing immediate help for the elite in meeting the demands of citizens but also being useful in terms of longrun growth problems. One thing this suggests, I think, is the need for more program aid and proportionately less for projects. Project aid for roads and dams and other infrastructures can be more easily monitored and evaluated, but the effects of such aid are also primarily long term. Program aid, by contrast, has a more immediate impact but is also beneficial as part of a growth strategy. And needless to say, there are many circumstances in which such aid can be imperative (e.g., to buy raw materials to run underutilized plants or to buy other needed goods when debt burdens consume available foreign exchange).

Since the correlation between economic growth and investment in nonhuman capital has been poor and since it has become clear that investments in human capital (i.e., current consumption in one or another form) are more important for growth, aid designed to meet immediate human capital needs also serves a double purpose.[23] It may make the impact of aid harder to measure but more fruitful in both the short and the long term. This kind of aid, which seeks to relieve problems of malnutrition, disease, illiteracy, and

23. See Theodore Morgan, "Investment versus Economic Growth," *Economic Development and Cultural Change* 17, no. 3 (1969):407 ff.

the like, is not the same as emergency aid for the relief of famine or drought.

This shift in emphasis to programs that serve both short- and long-term purposes may also explain part of the attractiveness of a redistribution strategy. Benefits for the mass of the people are immediate; the threat to the government is minimal, for it does not give power to its enemies (and may quiet dissent if expectations are not excessive); and the long-run implications for the creation of an integrated and just national society are not necessarily worse than the implications from conventional growth strategies.

What clearly needs to be drawn from this discussion is not support for a particular policy or set of policies or for the priority of one time period rather than another. The critical point is the need to try to think in the operating context of the elites whom we want to move in certain directions: Can we devise or discover policies that take account of their needs and fears but do not sacrifice all the goals we seek to achieve? In some cases the answer may be that there is only an either/or choice between present and future; in other cases, as I think with redistribution, we may be able to choose policies that benefit both present and future. Finally we should never forget that balancing present and future values is implicit in all our choices and that the only argument that is always wrong is one that asserts that the problem does not exist or that it has an easy resolution.


## A NORM OF PARTICIPATION

One of the most important political norms concerns the right to participate in decisionmaking. Few weak states have contested the notion that the wealth and power of the industrial countries justify special responsiblities on important issues. The stronger states have frequently, however, seemed to use that responsibility to protect their own interests and not to defend a more general "public interest." The apparent shift in bargaining power between the resource producers and the industrial countries in the past few years has encouraged increasingly extreme demands for a revision of decisionmaking procedures in the international system. The poor countries have begun to demand more and more voice on matters that directly (and sometimes not so directly) affect their existence. I think it is necessary to respond to these demands in a positive fashion because they reflect genuine grievances in some cases and because a more cooperative international system must begin to create patterns of decision based not only on wealth and power but also on authority, legitimacy, and interest. In this case we shall also need a companion norm, for the concessions that the industrial countries grant on participation in decisionmaking could easily be vitiated if the poor countries do not accept some constraints on their own behavior.

When the poor countries have acquired greater weight in some arenas like the U.N. or UNCTAD, the rich countries have responded by moving the true locus of decision to narrower arenas wholly within their control—the OECD, the Committee of Ten, the SALT talks, and so forth. This is understandable, and in some cases justfied, for many issues cannot wait upon a resolution of procedural disagreements between the haves and the have-nots. But it is also a response that can be shortsighted, for it may encourage the irresponsible behavior it purports to avoid. No one, great or small, will freely acquiesce in exclusion from decisions that fundamentally affect one's existence, unless the benefits of doing so are tangible and overwhelming. In the international system, however, the weak have been excluded because they lack power and wealth, not because exclusion necessarily guarantees better outcomes. As a result the poor countries are compelled to use whatever influence they have—which thus far has mainly been the power of the rhetoric of the many—to force some concern for their problems.

This issue of participation needs to be refocused in an international system that hopes to proceed by persuasion and cooperation. Surely this cannot be taken to mean equal representation for the poor countries on all issues, for that only guarantees a search for alternate arenas of decision on the part of the most powerful countries. On all matters directly affecting the fate of the poor countries, what seems necessary is acceptance of their right to be consulted and to participate in the decisional process from the start. This can be usefully done only if the poor countries themselves are able to vote for their representatives in any negotiation forum, perhaps through the medium of the "Group of 77" at UNCTAD or through a caucusing group at the U.N. itself. Representation need not be equal—four industrial countries, four underdeveloped countries, etc.—but it might be set at a number that guarantees the ability to veto actions or principles of behavior.

There is no doubt that the industrial countries would now greet this proposal with horror, for it would seem to provide the poor countries with a built-in capacity for blackmail. There are, however, constraints that might keep this capacity from being misused, for the underdeveloped countries need the cooperation of the rich countries even more than the rich countries need their cooperation. Acceptance of the principle itself could be taken as an important indication of good faith on the part of the most powerful countries. Moreover, this principle is not engraved in concrete: The poor countries would be well aware that obstructionism in instances when they could not make a good case for their views would rapidly create a movement toward decisions by and for the rich countries themselves.

There may be some arenas in which this principle should not apply at all. Issues directly affecting the East–West strategic balance are a case in point; so, too, are issues like mutual security in Europe. On other issues, especially economic matters, exclusion is morally wrong—for we have no superior wisdom that would justify only actions that meet with our approval, especially on issues directly affecting the poor—and practically unwise, for it engenders resentment and bitterness that can undermine any actions taken. Indeed, on some issues, a case might be made that the poor countries ought to be given the controlling voice on outcomes. As an illustration, take the disagreements at the Law of the Sea Conference on the control of seabed resources. The rich countries want an international authority that will guarantee them access when they want it and a fair return on their investment. For many LDCs, however, the successful mining of manganese nodules, for example, could virtually destroy their economies—unless they control the process and are assured of substantial benefits from it. The underdeveloped countries, particularly the raw materials exporters, cannot afford not to have a strong voice in any organization that controls these ventures. In cases like this we ought to be willing to temper our needs and our superior technologic capacity with a much more sympathetic understanding of the position of the poor countries. (But, again, an aggressive cartel strategy or efforts to take radical rhetoric seriously by the developing countries would justify actions by the developed countries to protect their interests.)

Participation in decisionmaking by the poor countries is not a principle that can be stated with complete clarity or precision. Nonetheless acceptance of the principle would begin the slow process of institutionalizing conflict within a collective bargaining system, that is, a process of joint decisionmaking. It would make it somewhat easier to make decisions by rules, through an organizational structure, and with the assistance of expert advice. This may diminish some elements of ideologic and rhetorical conflict and may decrease some elements of personal tension that appear in direct conflict. The establishment of a continuing relationship of this sort may also create incentives to compromise, for each side may begin to see that exploitation of shortrun advantages can hinder the creation of a longrun relationship from which both sides benefit. Recent recommendations (May 1975) by an international panel of experts on structural changes in the United Nations include a number of suggestions about voting that seem to me a step in the right direction. One suggestion, for example, advocates increased voting power for the underdeveloped countries in the World Bank and the IMF so that a single country—the United States—cannot dominate all decisions. Another proposal attempts to avoid the voting contests that have dominated the General Assembly by advocating the creation of small negotiating groups that would seek in private and over a period of time (1 or 2 years) to resolve deadlocked issues.[24]

There is a possible pattern of decisionmaking on rich–poor issues that makes sense to me because it is likely to be fair to all concerned and because it introduces an element of order into the

24. See *A New United Nations Structure for Global Economic Co-operation* (New York: United Nations E/AC.62/9, May 1975).

current proliferation of decision forums (or nondecision forums, where the existence of alternate arenas of decision is used to avoid decisions by arguing that a particular issue cannot be resolved, say at UNCTAD because, say, the Paris Conference of producers and consumers may deal with it—and vice-versa). Large fora like the General Assembly and the UNCTAD (or ILO, UNIDO, etc.) Conferences should be limited to studying and discussing issues until a consensus emerges that a particular issue has reached the point where binding negotiations should take place. But the negotiations themselves ought to be carried on in smaller arenas, perhaps on the basis of constituency representation: Each concerned group would select (and instruct) a smaller number of representatives to conduct the actual negotiations.[25]

This process would have a number of virtues. The larger fora would still have an indispensable role to play in "consciousness raising" and in establishing the range of contention around an issue. The negotiating groups, in which each side would have a veto, would ensure that no single group could impose its will on issues that affect the others in a substantial fashion. The fact that negotiating groups would be established only after a general consensus had emerged in the larger organizations might also inhibit the *ad hoc*, random proliferation of negotiating or quasi-negotiating fora that now occurs; this would reduce confusion, avoid buckpassing between different arenas, and save much money and time. The constituency pattern of representation would also help to conserve and enhance one of the Third World's scarcest resources: sufficient expertise to negotiate on equal terms with the industrial countries.[26] Finally the negotiating groups could be established and ser-

25. John White, "International Agencies: The Case for Proliferation," in G. K. Helleiner, ed., *A World Divided: The Less Developed Countries in the World Economy* (Cambridge: Cambridge University Press, 1976), pp. 275–93, argues the need for more specific, functional institutions but dismisses the role of the larger institutions like UNCTAD and FAO too easily. I believe that the functional institutions by themselves are not sufficient, for they cannot set general directions or set consistent targets among themselves.

26. Perhaps agreements negotiated in this fashion should also have sanctions included for violations of various sorts. The most that would be acceptable to the developing countries is graduated and differentiated sanctions (i.e., different degrees and kind of sanctions for themselves), but sanctions could have a useful disciplining effect. They have occasionally been used in commodity agreements with marginal

viced by the larger organizations like UNCTAD (a result that would be more acceptable to the industrial countries if the Third World set up its own research organization, so that the UNCTAD staff would no longer be identified, fairly or not, as spokesmen for only one point of view).

The pattern of institutional decisionmaking I have just outlined also puts a somewhat different perspective on the criticisms that have usually been directed against organizations such as UNCTAD, UNIDO, and the FAO. If such organizations are meant to be primarily fora of discussion and preparation, then some weaknesses—such as the process of group negotiating that inhibits quick results, or staffing that is partially determined by political and geographical consideration, or the difficulty of defining specific and negotiable goals in institutions with very different kinds of members, or the staff's inability or reluctance to play a mediating role between the main adversaries—may be less disturbing. The central point is simply that it may be necessary to accept or work with these weaknesses if the goal is to achieve a sufficiently wide consensus and to ensure that each group feels that it has had a voice in the proceedings. In any case, since rapid change in the way these organizations are run is unlikely, we may make a virtue of necessity: Rather than change the organizations, we need to change our perceptions of what can reasonably be expected from them.

## A NORM OF RESTRAINT

The principle of participation in decisionmaking can so easily be misused that a special collateral principle of restraint may be necessary. This is particularly true because the underdeveloped countries are so intent on establishing their right to be consulted and to participate that the obligation to use the right intelligently

---

success (e.g., by cutting the export quota of the guilty party). At any rate the matter may be more important symbolically than practically, for the usual sanction in these agreements is sufficiently strong: the end of the agreement (except in cases where the "free rider" problem exists, but even here the paying riders continue to pay only as long as they still benefit).

may be forgotten. Thus attempts on the part of the poor countries to force more and more issues into wide arenas like the U.N. or UNCTAD, while understandable as an effort to make use of the only leverage they have had, may also be self-defeating. Attempts to demand equality of participation on all issues are also likely to make participation a formal charade without real meaning.

What happens when contentious issues are forced into an arena like the U.N. is that the underdeveloped countries can agree among themselves only on "highest common denominator" proposals. The recent "Declaration on the Establishment of a New International Economic Order," passed by the General Assembly in May 1974, illustrates the problem: It includes so many demands, some sensible, some foolish, some unclear, that the rich countries can avoid a serious response by pointing to the obvious unrealism of the total package of demands. Acceptance of all the demands would disrupt the entire economic order for the primary benefit of the underdeveloped countries. But attempts to reverse the traditional pattern of relationships radically—not all of which have been or need to be exploitative—are wildly utopian; there is no way of knowing whether they would in fact create a better order if they could be implemented, and they divert attention from real problems that must be dealt with as quickly as possible. Furthermore both the rich and the poor countries recognize that neither side is really taking such revolutionary proposals seriously, which does nothing for the quality of an international dialogue already sufficiently debased.

The poor countries also need to develop a more coherent institutional strategy among themselves. For example, there was a good deal of fear that meaningful negotiations at UNCTAD-IV in Nairobi would be undermined by the fact that the Paris Conference on International Economic Cooperation was covering the same issues and in the smaller, more manageable forum I have already advocated. Many of the UNCTAD staff and many developing countries saw this as a conspiracy on the part of the rich countries to avoid commitments at Nairobi. This may be true in that the opportunity was there, but it needs to be emphasized that the developing countries themselves insisted that Paris not be limited to the energy question alone. In part this conflict between the two Conferences was simply the result of bad coordination within the Third World: OPEC and the Group of 77 in New York pushing for a wider Paris Conference, the Group of 77 in Geneva failing to be sufficiently aware (or powerful enough) to protect UNCTAD's interests. According to my argument the problem is not the existence of two fora but the timing of their existence. Paris should have been convened to negotiate seriously on general agreements that had been established at Nairobi. As it is, the two Conferences have been in competition, discussions at Nairobi were clearly affected by the desire to reserve some issues for Paris, and the results achieved at Paris may be challenged by some Third World countries that feel their interests are not being adequately represented.

The sharp adversary relationship between the rich and the poor countries has also penetrated into a number of smaller forums. Thus the Algerian delegate to a preparatory conference for the Paris Conference declared:

> For the first time, the Third World has a high card to play. That is the oil card that the producing countries are employing on behalf of the entire Third World. We will not be put off. We have the card, and we are determined to play it now before there is a risk that it will lose its value.[27]

I have already expressed substantial doubts in chapter 1 that OPEC is working "on behalf of the entire Third World."[28] Here I want only to note that when (or if) we pass the time that the "high card" has been trumped, the attempt to carry over the rhetorical cannoneering that has frequently characterized UNCTAD and the U.N. into smaller arenas of discussion could be disastrous.

I have stressed the dangers of posturing in small decisional arenas because, as I have already indicated in the preceding principle, I believe it might be easier for the poor countries to act in a re-

---

27. Quoted in the Washington *Post*, April 13, 1975, p. 22. And see Manuel Perez Guerrero's recent threat to use energy power "to obtain concessions from the West impossible until now," failing which, "we will not fall into the river alone." *The Economist*, Feb. 21, 1976, p. 84.

28. There are many figures, not all of them perfectly consistent, that indicate how much of the burden of rise in oil prices is borne by the non-OPEC LDCs. Total indebtedness in 1974 caused by the oil price explosion was in the neighborhood of $55–60 billion. The LDCs buy only about 10 percent of the world's oil imports, yet they owe around 40 percent of the oil debt. The reason is, of course, that the industrial countries have been able to adjust much more easily to the oil crisis.

strained and prudent fashion if they began moving away from general negotiations in universal arenas toward more functional arenas where narrower interests can be negotiated and compromised. There are some issues—like the future of the oceans—for which wider arenas are likely to continue to be appropriate, but for many other issues the interests of the underdeveloped countries themselves are so different that only small groups can develop joint proposals. This would simply recognize the fact, as I have already argued earlier in the last chapter, that the Third World itself is liable to break up into at least four different groups in the next decade. Whether in the smaller or the larger arena, I would still maintain the principle that the LDCs ought to be given special participatory rights and a weight commensurate more with their interests in an issue than with their power to determine the issue; the point here is that it may be easier to keep that principle from being misused in small groups where the necessity of making grand statements has not yet become conventional.

Some movement toward smaller, more functional decisional arenas might also have other virtues. The principle of unity has become virtually a fetish within the Third World. But in smaller arenas where shared interests were more tangible and negotiable the quest for unity might be less inhibiting; that is, the result need not be limited to general affirmations of principle that are rapidly forgotten when actual negotiations begin. Smaller arenas are also less apt, I believe, to engender or facilitate grand confrontations designed (ostensibly) to revolutionize the existing order. This tendency toward unrealistic goals, already too prevalent in organs such as the General Assembly and UNCTAD, expects too much from institutions in which majority votes are not binding on dissenters; perhaps it can be ameliorated within institutions that have more narrowly defined roles and expectations.

## A NORM OF INTERVENTION

The international system that may emerge by the early 1980s could be fragmented and unstable, with wide disparities of power and sharp conflicts over both ideological and practical matters, but nonetheless highly interdependent in some critical areas.[29] By its very nature this is a system in which the quest for universal rules and general settlements is bound to be futile, for there is no agreement on the vocabulary in which such rules or agreements could be specified nor any trust that they would survive the next crisis. If nuclear weapons begin to proliferate rapidly, if some poor countries become increasingly desperate, if the growth rates of the industrial countries do not revive, and if the industrial countries do not begin to take adequate steps to remedy resource scarcities, the system could begin to move sharply toward disaster.

This is an international system that may begin of necessity to develop a strong bias toward intervention. What the rich countries might seek in an environment dominated by so much uncertainty is the reassertion of a degree of predictability and control—which is apt to mean either direct intervention or the creation of satellite regimes in a few salient Third World countries. The evident facts that power disparities are increasing, that the need for resources owned by the poor may increase, that irrational behavior by the poor could create dangerous instabilities, and that domestic divisions within the LDCs always provide groups willing to "invite" outsiders in may make the decision to intervene increasingly likely.

Apart from the behavior of the Great Powers, objective economic conditions are also making intervention increasingly probable. For example, almost all the priority issues on the agenda of UNCTAD-IV—an organization ostensibly concerned only with trade in relationship to development, not (as its title suggests) trade and development—involve extensive intervention in domestic policymaking systems. Thus debt relief is impossible without some judgments about a country's development plans, its import needs, and its export prospects; improvements in the transfer of technology require substantial changes in national legal structures; commodity agreements may involve export quotas and efforts to diversify the domestic economy; and collective self-reliance will require

29. Oran R. Young, "Intervention and International Systems," *Journal of International Affairs* 22, no. 2. (1968):177, 187, is interesting and stimulating on the whole intervention problem.

joint planning and harmonization of domestic policies. In general many of these proposals involve efforts to intervene against the operation of market forces that reflect the existing distribution of power and wealth, and this cannot be done without judgments about, and interventions in, the domestic policies of both the rich and the poor countries. The reluctance of the rich countries to accept these conditions may be slowly altering, at least in their relationships with each other, but the reluctance of the poor countries is even more severe, because of instinctive reactions against intervention and perhaps because of fears of its effects on domestic political and economic power. The poor countries now consider only intervention to assess the record of the rich countries in meeting international obligations as acceptable.

On a certain level increased intervention could obviously be an unfortunate development. The principle of nonintervention not only is already a very frail reed but also is a psychic symbol of great importance for small, poor states. Thus the LDCs would be unlikely to accept intervention without severe efforts to recapture their freedom. Yet it is also possible to ask, I think, whether nonintervention is too absolute a principle for the international system we are discussing. Must we not also concede that there are values at stake in the international system that may be more important than nonintervention, that some weak states want (and need) intervention to help them survive and prosper, and that the strong states have an impact on the weak whatever they do—whether they intervene or whether they choose isolation and self-preoccupation? These objections suggest that in a dangerous and fragmented world an absolute principle of nonintervention is neither necessarily wise nor morally superior. But it is also clear that an unlimited right to intervene is not any better.[30]

A useful compromise might rest on the need for procedural agreement. Unilateral interventions ought to be proscribed, but since it is unlikely they they will be or that the proscription will deter a Great Power intent on acting, it may at least be a minor vir-

30. The dangers of *not* intervening, and the cowardice and irresponsibility of various international institutions afraid to endanger established relations with a corrupt and incompetent Ethiopian government, are vividly described in Jack Shepherd, *The Politics of Starvation* (New York: Carnegie Endowment for International Peace, 1975).

tue to remove the euphemism and compel honesty about actions dictated by perceptions of higher necessities. What is really needed, however, is a serious effort to establish a principle of accountability: Intervention ought not to be individually determined but must meet some generally agreed standards of behavior. Perhaps this could be facilitated by moving the right of intervention into the hands of regional and international organizations, which might give it some semblance of legitimacy and the appearance of reflecting a degree of community interest.

I expect that procedural agreement on intervention is not likely to be sufficient (or acceptable to many states) unless we also begin to treat intervention in a more differentiated fashion. In current circumstances the debate tends to proceed in terms of large abstractions: a good nonintervention against a bad intervention. This is not very useful, because the abstractions are poor reflections of what is actually happening within the international system. While I cannot do more here than leave the issue unsettled, it does appear to me that we must add to the quest for procedural agreement on how to intervene a quest for meaningful distinctions between various kinds of intervention. Differentiating the concept of intervention to reflect those that are unacceptable, those that are acceptable, and those that may be either good or bad but are inevitable because of secular trends in the world may be a useful first step toward a more sensible concept.

Because intervention is so likely, and yet so dangerous, there is a strong need to get it "out of the closet"—that is, to discuss it openly, to think about it in a more sophisticated fashion, and to establish conditions and procedures of implementation so that every act of intervention does not create an immediate crisis and an aftermath of bitterness. There is no perfect solution to this problem, but there are surely better and worse ways of living with it.

## A NORM OF LEADERSHIP

One price of leadership is the willingness to sacrifice shortrun gains. The leader must be the most persistent advocate and defender of the general interest, for no other state can or will do it. If the leader's perceptions do not extend beyond protecting its own self-interest, neither will anyone else's. Negatively, if the leader takes actions that injure the interests of others, the leader ought to accept the obligation of bearing the costs and of not transferring them to weaker states (e.g., by high levels of protection for domestic agriculture). Positively the leader should be willing to prevent actions that endanger the system or to inflict penalties on offenders (e.g., on states that develop nuclear weapons or on nuclear states that sell reprocessing facilities or fuel or missiles without safeguards).

Many issues now on the international agenda or likely soon to be are unlikely to be resolved or are likely to fester and accumulatively worsen unless—at least as a necessary condition—the leader is willing and able to act now to avoid future problems. The prospects for nuclear proliferation are a negative illustration of how to avoid facing the implications of our own and others' actions. And in the context of relations with the underdeveloped countries we can see similar issues arising: over access to resources, over debt problems, over the transfer of technology and the uses of the patent system, and perhaps even over the need to begin visualizing a new industrial geography as a result of converging comparative cost structures and the implications of this for the presumably neutral principles of comparative advantage. Problems will probably arise with all these issues within the next decade; we might be able to avoid or ameliorate these problems if we were willing to pay an insurance premium now. At any rate we will not be able to resolve them if we seek to treat such issues in narrow commercial terms or if we seek immediate compensation for all concessions.

The difficulty of the leader's role is apparent, for the willingness to sacrifice to implement a vision of a more orderly and cooperative future is frequently in conflict with the leader's own domestic imperatives. The increasing interpenetration of domestic and foreign policy has made the leadership role increasingly difficult, for it is no longer easy to justify shortrun domestic sacrifices by vague allusions to the "primacy of foreign policy" or the "defense of the national interest." No one needs to be reminded that the current mood in foreign policy is nationalistic, averse to external commitments, and reluctant to sacrifice anything for anybody; we may be in the process of relinquishing a world role just as it has become truly imperative. Without leadership the prospects for trade wars, the creation of rigid blocs, desperate confrontations between rich and poor, and all the other attendant evils of a highly unstable and insecure international system will surely rise.[31]

The leadership of the United States has become increasingly problematic, not only because of domestic constraints, but also because we have not devised a coherent policy toward the Third World. We are clearer about what we are against—communism, expropriation of American investments, excessive nationalism, resource cartels, and so on—than about what we are for. Consequently we have allowed what we ought to be doing for the Third World to be defined by various Third World spokesmen or various international secretariats. Such demands are not necessarily against our interests, but they are also frequently impractical, conflicting, or narrowly self-interested. In any case we surely need a policy that is more than a minimalist reaction to demands articulated by others and that rests on a careful consideration of our own interests toward the Third World.

Since this is not a book that is explicitly about American policy, although it contains material that I believe must be considered in any attempt to create a policy, I do not set down here a detailed comment about our interests and goals. Nevertheless, in a broad sense, the outlines of a policy have already appeared in this book. If it is in our interest to create viable societies that can provide for the needs of their own citizens and thus diminish the need for massive external change to right massive domestic failure, this can be done only by domestic efforts at immediate and widespread redistribution, joined to international measures that offer generous help to those who are able to use it effectively or who suffer from developments for which they are not responsible. And it is in our interest to support governments that seek redistribution and to oppose those who do not, for international redistribution without domestic

31. For an interesting argument about the consequences of the failure of leadership by the United States during the Great Depression, see Charles P. Kindleberger, *The World in Depression, 1929–1939* (London: Allen Lane, 1973).

redistribution only succeeds in shifting resources from the rich countries to the rich of the poor countries. Our moral interest in helping to provide for the basic needs of the great mass of the populace here coincides with our practical interest in creating a more stable and more just international order: The latter cannot be achieved in isolation from the former.

Whatever the choice, the need for a coherent policy is imperative. Without it, we have only a tactic of reaction and avoidance; with it, we have a strategy, reflecting our interests and values, with which to evaluate individual decisions.

---

The burden of the argument I have been making throughout this discussion of norms and practices is that in the international system that may be emerging in the next few years we have practical reasons to be visionary. More than moral or humanitarian arguments justify some willingness on our part to make concessions to the poor countries that might begin to create some faith that a more cooperative international system, in which the benefits for all would increase, could be established and maintained. The possibility that any or all of the norms we have been discussing will be adopted in the near future is obviously low. Still, if we agree that they represent a "soft" option worth trying, if only because the "hard" options are so frighteningly unappealing, we ought to try to think about ways in which these new norms could be made increasingly attractive to practitioners beset by contrary pressures.

The international system is self-regulating, which means that norms begin to acquire force only when the members of the system see important elements of self-interest in obedience. In the first instance a norm is usually developed to deal with some persisting problem that cannot or has not been dealt with by habitual modes of behavior. The norm survives to the extent that obedience seems less costly than any other alternative. This does not mean that sanctions for disobedience need to be specified beforehand, for, as Barkun notes, "norms, the evidence indicates, precede rather than follow the means for their enforcement . . ." [32]

32. Michael Barkun, *Law Without Sanctions—Order in Primitive Societies and the World Community* (New Haven, Conn.: Yale University Press, 1968), p. 164.

Norms also need not be accepted for the same reasons. For example, Robin Williams has argued:

> Persons in weak positions, fearing exploitation by the stronger, often favor predictable norms and sanctions. Persons in positions of authority and power often desire reliable conformity that is not dependent upon continual surveillance and coercion; they may therefore favor establishment of norms even if their own caprices are thereby curbed.[33]

The analogy with relations between the weak and the strong in the international system is instructive. What is critical here is whether different groups see a similar interest in obeying common norms, not whether they obey for the same reasons.

The international system must operate with a low degree of consensus. This makes the adoption of new norms even more problematic, for norms that reflect a high degree of consensus obviously stand more chance of being obeyed. There is something of a paradox here, for the complexity and unpredictability of an unstable system create a demand for new norms but simultaneously undermine their force. The members of a system will accept new norms and use them as criteria for settlement of disputes only if they believe that others see them as authoritative, but without a wider consensus on values there is little likelihood that many members will take the risk of doing so.

The need for norms to deal with increasingly confusing and unprecedented situations is on the rise, but the capacity for reaching agreement on such norms seems to be declining. The learning process by which the Soviet Union and the United States worked out a few tacit norms about acceptable behavior in strategic arms interactions perhaps provides some grounds for optimism: if the area of shared interest is salient enough, even direct adversaries can agree on certain minimal rules of the game. But the issues that may require this kind of learning process in the years ahead could be a good deal less obvious; indeed, the stronger powers might be able to force the weaker powers to pay the costs of "interdependence." In addition the process of "normal" learning may be too slow and

33. Robin Williams, Jr., "The Concept of Norms," *The International Encyclopedia of the Social Sciences* (New York: The Macmillan Company, 1968), p. 207.

too haphazard when failures or miscalculations could lead to major crises.

There may be some utility in speculating about the characteristics that might make the acceptance of new norms or principles more probable. The most obvious characteristic, and one that appears in many discussions of norm creation, is perceived mutual benefits.[34] But I think this is likely to be insufficient for rich–poor relations because the poor have so little to give in return (except access to raw materials, which only a limited number can offer) and because felt perceptions of exploitation may make the poor suspicious of apparently equal trade-offs. Consequently one necessary characteristic of these new norms may be a deliberate concentration on special gains and dispensations for the poor. A revised Pareto optimal formula is operative here: What is acceptable is what benefits the poor countries but does not inflict (major) costs upon the industrial countries.

The attempt to place the norms in a formal, binding agreement may also be important in this context. This would do two things: It would enable the poor countries to apply some pressure when the norms were violated and would provide elements of certainty about the duration of the norms and clarity about their content. For weak countries that fear risks and distrust their bargaining partners, such characteristics could be important. We would seek to institutionalize our commitment as a token of persisting concern. In addition, as McKean observes, it may be important to make an effort to publicize all relevant information about particular agreements, which is particularly important for developing countries short on expertise.[35] As one illustration, all of these characteristics are part of UNCTAD's efforts to negotiate a binding code on the transfer of technology or of other efforts to control the behavior of multinational corporations.[36]

34. See the useful discussion in Roland N. McKean, "Economics of Trust, Altruism, and Corporate Responsibility," in Edmund S. Phelps, ed., *Altruism, Morality, and Economic Theory* (New York: Russell Sage Foundation, 1975), pp. 29–44. McKean discusses the issue within the context of personal interaction, but some of his ideas are suggestive in a wider context also.

35. *Ibid.*, p. 42.

36. For one illustration, see *An International Code of Conduct on Transfer of Technology* (UNCTAD, TD/B/C.6/AC.1/2/Supp. 1/Rev. 1, 1975). As with many other Third

In the short run it would be utopian to expect agreements that reflect all these characteristics or that can settle the substantive issues in dispute. What I have suggested, then, is no more than a general standard by which to guide and evaluate our actions. In the near future the most that may be possible is to articulate and emphasize the practical reasons that we have for developing agreement on "how to" norms; agreement on "what" or "why" norms must be left until there is a wider consensus on the values that the members of the system want to accept. Until some consensus is apparent, the leadership role is crucial, for only a powerful and wealthy state can afford to take shortrun risks and to make shortrun sacrifices, and only the leader is likely to have a large enough vision of a global order to understand what norms ought to be consciously and deliberately stressed along the way.

No one can be very optimistic that the United States will once again be able to assume a leadership role in the international system. At a minimum we should be willing to confront the implications of our choices. If the industrial countries continue to avoid difficult decisions about the future—praying somehow that we will "muddle through"; if they continue to seek shortrun solutions to complex and interdependent problems; if the underdeveloped countries continue to seek to overturn the existing international order; and if they do not make a more serious effort to establish what their real problems are, what they can and cannot expect from the international system, and what policies make most sense for themselves, prospects for the future are grim. What is most likely in these circumstances, I think, would be ruthless control by the rich countries of whatever underdeveloped countries they needed, indifference to the rest, and deliberate and desperate disruptive actions by the poor countries to call attention to their problems. The first order of business for both groups of countries is to reorder their current priorities and to think through the implications of their current behavior. Without such an effort the norms I have dis-

World demands, there are also dangers of demanding too much too quickly here—of the best being the enemy of the good. Thus the long range goal of creating a binding code of conduct on technology may be sensible, but demands for immediate acceptance and implementation of such a code may succeed in ending or diminishing the process of technology transfer—not facilitating it.

cussed in this chapter are bound to be irrelevant; with such an effort these norms may at least play a small but meaningful role in moving us toward a relatively more benign future.

----◄••••►----

I began this chapter with a strong qualification: No changes in the international system, however justified, are likely to mean much to many developing countries if these countries themselves do not make a more serious effort to deal with their own domestic problems. But the qualification could be stated even more strongly. The external changes, by themselves, might even be pernicious if they succeed only in deflecting attention from more fundamental domestic problems or if they enable corrupt and reactionary elites to buy time to stave off domestic reform. The developed countries, by acting more justly within the international arena, would have succeeded only in allaying bad consciences for past depradations, but simultaneously they would permit more or continuing injustice within the developing countries. This is not to denigrate external reform, but rather to set the limits within which it can yield useful results. The case for international redistribution—when it merely shifts more resources to the rich in the poor countries—is not strong in isolation from domestic redistribution.

Some elites within the developing countries will understand the double imperative of change and will respond to it. Some will not understand it at all. And a great many are likely to waffle uncertainly between the dangers and the opportunities. If the developed countries are to avoid wasting scarce resources and supporting countries that have no moral claim on our support, making the right kind of decisions about whom we want to help will become an increasingly critical—and problematic—issue.

# Index

# INDEX

# INDEX

# INDEX

*The Weak in the World of the Strong* is one of a series of studies sponsored by the Institute of War and Peace Studies of Columbia University. Among those Institute studies also dealing with war, peace, national security, and future world order are *Defense and Diplomacy* by Alfred Vagts; *Man, the State and War* by Kenneth N. Waltz; *The Common Defense* by Samuel P. Huntington; *Changing Patterns of Military Politics* edited by Samuel P. Huntington; *Strategy, Politics, and Defense Budgets* by Warner R. Schilling, Paul Y. Hammond, and Glenn H. Snyder; *Stockpiling Strategic Materials* by Glenn H. Snyder; *The Politics of Military Unification* by Demetrios Caraley; *NATO and the Range of American Choice* by William T. R. Fox and Annette Baker Fox; *The Politics of Weapons Innovation: The Thor-Jupiter Controversy* by Michael H. Armacost; *The Politics of Policy Making in Defense and Foreign Affairs* by Roger Hilsman; *Inspection for Disarmament* edited by Seymour Melman; *To Move a Nation* by Roger Hilsman, jointly sponsored with the Washington Center of Foreign Policy Research, Johns Hopkins University, *Planning, Prediction and Policy-Making in Foreign Affairs* by Robert L. Rothstein; *The Origins of Peace* by Robert F. Randle; *European Security and the Atlantic System* edited by William T. R. Fox and Warner R. Schilling; *American Arms and a Changing Europe: Dilemmas of Deterrence and Disarmament* by Warner R. Schilling, William T. R. Fox, Catherine M. Kelleher, and Donald J. Puchala; *The Cold War Begins: Soviet-American Conflict Over Eastern Europe* by Lynn E. Davis; *The Crouching Future: International Politics and U.S. Foreign Policy—a Forecast* by Roger Hilsman; *Germany and the Politics of Nuclear Weapons* by Catherine M. Kelleher; *Developing the ICBM: A Study in Bureaucratic Politics* by Edmund Beard; and *Technology, World Politics, and American Policy* by Victor Basiuk.